491

This book is dedicated to a quartet of courageous men whom I shall admire and hold dear until the day I die: John Simonds, Richard Lauffer, Kent Carroll, and Herman Graf. These men made the cowards look like fools, and I am grateful.

Acknowledgments

In the process of writing this book, I came to know and admire Bobby Tolan and the men who took a big risk by trusting me as I eavesdropped on their intimacies and made notes of their conversations about their lives playing in the fascinating world of professional baseball. To the Pelican players, my admiration goes out to each and every one of you.

I also fell in love with the city of St. Petersburg, and became part of the Pelican family because the officials—Jim and Mark Morley, Phil Bensen, Mike and Reggie Marek, Charles Yancey, Seve Delich, Judy Nunez, Mike Mays, Jim Forbes, Hank Touhy, and Frank (Fireball) Smith—made me feel that way.

During the season I was afforded special access and provided hospitality by league and visiting club officials, including Curt Flood, Rick Horrow, Rick Remmert, Peter Lasser, Ray Negron, Rick Langford, Chuck Malkus, Mark Stewart, and Wynn Dillard.

I was also fortunate to get an opportunity to share radio broadcasts with Jack Wiers, professional sportscaster, over WDAE. We had eighty thousand listeners a night. Hopefully, this year they will all come to Al Lang Stadium to watch the Pelicans play.

In addition to the Pelican players, I took the opportunity to interview a host of opposing players. As it turned out, the Pelican players provided me with so much material I was not able to use much of the information imparted to me by the others. Nevertheless, their conversations gave me many interesting insights, and I wish to convey my deepest appreciation to Pete Broberg, Gates Brown, Chuck Fick, Ed Figueroa, Bob Fralick, Toby Harrah, Clint Hurdle, Tim Ireland, Mike Kekich, Pete LaCock, Tippy Martinez, Felix Millan, Joe Minceberg, Phil (The Natural) Nerone, Al Oliver, Amos Otis, Ron Pruitt, Mickey Rivers, Rick Waits, and Ron Washington. My deepest heartfelt appreciation to you all.

Thanks also to the Benins—Peter, Gini, Andrea, and Chris—and to the Rothschilds—Jim, Vida, Aaron, and Haley—for all your support during some trying times, and to Hillel Black, my editor, to Mark Hurst and to Jeff Mitchell, my extra pair of eyes, to Bill Adler, my agent, to Neil Reshen, my guardian, and to Rhonda, Chunkie, Sparky, and Mickey.

PETER GOLENBOCK
St. Petersburg, Florida
August 1990

Contents

Author to Reader

$\mathbf{F}$ew worthwhile endeavors come easy. *The Forever Boys* was no exception. The idea for the book came to me in midsummer 1989 when I read a short blurb in *USA Today* about the aborning Senior League. Beginning in November in various cities around Florida, about two hundred former major league ballplayers would be returning to the diamond after a hiatus from the game they loved.

I believed that if I could spend the season with a team riding the bus, living on the road, sitting in the dugout, and interviewing the players about their lives in and out of the game—I could describe what it's like to be a professional ballplayer in greater detail and with greater understanding in a special way.

The league founder, Jim Morley, invited me to attend the league meetings in Coral Gables, Florida, just prior to the opening of the season.

"It should be no problem finding an owner to cooperate," he said. "Come to the meeting and tell everyone what you'd like to do."

I stayed overnight at the magnificent Coral Gables Biltmore, where the meetings were being held.

When I entered the meeting room at noon, everyone was eating sandwiches. The only official I recognized was Curt Flood, the Senior League's commissioner. Between bites I told him about the idea behind my book. I congratulated him on his courageous autobiography, in which he described his ordeal as he challenged baseball's reserve clause, which enabled a team to own a player in perpetuity. For his efforts Flood was blackballed from baseball. Flood seemed a strange choice to be commissioner of a league that desperately would need the assistance of the major leagues. Later I would discover that many of the players considered themselves outcasts from baseball, so perhaps Flood's choice as commissioner had been fitting after all.

As Morley had promised, I got a chance to speak.

"It's a book about the love of the game," I said. "Here are men who give up everything to come back and play. I think that's pretty terrific." I added that the book would provide excellent national publicity for the league and for whatever team I chose to follow. Looking about, I thought I saw some heads nodding in agreement.

Two of the biggest names committed to the league were Earl Weaver and Dick Williams. I inquired whether either manager might be interested in letting me chronicle his season. Representatives of Gold Coast and West Palm Beach assured me that they were not.

"You can write about my team," Jim Morley, the owner of the St. Petersburg Pelicans, said. "Bobby Tolan's our manager, and he won't mind. And it will be great publicity for the Pelicans. Let me get back to you." It was a week before the season was to begin.

Without hearing from him again, my family and I packed up the following day for the two-day marathon drive to Florida. I plunked down the rent for our three-month stay, dropped off my wife, Rhonda, and two-year-old Charlie, and drove to Stengel Huggins Field, where the Pelicans were practicing.

The wooden clubhouse where Mantle and Maris, Ruth and Gehrig, Skowron and Kubek, Richardson and Boyer once walked still stood. After gaining entrance to the inner sanctum, I could see the rows of individual lockers taped with familiar yet distant names such as Wilcox, Howell, Randle, and Hendu, which is short for Henderson—but which Henderson was it? I didn't know.

Some names I held dear in memory: Jon Matlack and Pat Zachry, former Met pitchers, and Dock Ellis, once a successful pitcher with one of the Yankee pennant winners, and Steve Kemp, another former Yankee whose career ended prematurely several years after he was hit in the eye with a ball during batting practice. And there were other names that meant nothing to me at all: Williams, Contreras, Gomez, and Ferrer.

Self-consciously I stood in the middle of the clubhouse as these mostly large men prepared themselves for the coming practice. Some were in the middle of the dressing ritual, and others wandered in and out of the trainer's room, joking with each other with an easy camaraderie.

I discovered the boyish Jim Morley in a maroon-and-white Pelicans uniform lying facedown on the trainer's table. He seemed young—at thirty-three he was still two years too young to play in the league—and immediately I was impressed that someone so young could begin a venture so adventurous as the Senior League.

We shook hands. "Bobby and I have to talk to you," he said.

"Fine," I said. I didn't pick up on any warning signs.

"Let's go into Bobby's office," Morley directed.

Morley and I crossed the length of the locker room. A few of the players looked up, but most didn't notice. I had no inkling of what was to follow.

The manager, Bobby Tolan, sat at his desk. I had remembered Tolan from his playing days with the Big Red Machine in Cincinnati. He had once stolen a large number of bases to lead the league, and I was aware of his fights with the Reds' front office that had caused him to be banished. Most of all, I recalled a man who could swing a bat with the best of them.

Morley and I sat down. "There's a problem," Tolan said. "Jim and I both like the idea of your book, but we talked it over with the players, and none of them want you here. I'm very sorry."

I thought to myself, *None of them?*

At that moment Dock Ellis, a towering, hulking figure, entered Tolan's room. I didn't realize it at the time, but Dock was Bobby's pitching coach. Dock glared at me and said in a singsong, "Writer loser." And he walked out, closing the door behind him.

Tolan chuckled. Dock was one of his oldest friends, and he knew Dock was messing with my head. Dock had succeeded too.

Morley was contrite but firm. "The players don't want some writer invading their privacy. They don't want anybody with them while they're on the road. Baseball players are funny that way."

There was always the possibility of going across the causeway to the Bradenton team, but I liked Jim Morley, and I liked the mix of players on the Pelicans. I also liked my new house on the beach in St. Pete.

"May I have one chance to talk to the players?" I heard myself asking Tolan. He agreed.

"But if they say no," Tolan said, "you have to agree not to come back and hang around." I told him I had no interest in doing that.

Back in the main room the players were dressed, milling around waiting for the clock to signal the start of practice. Bobby Tolan, Jim Morley, and I exited Tolan's office.

Tolan said, "May I have your attention? This is the writer I was telling you about. I told him he could have five minutes to speak to you."

I was standing in the middle of the room, one row of lockers in front of me, another row behind me. The former major league players—some of whom had been burned badly by their local sportswriters—sat on stools, waiting to hear what this interloper was going to say. The room fell silent. At the far end I could see Dock Ellis still glaring at me.

I gave my name and told of some of the players I had written books with: Sparky Lyle, Graig Nettles, Davey Johnson, Ron Guidry, Billy Martin.

I began, "I don't give a damn what you guys do after the game. That's not what this book is all about. What this book is about is how players are treated by baseball." I paused. No one walked out. I had their interest.

As passionately as I could, I described what I knew to be the truth: that many careers ended too soon, either because a team changed managers and the new manager wanted his own people, or because a team changed general managers and the new guy wanted new players—or in the case of a black player, especially the utility players, he might lose his job because a white manager would prefer a white guy.

I paused. From the row of lockers in front of me one of the players said, "Or because you're a player rep." It was Dick Bosman, who, I remembered, had once pitched a no-hitter for Cleveland.

I repeated, "Or because you're a player rep."

I went on, "And there's something else. Baseball takes its toll on families. It isn't easy being a baseball player. You know that. I know that. But I'm not sure the public knows that."

"I can tell you how baseball broke up my family," said a player behind me. It was Steve Kemp.

"I'd like to hear about it," I replied.

"Each one of you has a story, and it's a story that deserves to be told. If you were Reggie Jackson, you could write your own book, but none of you is Reggie Jackson—well, I know Dock Ellis has written a book, and so has Ron LeFlore—but I want to write a book about baseball that's never been written before."

My five minutes were up. Bobby Tolan came out to break up the meeting. The Pelicans had a practice game against a local St. Pete semipro over-thirty club. Tolan still had some roster cuts to make, and the start of the season was approaching fast.

Several of the players clattered out the front door toward the field, but others came over to me to talk. Alan Bannister, a former star utility player for several teams, including the White Sox and the Phillies, looked me in the eye and said, "I hope you get to do this book." I thanked him. He will never know how sincere my thanks were. Another player, whom I didn't recognize, said he was all for it. Then he went out to the field.

I sat in the locker room as it emptied. Only a few players remained. Coming toward me was Dock Ellis. He was looking fierce. As he approached, the ferocity faded, and his face split into a grin. He stuck out his hand. I shook it. Then Dock turned and walked out of the locker room.

Bobby Tolan had told me that the players would take a vote, but there was no vote. I showed up for practice the next day, and the next, and when the bus was ready to leave for Winter Haven to open the season, I was on it. I remained for the entire season, which lasted from November 1, 1989, through February 4, 1990, when the Pelicans defeated West Palm Beach to become the first Senior Professional Baseball Association champions.

For me it was an extraordinary experience. Professional baseball players are heroic figures, and not only for what they do on the field. They give up so much for the game, and it seems that too often their final reward is bitterness.

I can never look at baseball again the same way. On one level it can be so wonderful, and on another so cruel.

Just like life.

It breaks your heart. It is designed to break your heart. The game begins in the spring, when everything else begins again, and it blossoms in the summer, filling the afternoons and evenings, and then as soon as the chill rains come, it stops and leaves you to face the fall alone.

A. BARTLETT GIAMATTI

St. Petersburg Pelicans 1989-90

Bottom row, from left to right: Batboy Charlie Hoffmeyer, Elias Sosa, Tex Williams, Luis Gomez, Hoot Gibson, Alan Bannister, Lenny Randle, batboy Brian Wilcox.

Middle Row: Mark Morley, Ivan DeJesus, Nardi Contreras, Butch Benton, Kenny Landreaux, Dave Rajsich, Steve Kemp, coach Ozzie Virgil, Sr., manager Bobby Tolan, trainer Brian Ebel, clubhouse manager David Chavey.

Top row: Charles Yancey, Pat Zachry, Jim Forbes, Lamar Johnson, Dick Bosman, Randy Lerch, Dwight Lowry, Peter Golenbock (author), Milt Wilcox, Steve Henderson, Dock Ellis, Roy Howell, Jon Matlack, Ozzie Virgil, Jr., Jim Morley, Phil Bensen.

CHAPTER

1

Beginnings

The players who strolled onto the bus were strangers. The overwhelming majority had played major league ball before, but on different teams, in different leagues, during different eras. In their cities once they had been household names, but the roar of the crowds had faded and so had the rush of adulation. This time almost all of them were playing for the money, but more important, they were attempting to rekindle what they once had, a joy from life that centered around doing the one thing they were meant to do—play baseball. This was a chance to be themselves again: professional athletes fighting for a pennant in front of fans who cheered them and before television cameras for the nation to see and admire. Their pictures would be on baseball cards. At the ballparks once more they would be asked to sign their names on little scraps of paper, grumbling about the foolishness of the exercise, but secretly wishing it would go on forever. Dreams do come true.

It wasn't that being a professional athlete was a cushy job. The public only gets to see the glamour. It isn't privy to the toughest part of the game: the politics, backstabbing, and blatant unfairness. The disappointments, heartbreaks, and feuds with managers and anger at men in the executive offices remained, and for some the bitterness continued to bubble under the surface.

Furthermore, it is said that athletes die two deaths: one when they stop playing and one when they stop breathing. All athletes suffer from being separated from the game. It is only after their careers end that the exballplayers realize that retirement has sentenced them to a routine of mordant sameness and crushing monotony. Once they are finished on the field, the highs become all too infrequent, and for some the series of unimaginable lows becomes a life sentence. For most it is as though someone else has taken over their bodies. After they are no longer wanted by the Tigers or Phillies or Yankees or Braves or Rangers, they are transported into otherworldly lives: construction workers, security guards, airport bellhops, purveyors of women's clothing, sellers of real estate and insurance and used cars, and in some cases lost souls unemployed, unwanted, no longer alive.

That November 1 bus ride, from St. Petersburg to Winter Haven, revealed little about these men, who had been resurrected as the St. Petersburg Pelicans. The team had been named after the funny little winged creatures whose presence darting and diving and flapping and waddling helps make the city of St. Petersburg, Florida, so special. These Pelicans were baseball players, pioneers of a grand new experiment: Senior Baseball. As it was conceived, the plan was to start a league for retired or discarded ballplayers over the age of thirty-five. (Catchers could be thirty-two or older.) The theory held that fans would flock to Florida ballparks during November, December, and January, when there was no other baseball being played, to watch their former heroes play again.

For the ballplayers the concept would give an opportunity for Reggie Jackson, Jim Palmer, Joe Morgan, Johnny Bench, Brooks Robinson, and many former retired major leaguers to put on the spikes and extend their careers. Players would get between $2,000 and $15,000 a month to play. The red ink per franchise that first year would be only about $1 million at worst. A draw of two thousand fans a game would break even. How could it miss? It had worked for the Senior Tour Golf. Why not for baseball?

The concept had come from a young Colorado real estate wheeler-dealer while he was ogling tits and ass on a nude beach in Manley, Australia. In April 1989, with waves crashing and gleaming bodies sunning around him, Jim Morley was staring at the scenery, at the same time devising the return of his childhood baseball heroes in a league for retired players.

On the flight home from Australia, Morley filled thirty-five pages of legal paper with his design. He would first contact the players, then get the empty, unoccupied stadiums in Florida, and after doing that, he would seek owners. Based on the demise of the United States Football League, Morley knew that disunity among owners could be a prime

Tom DiPace

Bobby Tolan and Jim Morley

reason for failure. He figured that if he set everything up and then got the owners, he had a shot at opening the gates for business that November.

Morley wrote to hundreds of former players over thirty-five. A week later he had one hundred and thirty yeses. Vida Blue, Luis Tiant, Bert "Campy" Campaneris, and Dave Kingman were among the first. Morley announced the names on the wire services. Reporters started calling. More players responded. Former Manager Dick Williams heard about the league and said he wanted to participate.

Morley called a press conference in New York on May 31. Steve Yeager, Rick Manning, Al Oliver, Jerry Grote, Bill Lee, and Dick Williams attended the meeting at Gallagher's restaurant in New York City. Howard Cosell was the first to arrive. Seven film crews came, along with 105 members of the press.

After the publicity from the press conference, Morley received inquiries from seventy-three groups interested in owning a team. He selected seven. By July, there were seven hundred players from which to choose.

A little more than six months after its conception, the Senior Professional Baseball Association became a reality. There were eight teams in the league, four in St. Petersburg's Northern Division, four in the other, Southern Division. The schedule was seventy-two games long. The designated hitter found another good use. And for the first time in America in November, December, and January, there would be world-class professional baseball. Thanks to Jim Morley's ingenuity and drive. As his reward, Jim Morley would keep the Pelican franchise. As part of their $1 million entry fee, the other owners paid him to run it.

Jim Morley was born in Detroit, grew up in Farmington, Michigan, adored the Tigers' Al Kaline, then moved to Phoenix when he was twelve. He was a high school baseball star. He went to the University of San Diego on a baseball scholarship and hit .320, but returned home after his older brother, Richard, was killed in a car accident. He transferred to Central Arizona, where the team was the NAIA national champions. The next year he went to the University of Arizona as a walk-on. His senior year he started every game in center field and upon graduation signed with the San Francisco Giants, where he played for Fresno in Class A. After two months the Giants released him. His baseball career was over.

"I wasn't as good as Chili Davis or Dan Gladden," Morley said.

Baseball may have been his first love, but as far back as high school Morley showed an aptitude for business. During a period of skyrocketing silver prices, he would drive to Nogales, Mexico, buy all the silver he could find from Mexican shopkeepers, head back across the border, and sell the silver for a profit.

Another of his schemes involved buying and selling airline half-fare coupons. Morley took out ads in the local paper—one for selling, one for buying. He hired two high school students to pick up and deliver the coupons.

"My delivery boys got out of high school at noon. They'd go to your house and buy three from you and walk next door and sell them to your neighbor," Morley explained.

When he graduated from college, Morley interviewed with a Colorado Springs real estate firm. The morning of the interview he discovered he didn't have the right shoes or a belt. Moreover, he needed the money he had to buy gas to get home.

He went to J.C. Penney's, ordered shoes and a belt that were three sizes too large, went to the interview, and afterward returned the garments, saying they were the wrong size. He got his money back, bought gas, and drove home.

Morley worked for the real estate firm for seven years, and then he and his brother Mark opened their own firm in 1987. In three years they accumulated $5 million in real estate holdings.

There were many questions concerning Jim Morley's Folly as First Class Bus 271 motored across Florida's Interstate 4 east toward Orlando. These players were old by baseball standards. Could they still play quality baseball, or was this to be a glorified beer league? No one knew if the pitchers could get anybody out. For that matter, no one could forecast whether the batters could hit the ball beyond the infield. It was as though baseball had been reinvented.

Question: Even if the players could perform close to their old standards, could they withstand a seventy-two-game schedule, playing almost every day?

Bigger questions: Would fans come out to watch them play? Would the weather be temperate enough? Would the owners have enough money to last the season? Would the games be competitive and interesting, or would they become an embarrassment to all involved?

Biggest question: Would the Senior League be a one-year wonder, or would it survive and flourish and become the resuscitator of old ballplayers' lives?

The answers would come shortly.

Floating above the cluster of general concerns was the overriding personal thought, the possibility that had brought many of these veterans to the land of Ponce de León, a dream about the future so tantalizing it was almost too incredible to contemplate: *Maybe if I shine in the Senior League, I can go back to the majors.*

When the bus reached the big Ferris wheel at Baseball and Boardwalk, it turned right and headed south toward Winter Haven, a boring stretch of superhighway. Then the bus traveled another fifteen minutes along a two-lane road until it turned left at an ugly orange-domed building, where the ballpark stood. It is called Chain O'Lakes Stadium. That is where Ted Williams and Carl Yastrzemski and Carlton Fisk and the rest of the Boston Red Sox went each spring to get ready for the season.

The field was radiant. The grass seemed a sparkling green, like the color of emeralds. The lines from the plate down into the corners were fresh and white and straight, and the moribund scoreboard in center field awaited its string of numerals. Wooden and ancient and charming, Chain O'Lakes looked as it did when the ballpark was built before the land rush. Only when you look beyond the park do you discern changes. Beyond the right-field fence orange groves once gave up their fruit. Now in their place are condominiums, beige with gray roofs. Civilization had come to central Florida.

Inside the locker-lined Pelican clubhouse, the players began the pregame ritual. The opening game would start at 7:05 P.M. sharp. It was only about 3:30 P.M. But as soon as the twenty-five Pelicans left the bus and settled into their cubicles civilian clothes were shed. With the donning of their regalia—the undershirt, the sannies, the maroon-and-buff shirt and pants, the spikes, then finally the maroon cap—the haberdashery transformation had been completed. The men grabbed their gloves and headed for the outfield to run and stretch. Perhaps the renewal would only last for three months. Dressed in uniforms, they put away any doubts. They were professionals, and they had one thing to focus on: today's opponents.

Pelican manager Bobby Tolan didn't know who was starting for the Winter Haven Super Sox because Super Sox manager Bill "Spaceman" Lee chose not to name him before the game. Naming the starter the day before is baseball custom. The press wants to know. So do the fans. It is a courtesy to do so. Lee, while still with the Red Sox, had admitted to sprinkling marijuana on his cereal in the morning and had publicly backed the federal judge who ordered forced busing in Boston. Not surprisingly, he had been bounced off two major league teams in Boston and Montreal—for his iconoclastic behavior and words. Now he was in charge, and he was in character.

If Tolan was ruffled, he didn't let it show. After the Super Sox completed their drills, the Pelican starters took their positions on the field for practice. Of the four infielders, Roy Howell, Luis Gomez, Lenny Randle, and Gary Rajsich, only Randle, the second baseman, could be described as a national figure. Lenny had made headlines for himself by punching out his manager, Frank Lucchesi, when Lenny played for Texas. Lenny also made the "Game of the Week" highlight film a few years later when, playing for Seattle, he huffed and puffed and tried to blow a bunted ball foul.

Howell at third and Gomez at shortstop had played together for bad teams in low-profile markets, and first baseman Gary Rajsich had had a cup of coffee with the Mets. Despite their lack of marquee recognition, when they began fielding the ball and throwing it around, the practice didn't *look* any different from a major league infield drill. As the ball moved crisply from player to player, it flew on a straight line, not arched, popping in gloves. Throws were sure and hard and on target.

Behind the plate the Pelican catcher, Dwight Lowry, seemed imposing. Lowry, who towered at about six-foot-four, had been a scrub for the Detroit Tigers behind their Franchise, Lance Parish. It was clear Lowry was a pro, as his throws to second snapped past his ear and to the bag in an eyeblink. In the outfield the name player on the team, Steve Kemp, once a Tiger star, later a Yankee disappointment, caught everything hit to him and always hit the cutoff man.

Jerry Martin, who had been a starting center fielder in the majors with Philadelphia and Kansas City, showed a strong arm. In right field Steve Henderson, the Henderson who wasn't Dave or Rickey, fired a long throw that sailed past the ear of the cutoff man by the mound and took a quick bounce and landed right in Lowry's glove, a foot from the plate.

This was serious business. The Pelican players were talking to each other, shouting encouragement, yelling where to throw the ball. They hadn't played their first game, and it was clear this was not going to be any over-thirty semipro league. These were professional baseball players, and they were showing that they knew how to play the game only one way—ballplayers had a favorite, cherished cliché for it—"110 percent." Still, it was only practice. A ball had yet to be thrown in anger. There had yet to be a mad dash to first by a batter. (Would their bodies hold up? A hamstring tear acquired during one run down the line in the first game could end a season.)

As 7:00 P.M. neared, Bobby Tolan, the Pelicans' manager, took another look at his posted lineup. A right-hander was starting for Winter Haven, and Tolan was ready. He sat on the end of the bench in the third-base dugout within shouting distance of home plate. He was alone, except for the batboy, a kid who was about ten years old.

"Are you nervous?" Tolan asked.

"No," the kid said. "Are you?"

"I'm too old to be nervous," Tolan replied.

From the beginning of training camp Bobby Tolan had made himself unpopular with some of the players with his no-nonsense Dick Williams type of approach. Tolan once had coached under Williams at San Diego, and he admired the man both for his success and his "It's-my-way-or-the-highway" style.

Before camp Tolan refused to sugarcoat his regimen. He told the prospective players, "I have two weeks to pick players. You come at your own expense. If you aren't in shape and you don't make it, it's your own fault." And when he carried out his threat, they resented it.

He began camp with calisthenics, and he made them run. When they finished running Tolan put them through drills—covering first base, pickoff plays, rundown plays, first-and-third double steals, the regular major league spring training routine. It was more work than some of them had expected or desired. The Pelicans under Tolan would be in shape or they would be gone, and they would play heads-up ball or face Tolan's sharp, critical tongue.

After just three days of practice, during which the team played but one intersquad game, Tolan cut seven pitchers, including some name players: the Phillies' Al Holland, the A's Blue Moon Odom, and the Giants' Ed Halicki. Halicki had pitched a no-hitter in 1975. Odom combined with Francisco Barrios to pitch one in 1976. But Tolan believed that for the team to be successful, he had to be ruthless. He realized some decisions were not fair, but he was a keen analyst of situations. The way he saw it, the team had exactly two weeks to prepare and if he didn't make cuts early, even if his decisions were wrong, the pitchers he wanted would not get enough work. Tolan made the cuts and took the heat.

Owner Jim Morley and Tolan had put together the team. Morley, who grew up in Arizona, was both practical and sentimental. He sought players from the Philadelphia Phillies and Arizona. The Phils used to play in nearby Clearwater, and he felt the fans would turn out to see their old heroes, so he tried to recruit players such as Randy Lerch, Bake

McBride, Al Holland, Larry Bowa, Jerry Martin, Alan Bannister, and Tolan. Morley had gone to the University of Arizona and so he chose former collegiates from the state of Arizona such as Gary Rajsich, Lenny Randle, and Bannister, who was doubly qualified.

Tolan didn't give a damn where the talent came from. He just wanted it youngish and fit. He wanted players as close to the age of thirty-five as possible, but he wanted *name* players. If he didn't recognize the player's name, he didn't want him. Except for Dock Ellis, his close friend and the man he chose both as a pitcher and as his pitching coach, Tolan refused to consider a player his own age, forty-four, no matter how big the player's name.

Tolan had to pare more than fifty candidates down to the remaining twenty-two roster spots. In the afternoons after the preseason workouts, Tolan, Dock, third-base coach Ozzie Virgil, Sr., and Morley each listed his choice of players on a sheet of paper. If the same name showed up on all four lists, that player made the club. By the final day of the season, the Pelican roster was set. In the end Tolan got the players he wanted and with two exceptions rid himself of the ones he didn't want.

In addition to his first-game starters, second baseman Randle, shortstop Gomez, first baseman Gary Rajsich, third baseman Roy Howell, catcher Dwight Lowry, and outfielders Kemp, Martin, and Henderson, he kept former valuable utility man Alan Bannister, Cards and Phillie outfielder Bake McBride, a lifetime .299 hitter, shortstop Sergio Ferrer, once a Twin and a Met, and catcher Butch Benton, a righty hitter who would platoon with Lowry.

Benton, who lived in Tampa, had once been the Mets' number one draft choice. Mark Corey, who played outfield for the Baltimore Orioles and in Japan, was on the squad as a designated hitter because, at age thirty-four, he was too young to do anything but catch. Catchers could be thirty-two because the beating they took behind the plate aged them prematurely. The problem was, Corey couldn't catch. He was an outfielder. But Corey and owner Jim Morely had been college buddies, so Corey was on the team. Tolan did not know what he would do with him.

The pitching staff provided an interesting array of once-well-known names. The starters were Randy Lerch of the Phils, Milt Wilcox of the Tigers, Jon Matlack of the Mets, Elias Sosa, who had relieved well on quite a few teams, and Gerry Pirtle, who had only pitched one season for the Montreal Expos but who had showed a good fastball and good control.

In the bullpen he had Dock Ellis, a classic starter who hadn't pitched since he cleaned himself up from drug use nine years earlier and who was penned in to relieve because of his age. Also Joe Sambito, a great left arm who had starred for the Astros. Sammy Stewart had been an important part of Earl Weaver's bullpen for years. Dave Rajsich, Gary's baby brother, had spent most of his career in the minor leagues, but he threw hard and nasty, and Mike "Tex" Williams, who got as high as Triple A for the Dodgers, had left baseball after being accused of gunrunning in Mexico. Dock liked Williams's arm, work-hard attitude, and wiseguy personality. Tex made the team over Al Holland, the former Phillies star who Tolan thought was overweight.

Bobby Tolan's reputation as a manager would rise or fall with these guys. To be successful Bobby would have to curb his sharp tongue, treat his players with diplomacy, and avoid personality conflicts, things he had failed to do while managing in the minors for San Diego and Baltimore.

In the past, when he was both a player and coach in the majors, he had bucked management, taking stands that got him traded. Once he and one of his star players, Phil Bradley, locked horns. At Bradley's insistence, Tolan was fired as batting coach. As a manager in the minors, politics twice had sunk him. With the Pelicans Bobby Tolan needed to be political. Could he be when he never had been before?

Tolan had most of the credentials to be a big league manager. He had been a very good player, and for a couple of years could have been described as a genuine star. As a player, he had helped lead three different teams to postseason play. One year with Cincinnati he led the National League in stolen bases and hit .316. Also in one year he hit .305, slugged 21 home runs, drove in 93 runs, and scored 104.

For two years he had been an integral part of the Big Red Machine. He knew the inside game, bunting, hit-and-run, stealing bases. He understood strategy. An excellent cardplayer, Tolan had a killer instinct. He was an arrogant winner.

But he also had liabilities. He was stubborn and willful. He wanted what he wanted. He wouldn't back down. And if challenged, his tongue could cut like a switchblade.

Tolan's primary problem was one he could do nothing about. He wasn't just a manager. He was a black manager. Compounding this fact of life was his choice of a black militant pitching coach to run a lily-white pitching staff.

Bobby Tolan had seen racism and, like many of the black players who came out of Los Angeles, had emerged gung ho to challenge it wherever it appeared. He was wary of the smallest slights, supersensitive to put-downs. His reaction to situations in which he felt he wasn't being respected or was being taken advantage of bordered on what many might label as paranoia.

But the whites in and out of baseball didn't have the sort of experiences the blacks did, so when Tolan would quickly retaliate or show anger, his mercurial temper would not be forgotten or forgiven, no matter how successful his won-lost record. On a team where most of the second-guessing would come from white players, he would need to learn to curb his tongue.

For Bobby Tolan politics would always be a white man's game, try as he would, because the words would come tumbling out whenever he felt he needed to stick up for himself. Whether this would get him in trouble with management or his players in the Senior League remained to be seen. It certainly had hurt him in the past.

In the clubhouse before the game Dock Ellis seemed calm on the outside. A hulking presence with a shaved head, he stood in front of his locker, shirtless, revealing a tattoo on one arm that read *Manhattan Dock*. He slowly dressed into his uniform. Dock did not expect to play this day, because as pitching coach he had not spent much time getting himself ready for the season, so focused had he been on paring away pitchers until he had the staff he wanted.

Bobby Tolan had been controversial as a player, but he had been a choirboy compared to Dock. Dock had had the talent and personality to be a popular and adored figure. Dock oozed charisma and presence. No one looked like Dock. No one talked like Dock. Even though he was black, and even though he played most of his career in Pittsburgh, a blue-collar city given short shrift by the national media compared to New York or Los Angeles, he was such a magnetic presence that writer Donald Hall wrote a book about Dock called *Dock Ellis in the Country of Baseball*.

One more thing about Dock: He could pitch. He threw hard, and he threw nasty. Dock had Hall of Fame stuff, but he had damaged his career by playing virtually his entire professional career on drugs. Dock even admitted that when he pitched his no-hitter for the Pirates in 1970 he had been under the influence of the hallucinogen LSD. He was so zonked, when it was over, he didn't even realize what he had done. Dock could have continued pitching after he quit, but the drug problem remained. With his reputation, no owner wanted him around.

Dock had been sober for many years and had been attending daily

Narcotics Anonymous meetings, but his sobriety had not dimmed his ferocity in his never-ending search for Truth, Justice, and the American Way. Dock was a man who hated: He hated bigots, he hated phonies, he hated liars, he hated self-deceivers. He hated anyone who strayed from the narrow path. Like many who turn their lives around, he disdained drinking and drinkers, drugs and druggies, and he kept an eye out for "the truth." If he thought you were conning him, he would call you on it. If he thought you were trying to put one over on him, he would explode.

Dock, who dished out more than most, didn't put up with much. He had a temper even worse than Tolan's, and admittedly Dock liked to "fuck with people," a characteristic not usually found in a pitching coach.

Dock Ellis as pitching coach?

Difficult to imagine, for he had been a member of the stoned generation. But remembering that Tolan had once punched out a top official of the Cincinnati Reds, once had been suspended by Sparky Anderson for growing a mustache, and once had been suspended by the Phillies for showing up manager Danny Ozark, then how did Tolan get hired?

Fortunately for both, Pelican owner Jim Morley didn't care. Morley had founded the league, whose purpose was to give former players a second chance. He was putting his philosophy into practice, but on a more practical level, he also didn't care because the two men displayed an attitude he admired. They were persistent—Tolan had called every day for a month to get the job—and they were competitive and tough. Tolan and Dock had grown up together as kids in Los Angeles, and Morely knew Dock's approach to the game would help recruit pitchers.

As far as Tolan was concerned, whether the players liked him and Dock didn't matter all that much. Winning, that's what Morley cared about, and that's what mattered to both Tolan and Dock. As Bobby had said about both of them, "Dock is a good person, but people won't ever, ever get a chance to know Dock. But he can be a prick too. We both can."

Dock was not someone to calm Bobby, and so Tolan was smart enough to hire as his third-base coach the popular, fatherlike Ozzie Virgil, Sr. Being a buffer was nothing new for Ozzie. For eleven years Ozzie had played that role between manager Dick Williams and his players at Montreal, San Diego, and then at Seattle.

Ozzie had begun his baseball career as a player with the New York Giants in 1956. He had stayed in the game ever since. He knew baseball, knew the politics of the game, and knew how to keep simmering conflicts from exploding into something worse. Ozzie had been with Bobby when both had coached under Dick Williams in San Diego.

Ozzie knew Bobby's moods. Ozzie was aware that Bobby would need his help, both strategically and emotionally. Bobby, inexperienced at this level as manager, was glad to have Ozzie's advice and support. Bobby Tolan realized that by hiring Ozzie Virgil, he had as his right-hand man one of the soundest baseball minds in the game.

"Give it up," Ozzie would shout to the players while he pitched batting practice or hit ground balls. Whatever that meant, they loved him for it and they would smile.

The Senior League season opened on the first day of November in the year 1989 under clear skies and cool breezes. A local Winter Haven high school marching band blanketed the field, prompting grumbles from some of the players, who wanted the band to "get the fuck off the field" so the game could begin. The owners of the Super Sox were Broadway play producers, so a singer from *Les Miserables* was flown from New York to belt out "The Star-Spangled Banner" before the receptive crowd of 1,428 curious fans. A twenty-one-gun salute followed, and the loudspeaker piped up a rousing rendition of the jazzy new Winter Haven theme song, with the ending lyrics: "It ain't over till it's over, that's Super Sox baseball." Yogi Berra would have been proud.

In the stands were kids and autograph seekers and many old folk. Part of the quandary for the Senior League brass was to decide whether to play the games in the afternoon or the evening. To generalize: Play in the day and you get the retirees but don't get the working class. Play at night and the retirees can't stay for the whole game because they go to bed early. What to do?

On this night there were some kids and families, but the crowd was made up predominantly of chipper blue-haired golden agers who shunned early sleep. The crowd was excited and polite, not rowdy.

Pelican relief pitcher Joe Sambito surveyed the crowd and noticed the bent toward the Danny Kaye generation.

"People come to St. Pete to retire," he mused. "They come to Winter Haven to die."

The Super Sox's lanky Jim Bibby, who celebrated his thirty-sixth birthday just four days earlier, came out to pitch. Bibby, at six-foot-five, had once thrown a no-hitter for the Texas Rangers. In 1980 he won 19 games.

The umpire called, "Play ball," Bibby stared in, and the switch-hitting Lenny Randle, batting left-handed, became the first Pelican to come to bat in the Senior League. He pulled the first pitch, a fastball, at right fielder Gene Richards, the former San Diego outfielder. There were two sweet sounds, the hard *thwack* of the bat hitting the ball, followed immediately by the softer, duller *thud* of the ball landing in Richards's glove.

Bibby then completed the inning by striking out designated hitter Bake McBride and Steve Kemp, both swinging.

In the dugout Pelican pitcher Milt Wilcox was not impressed. Wilcox said, "As short as everyone is for pitchers, if he could still throw eighty-eight miles an hour, he'd still be in the big leagues."

The Pelican starter, Randy Lerch, the young-at-heart man-about-town who called himself The Blade, didn't start out as well. A tall, thin left-hander who always looked like he had his fingers in the cookie jar, Lerch's pitches cracked the catcher's glove, but the throws were off the plate. He walked Richards to lead off the inning, and then he allowed a single to dribble along the infield grass without a play. The Super Sox were threatening. Al Bumbry's grounder to short resulted in a force at second, but Bumbry, the former Oriole speedster, beat the relay to first. The Sox looked certain to score.

Leon Roberts was the cleanup hitter for the Super Sox. Roberts had once hit 22 home runs for Seattle and he looked like he could still swing the bat. Lerch threw, and Roberts powered a ball up the middle that seemed headed for center field. Unexpectedly the shortstop, Luis Gomez, glided left into the middle and extended himself, diving to the earth. With his glove outstretched, he managed to ensnare a ball that had seemed determined to get by him. That was amazing enough.

But then Gomez quickly righted himself to his knees and made the throw to Randle at second, and when Randle completed his relay to first, the Pelicans had completed a spectacular rally-killing double play that even had the local Super Sox fans on their feet, clapping.

A young Super Sox fan was both impressed and angry that Gomez had made such a great play. He delved into his scorecard, trying to find out something about him.

Who is this guy? he wondered.

Gomez was born in Guadalajara, Mexico, but raised in the Chavez Ravine section of Los Angeles in the shadow of Dodger Stadium. He was an All-American high school quarterback. After attending UCLA on a baseball scholarship, he played eight years for Minnesota, Toronto, and

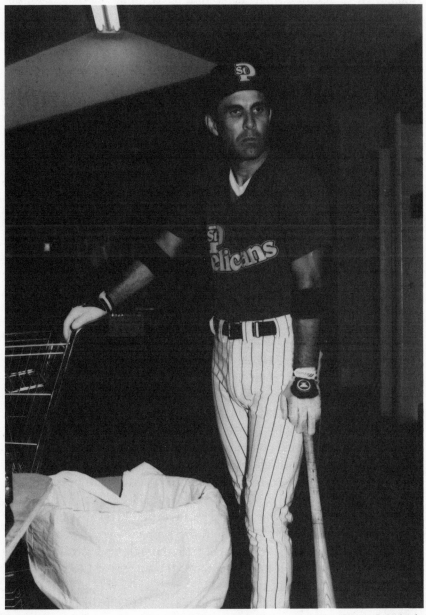

Peter Golenbock

Luis Gomez

Atlanta. He didn't hit a single home run, never hit higher than .246, but because of his excellent glove, his willingness to perform whatever role was asked of him, and his self-effacing, silent demeanor, managers wanted him on the team.

The fan looked up from his scorecard. He said, "Number two. Luis Gomez? Never heard of him."

The first Pelican run of the season came in the second inning. First baseman Gary Rajsich led off the inning. When Bibby couldn't throw an inside fastball past him, Rajsich, who toiled in the minors forever without ever getting a chance to play regularly in the majors despite All-Star seasons, got his teammates off their feet when he launched a line drive that soared about 380 feet away into the screen in right field for a home run.

It's funny what Senior Leaguers shout at a teammate who has just hit a home run, because they say the exact same things that Little Leaguers say:

"Attaboy, Gar, way to go!" "Nice shot, Gar-ee!" "Way to go!" "Allll-right!"

With the Pelicans up, 1–0, Cecil Cooper led off the bottom of the second inning for Winter Haven with a line drive that looked like it was going to land in right-center and take a short hop to the wall. Jerry Martin, quick off the mark, ran hard to his left at the sound of the crack of the bat, extended his glove, dug his spikes into the ground, and pushed off. Diving horizontally yet still in control, he somehow captured the ball moments before sliding on his stomach and incurring grass marks on the front of his clean Pelican uniform.

Jerry Martin was a serious, no-nonsense, sausage-and-gravy kind of guy who had the pedigree to be a ballplayer. His father, Barney, had pitched two innings in the majors with the Cincinnati Reds. Jerry remembers his dad telling him about the time he faced a young Hank Aaron. "He told me Hank hit the ball back through his legs, and he said when he turned around the ball went over the center-field fence—which we all know is a bunch of bull."

Jerry's mother (yes, his mom) had been a star basketball player. In high school football his senior year Jerry scored 100 points and in basketball averaged 26 points and 17 rebounds a game. He ran track, starring in the long jump, and played baseball. He was offered full scholarships in each of the four sports.

The Pelicans

Jerry   Martin

At Furman University, Martin led the team to its first Southern Conference championship. He was a strong, fast guard, scoring 37 points in a post-season game against Davidson.

Fate kept him from pro basketball. Jerry came from Columbia, South Carolina, and Frank McGuire, head coach at the University of South Carolina, had made plans for Jerry to play pro ball in Italy. But in the summer of 1971 McGuire got sick, so Martin called the baseball scout who had signed his brother Mike, the top left-handed pitcher in the country the year before. After working out with the Phillies, Jerry was signed by farm director Dallas Green.

Green told Martin, "Just because your brother was the number one pick for us last year, don't think we're going to do you any favors." The irony was that Mike Martin hurt his arm and never made it to the Phils. Jerry Martin made the Phillies and was an eleven-year major league player for several teams.

Martin was a member of the Philadelphia Phillies when the team won three straight division championships in 1976, 1977, and 1978. He might have been a better-known player had his Phils made the World Series any of those three years. It never happened.

Though Martin's Phils won the Eastern Division in 1976, '77, and '78, "we always seemed to come up short in the playoffs." Martin came closest in 1977. Instead the Dodgers went. Martin admits that he still has nightmares about the one crucial play that he could have made that would have sent the Phils to the World Series against the New York Yankees. He didn't make the play because he wasn't in the game.

It was Game Three against the Dodgers. Habitually his manager, Danny Ozark, had sent him to left field on defense for Greg Luzinski. The Phils led by two runs in the ninth inning, and Martin was ready to go in again, but this time Ozark either forgot to or didn't want to make the switch.

The Phils got the first two outs. Vic Davalillo singled. Manny Mota pinch-hit. He smashed a ball to deep left, and Bull Luzinski broke in then went back, and the ball hit off his glove at the wall. Mota got a double, and after two more singles, the Dodgers ended up winning the game.

Martin said, "Had I been out there, I would have caught that ball very easily and we would have been in the driver's seat to go to the Series. Yeah, I have nightmares about that. I go in slow motion, and I see the ball being hit out there, and I'm wondering why I'm not out there, and I see the ball hit off Bull's glove. I'm seeing the ball go in my glove and thinking, *All right, one more game and we're in the World Series.*"

Martin was a fourth outfielder with the Phils. He forced a trade to the Chicago Cubs, where he started for two years, averaging twenty home runs a year, and watched Dave Kingman hit even more. When the Cubs refused to reward him, Jerry Martin fled to the windy cavern of San Francisco's Candlestick Park for a year and then moved on to Kansas City, where he had a pretty good year playing for Dick Howser. Then he and Willie Aikens and Willie Wilson got busted for drug use, and it was on to a final stop in New York, where he watched Dwight Gooden begin an illustrious career with the Mets.

When Martin came in from the field, his teammates greeted him with high-fives and congratulatory greetings of "Way to go, Mud." Mud Martin. Gets his uniform dirty. Plays hard. Makes the big play. If only he had been in the game instead of Luzinski.

The Pelicans led 3–0 in the sixth and scored four more runs to make the game a rout. With two outs and runners on first and third, Steve

Kemp came up to bat. For the $9,000 a month he was getting from the Pelicans, Kemp was penciled in to start in left every day.

Kemp had been a star attraction for several years for the Detroit Tigers. A complex man with a strong personality, Kemp's promising career had been curtailed during batting practice one afternoon in New York in 1983 by a line drive off the bat of Yankee teammate Omar Moreno that struck him near his right eye and fractured his cheekbone. He eventually had been run out of the game because general managers were convinced that Kemp could no longer see. True, he did have trouble during day games when his pupil would not contract, making it difficult for him to see the baseball. Nevertheless Steve Kemp insisted it was not enough of a handicap to keep him from being successful in the majors.

Kemp was known as an astute negotiator who gained fame and notoriety by signing a five-year contract calling for him to make $5.5 million. He hung on as long as he could, but at the end general managers could talk about nothing but his bad eye. He retired in 1988 after being demoted to the minors. Kemp was one of the few Pelican players who truly didn't need the money because he had made millions and was lucky that advisers hadn't squandered all of it in bad investments. What Kemp wanted most of all was to prove to himself, and to anyone else who opted to notice, that he was still a big league hitter.

Kemp stood at the plate, swinging his bat like a scythe, holding his hands low and cocking his wrists just as the pitcher delivered the ball. It was a unique swing, dangerous to copy because the hitch was so pronounced. Kemp had kept his batting style since he played high school ball and had always been so successful that no one ever had the nerve to suggest he change it. Not that Steve Kemp would have gone along had he been asked.

"I've always swung left-handed, with that big swing," Kemp said, "and people always commented on all the movement I had in my bat, but it was totally natural, something I have done from day one, like a timing mechanism. It's where I get all my power. That's why I'm the type of player who has to play every day. When I play every day, my timing is there."

The pitch came in, and he lined a clean single to center, plating the fourth Pelican run. In the sixth Kemp again singled cleanly into the outfield. In the eighth he drove in what would be the Pelicans' eighth run of the day with another ringing hit, a double that he pulled down the right-field line.

The Pelicans won the opener easily. Winter Haven showed itself to be weak in every area, hampered by its owners' grand plan to stock the team with former Red Sox players—many were too old—hoping to attract fans through their association with the Boston team. But the Winter Haven owners learned, too late, as other owners did, that show biz and glitz don't attract fans nearly as successfully as a winning ballclub does. The Pelicans had won the game, 9–2. By the end the Winter Havenites didn't have a whole lot to cheer about.

The winning pitcher, left-hander Randy Lerch, threw six innings, gave up four hits, and didn't allow a single run. Throughout his eleven-year major league career Lerch had always had a live arm and superior stuff. His fastball moved, and the curve broke sharply. The question on any given day was whether he could find the plate. On this day he gave up a walk or a hit each inning, but the defense behind him had prevented several runs. His control was good enough to keep the Super Sox at bay. Not bad for a man who hadn't pitched a baseball in three years.

Like his teammate Steve Kemp, Randy Lerch does not fit the mold of the typical stoic athlete. He is a bundle of emotions, and he wears his heart on his uniform sleeve. "I'm the nut on the team," he quickly will say. "They probably think I'm the superflake."

To hear Lerch yakking and joking in the locker room or on the bus, one might think that. But scratch deeper, and there is a lot of little boy and a lot of hurt inside the man. Randy Lerch is what literature calls a "tragic clown." His was a career that began with much promise and ended with a series of bitter divorces—from baseball, his dad/coach, and his wife. Randy Lerch came to Florida not only to play baseball again but to resurrect his life.

Not a second after the final out, the banks of lighting at the Chain O'Lakes park went to black. The Pelican participants from the game were still in the dugout, while those in the bullpen milled about down the third-base line near the left-field fence. The clubhouse was a short walk from there. When the lights suddenly went out, everyone had to stop what they were doing. It was too dark to see.

Roy Howell said, "I figured it was because we kicked their butts and they didn't want to shake hands."

After their eyes adjusted to the sudden darkness, the Pelican players were able to begin their walk to the clubhouse down the line past third base. As they strolled, the first salvo of some very powerful fireworks erupted from behind the left-field fence and exploded in a dazzling array of colors overhead, the noise of the concussion deafening—*bah boom*—

and a little scary. The fans, still in their seats, oohed and aahed, but the exposed players reacted as though they were being fired upon. They made a break for the clubhouse. As they reached the door, the sounds of the crunching of gravel under their cleats made a racket.

Safe inside the locker room, with the sound of the projectiles whistling above, Joe Sambito, who had seen a lot in baseball, commented on the Opening Day festivities in Winter Haven.

"They have shot their whole wad on the marching band and the fireworks," he said. "Tomorrow they'll have nothing, and two hundred fans. It'll be just like Cleveland."

Third baseman Roy Howell, standing next to him, slowly peeled away his uniform. Howell had gotten three hits and showed both range and a strong arm. He hadn't been impressed with the Winter Haven team.

"They were all show," Howell said. "And we played hardball."

Joe Sambito had been right about Winter Haven blowing its wad the first day. For the second day of the season the sun beat down on Chain O'Lakes park, and though it was a magnificent day, attendance totaled 324. The Senior League owners were going to find out that it wasn't enough to throw open the ballpark. They had to advertise and promote and produce a winning team.

"Nice and cozy," mused Bobby Tolan. "Just the families."

Ferguson Jenkins pitched for the Super Sox against the Pelicans' Milt Wilcox. Jenkins, tall and elegant, threw with an easy, smooth motion. His 284 wins over nineteen years of play would have made him a first-ballot shoo-in for the Hall of Fame, except that one afternoon in Toronto while playing for the Texas Rangers, he was arrested for drug possession after customs officials inspected his bags and discovered a small amount of cocaine and marijuana. The incident will probably put off his election for several years even though the charges were later dropped.

While Fergie warmed up before the game, Pelican second baseman Lenny Randle entertained his teammates by talking about Jenkins. The two had been together at Texas.

Randle, a joyous, outgoing person, was the mouth of the Pelicans. On the field he was its spark. His game was akin to that of Cincinnati Reds star second baseman Joe Morgan, though one important skill Morgan had that Randle lacked was Joe's ability to hit home runs.

But the accomplishments of Lenny's twelve-year career were overshadowed by one incident of madness. He is remembered most vividly for being one of the few players ever to punch out his manager, Frank

Lucchesi. When you get to know Randle, it's impossible to reconcile the everyday Lenny Randle, a laughing, caring, bubbly personality, with his image as a ruffian. Moreover, Randle is such a multitalented player—he can bunt, hit-and-run, steal bases, hit in the clutch, and field like a dream, plus he has a sense of the game that borders on genius—that it's equally hard to imagine a manager sufficiently offbase to give a talent like Randle cause to hit him.

Glib, intelligent, and quick-minded, Lenny occasionally performed standup comedy after his retirement from baseball. In the dugout, Lenny was giving a performance, describing how pitchers differ from infielders, how catchers are different from outfielders. Listening to him, you are amused but at the same time you think, *Yeah, he's right.*

"Pitchers," Randle said, "are very critical. Every ball should be caught, every ball should be an out, every pitch is a strike. And nothing is ever their fault. 'If you don't get me five runs, it's your fault.' 'I'm not taking the blame. You should have hit a home run.' 'Run into the wall and catch the ball.'

"Pitchers are in their own world. Pitchers are artistic. I respect that. They have an artistic viewpoint of their craft. They are like painters, sculptors, actors, people who are very sensitive, easy to set off balance. You can intimidate them, psych them.

"Infielders are different. Infielders are competitive. They have a relationship. They have a chemistry, an aura, both second basemen and shortstops. There's a drive to be the best you can be out of your abilities, to dive and to hustle, on or off the field. Infielders have an intuitiveness that goes beyond just playing. Very competitive. Infielders piss off a lot of pitchers, because they are usually the guys who beat you, the scrappy guys who will do anything to win. They'll cheat. They'll steal a base or steal a candy bar. They're survivors. And those are the guys the managers want to score the winning run. They can get the hit or the sacrifice, bunt, squeeze, just make things happen.

"Catchers are more like Henry Kissinger. Diplomats. They all have broadcasting jobs. They always end up in the booth. They're articulate, and they analyze a pitcher's philosophy or why he throws a pitch. They think like managers. They are individuals and team spokesmen at the same time. They're mayors.

"Outfielders? They're alienated. Each one is an only child. I mean, I would love to have them sit down with Dr. Ruth or Joyce Brothers and get counseling. They stand out there, spaced out, looking at shadows, thinking about their hitting. They're like pilots in a cloud. When it's time for them to hit, they land."

Lenny smiled broadly. Later, seeing his former teammate Fergie Jenkins warming up, he had several of the Pelicans chuckling as he recounted what it was like when Texas pitching coach Art Fowler would come to the mound in the middle of a game to give instructions on the orders of their demanding, critical manager, Billy Martin. Fowler, a good old boy from the Carolinas, knew there was little he could impart to a consummate pro like Fergie, but Billy had told him to go out there, and Art was just doing what he had been told. Fans assumed Art's role was to sit and drink with Billy. He did that, but his primary role on the team was to break the tension Billy created with humor.

" 'God dang, Fergie,' " Lenny began in his best Art Fowler drawl. " 'I don't know what the hell I'm doing out here. Shoot, I'd rather be shooting quail, but Billy sent me out here to talk to you, and I don't know what the hell I can say. You're going to the goll dern Hall of Fame. What the fuck am I doing out here? Shoot, I'm just stalling. What do you want to do, talk? Ya wanna get this guy out?' "

Roy Howell and Joe Sambito and a couple of others listened and laughed.

Randle led off the third inning of the scoreless second game. Ozzie Virgil yelled out at Lenny, "Go with him. Don't pull him. Take him to left." Jenkins was throwing hard, and Ozzie wanted the left-handed Randle to hit Fergie's fastball to the opposite field.

Randle took the next pitch right up the middle for a single. Though Lenny was not forty years old, when Jenkins threw home to the next batter, Lenny Randle broke for second, sliding headfirst safely ahead of the throw. It was hard to imagine—even at age forty—that Lenny couldn't help a major league team.

Randle led off the fifth with another hit, and he scored the first run of the four-run inning, as Kemp, Howell, and Steve Henderson drove in all the runs and started the Pelicans on their second straight rout of the Winter Haven Super Sox. A leadoff single by Randle in the eighth led to six more runs. The final score was 12–2.

The beneficiary of this largess was Milt Wilcox, once a star pitcher with the Detroit Tigers. Wilcox, thirty-nine years old, had pitched for sixteen years in the majors. He won 11 or more games for seven years in a row. In 1984 he won 17 games under Sparky Anderson and helped pitch the Tigers to a World Series victory over San Diego, winning a game in the playoffs against Kansas City and another against the Padres in the Series.

Wilcox threw the ball with a jerky motion, but his follow-through was smooth, and his fastball seemed to rise, even though aerodynamics experts say that this is impossible. His curveball, now his bread and butter, came at batters at several speeds and kept them guessing.

Only one time, in the fourth inning, did Wilcox appear to be in trouble against the Super Sox. With one out, he had allowed two singles and a double for a run. Left-handed outfielder Pete LaCock was the batter. After a conference with manager Bobby Tolan, Wilcox issued a free pass to LaCock, loading the bases.

Former Red Sox third baseman Butch Hobson came to the plate. It was righty against righty, and Wilcox threw sidearm, low and away. Hobson hit it hard, but right to shortstop. The ball went six-to-four-to-three, short-to-second-to-first, a double play, before Hobson could get three-quarters of the way down the line. Wilcox was out of the jam.

Wilcox told the press after the game, "It was something I had to do and I did it. We're out here to win ball games. That's what we're here for."

Milt, the old pro, was in midseason cliché form.

The day did not end without controversy. The Super Sox owners had decided to build their following on the cult of manager Bill Lee, the former Boston Red Sox and Montreal Expo pitcher. During the game they gave away Bill Lee autographed balls, Bill Lee autographed posters, and autographed copies of Bill Lee's autobiography, *The Wrong Stuff*. It can be a problem when a team's identity revolves around one man. The one man had better perform on the field. In this game Lee had relieved Fergie Jenkins in the fifth inning with the score tied, 1–1, and he proceeded to get lit up. By the end of the inning the fans were shouting, "Take the pitcher out."

Lee, a competitor of renown, was stomping around on the mound, angry at himself, angry that his team was being shown up. At the end of the game he allowed his frustrations to get the better of him. In his own mind Lee had envisioned the Senior League to be a fun league, where he would pitch a little, play outfield or first base, where he could get up and hit. He hated the role of the designated hitter because it had prevented him from showing his batting skills. But Lee's kinder and gentler idealism was being ruined by Bobby Tolan's vision of a league where his team would, as Dock Ellis put it, "kick ass and take names." As a result, Lee was upset.

After the game Lee told the writers, "I think the Pelicans are assholes. They're good ballplayers, but that doesn't make them nice men. It's a damn militaristic regime over there. Tolan makes them shave their mustaches. He's a Hermann Goering. He's an anal retentive black man. He should take a shit somewhere and relax."

Lee said, "We play hard and we play to win, but we don't scrape, crawl on our bellies, and sell our souls to the devil to win. You can be good winners along with being good losers."

Lee added, "I guarantee you we'll have a better attitude losing than some of their guys do winning." Then he said, "Some of their guys have come over and said they want to play for me."

After the reporters wrote down what Lee had said, they scurried over to the Pelican dugout to get a response from Bobby Tolan, who was mystified at Lee's remarks.

"What does he have against me?" he asked. "What did I do? We kicked their butts, and we were better prepared. That's why he's so upset."

CHAPTER

2

The Skipper

It was ironic that Bill Lee had called Pelican manager Bobby Tolan a fascist who ran a "militaristic regime," because during his entire playing career, Bobby Tolan had been a thorn in the side of management. Tolan had decreed there would be no mustaches on the Pelicans. Yet when he was with the Cincinnati Reds, the incident that sealed his departure was his insistence on growing facial hair despite manager Sparky Anderson's rule that all players must be clean-shaven. Tolan had grown his mustache specifically to flaunt authority. This was different. This time, he was the authority, and he wanted his team to be disciplined, something he had always believed in, so long as *he* was not the target.

Discipline. The word has a number of meanings in baseball. For a manager, it can be the rules laid down to keep the players in line: No mustaches, bed checks, everyone must wear shirts and ties, everyone rides on the team bus.

And yet a team can have discipline on the field, even when none of the rules are enforced. For Tolan, it was the discipline on the field: Throw to the right base, hit the cutoff man, know the count and how many outs, hit to the right side with a man on and less than two outs, swing at good pitches. That was his credo. It was the on-the-field discipline that had been his watchword since he played on his first organized baseball team. Execution. Fundamentals.

As a boy, Tolan had so much ability that adult coaches pleaded with him to play on their teams. When he was eight he was recruited for a team called the Millie Tigers. It was sponsored by a hamburger stand. On the uniforms a big hamburger had been stenciled over the heart. Tolan had been sitting in the stands, eating potato chips and watching his friends play, when the coach of the Millie Tigers came over, bummed a few chips, and asked Bobby to take some swings on the field.

"Finally I did, and the first two swings, I hit the ball out. When practice was over, he handed me a jersey," Tolan said.

The manager of the team, Theodore Webb, taught his players the fundamentals of the game.

Tolan recalled, "He taught us bunting. He would take us out into the field and station us where the cutoff man should be. Taught the shortstop how to back up a stolen base attempt—things that were not ordinarily taught at that age—so we were more advanced than other teams, and that's why we won. We executed. We threw a lot of runners out at the plate because we always tried to get in position and we didn't miss the cutoff man."

In the three years Tolan played on the team, the Millie Tigers rarely lost. At a young age, Bobby Tolan learned what it took to win ball games. He saw that on the baseball field he was royalty.

"One year," he said, "we played about sixty games, and I had forty-two home runs. Most of them were line drives in the gap that rolled until the ball stopped."

When Tolan got too old to play on the Millie Tigers, he moved up to a team called the Thompson Tigers. Tolan was the team's star pitcher and hitter. When he defeated a team coached by former Negro League pitching star Chet Brewer, Tolan found himself on the fast track to the major leagues.

"We were winning all of our games," he said, "and there was another team, the Pirate Rookies, coached by Chet Brewer, who was a bird dog for the Pittsburgh Pirates. We had never played each other. People kept saying, 'Wouldn't it be nice if the Thompson Tigers played Mr. Brewer's team.' And I didn't know if they were avoiding us, but finally it happened. I was the pitcher. I shut them out. Then the next day the coach told me Mr. Brewer wanted me to play for his team. I figured, 'Hey, this will give me a chance to be more exposed,' because I wanted to play professional baseball. Mr. Thompson didn't mind me leaving his team, 'cause eventually the two teams worked hand in hand and it was almost like a franchise."

The Pittsburgh Pirates sponsored Brewer's team, supplying the

The Pelica

Bobby Tolan

uniforms, bats, and balls. Chet Brewer recruited all the best young players in the Los Angeles area for the Pirate Rookies.

"We had an awesome team," Tolan said. A remarkable number of his teammates ended up playing in the major leagues.

"I played first, Davy Nelson played second, Ricky Smith was at short, Bob Watson was the catcher, Dock Ellis was a pitcher, Willie Crawford was in the outfield, and we had pitchers named Gary Boyd and Leon McFadden."

Because his players came from the black areas of L.A., many from Watts, Mr. Brewer's team played mostly against other black teams. Some white teams would schedule games, but never in the black neighborhoods, so the Pirate Rookies did a lot of traveling, to Glendale, San Bernardino, and other areas. Whether their opponents were black or white, the Little Pirates rarely lost. It was a continuation for Tolan of unlimited success on the ball field, feeding his belief of personal invincibility that is common to many professional athletes.

Tolan recalled, "Over the years with the Millie Tigers, the Thompson Tigers, and Mr. Brewer's team, we won somewhere between a hundred and fifty and two hundred games and didn't lose more than ten games. It was like we were the L.A. All-Stars. Here we were fifteen, sixteen years old, high school age mostly, and we played teams of older men, thirty years old, and we'd hold our own, and a lot of these guys had come back from pro ball.

"I had to play guys older than me to get anything out of the game." He wasn't bragging. He was being matter-of-fact.

"But I was always pretty level-headed. I could handle the pressure of tight situations. I never got too upset. I felt that, knowing my ability and deep down inside being honest with myself, I could make it to the major leagues if I was given the opportunity. And my first day in the major leagues, I was nineteen years old, which says something."

Tolan went on to star at Fremont High School. His teammates were Willie Crawford, who played with the Los Angeles Dodgers, and Bob Watson, who was a star at Houston for many years before being traded to the Red Sox and then signing on as a free agent with the Yankees.

Like Theodore Webb with the Millie Tigers, his high school coach, Phil Pote, stressed fundamental baseball, poverty-style.

"We learned discipline." Tolan said. "He taught us to be very selective as far as swinging the bat, because of the budget. If you broke a bat, he'd stop and make the whole team do push-ups. Hey, I loved the game, and it didn't bother me. To me it was just another form of exercise."

Coach Pote was a fanatic about baseball, and Tolan was thrilled that his coach's passion about the game matched his own. Inside the school building Tolan would be walking from one class to the next, and if Pote saw him, the coach would yell, *"There he goes,"* which meant an imaginary runner was stealing second. In the hallway Tolan, the team's star pitcher, would stop, drop his books, get in a set position, whirl, and pretend he was throwing to second base.

"People thought I was weird," Tolan said. "'Hey, this fool is dropping his books,' but it kept me sharp. I wasn't going to balk. I'd hear *'There he goes,'* and I'd drop, turn, and throw. At times I would get harassed by kids who would walk by me and yell, *'There he goes,'* and I'd do it, and it wasn't the coach. But it didn't bother me. We were taught to react, not to think, so that when a situation came up, it was automatic. We were programmed, like a computer."

Pote was fanatical about another aspect of his players' lives. He demanded that they have satisfactory grades. Pote kept in touch with his players' teachers, and he would check up on the players in school to make sure they were doing their homework during study period and not goofing off.

Coach Pote's players were required to show him their report cards. If a player didn't pass a course, whether he was a star or a scrub, that player didn't play. Even Willie Crawford, the team's star outfielder, wasn't exempt. Not all of the players, including Tolan, understood, but to his credit Pote remained firm.

"We had a real key game one day against one of the tougher schools," Tolan said. "We were at the five-week point, and Willie Crawford was failing one course. Mr. Pote said Willie couldn't play. I told him, 'I think the teacher will say that Willie will pass.' He said, 'No. He's supposed to have a passing grade, and he's not playing.' It hurt Willie. I was hurt too because I thought the coach could have bent the rules a little bit to let him play. But he didn't. We won the game anyway. Willie got his grades back up, and he kept them up the rest of the year. Once we found out Coach Pote wasn't kidding, we got our work done."

During Tolan's senior year, Fremont High won the city championship of Los Angeles. Tolan did most of the pitching. In the semifinal game against Dorsey he went into the seventh losing by a run, but Bob Watson hit a bases-loaded double off the top of the wall for a 6–4 win.

The championship game was played on the home field of the University of Southern California, and a lot of scouts were there. Tolan again was the pitcher, the last game he would ever pitch. The opponent was Banning High School, which had defeated Fremont in an exhibition game. But this day Tolan pitched a shutout, hit a three-run home run in the first inning, and struck out fourteen.

At the time—this was 1963—there was no major league draft. A high school grad could be signed by the highest bidder. On June 20 Tolan graduated. He had been interviewed by scouts from Cleveland, St. Louis, Houston, and California.

"They all said they weren't going to try to sign me, because they felt I was locked up with Mr. Brewer and the Little Pirates," Tolan recalled. "It didn't make any sense to me. I was just looking for the highest bidder. But nobody else approached me, and I figured the only team that wanted me was the Pirates."

The night Tolan graduated high school, the Pirate scouts came over to his house and offered him a contract. It was for $10,000, and Tolan said for him "that was a lot of money."

Which it was. But the fact that none of the other teams had opted to challenge the Pirates in a bidding war upset his sense of fair play. Tolan felt that whitey was doing a number on him.

Afterward, remorse and bitterness set in. All those years he had won ball games, had been a superstar. Now that he had signed a professional contract, he was convinced that he was being ripped off.   •

Tolan said, "I felt I could have gotten more. I felt I had signed my life away. The scouts said, 'What's the matter?' I said, 'I'm just not happy. I need more money.' They said, 'You already signed a contract.' I said, 'I don't think it's fair.'

"They said, 'If you don't think it's fair, here's the contract. Tear it up.' Which they didn't think I would do. I tore it up. They said, 'That's the last time you'll hear from us.' "

But of course it wasn't. Gamesmanship is an important part of any negotiation, and the Pirates weren't about to let Bobby Tolan slip away.

That evening was graduation night for Fremont High, and the senior class went to a local amusement park. When Tolan arrived, standing under the Ferris wheel and the roller coaster waiting for him were two Pittsburgh scouts. They offered him the same $10,000.

Tolan, chastened or resigned, again put his signature on the document.

The next day a scout from the California Angels really messed with his head. Scout Rosie Gilhousen came over to his house and offered him a contract for $25,000. Tolan believed the scout was only toying with him.

"I suspected Gilhousen knew I had already signed with the Pirates and was trying to make me feel bad," Tolan said. But he wasn't sure.

He reluctantly turned down Gilhousen's offer and honored his new pact with the Pirates.

"It didn't seem right. I was seventeen years old. I thought, *If only I had waited.*"

Later Tolan asked the Pirates why he was only offered $10,000, despite his high school heroics. They told him, 'If only you were three inches taller, you could have gotten $15,000 more.' Tolan at five-feet-eight, 120 pounds, was small, but all his life he felt he had been cheated.

Once he signed, Tolan immediately went off to pursue his siren.

Pirate scout Jerry Gardner drove him to Reno, Nevada. They arrived just as the game against the Modesto Astros was to begin. In the sixth inning, Tolan was sent up as a pinch hitter. He got a broken-bat single over second. His pro career had begun. Never again would his life be so carefree. To the end, controversy and acrimony would follow.

CHAPTER

3

Manhattan Dock

When Dock Ellis heard from the two chortling reporters the remarks Bill Lee made about Bobby Tolan, he was blazing. Dock had focused on Lee's comment that Bobby was "an anal retentive black man," but he hadn't heard the words quite right, and he was asking, "What's an analitic black man? What does 'analitic' mean?" Instinctively Dock knew Lee wasn't being complimentary.

Like Bobby, Dock wondered aloud, "Why would he say a thing like that?" In the clubhouse Dock had showered and appeared placid as he dressed, but inside him the maelstrom churned. Before getting on the bus for the return to St. Petersburg, he was saying loudly, "I'll hit him in the head. I will. He better watch his mouth. Talk like that can get you killed."

Coming from Dock Ellis, this was not idle chatter. All his life Dock had been retaliating against whites who made the wrong kind of remark.

Dock grew up in what he calls the Neighborhood, two city blocks between 135th and 139th to the southeast of Los Angeles, near the cities of Gardena and Compton. The Neighborhood was prosperous, middle-class. No ghetto.

Dock Ellis's father always pushed for Dock to get an education, so when it was time for him to go to high school, his father sent him to the white school, Gardena, rather than the mostly black school, Fremont, where Tolan attended. Ellis's father figured the education at the white school would be better. What he didn't foresee was the verbal harassment his black son would have to take from the white students who called him "nigger" and "Watusi" as he strolled the school's corridors.

Dock had intended to play on the varsity baseball team and went out as a tenth grader, but he hadn't been wooed by the coach as Tolan had been. Tolan had a coach who was black, and they were simpatico. Dock had a white coach who tended to feel more at ease with white players, so Dock did not get the TLC Tolan received. Nor did Dock get his coach's support when Dock was taunted because of the color of his skin, something Tolan didn't have to face at Fremont High.

"I knew I could play on the team," Ellis said, "but one of the senior pitchers on the team called me a 'spearchucker.' I didn't know what that meant. I asked, and when they told me, I knocked him out."

Dock decided, "I don't want to play for *them*." He dropped off the team. Dock never stopped playing, though. Since he was fourteen, he had played for Chet Brewer's team. It was where Dock and Bobby Tolan first played ball together.

Ellis got his first opportunity to pitch for the Little Pirates when the star pitcher, Waco Jackson, who had signed with the Pittsburgh Pirates, was fatally shot in the head. Waco was sitting in a restaurant in the black section of L.A. when an argument started across the street. Suddenly a shot rang out. Waco was dead before his food arrived. The following day Dock started in his place.

Chet Brewer became a second father to Dock Ellis.

Ellis recalled, "Mr. Brewer was a great pitcher himself, and he taught pitching all the time to me, because what he saw in me was himself. See, we had a team that played grown men, and those men taught us how to play baseball. I learned that, no matter how hard I threw the ball, they were going to hit it over the fence, so I had to come to my senses and say, 'Hey, I have to throw something else.' We had hitters like Reggie Smith, Willie Crawford, Tolan. We played against guys who had played Triple A, and we beat them. Here came Mr. Brewer and all these fucking kids, and Mr. Brewer was just laying back laughing, 'cause we were whupping their ass.

"I remember we'd go to towns, and they'd turn the lights out so they wouldn't have to finish playing against our team. We were so good that white teams wouldn't play us. So Mr. Brewer fixed their ass. He started getting some white players, like Billy Rohr, who played with Boston and Cleveland, and a dude named Lillywhite, who was from Arkansas but never signed. He should have. He could play some baseball.

Tom DiPace

Dock Ellis

"Under Mr. Brewer every game was a championship. That's the way he billed it. That's the way he pumped us."

Dock Ellis hasn't seen Chet Brewer in years, but he continues to harbor a deep resentment that the Pirates treated his old coach shabbily. As Dock saw it, Brewer found a lot of talent for the Pirates but was paid relatively little for his efforts.

"They didn't compensate him but maybe two or three hundred dollars a month," Ellis said.

After the Pirates won the World Series in 1971, Dock encountered a man wearing a World Series ring who informed him he was a scout in the California area. Dock blew up. He didn't know the man. He said, "Man, who *are* you? I ain't ever seen your face."

The next year, when the Pirates were visiting L.A. to play the Dodgers, Chet Brewer came to Dodger Stadium to visit Ellis. They were standing in the visiting dugout, and Dock asked Brewer about his World Series ring. Brewer, naturally, had no idea what Dock was getting at.

Dock told anyone within earshot that he wasn't going to pitch another game for the Pirates unless Chet Brewer got a World Series ring. When the Pirates didn't give Brewer the ring, Dock mutinied and didn't pitch.

When Ellis returned to Pittsburgh, general manager Joe Brown called him into his office to discuss the matter. Dock told Brown, "All those motherfuckers got World Series rings, and Mr. Brewer doesn't have one. Take it out of my pay, and buy him a ring." Chet Brewer got his ring.

But at the same time Chet Brewer had been afraid that Ellis's stand to get him the ring was jeopardizing his position with the Pirates.

Ellis said, "Mr. Brewer was crying, because he said I was jeopardizing his chumpchange they were giving him. But Mr. Brewer had the nucleus of a major league team on one fucking team, and all he had to do was say, 'If you don't give me $100,000, they ain't gonna sign.'

"He saw it as an opportunity," Ellis said.

Dock saw a black man being taken advantage of. It was probably both.

Dock Ellis is proud of his arrogance and cockiness. He sees these traits as a badge of courage coming from his roots in Southern California. He points to his peers, Tolan and Crawford, and contrasts them with the young players who came from the north of the state.

Ellis said, "They weren't arrogant and cocky like the guys from my part of California. If we would have been like those guys, there would have been a lot of us going to the Hall of Fame, but we were all labeled troublemakers, 'cause we didn't take no shit.

"I grew up in it. Prejudice. Racism. It was like Mississippi or

Alabama. Only they didn't hang me. It was subtle. We played ball with a chip on our shoulders, and we dared somebody to touch it. Every one of us but one, Bob Watson, played that way, and that was because he was raised by his grandparents, so he wasn't exposed to street life as much as we were."

With Dock's reputation made with Chet Brewer's Pirates, the baseball coach at Gardena High naturally wanted Dock to play, but Dock refused. After boycotting his junior and most of his senior years, Dock ended up playing his senior year only after he was caught drinking wine in the boys' lavatory. Faced with the choice of playing on the baseball team or being suspended from school, Dock opted to play ball.

Dock pitched in three league games and then in the city tournament, where he was asked by Dodger scout Kenny Meyer to sign a professional contract. Dock, who loved basketball more, intended to go to college to play hoops.

"I used to make people look like an ass, like Magic Johnson," Dock said. Dock told the Dodgers, "I'm not signing shit." Nor would he sign with the Cleveland Indians.

The Indians offered him $12,000, but L.A. high school star Bob Bailey had received $200,000 from the Pirates. Dock and his friends knew "Bailey couldn't hit me with a banjo." If he was going to play baseball, he wanted what Bailey was getting. Dock's hoodlum friends told the Indian scouts, "Get the fuck out of here."

As bright as he was, Ellis only had a 1.9 grade-point average. When the college scholarship offers came in, the vice principal tore up his scholarship applications, saying, "You can't get a scholarship with a 1.9."

"No one was counseling me," Dock said. "Today, I would have taken college preparatory courses. Back then, my family didn't know, and the people who knew never passed it on to me. I had a cousin who was a journalist. He took college preparatory courses. My nieces and nephews are all going on to college. But I was not told this, and that's the system."

At Gardena High, the whites studied for college. The blacks took woodworking, shop, and ceramics.

"I remember breaking into a teacher's desk with a friend and finding the IQ scores," Ellis said. "My friend said, 'Look, we're up in the 130s.' I said, 'Why didn't she tell us?' And yet she *was* telling us. She would say, 'You must study harder. Stay after class. I want you to.' I'd say, 'Fuck that.' She wanted me to be a writer. I said, 'Nah, I don't want to be no writer.' I wrote a story about a player who went to USC and who went on to play for the Giants, and she put the article in the school paper. She might have been the only teacher who tried to encourage me and my friend, Horace Mack, but we didn't respond because we didn't understand.

"I have a lot of resentments," Ellis said. "I deal with them every day."

One of those resentments concerns how the Pittsburgh Pirates got him to sign for so little money. When his father died, the litany was: "All he ever wanted you to do was play baseball." So when the Pittsburgh Pirates came to him with an offer of $2,500, he signed.

Chet Brewer told him, "It's an opportunity. You say you can pitch. If you can, you'll be in the big leagues, so don't worry about it. Just make them pay later."

When Ellis arrived in camp, he saw how badly he had been ripped off. It still makes him angry.

"I saw these motherfuckers who couldn't do shit, who they had given all this money to, and then I went crazy. I cussed them out, man. Hundred-thousand-dollar bonus babies. I'd tell them, 'Go back to Ohio and buy some apartments, punk, because you ain't gonna make no money playing baseball.' And they'd be gone in a year."

Ellis began his minor league career at Batavia, New York. It was where he learned to pitch and how to handle living in an inhospitable world. He discovered the pleasures of alcohol.

"There were no more than fifty black people in the town, but it wasn't bad, because I could drink. When I found out the drinking age was nineteen, I said, 'I don't want beer. I want what they're drinking *at the bar*, the green stuff.'" That was crème de menthe. Dock would steal the team car and go to Buffalo and Rochester.

Midway through the season the team sent Dock home and ordered him to lie and tell everyone who wanted to know, including and especially scouts from other teams, that he had a bad arm. Unlike Bobby Tolan, whom the Pirates would lose after his first season, Dock Ellis was kept by the Pirates, through deceit.

When Ellis returned for spring training, he once again found himself face-to-face with a white kid who called him a "nigger." It's quite likely the player never again called another black person a nigger.

"He was an older guy, a year ahead of me. His name was Shoemaker," Ellis said. "I tried to kill him.

"I almost knocked him out, and I took a knife and just started cutting him. I cut a heart-shaped circle over his heart, dug into him a little, and told him, 'The next time I'm going to go this deep,' and I held my thumb and finger about three inches apart.

"When they called me into the office, I said, 'Fuck you. Don't call me into no motherfucking office. Call him.' And they didn't say shit to me."

Dock had two skills: He could pitch, and he could get in trouble. With Kinston in '65 he was 14–8 with a league-leading 1.98 earned-run average, and in '66 with Asheville he was 10–9 with a 2.76 ERA. The next year he moved up to Triple A Columbus, where trouble became his middle name.

Late in the season Ellis was hit in the leg by a vicious line drive. Unattended, after a week the leg pained him so much that he insisted the trainer look at it. When the trainer made an incision at the spot, a jellylike substance oozed out.

As the team readied itself for the playoffs, Columbus management wanted Ellis to pitch. He refused, saying the leg hurt too much. Part of his reluctance was his belief that, had he been a white player, he would have gotten the proper treatment.

When his teammates insisted he pitch, he went to the bullpen and worked out. "You can pitch," said Ed Hobaugh, one of the other pitchers.

Ellis said, "You want me to pitch because you can't pitch, you motherfucker. I ain't gonna pitch."

Hobaugh, who had formerly pitched with the Washington Senators, began circulating a petition to kick Ellis off the team. Other signatories were shortstop Ernie Bowman, a pitcher named Acker, and about five others, including shortstop Freddie Patek. Ellis found out about the petition from another former Washington Senator, pitcher Pedro Ramos.

As a result of the petition, Ellis was suspended. Columbus went on to win the playoffs without him. Ellis was not voted a share in the winnings, and feelings became so acrimonious that Columbus management threatened to charge Ellis for the hotel room he lived in.

"That's when I threatened to hurt someone," Ellis said. "They paid the bill, and I got the fuck out of there. And I swore to get every one of those motherfuckers. If I ever played against them, I would hurt them."

Over time, Dock Ellis kept his word. He broke the arm of one, the leg of another. One time he almost killed Bobby Cox because Dock thought he was Ernie Bowman. "Cox was the third baseman, and I thought it was the shortstop coming up to bat. I hit the helmet with the pitch, and he came out of his helmet. They thought I hit his head."

The only signatory he didn't hit was Freddie Patek, a Pirate teammate from 1968 to 1970. But he held a grudge anyway.

"I was with the Yankees when I finally faced Patek," Dock Ellis recalled. "Patek was with Kansas City, and every time I pitched against them, he would scratch himself. He knew I was going to try to kill him. He knew me. He knew I wasn't bullshitting.

"And just before we played them in the playoffs, Hal McRae begged me. He said, 'Dock, you're a man. That man is scared of you. He is frightened to death. Let's think about that. At one time you liked him.'

"So I told Hal I wouldn't, and when I pitched against them, Patek was in the lineup, because he knew if I said it was over, it was over. The motherfucker hit two doubles off me."

Despite Dock Ellis's scrapes with just about everyone wherever he went, he still made the Pittsburgh Pirates in 1968 at age twenty-three.

Had he been even-tempered, political, placid, and straight, rather than aggressive, loud, antagonistic, and on alcohol and drugs, Dock Ellis probably would have been ranked with the best pitchers of his generation. That was the kind of tremendous talent he had. He needed to be Joe Louis, not Jack Johnson. Despite the fact that Dock was the raging avenger, made enemies, and was on drugs his entire career, he still managed 138 wins and twelve years in the majors.

"They knew my talent," Dock said, "and I knew my talent. I knew as long as I could throw, I would be around, no matter what the fuck I did. Like I told them, 'When the arm no longer can do what you think it can do, I'm gone, and I'm gonna kiss your ass. But right now, you can kiss my ass.'"

CHAPTER

4

What Made Sammy Run

Home after two successful games on the road, the Pelican players drove from their hotel rooms, rooming houses, YMCA residences, and rented condos to arrive at the maroon Pelican locker room at St. Pete's Al Lang Stadium. They arrived around three in the afternoon on November 3, excited to be playing before their own fans.

To keep expenses down the league had established a salary cap for each team of $550,000. Based on their projections, the same officials predicted that if the teams could average two thousand fans a game, the league would prosper, and on this day the ticket office gleefully reported brisk sales. Attendance above four thousand was expected for the evening's contest. Optimism was high.

The clubhouse at Al Lang, where the St. Louis Cardinals trained in the spring, proved spacious. Once they had put on their uniforms, the players turned right at the exit. After a short walk down a hallway, they had a choice of three openings: left to the whirlpool, straight ahead to the trainer's tables, and right to the dugout and the field. A table with chewing tobacco, sunflower seeds, and coffee sat in the hallway. Some of the players grabbed the traditional tins of Red Man and Copenhagen. An equal number chose paper cups of the seeds, which they would stuff in their mouths and chew like cud. They would swallow the meat and then spit out the shells onto the floor of the dugout.

Equipment manager David Chavez had set up the clubhouse as though it were for a major league team. He had had experience as clubhouse manager in the Triple A cities of Denver and Des Moines, Iowa, and he was aware how finicky the players could be. He tried to arrange everything perfectly, and he almost succeeded, until the uniforms arrived. The uniform pants were uniformly the wrong size—too loose— and everyone complained. A harried, conscientious Chavez personally took as many pairs of pants as he could to his local tailor. By the start of the game, most everyone—even Steve Kemp—had been mollified.

Al Lang Stadium shone. It is a modern structure, poured concrete, with rows of red seats and then higher navy blue seats and still higher silver seats that gleamed under the Florida sun. Towering poles of lights ringed the field. Beyond the green fence with the local advertising signs rose palm trees that lent an exotic, tropical atmosphere. Behind the scoreboard in left-center was a cultural center, the Bayfront Auditorium, and beyond that white boats sailed lazily on placid Tampa Bay.

In the dugout stood a large, energetic man with a sizable girth and a big grin, entertaining anyone within earshot.

"Good afternoon, ladies and gentlemen," he intoned as if he were the PA announcer. "Welcome to Al Lang Stadium." He paused. "Today's trivia quiz." He grinned wider and paused again. "Who the hell is Al Lang?" Sammy Stewart asked.

Those around him laughed. "Who in Christ is Al Lang?" asked another Pelican. Shoulders were shrugged. No one seemed to know—or really care.

Outside the stadium, a small plaque reads:

This stadium dedicated March 12, 1977, in honor of Albert Fielding Lang, 1870–1960, Florida's sunshine ambassador to major league baseball. It was through his dedication, vision, and love of the game that the big leagues discovered Florida's excellence as a conditioning site and St. Petersburg became baseball's spring training capital.

Sammy Stewart, who had pitched most of his career for Earl Weaver in Baltimore, and later in Boston and Cleveland, had always been known for his devil-may-care approach to life. Once again he had found humor in his surroundings and made others chuckle. Stewart explained, "I've always had a loose kind of attitude where I come and try to pick people up. If I can make somebody smile, have a good time at the ballpark, it makes for a better atmosphere."

He thought about some of the things that had happened to him in the major leagues, and he added, "I never worried about getting released or nothing."

Stewart's reputation preceded him. He occasionally missed team buses and planes, often showing up at the park last and leaving first.

Sammy enjoyed being the life of whatever party was going on. Once he was arrested for drunk driving, another time for having a gun in his car. He outwore his welcome in Boston in just one season after he spit in the face of the Red Sox traveling secretary, who had ordered the bus to leave without him on a day when Stewart was a tiny bit late.

On the mound—to Stewart the only place that counted—he was a tough, almost mean competitor. He became an important cog in the Orioles' strong pitching combine, setting up games for Earl Weaver's closers, keeping the Orioles in games whenever a starter faltered early.

There was also the poignant side to the man. His son, Colin, born in 1979, developed cystic fibrosis. Sammy would spend hours in the hospital with him. The illness also cost Stewart huge sums of money.

Stewart left baseball after the 1987 season, found no employment in

Sammy Stewart

The Pelicans

1988, and hoped major league brass would be impressed by his work in the Senior League. Jim Morley had offered Stewart $500 a month more than Earl Weaver's Miami Gold Coast team. An enigma, Stewart seemed desperate to make an impression. Though he arrived in camp too heavy to be at his best, he had lost enough weight to make the team. Bobby Tolan hoped Stewart would become an integral part of his bullpen.

Stewart began his career in 1975 when he signed as a free agent with the Baltimore Orioles. After high school he had been asked to go to Kansas City's Baseball Academy, but he turned the Royals down because he and his father didn't think the $7,000 signing bonus sufficient. He went to Montreat-Anderson Junior College in North Carolina, led all junior colleges in earned-run average with a 0.36, and signed with the Orioles. This time he got $4,000 and was sent to Bluefield, Kentucky. Stewart hated it there.

"Bluefield was no fun, really. It was a like a second armpit to Cleveland," Stewart recalled. "It was a challenge because they said they'd give me more money when they saw how my arm compared to their top draft choices, Dave Ford and some boy named Dyer, I forget his first name, but they signed for big bucks and I didn't. Shoot, I beat them both to the big leagues. I saw all these youngsters, and they didn't have the mental capacity for the game that I did. I knew what baseball was about. I saw that all these top draft choices were getting scared. 'Uh-oh, I had a bad outing. I'm going to get the pink slip.' I'd say, 'What are you worried about? Sit down and have a beer. Go home, think about what you did wrong, and try to correct them.' And they'd hang their heads. I'd say to myself, *Well, the world needs ditchdiggers too.*"

Stewart next went to Miami, where former Oriole hurler Ray Miller taught him how to pitch, and became a big winner in the minors as a starter. In September 1978 the Orioles brought him up. In his very first game Sammy Stewart struck out seven batters in a row over the second, third, and fourth innings. Stewart said, "I had relatives coming out of the woodwork saying, 'You're the hero of this town. You broke a major league record.'"

According to Stewart, after he started and won his first two games in 1979, he was replaced in the rotation by Steve Stone. Stewart fumes about losing his starter's job to this day.

A check of the record books, however, tells a different story. Steve Stone, a starting pitcher his entire career, signed as a free agent with the Orioles on November 29, 1978, and started 32 games in 1979. He was

11–7. In 1980 he won the Cy Young Award, going 25–7. How can you quibble with that? Stewart nevertheless tries.

"Stone had been nothing but a .500 pitcher," Stewart said. "Then in 1980 he won the Cy Young Award—and that was my starting position. I became the middleman and a spot starter. If Jim Palmer slept on a foam rubber pillow and his neck was sore, I had to take over. I did that for seven years for Baltimore."

There is no indication that Stone was anything but a starter for the Orioles or that he ever "replaced" Stewart in the rotation. Sammy's hurt appears to come from within and seems to have clouded his perception of past events.

Whenever Stewart told Earl he wanted to be a starter, Weaver knew the right words to calm him down. Weaver would tell him, "We have Jim Palmer, Mike Flanagan, Scott McGregor, Denny Martinez, and Steve Stone, and if you start I lose you. I need you three times a week, not once."

Stewart would capitulate. Earl told him, "I want you to be my Mr. Everything."

For most of Stewart's years in Baltimore his manager was Earl Weaver. Sammy prospered under The Earl. Like his counterpart, Billy Martin, Earl Weaver preferred his players to be men's men. Sammy was a drinker and Earl was a drinker. That may have been one of the reasons they got along so well. Stewart admired him greatly.

"Earl is a little man who thinks he's seven feet tall, and in the game he could very well be," Stewart said. "People said he had a lot of players who made him a winner, but he got the best out of you. I didn't care whether he got drunk.

"I remember one time in Texas John Lowenstein and I were waiting for the elevator. The doors opened, and Earl was in the back of the elevator, and he was going, 'Eee-le-ven. Eee-le-ven pleash.' We said, 'Earl, there are only four stories in this hotel.' Earl said, 'Ahhhh, eee-le-ven, push the eleventh button pleash.' I said, 'Why, ain't you tall enough to reach the elevator button yourself?'

"Finally he got to his room, and half an hour later we found him half in and half out the door. We put him to bed.

"He would go home and get drunk and fight and come to the ballpark and put up the best lineup. If Mark Belanger hits Jim Kern, he'll be hitting first, and sure enough Mark will get a double to win the game somehow."

Stewart continued, "But he was a little man. I remember him coming

out to the mound in the World Series and saying to me, 'I'm fifty-three
fucking years old, and I can still throw the ball over a fucking seventeen-
inch plate. You suck. Go take a shower.' That was his way. I mean, he
used to stand on top of a stool to argue with Rick Dempsey. 'Listen here,
you...' He wanted to be bigger.

"And he would say things like that whenever I had a bad outing, but I
could take it because he was right. I never liked to throw the ball right
down the middle of the plate. I liked to play Whiffle ball with the batters.
I liked to say, 'Hey, hit this,' and if the batter didn't swing, he'd walk.
But I had a great pickoff move. I picked off sixteen at second base and
seven at first. So I kept runners close. And I always thought I'd get a
ground ball when I needed it. That's how confident I was in my pitching.

"But Earl Weaver was fun to play for. He loved to argue with Jim
Palmer, our star pitcher. Palmer would say, 'The only thing I know is you
have to pitch this guy up and away.' And Earl's favorite comment was
'And the other way is...' and he'd tell him another way to pitch him.
Earl would never agree with Palmer, because they were kinda alike. Earl
knew if he threw it high and away, he'd blast it, so Earl wouldn't let him
get away with that. 'Oh no, you've got to get him out the other way too.'
Earl wanted him to mix it up. And Palmer himself was very stubborn.
They were always fighting."

Sammy's string of troubles began in 1983. Earl Weaver was gone. Joe
Altobelli had replaced him, and Joe Altobelli was different from Earl.
Stewart did not respect Altobelli.

"Joe was very, very lackadaisical. He'd go, 'Aw, I should have pinch-
hit right there.' We'd go, 'Oh-kay.' But we won the thing in 1983. He
made some good moves. He fined me one time the next spring training.
See, I've had the bad habit of being the last one to the ballpark and being
the first to leave. I always said I never cared about nothing except
between the lines, and in the clubhouse I care about all the guys.

"But this one time in spring training, we had two days to go, and the
hotel manager said, 'You're going to have to get your stuff out,' and I
said, 'What about doing it tomorrow?' and she said, 'I have people
coming in now.' So I rushed. I thought I had enough time, but I got to the
ballpark just as Eddie Murray was in the locker room putting on his
shoes."

"It'll cost you $250, and it'll cost you $250 every time you're late,"
Altobelli told Stewart.

Stewart hollered back, "You can take the money and shove it up your ass. I don't give a shit. You don't treat people like that."

Then, during the All-Star break, Stewart was stopped by a policeman at five in the morning when his car was observed to be weaving. Stewart was arrested for drunk driving.

"My little son was in the hospital," Stewart said. "My friend had a birthday party. They kept a bar open, and I got caught hitting a couple of lanes."

The Orioles checked his urine every other day. In 1983 Stewart won 9 games and saved 7.

"Every day I came to the ballpark my head was clear. I'd go to the park, make someone laugh, come home, enjoy the kids, and I pitched great. I made everything happen great. I didn't drink, and it was just a magical time. In the 1983 World Series against Philadelphia, for the second time I didn't get scored on. I remember Mike Schmidt and Garry Maddox said I should be the Most Valuable Player because I came in at tough times and shut the door on them."

It was to be his last great year. His relationship with Joe Altobelli deteriorated.

Stewart recalled, "He had taken all the fun out of it, because he would constantly say remarks to me, like 'Don't be late.' He would single me out. 'Tomorrow everybody be dressed by ten. Sammy, you too.' And I hadn't been late. But he would pick me out, and it upset the whole atmosphere as far as me and him being able to look each other in the eye and play ball."

When Altobelli was fired, the players expected Cal Ripken, Sr., to take over. "Everybody was ready for him," Stewart said. But Ripken didn't get the job. Instead, the Orioles brought back Earl Weaver. It was a difficult time for everybody.

"The atmosphere just wasn't there," Stewart said. "People were saying, 'What's he coming back for? Does he think he's going to pull off a miracle?' 'Cause we really didn't have that good a team."

Earl had no miracles to perform. But Stewart enjoyed playing baseball again. In 1985 Earl used him in a stopper's role, along with Don Aase. With Earl in his corner, Stewart felt certain he would remain with the Orioles. Instead, they traded him to Boston. "I went there and made a mistake," Stewart said.

Stewart's last contract in Baltimore called for him to made $390,000 for the year. Because he believed he would be making that kind of money for years to come when he got to Boston, he bought a house for $300,000.

That house became Sammy's misfortune because he alienated himself in Boston when he spat on traveling secretary Jack Rogers. Boston is a very proper town, and the Red Sox a proper organization. Spitting on a Red Sox executive ruffled some feathers—big-time.

"I came to the ballpark one day after being with my little boy in the hospital for about three hours," Stewart said. "The team bus was parked outside, waiting to go to the airport. I put my carry bag onto the bus and went to park my Cadillac. I came back, and the bus was gone...even though they knew my carry-on was there, and they knew I was there. It made me so mad. I had to take a cab to the airport."

Once Stewart got to the airport, he told manager John McNamara he didn't appreciate being treated that way.

When McNamara told Stewart that Jack Rogers had made the decision to leave him, Stewart replied hotly, "Wait a minute. You're running the team. You never ran off and left Jim Rice when he was late. You don't do this. I haven't been late. Why did you do this?"

McNamara told him, "You have a reputation for that."

Stewart answered, "I may have had a reputation for that, but I haven't been late for you, have I?"

McNamara said, "No, you haven't." Mac then reasserted that Jack Rogers, not he, had left Sammy behind.

Stewart said, "I'm a country boy, and I have a temper, and I believe if it comes to hands, I'm not scared to throw them.

"Well, Jack Rogers came up to me and said, 'If you get off your ass and get to the ballpark on time, that wouldn't happen.' I thought to myself, *And if they can't wait till I park my Cadillac and come back through the tunnel to get on the bus, there's no use me playing for a team like that.* I spit on him. I mean, I was going to hit him, but he was seventy years old. I went: *Pttui.* It was a very despicable and very stupid thing for me to do."

It was particularly stupid because at the start of the season Sammy Stewart had become a very popular player in Beantown. In one period in April and May he had nineteen and two-thirds scoreless innings, and during that stretch the team went into first place and never lost it.

"I was working my tail off," Stewart said. "I did everything for the people in Boston. I have a shirt that says '53 will always be Number 1 in Boston.' People liked me, and I really thought I was going to stay there."

But after the incident with Jack Rogers, John McNamara stopped using him, except in one-sided games. Stewart also was kept out of the 1986 World Series against the New York Mets.

"I had been scoreless in two World Series," Stewart said, "and a lot of people said that if I had pitched we could have come out a little better. When you talk a little better, you're talking one ground ball. If this hadn't happened, the thing with Buckner might never have happened."

What Stewart was referring to, of course, was the ball hit by the New York Mets' Mookie Wilson that went through first baseman Bill Buckner's legs and cost the Red Sox the World Series.

"I was sitting in the bullpen when that happened," Stewart said. "When we saw the ground ball, we jumped up, ready to holler, and then, *'No! No!'*"

When Stewart came to Boston, the first day he walked into his supermarket, one of the clerks recognized him and said, "You guys are going to blow it again."

Stewart replied, "Wait a minute. This is my first year here. I'm coming over from the winningest team in the last twenty-five years, the Baltimore Orioles. I'm a winner, and you have to give us a chance."

The clerk wasn't buying it. "No, forget it. you guys will blow it again," he said.

Stewart remembered, "When we lost the Series, that's when I said, 'They got more than clam chowder up there. They know what they are talking about.' I thought, *Now I have to go home and listen to: 'We told you so.'*"

The Red Sox had told Stewart they were going to keep him for several years, but after he spit on Jack Rogers and was caught with a gun in his car, they released him at the end of the 1986 season.

Stewart initially was elated, because he had become a free agent and believed he would be sought by a number of teams, resulting in a salary even bigger than his $390,000 from the year before. He thought, *It's finally my chance.* But his agent kept saying, "Sammy, it's a bad time right now. Nobody's going after anybody, not even Tim Raines." Raines, an outfielder for the Montreal Expos, was a superstar.

Stewart replied, "You've got to be kidding me."

The agent wasn't kidding. Stewart worked out that winter and was in great shape. At worst, he figured, he would re-sign with Boston like catcher Rich Gedman.

Unfortunately for Stewart, he had worn out his welcome in Boston, and the fallout would be devastating. After three months of waiting, Cleveland called with an offer of $147,000. That's a lot better than zero, but it was a deprivation after making $390,000 a year, what with the size of his mortgage and his ailing son's medical bills.

Stewart moved to Cleveland and left the rest of his family back in Boston. His troubles worsened.

"They foreclosed on the house. It messed up my whole family situation. My boy was getting sicker, and things weren't working out right."

In Cleveland, Stewart didn't get along with manager Pat Corrales. The problem arose, according to Stewart, when Corrales ordered him to throw at and hit members of the Kansas City Royals.

Stewart said, "I was very sour at that, because here I had been out of baseball two months. He's got some problem with the Kansas City Royals, and he asked me to drill Danny Tartabull and Frank White because we were getting our butts kicked. Those are two people I like. I don't play the game like that."

Stewart knocked Tartabull and White down and hit Jamie Quirk on the hand. He told the Royals' players, "I want you fellas to understand that if I want to fight, I'll come up and we'll fight in the outfield. But I'm not going to hit you with a baseball just to get you mad. 'Cause I don't do that. I don't want to take anybody's career away."

The Royals' players told him, "We had trouble with Pat Corrales before when he managed Texas."

Stewart won four games for the Indians in 1987, but because he missed spring training and the first two months of the season, he left himself vulnerable to injury. He hurt a rib cage muscle. After that, he never got a good chance to pitch.

"Nothing but in blowaway games," Stewart said.

Stewart's career went up in flames because of a proverbial bridge that he had burned behind him. When he was traded from Baltimore to Boston, Stewart told off Orioles general manager Hank Peters. Stewart told Peters that under his leadership the Baltimore organization was heading for the dumper. Stewart was not wrong. The Orioles fell to the bottom, losing 107 games in 1988. When Peters was hired as Cleveland general manager, Stewart's days were numbered. At the end of 1987, he wasn't offered another contract by the Indians, or by anyone else.

"All of a sudden, I'm out of baseball," Stewart said. "I worked out very hard the first three months of 1988 and then gave up."

There was a recent British movie in which the protagonist says, "I'm not afraid of growing old. I'm only afraid of growing bitter." It was a poignant line. Bitterness makes you mull over and over the question "What if?" What if Sammy's son hadn't come down with such a serious illness? What if Baltimore hadn't traded him? What if he hadn't spit on

Jack Rogers? What if there hadn't been collusion and another team had picked him up for the same $390,000 a year? What if? "I was just getting ready to make the big money, and that's when collusion set in," Stewart said. "I now have a $1.4 million claim, and I hope I receive a big portion of that. Because I think I deserve it. They took my career right out of my hands when I was in my prime. I did everything any organization ever asked me to do. I signed autographs. It's so disappointing."

With the Pelicans Tolan pitched Stewart only once when it mattered. In the second Pelican home game the Pelicans were leading by two runs in the ninth inning. With one out and a runner on third, Tolan called on Stewart to retire four-time National League batting champion Bill Madlock of the Orlando Juice. At the age of thirty-eight, Madlock's tummy may have bulged some, but he still carried a lethal bat. If Madlock weighed too much, so did Stewart. At the start of the season Tolan told all the players that he wouldn't tolerate anyone being over-weight. Sammy was pushing 250, and he was trying Tolan's patience.

Stewart tried to come inside to Madlock, but Madlock was ready and lined a hard single to left, scoring a run. Quickly Tolan returned to the mound and gave Sammy the hook. It was an inauspicious outing for Stewart. He was hanging on to a job by a thread. Stewart had hoped to pitch well enough in the Senior League so he could get another shot at the majors.

However, when Sammy Stewart arrived in St. Pete to play for the Pelicans his financial condition had deteriorated and his behavior had turned erratic. He leased a car from a local Dodge dealership and smashed it up. He began borrowing money from the other players, $100 here and $50 there, calling at odd hours with odd explanations why he needed the cash.

Pitcher Elias Sosa had been one of the Pelican players from whom Sammy had borrowed money. It was one in the morning, and the phone rang in Sosa's hotel room.

"Can I borrow $100?" Sammy said. "I owe the cab driver money." Sosa, trying to be a good teammate, agreed to lend Stewart $50. Stewart came up to his room and got the money.

An hour later Sosa's phone rang again. It was Stewart. "Can I borrow another $50?" This time Sosa told him no and asked him to please stop calling so he could get some sleep.

Several days later owner Jim Morley and manager Bobby Tolan called a meeting of the Pelicans in the Al Lang clubhouse. It was both an angry and sad event. Sammy Stewart was in trouble again, and this time it was going to cost him his job.

At the meeting it was revealed that Stewart owed fourteen Pelican players close to $2,000. He had also borrowed money from the clubhouse manager and from the trainer, and he wasn't paying anyone back. Now everyone was wondering whether it was because he needed the money to feed a drug habit. Tolan said he was leaving the Pelicans no choice but to release him. "And our money?" Tolan was asked. The manager could only shrug his shoulders.

After Stewart's release by the Pelicans, he next went to nearby Bradenton to play. A week later he was released again. He had borrowed $500 from a former Baltimore teammate playing on the Explorers. He too would not be repaid.

A short time later Stewart was arrested and jailed in Sarasota for striking his wife. A month later, it was in all the newspapers that back home in North Carolina, Sammy had taken his wife into their car against her will and was holding her prisoner with a knife when the cops arrived. The pressures and problems of life—no income, no baseball, a sick child, a marriage on the rocks—had piled too high for the fun-loving Sammy Stewart from Swannanoa, North Carolina. He had crashed and burned.

5

Hurts
and Indignities

Experts covering the start of the Senior League predicted that the number of injuries to the players would help determine the success or failure of the league. In the early articles the color pieces centered around the novelty of "old men" returning. There seemed always to be the worry that these former players would no longer be in any shape to play the game. Would somebody get killed by a line drive or a pitched ball? Would a lot of players pull rarely used leg muscles when running down to first base to beat out an infield hit? Would somebody have a heart attack while trying to score on an inside-the-park homer?

In their home opener, their third game of the season, the Pelicans met the Orlando Juice, a team with talent but without pizzazz, pitching, or a strong defense. The Juice's key players were Sixto Lezcano, Jose Cruz, and Bill Madlock, all former major league hitting stars. Lezcano, a former Milwaukee Brewer star, was the player expected to supply much of the power for the Juice. But when the Pelicans' Elias Sosa hit Lezcano square in the left arm with a sidearm fastball, Lezcano's arm turned out to be broken. After just three games Lezcano went home to Puerto Rico, finished for the season.

The Pelicans beat the Juice two of three, giving them a 4–1 record as the Winter Haven Super Sox came to town to resume their feud. The opener was advertised as "Boo Bill Lee Night," and professionally printed signs that read BOO were distributed around Al Lang Stadium. Whenever Lee stuck his face onto the field, he was booed. It may have been bush, but the Pelican fans had read what Lee had said about their manager, Bobby Tolan, and booing him proved irresistible.

Sports Illustrated arrived to cover the game. The Pelican brass became excited because they assumed the magazine wanted to write about "Boo Bill Lee Night." All the league owners counted on positive press to help publicize the Senior League around the country. They were so in love with their product, they couldn't imagine anyone could write negatively about it. The owners were naïve. They underestimated how negative the sporting press can be.

To the dismay of all, the first question *Sports Illustrated*'s photographer asked was "Can we shoot pictures in the trainer's room?"

When league founder Jim Morley heard the photographer's request, he immediately knew what it meant. *Sports Illustrated* wanted to write about old men getting hurt. This was to be the storyline, in advance. It was not the sort of publicity the owners sought. "This is so unfair," Morley said.

And it was. But there was nothing anyone could do about it.

Young Brian Ebel forbade the photographer from entering his trainer's room and shooting him while he was at work, so the intrepid cameraman went to the visiting clubhouse and took his shots of the Orlando players. When the piece came out in the magazine, readers new to the league were left with the impression that the Senior League was semiserious and semilegitimate, a bunch of old men foolishly trying to regain their youth.

In fact, a lot of Pelicans *were* hurting—if only a little. Jim Morley had invented Senior Baseball in April. Just six months later, eight teams were playing. But because of the time crunch, the players only had two weeks to get ready. So the pulled muscles and strains and aches that would have disappeared after eight full weeks of training slowed the players on the field. Sometimes these minor hurts created a bad first impression for fans and critics alike, who saw players struggle to reach balls in the field or fail to run out ground balls when their legs were in great pain. You can try hard, but if you have a pulled leg muscle, you still do not appear to be running hard. A couple of players even had to excuse themselves from a game or two.

"I came down here in great shape," said shortstop Luis Gomez, "but I woke up this morning and my leg was sore. It's different when you're playing. You're going all-out." Sergio Ferrer, the other Pelican shortstop, got the start.

Steve Kemp too had a sore leg. As a result, Bobby Tolan inserted Ron LeFlore in left field and led him off, despite the knowledge that LeFlore had not yet recovered from leg injuries suffered during the preseason.

Orlando had bases loaded and no one out when Winter Haven shortstop Mario Guerrero hit a high fly to left to the gimpy Ron LeFlore, who ran in as if he were stepping on eggs. He just missed getting to the ball. A healthy LeFlore would have put it in his back pocket. The hit turned into a double, and two runs scored.

The next batter grounded wide of first. First baseman Gary Rajsich ran toward second to spear it, but when he turned to throw to the pitcher covering first, he had to hold onto the ball. Pitcher Randy Lerch's legs tightened as Jon Matlack's had the day before on a similar play, and Lerch never got to first. Everyone was safe. The bases were loaded again.

When another batter grounded wide to Rajsich, again Lerch couldn't get over in time, and the fans became derisive.

Later Gary Rajsich was heard to remark, "From now on I'm going to ask the pitcher when he goes out there if he's well enough to cover first base."

With the score tied, Winter Haven's Pedro Borbon pitched the bottom of the ninth. Borbon, once a fine reliever for the Cincinnati Reds, is also known for biting off a piece of the ear of an opponent he was fighting during a brawl on the field.

There was one out after a single, a botched bunt, and an intentional walk, and Super Sox manager Lee ordered the infielders to play in, hoping they could get a force at the plate.

The batter was Ron LeFlore. LeFlore, playing in his first game, had already slapped out two hits. Borbon threw two quick strikes, then a ball. All LeFlore had to do was put the bat on the ball and send it through the infield. Chances were it would get through. With LeFlore playing on still-sore legs, Lee would have been better off keeping his fielders back and going for the double play.

Borbon threw, and LeFlore did get the bat on the ball, slapping a hard bouncer in the direction of shortstop Tom McMillan, a career minor leaguer who had been the number two draft pick in the country in 1973. Before the season McMillan had been selling John Deere construction equipment. This night he could only watch in frustration as the ball quickly rolled by him. Had he played back, the Super Sox would have had their double play.

As it was, the Pelicans scored, and "Boo Bill Lee Night" turned into a joyous evening for Ron LeFlore.

The next night the Pelicans improved their record to 6–1 with a 16–3 clubbing of woeful Winter Haven. The Pelicans tattooed five Super Sox pitchers for 19 hits, dropping the team to 1–6.

The highlight of the game was Bill Lee's self-destruction as manager. With St. Pete leading by a run in the third, Winter Haven had one out and runners on first and third with its top slugger, Leon Roberts, scheduled to bat. Roberts had become ill and was throwing up in the clubhouse, so Lee decided to send a left-handed batter to the plate. The left-handed batter turned out to be himself. He would be confronting the Pelicans' Milt Wilcox.

Lee had prided himself on his hitting, but it also appeared that, by pinch-hitting himself, Lee was attempting personally to get back at the St. Pete fans who had booed him the night before. In actuality, Lee had wanted to pinch-hit Bernie Carbo, but the mercurial Bernie had forgotten his glove and refused to play that day. Lee had no other lefty batter on the bench.

Lee stepped into the batter's box with grim determination. Wilcox threw three pitches—*zip, zip, zip*—the third one looking. Two outs. A groundout ended the rally.

Many Pelican runners circled the bases as the game progressed. After Mark Bomback gave up nine hits and nine runs in less than three innings, and after Darrell Brandon let in a couple more, Lee, in his second unorthodox managerial move of the night, replaced Brandon with first baseman Pete LaCock while Lee went out to play in right field. Lee had played outfield for USC, and this was his chance to show those skills as well.

LaCock grounded out, but Ron LeFlore hit the third of his four singles to drive in two more runs. At 14–2, it was more than the principal Winter Haven owner, Mitchell Maxwell, could take.

Under the stands Maxwell turned apoplectic. Maxwell loved Lee, but he was a baseball purist who wanted his pitchers pitching and his outfielders playing the outfield. Maxwell had heard Lee when he talked about having fun and not giving in to the pressures of winning. But talk and putting words into action were two different things. Maxwell and his partners had invested $1 million in the Super Sox, and his boys were getting their brains beat out and laughed at in the bargain.

Maxwell screamed at Lee to get out there and pitch himself. Lee responded by quitting the outfield for the mound and gave up the last two runs.

After the game Lee tore up the clubhouse.

6

Ronnie Rebels

Joe Tinker Stadium, miles from Disney's rodents in both location and sensibility, was built in 1914 and looks the same as it did when it was refurbished in 1963, while the rest of the city of Orlando has changed and grown around it. Quaint and cozy in the heart of a low-rent district, it huddles in the shadow of the gray, hulking Citrus Bowl, for which the city fathers spent $20 million to add twenty-five thousand seats for one football game a year. The Minnesota Twins used to train at Joe Tinker Stadium, but the city refused to open its coffers to improve the facility, so the Twins left for a less dangerous, more elegant neighborhood in Fort Myers.

Joe Tinker, the Cubs' Hall of Fame shortstop who played with Johnny Evers and Frank Chance just after the turn of the century, became Orlando's most famous baseball player. During the summer the stadium is home to the minor league Orlando Sun Rays of the Florida State League.

The Senior League Orlando Juice drew fewer than five hundred fans a game. The reason whispered concerned Joe Tinker field's location, a predominantly black section of Orlando that was said to be dangerous. When a team fails to advertise and promote properly, this is often the excuse given.

It's also the red herring a team throws out when it wants to leave. That's what Mike Burke and George Steinbrenner, then owners of the New York Yankees, argued about the South Bronx before blackmailing the city of

New York into paying gadzillions of dollars to renovate and ruin the charm of Yankee Stadium. Now, as the Yankees seek to move to New Jersey, the crime statistics are being trotted out once more.

"The area is unsafe," said a Juice usher.

"Is it really unsafe?" he was asked.

"That's what everybody says," he said with a shrug.

But if the area was so unsafe, why did the town spend millions to fix up the adjacent football field?

The Pelicans, who marveled at the charm of the old stadium, won the first of their three games with the Juice. Starter Jon Matlack, his legs healed and the stiffness gone, once again pitched and played with his former elegance. After each successful inning, he transformed into the Mets' master of old, striding off the mound expressionless with his head down but with purpose in his step en route to the sanctity of the dugout.

Matlack received strong relief from another former Met pitcher, Pat Zachry, who had been on the disabled list all season long suffering from leg injuries. With the release of Sammy Stewart, the former National League co-Rookie of the Year was activated and struck out Bill Madlock to end one inning. In the following frame he fanned in order Tom Paciorek, Ike Blessitt, and Larvell Blanks, an auspicious beginning for any pitcher.

Pat Zachry was a player who wasn't what he seemed. To the public he was brusque and hard to approach, a salty Texan who enjoyed growling. He constantly wore a red ass. During the road trip to Orlando one morning, Zack walked across the street from the Holiday Inn and ordered bacon and eggs and grits. When the food came it sat on his plate, looking greasy and unappealing. He was so angered at its quality, he gruffly snapped at the helpless waitress, "I wouldn't feed this to my dog," and walked out.

To his friends, however, Pat seemed to be a different person, caring and sensitive, proud of his family, someone who missed his wife and children who were left back home in Waco, a man who loved to read and discuss books. On the bus, while most of the players listened to music or slept or looked out the window, Zachry was rarely without something to read. And when he wasn't reading, he enjoyed talking about authors and their craft. Some days he would have his golden retriever jump in the back of his pickup, and when he got to the park, they would roughhouse a little. The dog would wait for him to finish. They would return home together. Pat loved kids and dogs. It was the adults he wasn't too crazy about.

The season was only eight games old, and already the Pelicans were talking about winning the pennant. West Palm Beach, the power in the other division, finally lost, and the players noted how much they were looking forward to playing Dick Williams's combine. The players were also making fun of the fact that Bill Lee had been fired as manager of Winter Haven. Boston's Triple A manager, Ed Nottle, replaced him. The Pelican players were convinced no one in their division could beat them, even though they had yet to play a game against Bradenton.

When the Pelicans lost the second game of the Orlando series, the players tramped into the locker room, angry. They dressed quietly, purposefully. Milt Wilcox sat in his locker, analyzing the stuff of Orlando's winning pitcher Bob Galasso.

"He has a pretty good fastball," the big pitcher said, "Not much of a curve. Besides, he shows it. In a month we'll be on him."

Outfielder Ron LeFlore strolled into the trainer's room, where Brian Ebel began working on his still-sore legs. As LeFlore lay on his muscular back taking treatment, he began to regale some of the other players with a horrific story of how he had fallen asleep at the wheel doing over a hundred miles an hour, rolled the car over, and almost killed himself in 1985 after he was out of baseball. As he described what happened, there seemed to be a gleam in his eye and a smile on his lips, as though the danger had been something that had really turned him on.

At his locker afterward, LeFlore, who could be moody, grumbled. "I feel too quick at the plate. I'm not getting enough batting practice on the road."

From the beginning of the season LeFlore had been unhappy. An intense, complex man, the Pelicans had been counting on LeFlore to be one of the team sparks. He had been a well-respected leadoff batter for the Detroit Tigers, Montreal Expos, and Chicago White Sox, the only player in the history of the game to lead both leagues in stolen bases. In 1980 he stole 97 bases for the Expos, one more than Ty Cobb at his best, and only Rickey Henderson, Lou Brock, Vince Coleman, and Maury Wills had stolen more in a season in the entire history of the game.

Despite his salary, which made him one of the highest-paid St. Pete players, LeFlore had reported to the Pelicans' training camp weighing about 232, twenty pounds overweight. He had a rolling gut. Almost immediately he injured a leg running out a ground ball. Nevertheless, when manager Bobby Tolan didn't start him the first few games, he became upset.

His mood did not improve when on opening night all the Pelican players were introduced over the loudspeaker except him. One by one the players ran out onto the field to applause, as LeFlore was left standing by himself in the dugout.

After a long pause, the public address announcer realized he had omitted LeFlore's name. He intoned, "Number thirty-one, Ron LeFlore." Except that Ron was wearing uniform number eight. A proud man, LeFlore refused to go out onto the field. Instead, he sat on the bench in the dugout, glaring.

Ron LeFlore, above all, demanded that he be treated with respect. Omitting him from the roster during opening ceremonies was a slap. Not starting him was an affront.

But if Ron LeFlore was vexed by manager Bobby Tolan, the Pelican manager was equally, if not more, perturbed with LeFlore. Tolan had ordered him on a weight-loss regimen, but in a month he had only lost half a dozen pounds, angering the coaching staff and a few teammates as well.

"He wants the money, but he doesn't want to get in shape," complained one teammate. Coach Ozzie Virgil was equally peeved.

"You have to pay the price," he said. "If you're not willing to pay the price and work and work and work, you're going to get hurt, because your mind is telling you one thing, and your body does not react to what your mind is telling you. If I say I want to lose some weight, I can't have a case of beer every day. I can't eat pasta and spaghetti. I have to cool it, to sacrifice. If LeFlore got himself on a weight program, he could stay in pretty good shape. It all depends on the individual, if you want to pay the price."

The vibes against him were there. After LeFlore played two games, he showed he could still hit well, but everyone paid attention to what he wasn't doing in the outfield and on the base paths. In their opinion his performance did not match his potential because he wouldn't quit the beer and the baloney.

LeFlore, moreover, was seen as a "pain in the ass" by the Pelican management, because he often looked for favors, a free meal or free tickets, though what he asked for was no different from what a lot of ballplayers requested during their careers. Why LeFlore was being singled out for criticism wasn't entirely clear, except that there were times when LeFlore could be heard second-guessing Tolan's managerial decisions. The grapevine being what it was, surely that information got back to Tolan, and Tolan wanted to show LeFlore who was boss.

LeFlore, reacting to being put down by authority, became contemptuous, for Ronnie had always viewed himself as a star. He had resented it when he wasn't treated as one, even in Detroit or Montreal or Chicago.

Make no mistake—Ron LeFlore had been a *star.* In his prime Ronnie was the fastest man in baseball, a greyhound who could eat up the territory in the outfield and steal bases in bunches. Ron LeFlore was a force.

He was something else—a legend. After wasting six and a half years of his youth in federal prison for armed robbery, he became a major league ballplayer within a single year of release. That he got to the big leagues at all was amazing.

Ron LeFlore had a childhood like very few others who ended up playing major league baseball. He grew up in the projects of East Detroit, like Harlem all concrete. If you ventured more than two blocks from your turf, you had to fight. Every day Ron LeFlore had to fight or run. Only when the numbers were against him did he run. He acquired scars and gave them, and he developed an explosive temper.

His mom and dad were good, God-fearing people, and in school LeFlore wasn't a bad student, but he had a character defect. He enjoyed taking things that didn't belong to him.

"I just had the devil in me," LeFlore said. "I had little horns growing out of the top of my head. For instance, my parents would go to sleep, and I'd jump out a second-story window and go out and rob with my friends. My parents never knew what I was doing—until I got caught."

In East Detroit it wasn't cool to say no to your friends. The peer pressure proved enormous. The pressure also called for Ronnie to produce the most macho, courageous perpetration possible. LeFlore added, "And even if it wasn't the right thing to do, you didn't say no because you didn't want to be looked at as the sissy of the group."

When Ron was eighteen, he was a heroin addict. Heroin addiction requires money, and the stash he accumulated from a previous robbery was running out. In mid-December 1966, with Christmas approaching, LeFlore met a group of his friends in a pool room and suggested a robbery of imagination and daring. His friend Emmet had a 1965 Mustang, orange with a black convertible top. LeFlore appointed Emmet

The Pelicans

Ron LeFlore

the getaway man. At two in the morning, he and the others would stick up
a bar that cashed checks for then-prosperous Chrysler assembly line
workers.

LeFlore and his friends waited until just before the bar was about to
close. Then they pounced. They escaped with a bag full of money—how
much, they didn't know. They also did not know a silent burglar alarm
had been activated.

Emmet began driving slowly down an alley with the headlights off.
When the police arrived, they noticed the suspicious vehicle and took
down the license plate number.

LeFlore's gang returned to Emmet's home and counted out the money.
There was $36,000 in the bag.

They decided to wait until the next day to divvy up the swag. Emmet
removed a pipe, stuck the money behind it, and replaced the pipe, and
then LeFlore called for a taxicab. When Ron looked out the window for
his cab, he saw flashing red lights. The police. LeFlore thought, *Shit,*

every policeman in Detroit is here. The cops began to break down the door.

LeFlore decided to scam his way out of it. He ran upstairs and took off his heavy coat. When he came down the stairs he said to the policemen, "You woke me. Tell me, what's going on?"

A cop said, "There was a crime committed."

LeFlore said, "I'm not involved. I'm going to leave."

But just as he was getting ready to walk out the front door, Emmet ratted on him and he was arrested.

LeFlore recalled, "They stopped me, shook me down, and they took me to juvenile court. I was tried as an adult."

Ron LeFlore got five to fifteen years at the State Prison of Southern Michigan at Jackson, better known as Jackson State. The education he received at one of the country's largest penal institutions proved different than most. According to LeFlore, he learned that if he did not change his ways he would die—one way or another.

"When I got there, I had an attitude, and they tried to break me," LeFlore said. "The beds were metal and had little holes in them. They gave you two thin blankets, a pair of coveralls, and a pair of bottlesocks to wear. That was it. It was very cold in the winter, and if you weren't quiet they would open the windows and you would freeze.

"They had goon squads. Six or seven guys, the shortest six-foot-five, the lightest 250 pounds. They would come into your cell at three in the morning when no one could assist you, and they would beat you with their fists or clubs. The next morning the doctor would come in and see you.

"They had a silent system. If you were caught talking, they'd put you in the slammer, as we called it, which would be total blackness. They would leave you in there for seven days. They did that to me a few times. You would get two meals a day, half rations, so if you normally got six potatoes, you'd only get three. And after the third day the doctor would come and see how you were doing. After your time was up you'd go to classification, which we called Kangaroo Court. They would ask, 'Are you ready?' I'd say, 'No, I'm not ready,' and they would throw me back in there. It was because I was young and could not accept authority. The influence of the streets made me defiant."

The guards put LeFlore in solitary confinement because he refused to work. He hadn't worked as a kid, and so he didn't see any sense in working there. "Why in hell would I have to work in jail when I didn't

work in a free society?" he told himself. But after doing six and a half
months in solitary, he finally broke.

LeFlore hated prison, but prison got LeFlore off the streets and onto
the playing fields. Once his incredible talents were challenged, Ron
began a career that would catapult him to celebrity.

"I wouldn't wish prison on anyone, because it's the most injurious
thing in the world for you to be locked up in a cell," LeFlore said. "You
look out a window and see people walking around free as a bird.

"But you get a chance to get into yourself and find out who you really
are and what you want to do in life. If you have any sense at all, you don't
want to continuously go back and forth to jail. And it's tough to be
accepted back into society, because they have it in the back of their
minds: *Can this guy really be trusted?* I'm sure that when I was first
released and started playing ball, the thought was there: *Is this guy going
to be straight?*"

LeFlore played sports at the prison, starring in basketball, football,
and baseball. "I was winning trophies all the time, Most Valuable Player
of teams, best running back, best defensive back," LeFlore said. "We
had field events on the Fourth of July, and I was the fastest runner in the
institution. When I was a student at Eastern High School, I had been a
phenomenal running back. I had gone to school with Frenchy Fuqua, a
pro football player with the Steelers. We had Bill Yearby, an All-
American at Michigan and a Pittsburgh Steeler, and Reggie Harding,
who was a seven-foot center who had played with the Pistons in the NBA.
Matter of fact, Reggie and I were in prison together, and just before he
was released, he got another tryout with the Baltimore Bullets. He went
out and got caught up with street life again, and before he got to camp he
was shot to death. Reggie slapped a kid. The kid went home, got a gun,
and blew Reggie's brains out."

LeFlore was aware that he would meet a similar fate if he didn't turn
his life around. In the Detroit ghetto LeFlore knew a common end was
violent death.

"All my peers, the friends I grew up with, are dead," he said. "Every
single one of them. Josie Daniels was killed by the police department. He
was robbing a jewelry store. A friend named Larry Brown was killed a
couple of years ago. He owned an after-hours place in Detroit and sold
drugs. A guy owed him five dollars. He asked him for his money, and the
guy blew his brains out. I had one friend who was a contract killer, and he
informed the guy he was supposed to kill to save him. The guy he tried to

warn ended up killing him. Several friends died from drug overdoses. It's really weird. Like eight or nine guys who I grew up with, they all lived in the same neighborhood, and all of them are dead—all but me.

"I got away from East Detroit. I started playing ball. I had something good happen to me. They had never had the opportunity."

LeFlore began the rehabilitation process by writing to Detroit Tiger general manager Jim Campbell. Campbell often received letters from friends of prisoners, telling him about various phenoms. When he got LeFlore's letter, he wrote the usual polite response that he didn't have the manpower to send someone to Jackson State to scout him.

But LeFlore had a friend in the prison who knew LeFlore's talent. The friend told his friend, who knew Billy Martin, who was then the manager of the Tigers. It's hard to imagine that another manager would have given LeFlore the opportunity.

Martin himself had grown up tough, and he understood the streets. He wasn't turned off just because a man had a past. Martin had found baseball earlier than LeFlore. Martin knew that was the only difference between the two men. Without baseball, Martin once told me, he probably would have ended up like LeFlore. And Billy Martin held no prejudice because LeFlore was black. If he could play, he would play for Billy. Martin agreed to come to the prison to scout him. But on that day it rained and the tryout had to be canceled. But Martin gave LeFlore another chance. Martin said that if LeFlore could get a furlough, he would give him a tryout.

One day before LeFlore's twenty-fifth birthday, June 15, 1973, he was released for a trip to Tiger Stadium. Martin saw this powerful chunk of muscle hit towering drives to all fields. Those few in attendance that day wondered who he was.

Lew Matlin, the Tigers' public relations director, asked Martin, "Who is he?"

Billy replied, "He's my brother."

Matlin wanted to interview the tryout, but he couldn't, because LeFlore was still an inmate.

The following week LeFlore was granted a special furlough to play in a Tiger intrasquad game. That day he was timed at 6.1 seconds in the sixty-yard dash. He demonstrated a strong arm and power to right-center. If Ron could get released from prison, the Tigers agreed to sign him.

LeFlore had done six and a half years. LeFlore wrote to the director of corrections, and so did the Tigers. He was allowed to leave prison. On

July 2 he went to Tiger Stadium to sign a contract. He got a $10,000 signing bonus, which was assigned to his parole officer to make sure LeFlore didn't get involved in drugs again—and sent to Clinton, Iowa.

"I had made up my mind I was going to do something to better my life, and whatever sacrifice it took, I was going to do that," LeFlore said. "People had not turned their backs on me. I had something to give back to the people who cared enough about me to sign me."

When LeFlore arrived in Clinton, his past preceded him and his teammates were wary—if not afraid—of him.

"Guys didn't know how to respond to me," LeFlore said. "But I let them know. We were playing Cedar Rapids, and they had a player by the name of Freddie Mills. Everyone was afraid of him. He was supposed to be the bully of the league. In the first homestand we almost had a bench-clearing brawl, and I said, 'If it happens again, I'm going to go over there and challenge Freddie Mills.'"

"It happened again, and I went over to their dugout and told Freddie Mills to come out. I said, 'I'm going to kick your ass and anybody else who comes out with you.' And I never had any problems in baseball again. I was never thrown at intentionally. I was never ejected from a ball game in my career."

Despite his reputation LeFlore had been a scrupulously clean player. He always played hard, but he never tried to show up an opponent. It went back to his philosophy concerning respect: So long as he was accorded it, he would reciprocate.

In 1974 LeFlore went to the Detroit Tigers' major league spring training camp. Though Billy Martin had moved on to the Texas Rangers, Tigers skipper Ralph Houk had been equally impressed. The Major helped LeFlore's confidence a great deal. He saw that LeFlore wasn't experienced and didn't know the fundamentals of the game, but he perceived LeFlore had a great capacity for learning. Houk told him, "I don't care how you're playing right now. You're learning. You're going to be my center fielder and you're going to play every day."

LeFlore began the season at Lakeland in Florida, where he played in 93 games, had 179 hits, scored 93 runs, stole 42 bases, and hit .339. He went to Triple A, was there nine days, played five games, and in his final game in front of the Detroit top brass told teammate Brian Lamb, "I'm going to get three hits today." He did. The last one was a home run. He stole two bases. That night in Boston outfielder Mickey Stanley broke an arm. The next morning Ron LeFlore was a Detroit Tiger.

"That was twelve months and a week to the day after I was released from prison," LeFlore said proudly.

Ralph Houk had kept his promise. And under Houk LeFlore thrived. "He knew you were going to have your good days and your bad days," LeFlore said. "Your character really came to the fore if you had a bad day, because he could tell if you took it to the outfield or to the plate. You can always tell when a guy is really down on himself. I never did that. When I wasn't hitting, I still ran hard. I never shammed. I never wanted out of the lineup, no matter how bad I looked or how many errors I made or how stupid I looked running the bases. I always wanted to go back out there and redeem myself. In the American League, when I faced Nolan Ryan, I struck out twenty-two times, and it didn't bother me. I'd face him every day, because I knew that eventually I would hit him. He was just better than I was. That's all there was to it. Then, when I went to Montreal and he was pitching for Houston, I hit Ryan like I owned him."

Two years after he made the majors, Ron LeFlore stole 58 bases, and in the following seasons he stole 39, 68, 78, 97, 36, and 28. In spring training he would talk to the masters, Lou Brock and Joe Morgan and Maury Wills. Morgan would say to him, "Tell me what you see from their delivery to give you a good jump."

LeFlore said, "I'd hit it on the nose every time and steal a base, even off Bob Gibson."

Watching Gibson in practice before a spring training game, Brock asked LeFlore, "What is Bob doing?"

LeFlore answered, "He collapses his back leg before going to the plate."

"Correct."

LeFlore got a hit off Gibson and he took off and stole the base cleanly. "I studied pitchers and I learned," LeFlore said.

In Detroit LeFlore was a workhorse on both offense and defense. "I was the only guy stealing bases," he said. "In the outfield I had to play center field, left-center, and right-center. Alex Johnson and Willie Horton were out there, and they were old and couldn't move, so I had to run around a lot, plus steal bases and score runs. By the end of the year, I used to be worn out. If I had played on a team with some young outfielders, my stolen base totals would have been even better. I would have scored more runs too, though for Detroit I averaged about ninety runs a season while I played, which wasn't bad."

In 1978 Ralph Houk stepped down as the Tigers' manager and was replaced by Les Moss, another easygoing man. LeFlore enjoyed playing for Moss. But Moss was fired, and he was replaced by Sparky Anderson, a high-powered dictatorial man. It was the beginning of the end for LeFlore, who needed a "relaxed, kicked-back guy." Houk and Moss did not hound him with rules and regulations. Sparky brought his rules with him from his winning days in Cincinnati. One rule was no mustaches. LeFlore was a free spirit, a rebel, a man not used to compromise. Looked at from management's perspective, he had a "bad attitude."

"Sparky wanted you to look totally uniform," LeFlore said. What especially angered LeFlore was the midseason change in philosophy. Moss had let him alone. LeFlore felt the rules had been established for the year. Under Sparky, the regimen had changed, and LeFlore thought his rules showed a lack of respect toward the players.

As you might imagine, Ron LeFlore refused to shave his mustache. As you also might imagine, Anderson shipped his ass out.

"I guess he thought I was being rebellious," LeFlore said, "that I couldn't take orders, because all the guys who kept their mustaches— Rusty Staub, Aurelio Rodriguez, me—were traded from Detroit that year. Sparky got the boys he thought he could win with, Kirk Gibson, Lance Parrish, and they won in 1984.

"I mean, I didn't see any sense in getting traded because you had a mustache. That year I hit .300, drove in a hundred runs, but Sparky didn't care. At the end of the season the Tigers traded me to Montreal for Dan Schatzeder. I was upset, but what could I do about it? Nothing."

There was one thing. He could have shaved off his mustache. It was the same with Tolan and the Pelicans. They wanted him to lose weight, but apparently that also was out of the question.

Ron LeFlore and his mustache went from Detroit to Montreal after the 1979 season, and from that point the winged-footed former inmate of the State Prison of Southern Michigan at Jackson began a slide that in three short years would see him traded to the Chicago White Sox and then out of baseball and back into the drug world.

LeFlore played one season for Dick Williams at Montreal. He was comfortable playing under Dick, and that season he led the league in stolen bases and was a superstar.

"The only people Dick Williams is tough on are pitchers," LeFlore said. "Pitchers throw home run balls. That's the way you lose games. But Dick knows what it takes to win. You play, and that's it. He's not concerned with what you do after the game is over. You feel comfortable playing for Dick, because all you have to be concerned with is just doing your job."

At Montreal LeFlore was happy because he played every day. LeFlore also liked the fact that his team had a winning attitude. There was racial tension on that Montreal team. Some of the black players resented Gary Carter for the disproportionate amount of attention the white star got from the Montreal media and local endorsers, but LeFlore didn't see a great deal of prejudice.

"The guys had to work together," LeFlore said. "Like I was talking with Steve Kemp. I said, 'In a few weeks you can go home and pick your own friends.' Steve said, 'Right, I won't have to be with these dickheads.' But it isn't prejudice. Even if a white guy *is* prejudiced to a black, he isn't going to show it. I work with him. Maybe he's prejudiced away from the park. I can deal with that. There are few athletes where you can notice the prejudice face-to-face."

What ended LeFlore's season and the Expos' chance to win the pennant wasn't emotional but physical. Injuries are always a variable. No matter how highly a team is rated, an injury to one or two stars can kill a team's chances. With twenty or so games left in the 1980 season, the Expos were five games in front.

Dave Kingman smashed a drive to left field, the ball hit in the stands, and LeFlore, running at full speed, was too close to the wall to stop in time. The left-field line in Olympic Stadium in Montreal is about two steps from the wall. When LeFlore arrived at the wall, he tried to stop himself with his hands. The impact of the collision broke a bone in his wrist. He played the rest of the game.

The next day he couldn't move his hand.

After he was disabled, the Expos didn't have a leadoff hitter. The Expos tried their young prospect Tim Raines, but he wasn't ready. Infielders Jerry Manuel and Rodney Scott didn't have LeFlore's skills and weren't good enough to lead them to victory. LeFlore had been the force, the intimidator. He would have broken the century mark for stolen bases in a season if not for the accident.

It was LeFlore's option year. The Expos wanted him to sign a one-year contract. LeFlore was afraid that if he had a bad year, he would blow his chance at the big money. He sought a multiyear deal. He signed a three-year contract with the Chicago White Sox. After he signed with Chicago, LeFlore received some bad press back in Montreal.

"You know how the media is," LeFlore said. "The media makes you or breaks you, and the majority of the time when you get older in your career, they break you."

LeFlore got his money in Chicago, but by changing teams and managers he was playing Russian roulette with his career. Whenever a player goes to a new club with a new manager, he is risking his job. If he had stayed with Williams, there was the likelihood that he would have remained a starter.

In Chicago, White Sox manager Tony LaRussa changed LeFlore's role. Instead of playing every day, in 1981 he became half of a righty-lefty platoon. Rudy Law batted against right-handed pitchers, and the right-handed-batting LeFlore played only against left-handed pitchers. Because there are more righty pitchers, LeFlore spent a lot of time on the bench. The thirty-three-year-old outfielder played in only 82 games.

LeFlore did not have the temperament to be a platoon or role player. The more he sat, the shorter his patience. Before long LeFlore and LaRussa were at odds.

"I started platooning," LeFlore said. "That affected me, because I was accustomed to playing every day. I was in center, and Steve Kemp was in left, and I guess my legs couldn't take it. I couldn't cover center *and* left for me and Kemp. And Chicago has a big ballpark. I was getting older, and my legs were taking a beating. It was inevitable, but I don't think I accepted it as well as I should or could have.

"I had a problem coming to the ballpark late at times, and LaRussa didn't like my work habits. One time my wife was pregnant. She had a miscarriage. I woke up and saw the blood and took her to the hospital. I didn't call the ballpark. Then things just went downhill. LaRussa didn't believe me. Then he stopped playing me—period.

"Sitting on the bench was the pits. It was just like me sitting in solitary. I had never been accustomed to that. It might have been different if I had been weaned into it, but it was an all-of-a-sudden move. I would come to the park knowing I wouldn't be playing, and finally I said something in the newspapers.

"One time LaRussa said I was going to play, and he didn't play me. I felt he had lied to me. Any human can only take so much, and then you just snap."

The White Sox released LeFlore in 1983 with one year left on his contract. It was the last day of spring training, the getaway day.

"I guess that's the way of really putting you down," LeFlore said.

LeFlore was living in Sarasota, and he saw Doug Rader, the manager of the Texas Rangers, who told him, "Go to Puerto Rico, and if you have a good winter, maybe I'll give you a chance." LeFlore got in shape, played well in Puerto Rico, went to the Caribbean series, and in the playoffs pinched the sciatic nerve in his hip. An injury at an inopportune moment struck again.

"Once I did that I just forgot about contacting him," LeFlore said, "because there was no way. The Rangers wouldn't have had enough time to see if I could play. It was just one of those things."

His agent called other ball clubs, but no one was interested. It was over. At age thirty-four.

LeFlore said, "What did I do? I'll tell you. I started using drugs real hard. Because I was depressed. I started seeing my money evaporate. I couldn't take a regular job. I was used to making so much money. It's tough to accept a job for $18,000."

He went to see a psychiatrist. "I wanted to find out if I was going to snap, because I had started to feel like committing suicide. Things had happened to me so fast. That was frightening."

LeFlore's marriage dissolved. When he and his wife parted, both stopped their drug use.

Ron added, "She went to a rehab center. She's a rehab counselor now. She's a reborn Christian, and she's got my kids. She's remarried and has a daughter of her own, and she's trying to let me get myself together."

LeFlore wants desperately to find a job, establish himself in society, and get his kids back. His outlook is positive, and he thanks the Senior League for what it has done for him.

"I can go out again and assert myself in life," he said.

LeFlore also has found some comfort in religion.

"I don't go to church every day, but I believe there is someone behind me. If not, I don't think I would be alive today. I can sit down and ask for forgiveness now, whereas before I wouldn't do that because I never thought I did anything wrong."

The next day before the game Bobby Tolan confronted LeFlore in the trainer's room.

"How much do you weigh?"

"Two twenty-three. Last week I was 227," LeFlore said. "I'm playing, so I have to eat."

Tolan was not impressed. "I've been in this game thirty years," Tolan said. "Don't give me that. As soon as I'm ready to play, you're going to be out of there." He paused. "And I'm going to be ready real soon."

Tolan brightened. "I'll tell you what. I'll race you for $100."

"Right now?"

"This is Sunday," the manager said, "and on Tuesday, we'll race for $100."

"You're on," said LeFlore, who headed for the dugout to get ready for another three-hit day.

Tolan grinned. "He's going to win the race," he said, "and I'm going to ask him for $100. I said I'd race him for $100, not beat him for $100."

As always, the manager would have the last say.

Ten days later Bobby Tolan stood on the grass in front of the dugout, lovingly holding his baseball bat. He squeezed it, turned it in his hands, took a few imaginary swings, and then posed with it, leaning on it like a walking cane. Then, seemingly absentmindedly, he hefted it again, swinging it over and over. Bobby Tolan may have been the manager, but in his own heart he was still a hitter.

That day Ron LeFlore led off the game for the Pelicans. He hit a ball sharply to first, and as he raced down the line, he pulled up, holding his leg. When St. Petersburg went out into the field for the second inning, playing in his spot was the manager, Bobby Tolan, doing exactly what he had threatened LeFlore he was going to do: replace him.

Another ten days went by. November 28 was a sunny, bright day. After playing on the road, the players had returned to St. Pete to spend one night at home. The following day everyone seemed to be in a good mood as the players got on the big bus in front of Al Lang Stadium to drive all the way across to the east coast of Florida to play St. Lucie.

Before the bus left, however, the Pelicans made a roster move. Despite his .362 batting average, Ron LeFlore was released by Bobby Tolan.

While the rest of the players lounged in their seats, waiting to leave, Ron stood outside, looking glum. He didn't appear to be angry, because LeFlore would never allow himself to lose face by showing emotion in front of the other players.

On the bus someone asked, "What happened to LeFlore?"

"He got put on waivers," was the answer.

No one expressed any feeling about it, not even a "That's too bad," which was curious, because LeFlore was usually cheerful and was never abrasive. True, he was overweight when he didn't have to be, angering the coaching staff, but there were other players sporting too much tummy. I could only think his shadowy past and his rough background had kept teammates at a safe distance emotionally.

And just like that, Ron LeFlore, who had been the Pelicans' primary spokesman at banquets and get-togethers before the start of the season, had been rendered a nonteammate.

Tolan enigmatically told the press, "There are a lot of good guys around here, but I'm not saying Ron is a bad guy."

Owner Jim Morley just couldn't understand why LeFlore had refused to lose the fat. "Where else could he make this kind of money?" Morley wondered. He was genuinely perplexed.

LeFlore was picked up by the Bradenton Explorers for half of his reported $9,000 a month Pelican salary. He played center field and continued his excellent hitting. He would be a factor in Bradenton finishing in second place after a horrendous start, and only in the last week of the season with the arrival of a younger, fitter Jerry Royster did LeFlore lose his starting position.

With LeFlore gone, Tolan had gotten rid of a burr in his side. Even though the Pelicans lacked an extra right-handed bat through most of the season, a bat LeFlore might have provided, Tolan was happier without him. In the game of baseball having a skill is rarely enough. Like with any other job, you also have to be able to get along with the boss. Or at least not piss him off.

7

Trade Blues

The Pelicans won the rubber match against hometown Orlando on November 12, giving St. Petersburg an 8–2 record and a two and a half game lead over the second-place Juice. The game featured two home runs by Pelican first baseman Gary Rajsich. Modest and unassuming, Rajsich is at his most expressive when he smiles, which is often. When asked about the home runs, he replied, "I got lucky." But before he reached the major leagues, he had spent seven long seasons in the minors, working to improve, struggling to get noticed, so that when he talked of "luck" you knew it was anything but.

One year he was Most Valuable Player of the minor league World Series, and another year in Triple A he hit 29 home runs and drove in 95 runs with a sweet left-handed swing. And yet, despite his excellent numbers and his talented first baseman's glove, no manager ever gave him the chance to show what he could do on a regular basis in the majors.

By the time he could convince someone he could hit well enough to play in the big leagues, he was past the prime age. When a player starts heading toward thirty, suddenly he gets downgraded from prospect to suspect. Rajsich finally made it, at the age of twenty-seven. By then he was labeled a part-timer and a pinch hitter, a job he did poorly. For all his efforts, he got exactly 296 at-bats in the major leagues.

Most players denied an opportunity after working so hard and long would carry the resentment with them, but Gary Rajsich is too secure for bitterness and too down-to-earth for recrimination. He always contended he played for the "love of the game," and if that was so, how could he complain?

In beating Orlando, Milt Wilcox earned his third win of the young season. Wilcox had pitched in the World Series at the age of twenty with the Cincinnati Reds. After ten games in the Senior League it was beginning to look as though Wilcox, at the age of thirty-nine, was going to be the ace of the Pelican staff.

The bus ride back to St. Pete was almost joyous in its intensity. Their record was 8–2, and most of those wins had been easy. Steve Kemp, Lenny Randle, and Steve Henderson all were hitting over .400, and catcher Butch Benton wasn't far behind. Five of the nine pitchers on the staff had wins. In celebration the players on the bus were drinking a little beer, Miller Lite mostly, and teasing each other gently and talking baseball, with periodic bursts of laughter coming from one group and then another. Only weeks ago these men had been toiling at some day job.

Back in their own world, free from suits and ties and from lunch hours and from bosses they didn't respect, they were not only ballplayers, but winning ballplayers. They belonged to a team and had teammates, and no one cared that it was a bus, not a plane, that it was a new league of old-timers with not many fans and no tradition, that it was Florida in winter and not New York or L.A. or Detroit or Philadelphia in summer. The Pelicans were playing as a finely tuned instrument. Several players may have been unhappy because they weren't playing as often as they wanted to play. But grumbling occurs on every team from Little League to the majors, and on the Pelicans the dissatisfaction seemed minimal.

Bobby Tolan had gotten his players ready better than the managers of the other teams the Pelicans had played. During training Tolan had annoyed some of the players with petty rules such as no beer on the bus after the game, and no mustaches or facial hair. He had quickly rescinded them when he saw they were getting in the way of the harmony he wanted to build.

The bus arrived back in St. Petersburg around midnight. The next day, Monday, November 13, was an off-day. The men stayed in town playing golf, barbecuing, or fishing in Boca Ciega bay. During this day of rest, owner Jim Morley and manager Bobby Tolan upset everyone's equanimity by engineering a four-for-one trade with the Orlando Juice.

They sent the Juice four players—center fielder Jerry Martin, who struck out too much for Tolan's taste, a gimpy Bake McBride, whose left knee, as he described it, was "bone on bone," pitcher Gerry Pirtle, who had pitched one season for the Montreal Expos, and former Baltimore outfielder Mark Corey, Jim Morley's former college teammate, who had been limited to catching duties with the Pelicans because he was only thirty-four years old and not eligible to do anything but catch and DH under the Senior League rules.

Unfortunately for Corey, a fun-loving free spirit, catching is a difficult position to learn at such an advanced age, and he hated putting on the equipment. "Is catching as much fun as they say it is?" he was asked.

"Take the worst case of hemorrhoids you've ever had and triple it" was his answer.

In return the Pelicans obtained perhaps the best center fielder in the league, former Minnesota Twins and Los Angeles Dodgers star Kenny Landreaux. Landreaux had been an impressive performer against the Pelicans. In the field he was fleet and sure-handed, and he had a fine arm. At bat his speed made him dangerous. He wasn't a home run hitter like Martin, but he made contact often and had extra-base power.

Mark   Corey

The Pelicans

On the surface, it appeared that Morley and Tolan had picked Orlando's pocket. Baseball is a game where speed helps you in so many ways, especially on defense and on the base paths. In the Senior League only a handful of players had major league speed. Landreaux was one of them. And what had the Pelicans really given up? Mud Martin was an everyday player, and Pirtle showed he could pitch, but he wasn't going to be any more than a so-so hurler. Bake McBride could still hit, but it wasn't clear that he could still walk. Corey could hit too, but because he had to catch before he could hit, he wasn't going to get to hit much at all.

It came down to Martin for Landreaux. Martin had made several excellent fielding plays, and in practice he showed home run power. But he was still rusty. If he was going to demonstrate that power, it would be with Orlando.

Ballplayers, no matter how talented, are at the mercy of the men who run the teams. For a player to have a long, successful career, he has to stay injury-free and he has to avoid getting trapped by the system.

All sorts of bad things can happen to a player without his having any say in the matter. Among the more disastrous is to get traded to a team that then treats you badly. This may happen because the new manager doesn't like you or your game or doesn't appreciate your talents or doesn't like the general manager who made the trade. He will then punish that general manager by keeping you on the bench.

You may also find yourself failing to play because you are acquired as insurance. So you sit behind a resident superstar and rot.

A rare but disastrous calamity occurs when a man is traded to a team for its Franchise player. Franchise players are superstars. They end up in the Hall of Fame. They play with the same team for years and are closely identified with that team. Players like Mike Schmidt, Brooks Robinson, Jim Palmer, Johnny Bench, Mickey Mantle, Ernie Banks, and Sandy Koufax come to mind. But there have been instances when teams on the decline trade a Franchise player for several prospects in an attempt to return to respectability. That's what the struggling New York Mets did in 1977 when they traded Tom Seaver to the Cincinnati Reds for four prospects. One of those four prospects was Pelican pitcher Pat Zachry. That trade turned Pat Zachry's life upside down.

Tom Seaver, the premier pitcher in the National League, was negotiating with the New York Mets for more money. For reasons known only to them, the Mets brass apparently decided that rather than pay Seaver, they would trade him. But because Seaver was a ten-and-five player (ten years in the majors, five on one club) he could not be traded without his permission.

The Mets sought to secure that permission by making it uncomfortable for him to remain in New York. Their strategy was to try to turn public opinion against him by slandering him in the newspapers, sullying his fine name, as the late Dick Young of the *Daily News,* an ally of Mets management, printed scathing criticism of the pitcher, even attacking members of Seaver's family.

When some nasty comments were printed about Seaver's wife, Nancy, Seaver cried "uncle." He agreed to a trade.

M. Donald Grant traded Seaver to the Cincinnati Reds for four youngsters, including Zachry and another Pelican, Steve Henderson, along with infielder Doug Flynn and prospect Dan Norman.

For Zachry, a young and sensitive man who went from a team of champions to a team of chumps, the experience proved terrible.

Pat Zachry was the only pitcher in the deal, so in the minds of many Mets fans the trade boiled down to Seaver for Zachry. Seaver had worn uniform number forty-one. Zachry wore number forty. Seaver arguably had been the National League's dominant pitcher of the decade. He had led the Mets to pennants in 1969 and 1973. He had come to symbolize everything that was right with baseball. Not only was he a Hall of Fame pitcher, he was a family man, intelligent, a good teammate. The Mets fans all knew Tom Seaver was the sort of player who came along once in a generation. The Mets would not see another player of his stature until Dwight Gooden arrived in 1984.

Seaver departs. Zachry arrives. The fans and the press wanted Zachry to be as good as Seaver. It was impossible. No one, except perhaps Steve Carlton, was as good as Tom Seaver.

The contrast between playing with a cheapskate organization like the 1977 Mets and arguably the best organization in baseball, the Cincinnati Reds, was great. To pitch as a rookie for the Big Red Machine was a dream come true for Zachry. Like many Reds rookies, Zack had some difficulty with the manager, Sparky Anderson. But Zachry accepted that it was Anderson's way, and it didn't bother him. He finished the season 14–7 with a 2.74 earned-run average and was named National League co-Rookie of the Year along with Butch Metzger of San Diego. It was to be his finest season in baseball.

When Zachry looked around him, he saw stars: Tony Perez, Joe Morgan, Dave Concepcion, and Pete Rose in the infield and George

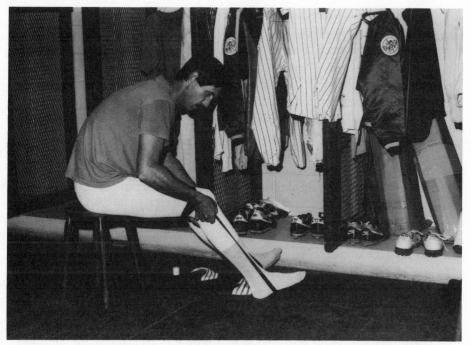

Peter Golenbock

Pat   Zachry

Foster, Cesar Geronimo, and Ken Griffey in the outfield. Johnny Bench was his catcher.

"It didn't matter who the other team put on that field," Zachry said. "We were going to win. It could have been guys in steel helmets carrying five-foot-long swords. We would have kicked their ass. It seemed destined that our ball club was going to beat the crap out of whoever they put on that field."

But after two years of winning championships, the Reds' management decided to tighten belts. They didn't want to pay Don Gullett. They took an ad out in the Cincinnati paper to say why they didn't want to pay Pete Rose. The Reds traded Rollie Eastwick and Will McEnaney. On June 15, 1977, Pat Zachry became a part of the housecleaning, sent to the New York Mets with three other players for the legendary Seaver.

The Reds may have been temporarily in trouble, but they righted themselves quickly. Tom Seaver had a big hand in that. Back in New York Pat Zachry pitched on a bad team run by an organization that was worse.

Joan Payson, the charismatic Mets owner, had died, leaving the team to inept relatives who delegated control to M. Donald Grant, who ran the team into the ground.

"When I first got to New York, they were cutting back on everything," Zachry said. "They would have put us on a wooden airplane with a rubber band for a propeller if they could have.

"We flew Allegheny Airlines. We called it Agony Airlines. At least we weren't taking the bus.

"I never enjoyed playing for the Mets. Here I was, twenty-five years old, traded from the penthouse to the outhouse, from first to last."

He was 7–6 in for the Mets in 1977 and then began the next season 10–3. He made the All-Star team. But then, in a pique after being taken out of a game, he broke his foot kicking the step of the dugout. His career went into decline.

At the end of his contract with the Mets in 1982, Zachry had a chance to become a free agent. Instead he opted to re-sign with the Mets, who promptly shipped him to the Los Angeles Dodgers for Jorge Orta. Zachry never did fulfill his destiny.

"I always felt playing for the Mets was unfinished business," he said. "There was always so much hope and promise. And not being able to reach that potential everybody tags you with." The frustration showed on Zachry's face.

Zack had high hopes when he was traded to the Dodgers, only to discover he had been acquired as an insurance policy. That first year in 1983 he was 6–1 with a 2.49 ERA, but he was frustrated because he wasn't a regular starter.

"They were concerned with guys who threw the ball ninety miles an hour, and I was past that," he said. "It was hard to sit around at the All-Star break and only have pitched fifteen or twenty innings."

In 1985 Zachry was traded to Philadelphia for Al Oliver. He became a mopup man. He was in the last year of a five-year contract. He was released one day before the player strike. No one else would hire him, not even for Triple A, because teams didn't want to hire high-paid veterans.

"They would rather take a young kid making the minimum and teach him," Zachry said. He was one of the victims of the owners' collusion of 1985.

"Everybody said, 'You want a lot of money,'" Zachry said. "I said, 'No. Just let me come to spring training. I'll pay my own way.'"

Zachry stayed home and went nuts. The Dodgers called and asked him if he was interested in being a minor league pitching coach. He coached for two years, at Vero Beach and then San Antonio. Then the Dodgers hired a new minor league director, Charlie Blaney, who told Zack he didn't fit the Dodger image.

"I couldn't really argue with that," he said. "I don't think I fit anybody's image."

Zack was out of ball again until the Senior League beckoned, giving him another chance to do the one thing he loved more than anything else: throw a baseball.

The morning after the Pelicans trade, a solemn Jerry Martin returned to Al Lang Stadium to retrieve his bats. In the empty locker room he stuffed his gloves in his red-and-white carry bag with the Phillies logo on it. With his bats under his other arm, he walked up the runway from the clubhouse and into the sunshine and his Jeep 4 × 4.

He opened the back and dumped in his equipment with a thump and a clatter. From the back of the truck he brought out a short stack of large St. Petersburg Pelican posters with the schedule of games on them. Expressionless, he walked to the garbage can outside the players' entrance and stuffed them inside.

Martin walked back to the driver's side, jumped in, slammed the door, and headed for Orlando.

Before the afternoon's game Gerry Pirtle stood in the parking lot outside the stadium, looking forlorn as the crowd headed for the gates and their seats. Tall, with a mustache, no one recognized him. Gerry had only managed a cup of coffee in the majors with Montreal, where he was 0–2 with a 5.88 ERA in 1978. Despite earning a Pelican victory, he faced rejection once again.

A nice man, Pirtle said quietly, "I'd rather be here."

"Have a good season" was the reply. What else can one say?

Figuring he had the club made, Pirtle only a week ago had plunked down three months' rent, nonrefundable, for his apartment, and now he was losing it. Orlando is two hours away, too far to commute. There is no players' union. There was nothing he or any other traded player could do about it.

In the clubhouse several hours before game time the raucousness of the previous bus ride was replaced by a somber, wakelike atmosphere. The Pelican players were visibly upset at the loss of their four buddies.

Pelican pitcher Mike "Tex" Williams particularly did not want to see

The Pelicans

Gerry   Pirtle

Mud Martin leave, and he didn't like the timing of the deal because the team was hot and why fool with success?

Tex had only gotten as far as Triple A Albuquerque with the Dodgers, but he was aware of the vagaries of the game. He had been promised his chance to be a Dodger by manager Tommy Lasorda, but that opportunity never materialized. For Williams the Senior League was his shot at playing with major league ballplayers. Dock Ellis had liked his fastball and his determination and his loosey-goosey personality and kept him for the Pelican bullpen.

Part of Tex's anger came from the realization that it just as easily could have been *him* going to Orlando. Tex himself had suffered from managerial manipulation. He hated when it happened to someone he liked.

"I say, 'You don't change something that's working,'" Williams said. "That's my own personal feeling. Jerry Martin is a great guy. He was just coming around. He started hitting the ball. He was playing slow-pitch softball for a long time. Now he's getting his swing back. I guess they didn't know how much longer it would take to get it back.

"I feel sorry for the guys who had to leave, because this club is going to win it all. I'd hate like heck to leave this club. I like all the guys here. I'm the minor leaguer. I feel I may be starting to fit in a little more, so I'm hanging in there and doing what they're telling me to do. I try to give 100 percent every time I go out there."

Tex was like a soldier on the front lines whose buddy had just had his chest ripped open by shrapnel. He had survived. His buddy was gone.

Even the hardened veterans were not immune to emotion after seeing four teammates jettisoned.

Jon Matlack, the thirteen-year major league veteran, was tight-lipped. "You're always upset," he said. "There's a sense of loss. You develop friendships, and they are sent away. You don't know whether the guy coming in will fit in. It's upsetting, but it's part of the game."

CHAPTER

8

The Roller Coaster

The four-for-one trade with Orlando dampened the spirits of the entire team—for one day. The first evening back there was no spark or life, the play lethargic. When the team was on the field, the specters of the four former players hovered in a dugout emptied of bodies. The extras had been sent away. It was as though they had died. The new player, Kenny Landreaux, was absent too. He was not expected until the following game.

That first game back in St. Petersburg took place against the Fort Myers Sun Sox. A team managed by Pat Dobson that featured some good pitching, it was led by left-hander Rick Waits, whose claim to fame was that with Cleveland he beat the Yankees on the final day of the 1978 season, which enabled the Red Sox to tie for the division title. Without Waits's win, Bucky Dent never would have had his chance to hit his home run off Mike Torrez. The Sun Sox featured Amos Otis, another young Mets prospect traded away to become a star for another team, in this case the Kansas City Royals, and Ronnie Jackson, a burly, powerful man who jumped from team to team around the American League for ten years.

Waits shut out the Pelicans. After the game, everyone dressed quickly and left. Clubhouses can have moods, and on this day it was funereal.

The next day, November 15, Al Lang Stadium was graced by the arrival of two newcomers. The first was Landreaux. Quiet, almost shy, Kenny Landreaux, unlike most of his new teammates, hadn't yet stopped playing pro ball. After Kenny's major league career ended in 1987, he took a job as a salesman for a premium distributing company, but quit to play in Culiacán, Mexico. In 1989 he tried out with the Baltimore Orioles. He played well enough to make the team, only to be told he was being released.

"They said they didn't have any room, that they had players to protect," Landreaux said.

He returned to Mexico and played summer ball for Aguascalientes for a month. He then signed with the Dodgers, playing at Triple A Albuquerque. "They said they were helping me out, doing me a favor," Landreaux remembered.

Here he was playing in Florida, so that in the last eighteen months, Landreaux had spent exactly two weeks away from baseball. When asked about the trade, Landreaux said only that it had been a surprise.

"I was the only outfielder in Orlando who was healthy," he said. "I didn't think they would trade me."

The Pelican players once more seemed in good spirits. They were back to their kidding, joking old selves. Steve Kemp showed up wearing baggy sweatpants made of imitation leopard skin. Kemp looked like a model from an all-men's magazine. The players, and Randy Lerch in particular, teased him about it. Laughter filled the clubhouse.

The old teammates were forgotten, the new one greeted warmly. It was a new night, a new ball game, and it was payday. Furthermore, Ted Giannoulis, once known as The San Diego Chicken, now The Fabulous Chicken, had come to town. The team of Al Schacht and Nick Altcock were the first jesters, entertaining their fans as they played for the Washington Senators in the 1920s. Later Max Patkin wore the mantle, scratching out a living, only to grow old and bitter as he watched Giannoulis become famous and grow rich.

The Pelican players had mixed feelings about The Chicken. They liked him because he was funny, but they didn't care for his interruptions, because they rightly felt the game always should be paramount. The team owners appreciated The Chicken because his presence usually would bring several thousand extra fans to a game, but they didn't like him because they had to pay him $7,000 an appearance. Few Pelicans made that much per month.

During the season, The Chicken made around two hundred appearances at major and minor league ballparks. Do the multiplication. It ain't chicken feed. Until the advent of the huge cable TV contracts, The Chicken had been one of the best-paid performers in the game.

Peter Golenbock

Ken Landreaux

For this game, 2,638 fans—a large crowd by Senior League standards—paid to watch him and the team. The mood was festive.

The Chicken entered the game in the middle of the second inning. He had an orange body, a yellow head, and a navy blue comb. He strutted, bowed, gestured at the ump, and made semiobscene gestures, which got big applause. Giannoulis is a brilliant slapstick comedian. Few other mimes in America can make people laugh like he can.

He led the enthusiastic crowd in rhythmic applause, coached first base, danced around, and picked his nose with a large foam rubber finger, wiping the imaginary residue on Fort Myers catcher Tim Hosley.

There was more. He dropped baseballs from his backside, beat up a foam rubber ump, and writhed on the ground after pretending to get hit in the nuts during fielding practicing.

Once there were Laurel and Hardy and The Three Stooges. Slapstick was still alive.

You couldn't say the same thing about the Pelicans after the Sun Sox beat up starter Jon Matlack for five runs in the fourth.

In the stands a young fan put the day in perspective. "The Chicken is all right," he said, "but we're losing."

A mark of a good team is its ability to scratch back. The Pelicans scored five in the sixth to take the lead. The new man, Kenny Landreaux, had a single to keep the rally alive. Steve Henderson drove in the game winner. Pelican reliever Joe Sambito got the final out of the game with the tying run on base when he retired Larry Harlow on a lazy fly ball.

The Fabulous Chicken and a victory too. What more could the fans have asked for? Sambito punched his glove. All the Pelicans rushed to the mound to congratulate him and themselves on a game they easily could have lost.

The next game pitted the two titans of the league, the Pelicans and the West Palm Beach Tropics, managed by Dick Williams, a supporter of the league from its inception. Because Williams got involved early, he was one of the first managers to prepare lists of players he desired for his team. Having managed in both leagues, he knew exactly who he wanted.

Williams had excellent starting pitching, with Juan Eichelberger, Pete Broberg, "Father" Ray Burris, and "the Giant," Tim Stoddard. His relief tandem of Rollie Fingers and Al Hrabosky proved equally outstanding. His defense was sharp. Ron Washington, the shortstop, hit over .400 most of the season, and Mickey Rivers in center played like he was a youngster. It seemed as though Mickey, now forty-one, never aged. Toby Harrah, a one-man inspirational force, played third.

Williams's Tropics had pitching, defense, and discipline. And, of course, it had Dick Williams, who managed at Boston, Oakland, California, Montreal, San Diego, and Seattle, and developed winners almost everywhere he went, taking a total of four division titles, four pennants, and two World Series.

For this battle of division leaders no more than five hundred fans showed up at Al Lang Stadium. No one could figure out why, except that The Chicken had left for another town and performance and Friday night in Florida traditionally means high school football. Also it was windy and cold, and when the temperature drops the dampness goes right through you. A Michael J. Fox movie, *Back to the Future,* was on television, and beyond center field, crowds were mobbing the Bayfront Auditorium for the annual boat show.

Baseball in winter was new, novel, and hadn't become a habit for many fans. Would it be soon? Would it ever be? What wasn't in dispute was that anyone who saw a Senior League game went home thoroughly entertained. And this night proved no exception, as the two teams scored twenty-one runs. It wasn't pretty, but it was exciting.

The Pelicans led by three when the Tropics went up to hit in the seventh inning. With two outs and runners on first and third, Mickey Rivers came up to hit. Mickey, skinny, sleepy-eyed, looked the same as he did when he played for the world championship Yankees in 1977 and 1978. Coming to the plate, Mickey still shuffled the way he once did. It was only when he put the ball in play that you were aware of his superior athletic skills.

Rivers hit a blooper to center field. Kenny Landreaux came racing in, dove, and appeared to make the catch, but the umpire ruled it no catch. Both Jerry White and Tito Landrum scored, the latter all the way from first.

Bobby Tolan came out to argue. Before he was finished, the umpires sent Landrum back to third. On what basis they did so no one in the dugout could be sure, except that the umps had blown the original call, and maybe this decision split the difference.

It didn't make any sense to Dick Williams either, and the silver-haired manager raced onto the field to argue his point. From umpire to umpire he went, arguing, gesticulating, until almost ten minutes had passed. Tolan, disgusted with the delay, called his players off the field. There Dick stood, arms waving, mouth moving, alone with the umps. Finally, unable to shoo him away, the umps threw him out.

Williams kicked dirt all over the plate. While he finished the throes of his protest, Pelican players took their positions. In all, nearly twenty minutes elapsed.

The game resumed, and no more runs scored that inning. Tolan's persuasiveness, and perhaps the umpires' lack of decisiveness, had kept the Pelicans in the game. Had Landrum been allowed to score, the Pelicans probably would have lost.

Going into the ninth, the Pelicans were ahead, 11–7, with runners on first and second and one out, when Dock Ellis came in to finish it off. Pitching deliberately, Dock took his time between pitches. He glared down at the batter, acting as though he hated the world. He was forty-five years old, pitching to other older men, but when he stood out there, he was a commanding figure to watch.

Mark Wagner popped up for out two, but the Pelicans would discover that Dick Williams's team rarely would lose easily. Toby Harrah, gritty, determined, a man who succeeded on the sheer force of his positive personality, doubled two in, and his sidekick, Ron Washington, the league's Most Valuable Player by year's end, doubled over Landreaux's head in center for two more runs. Now it was 11–10, with the tying run on second.

Jerry White, a slap hitter, was the batter. Dock took a deep breath, stretched, and came in with a fastball. White swung and sent a lazy fly ball to left field, ending the game. On this night Dock Ellis and the Pelicans had squeaked through.

Milt Wilcox beat the Tropics the next day for his fourth win, and the day after Elias Sosa pitched just as well, except that the Pelicans only gave him a single unearned run and it wasn't enough. Tropic pitcher Pete Broberg, the pride of Dartmouth and a former Washington Senator, showed he still could throw as hard as ever, as he pitched a shutout.

Having taken two out of three from powerful West Palm Beach, the Pelicans were sitting three and a half games ahead of Orlando, four over Winter Haven, and four and a half over Bradenton, managed by former Yankee star Clete Boyer, whom they weren't scheduled to meet for another five weeks. The Pelicans had a team batting average of .319, fifth in the league. The hitters were clearly ahead of the pitchers. Nine players were hitting over .400, including Steve Henderson, who was fourth at .426, and Lenny Randle at .417. Dan Driessen, Toby Harrah, and Amos Otis were one, two, and three.

The St. Lucie Legends, the worst team in the league, were next to play in St. Pete. Before the opener on November 21, a man of below-average height with a small bulge in the tummy and a receding hairline walked out of the home dugout wearing a Pelican uniform and a glove. It was about three in the afternoon, hours before the scheduled 7:05 P.M. start. He looked like a guy from a local beer league.

"Hey, Ozzie, who is this guy?"

"That's Mike Marshall," Virgil said. Sure enough, it was the former relief star for Detroit, Seattle, Houston, Montreal, Los Angeles, Atlanta, Texas, Minnesota, and the Mets. Marshall was best known for his expertise in kinesiology—the study of how anatomy relates to movement—his screwball, and his rubber arm. One year for the Dodgers he appeared in 106 ballgames, winning 15 games and saving 21 others.

Marshall, auditioning to make the Pelicans, went out to the bullpen in right field and began throwing. He didn't look fast, but his ball really moved, darting in to a right-hander, and the next pitch darting away. After about fifteen minutes, the noncommittal Bobby Tolan apparently had seen enough.

"You'll enjoy pitching for this club," Tolan told Marshall.

"If it doesn't interfere with my real work," he replied enigmatically.

It was the last time the Pelicans saw him until he appeared a couple of weeks later on the mound, throwing for the Winter Haven Super Sox.

In the dugout Roy Howell talked about his experience with Marshall. One year in Texas they were teammates.

"You gotta understand," Howell said, "Mike is one of those types of guys who just ... you know ... his shit doesn't stink. He was in his own program. That's fine and dandy. And if anyone was doing anything different than he was doing, then it was wrong. And you knew that over the years, and you'd just laugh and go about your business."

Howell remembered when Marshall joined the Rangers.

"I was sitting in the locker room, and Marshall saw my locker was next to his, and he said, 'I gotta get a new locker. There isn't anyone in this area that's intelligent enough to hold a conversation with me.'"

Howell told him, "So pick up your shit and leave."

He said, "That was my encounter with Mike. But I didn't care, so long as he could get them out."

In addition to Marshall's appearance, the day was also designated as "St. Lucie Legends Autograph Day." The St. Lucie team members were supposed to sign autographs for the fans. For those who came, it would be an autograph bonanza. The St. Lucie owner, Joe Sprung, had attempted to build his team around big-name former New York players, and he signed ex-Yanks and Mets such as Bobby Bonds, Felix Millan, George Foster, Jerry Grote, Fred Stanley, Walt "No Neck" Williams, Juan Beniquez, Clint Hurdle, and Oscar Gamble. Unfortunately for the Legends, someone forgot that pitching is a large part of the game. The Legend starters would provide some good innings, but their middle relief was weak and got beat up almost every night, so the team remained in last place in the other division.

The fans lined up in a snake of autograph seekers, but some of the biggest names on the team, including George Foster and Jerry Grote, were no-shows, opting to stay out of sight in the visitors' locker room.

Roy Howell and Joe Sambito watched the proceedings from the St. Pete dugout. They commented on the St. Lucie name players who were staying away from the autograph session.

Howell said, "Once an asshole, always an asshole."

"You know," Sambito said, "there are players who haven't even made it to the big show who won't sign autographs."

"Like who?"

"Robin Ventura. I heard Ventura wouldn't sign autographs because he didn't want to lessen the value of his signature."

Howell laughed. "He didn't want to flood the market."

Sambito said, "The value of his autograph has only one determination: performance. That's the only thing that counts."

"You got that right," Howell replied.

The day after Mike Marshall's tryout, several hours before the second game with St. Lucie, a wiry man in cowboy boots and street clothes stood in the Pelicans' dugout. He had a mustache, and he talked with a thick Texas drawl. He introduced himself. "Mah name is Hoot Gibson."

You felt like responding, "Yeah, and my name is Roy Rogers," but you didn't because he appeared to be made of hemp and rawhide and leather, and you suspected he could have pinched your neck off if he had chosen to do so.

James "Hoot" Gibson had been home in Bryan, Texas, when he watched one of the Senior League games on the cable. He had once been a college All-American at Texas A&M and had been drafted by the Montreal Expos. He had never pitched in the majors, in part because he had begun his minor league career with the Atlanta Braves at the age of twenty-eight. After reaching Triple A, he quit, returning home to Texas.

The players he watched on TV all had been ex-major leaguers. He thought, *It would be a gamble for me to spend the time and money to try out and then not make it.* He grabbed his shotgun and went hunting for a few days to think about it. When he returned, he discovered that his wife had packed his bags. He got in his Camaro and drove to St. Petersburg.

He figured, *The Pelicans seemed like the best team. Might as well try out with the best.* It wasn't until he arrived in St. Pete that he called to say he was coming.

Jim Morley's initial response was "Gimme a break ... a guy named Hoot?" Then he thought, *He's here, so why not?*

Twice Gibson threw for Bobby Tolan and Dock Ellis. He was smallish, but he had a big man's fastball and a tough, biting slider. They offered him a contract, but the official major league records showed he was thirty-four, too young to pitch in the league.

Gibson said, "When I signed with the Braves I lied about my age to protect Hank Aaron. Hank Aaron would have looked foolish signing a twenty-eight-year-old rookie. So they wrote I was twenty-five."

They asked him to prove it. A birth certificate solved the problem.

His wife, Vicki, said, "Don't you know Hoot's older than dirt?"

In the game against St. Lucie, Gibson pitched three innings, allowed nothing. Bobby Tolan had brought Gibson into the game to pitch to George Foster. There was one out. The bases were loaded.

I can't believe it, Gibson thought, standing out on the mound. *I'm pitching to George Foster. I mean, he's a real big leaguer.*

Gibson threw a hard slider, and Foster grounded to Roy Howell at third, who threw to Randle, who relayed to first. The inning was over. Hoot got his first victory in his first game when the Pelicans rallied for four runs in the fourth.

Gibson said after the game, "I used to dream about playing against these guys. And now I'm getting them out."

The arrival of Hoot Gibson left another pitcher, Dick Bosman, an eleven-year veteran with Washington, Texas, Cleveland, and Oakland, feeling blue. Bosman, who had once thrown a no-hitter for Cleveland, knew he should get a chance to pitch, but Bobby Tolan and Dock Ellis— the other Pelican pitcher to hurl a major league no-hitter—were making it obvious he wasn't in their favor.

Bosman was the pitching coach for the Baltimore Orioles' Triple A Rochester club. He had applied to owner Jim Morley for that job. He didn't get it. Tolan's pal Dock did. But Bosman was not the kind of guy to notice a flaw in a teammate's delivery and keep his mouth shut. And Dock was not the kind of guy not to notice Bosman's interference.

Bobby, who didn't like players second-guessing him or his staff, backed his pitching coach. Tension brewed between Bosman and Dock, and it grew throughout the season as Dock tried to assert his authority and Bosman tried to assert his in the form of pitching tips.

When the season began, Dick Bosman, despite his no-hitter and his American League leading earned-run average in 1969, found himself relegated as a standby player. He was given a job as color man in the radio broadcast booth with the vague promise of action "if a spot opened up." Well, a place had opened up, but a career minor leaguer named Hoot Gibson was filling it, and Bossie was having a tough time swallowing his considerable pride.

Dick Bosman felt he deserved more respect if only because of his career accomplishments. He had won 82 games for mostly bad ballclubs in Washington, Texas, and Cleveland. He had pitched that no-hitter. He had been around a long time.

Bosman began his baseball odyssey in 1963 when he signed with the Pittsburgh Pirates for $7,000. Jack Kennedy was still President. Bosman began deep in the minors in Kingsport, Tennessee, making $500 a month, living three to an apartment, making long bus trips to other tiny towns, but pitching well and showing promise. He was drafted by the San

Francisco Giants and then sold to the Washington Senators, where in 1966 his first major league manager was Gil Hodges.

Hodges, a tough Marine, had a scar on his neck, and Bosman remembered that whenever he got mad, the scar would remain white and the rest of him would turn red.

Bosman said, "He would start to shake a little bit, and you thought he might pinch your head off—Jesus Christ—and he would start to yell, and the volume would increase, and he'd get himself worked up. He would pace back and forth, getting louder and louder, and at the end it would reach a crescendo, and whoever the offender was would be cowering in his locker."

In 1969 the Washington Senators were sold to Bob Short, and Short brought Ted Williams, one of baseball's legends, out of retirement.

"Ted had never managed before, and there were a lot of things he did as a manager that were questionable, but as an instructor he was great," Bosman said. "He had made such a great study of hitting. He knew what was coming, because he knew pitchers are creatures of habit. He knew what was going on out there, because he watched, and I learned a lot from that."

Williams was the one who convinced Bosman he could be successful in the big leagues if the pitcher would throw more breaking balls and get ahead in the count more often. Williams showed Bosman how to set up hitters and told him what the batters were thinking about. They talked pitching strategy for hours.

Bosman recalled, "The guys said Ted could sit in the dugout and call the sequence of pitches that I was going to throw. 'Sinker away. Fastball off the plate. Slider for a ball. A fastball low and away for strike three.' And it would go on like that."

In 1968 Bosman had a rough year, going 2–9. He was a fringe player. In 1969 he came to spring training scuffling for a job. But after he sat with Williams and learned what he had to teach him, Bosman took the same stuff but with a better idea, and he was 14–5 and led the league in earned-run average with a 2.19 mark.

"So what was the difference?" Bosman asked. "I learned how to pitch from Ted."

Williams, a hardass, could be caustic. One time the Senators were playing in the old Kansas City ballpark and for a change had a big lead. Senator pitcher Casey Cox was on the mound, walking batters and giving up hits. In the dugout Ted got up off the bench and walked down to the other end, where he kicked the water cooler. Bosman was down there, taking a nap.

"It scared the shit out of me," Bosman said.

Williams growled, "You know, Bossie, as a player I hated fucking pitchers, and I'm having a hard time liking you pricks too."

In 1970 Bosman finished 16–12. He pitched 231 innings and finished the year with a 3.00 earned-run average. But because the Senators were a poor team, Bosman was denied the 20 victories he so badly wanted.

"I should have won twenty just throwing my glove out on the mound," he said. "But we faded at the end, losing thirteen in a row."

In 1971 Bosman pitched 237 innings but finished with a 12–16 record, largely due to lack of support by his teammates in the field.

In 1972 the Senators became the Texas Rangers, beginning a saga of poorly run, truly dreadful baseball. Williams became bitter when the Texas management made a couple of deals without consulting him. The press also turned on him. He quit after the season. Whitey Herzog replaced him.

Bosman spent parts of three seasons in Cleveland, playing for mediocre teams under cheapskate management. The highlight was the no-hitter he pitched on July 19, 1974, against the Oakland A's, who had won the World Series in 1973 and would win it again in 1974.

Bosman was traded to Oakland in 1975. He had had three goals: to pitch a no-hitter, pitch in the World Series, and win 20 games. Oakland had been world champs twice. He was excited to go.

The beginning of his two-year tour with Oakland began with so much promise. This was Bosman's chance, finally, to play on a winning team. In his very first game pitching for the A's, he went up against the Indians, the team that had traded him.

It was late in the game, the score 1–1, and as Bosman was walking out to the mound, his right fielder, Reggie Jackson, jogged by and, patting him on the ass, said, "Hold them right here, and we're going to get them." The next inning the A's scored four. And with the A's bullpen, Jim Todd, Paul Lindblad, and The Man, Rollie Fingers, there was no way the other team was going to catch up.

Bosman recalled, "The idea was to stick in there until the sixth or seventh and be ahead, and if you do that, guess what, brother? You win. And I did." Quickly Dick Bosman understood he was playing on a winner.

"I won my first six games and I hadn't met Charlie Finley yet," Bosman said. "After my sixth win, I finally met him. It was like meeting the Pope. I had an audience with the Pope, for Christ sake. And he was chirping. We had won three pennants in a row, and here we were, rolling again. There was me and Ken Holtzman and Stan Bahnsen. We were cooking. Everyone was still there, except Catfish Hunter, who had gone to the Yankees.

"We were a machine. You were carried along with the wave. It was an attitude. Alvin Dark was very positive, and he pushed the buttons. It was a wonderful experience."

Alvin Dark, the manager, had a stormy relationship with his players. Alvin was religious, but he was also a fighter. Clubs usually reflect the philosophy of the manager. The A's fought often. The fights were only a sideshow. They didn't impede the team's success.

"You know what winning does. You overlook a lot of things," Bosman said. "We were making good money for the time. We won every night. All these guys were winners, Rollie, Lindblad, Joe Rudi, Bill North, Reggie, Gino, Garner, Campy, Sal."

As a player, shortstop Alvin Dark had teamed for two years with second baseman Eddie Stanky, another scrapper, to anchor the New York Giants' infield. Both were disciples of Leo Durocher. Leo believed in beanballs and fighting and playing to win. So did Stanky and Dark. So did Dark's players. Bosman fit right in.

"Sal Bando, our third baseman, was a hard-nosed son of a bitch," said Bosman. "He knew how to play the game, and when Alvin fucked it up, he got pissed off. He'd smash a helmet or bust a bat. One night after a ball game, Sal felt that Alvin had screwed up and he kicked the garbage can and said, 'That son of a bitch couldn't manage a fucking meat market.' And he turned around, and Alvin was standing right behind him. And we had to break it up!

"The fighting in our clubhouse was real, because we had a lot of big egos. Each guy was a hero in the papers and in their own mind, and even in the stats. And Bill North was hard to get along with, because he had a big mouth and he swaggered a lot.

"One time he got in a fight with Reggie over tickets. North left tickets for a broad, and Reggie said something about their fucking the same girl, and they started yelling. Before you knew it, they were both on the floor of the clubhouse.

"Rollie agitated everybody. He had the greatest one-liners in the world. We hung out at the bars together. He had the loosest, happy-go-lucky attitude for a guy who went in there with the game on the line every night. One night he said something to Reggie. I was pitching. A guy hit a line drive to right. Reggie charged it and damn near got hit right between the eyes, never got the glove up, ducked it, and it ended up going to the wall for a triple.

"We won the game anyway. We were in the clubhouse afterward, eating the spread. Reggie looked at Rollie, like *I know I'm going to get ripped. What do you have to say?* And Rollie said, 'Jesus Christ, I could have caught the fucking ball with a straightjacket on.' The joint broke up.

"'Fuck you, you cocksucker.' It went on like that forever, just on and on."

The one teammate Bosman didn't respect was shortstop Bert Campaneris. Campy didn't play aggressively enough for Bosman's taste.

Bosman recalled, "Campy was a wimp. He would never break up a double play. He didn't want to cover second on a goddamn double play. Never did. Christ sake, I remember one night Boog Powell was the hitter, and Garner was playing four and five steps back on the grass in right field, and Campy wanted Garner to cover second."

Bosman did respect Reggie Jackson, who every once in a while was faulted for not hustling in the field.

"Let me tell you something about Reggie," Bosman said. "I watched that son of a bitch for years before I played with him. He was cocky, but you respected him because he busted his ass. He busted his ass out there every day.

"The only day I felt he didn't, we were going to clinch the pennant. We were in K.C. on a Sunday afternoon. It was me against Dennie Leonard, and Leonard beat me, two to one. George Brett pulled a sinker down the right-field line that Gino couldn't get at first. The ball got by Reggie in the corner, and Amos Otis scored from first base. I got beat.

"To me, I didn't think he hustled after the ball. And it was emotional for me, because I had been traded over there and I could have pitched the pennant clincher, and yet I lost.

"Those were the days when you lost, it was the end of the world. That's the way I was from the first day I ever put on a baseball glove. Back then it was all right to break a helmet or fire a bat or go nuts, because that's why you were out there, to win that ball game. I'll be a son of a bitch if you lost. Maybe I was wrong, but that's the way I felt. And I still feel that way."

Bosman had a solid season his first year in Oakland, finishing 11–4 for the A's, and at the end of 1975 Syd Thrift, then the minor league farm director, was appointed to negotiate contracts. He offered Bosman a $2,000 raise. It was one year before unrestricted free agency, a year before the revolution that would change the face of the game forever. Before free agency a team owned you. If you didn't sign with that club, you didn't play. Syd Thrift gave Bosman the usual pre-free-agency ultimatum, "Take it or leave it." Bosman signed.

In the spring of 1976 Bosman started the season in the bullpen. At the All-Star break he was 4–0. Then things deteriorated on the A's. Owner Charlie Finley began selling off his star players, one by one. Finley knew free agency was coming, and he didn't want to pay the huge salaries. He sought to sell Vida Blue, Joe Rudi, and Rollie Fingers for $1 million each, but Commissioner Bowie Kuhn stopped him "in the best interests of baseball." A's players came and went. It was a revolving door.

Major league careers end for different reasons. For Dick Bosman, his ended because he was conscientious and caring about his fellow players, believing strongly in the Players' Association. He had been a player representative in Texas and Cleveland, and in Oakland he took the job against his will because no one else wanted it.

In 1975 Bosman had been the alternate player representative. Going into spring training in 1976, Reggie Jackson had the player rep job. Reggie, realizing he was hurting his bargaining position in contract negotiations because he was player rep, stepped down. The team held a meeting to choose a replacement.

Third baseman Sal Bando refused to take it. He too was negotiating his contract. Bossie had been a player rep for eight years in Texas and Cleveland. They asked him if he would take the job. At first, he demurred. He didn't want the job either. He was aware that Finley was the sort of owner to hold it against you. "I served my apprenticeship," Bosman told the others.

When no one else volunteered, Bosman became upset. He looked around the room. There were big-name veterans, like Billy Williams, Joe Rudi, and Rollie Fingers. He wanted them to take some responsibility, to take the job, but he knew they would not.

Bosman said, "The reason I took this job nine years ago was that I was excited about our association and the things that got done and Marvin Miller and the issues we stood for. I've been through a strike, a lockout, a lot of things, I've been traded a couple times, and now look at you guys. I ain't gonna name names, but there are a lot of guys who have never been player rep. You've been in the game longer than me, and you've had better careers than I have, and you know, when things go wrong, you bitch to the player rep. You got your hand out for things. And when you finish in this game and become eligible for the pension, you're going to want to have it. But when you're asked to serve the association, you duck it. If you're

Tom DiP

Dick Bosman

pissed off at what I've said and the shoe fits, wear it. I'll take the goddamn job again."

Nobody said a single word to him. Less than a year later Dick Bosman was out of baseball, he believes, because he took the player rep job.

"But I don't regret it," Bosman said. "It's not sour grapes, because I believed in what I did, and as we speak, I'm taking my pension, and my daughter will go to the college of her choice because of that, and I'm proud."

Bosman finished the 1976 season 4–2. The next spring he was pitching well. On March 28, one of the final days of spring training, Bosman was scheduled to attend a player reps' meeting in Sun City, Arizona. He was packing to go when general manager Jack McKeon stuck his head out of the office and said, "Bossie, Charlie's on the phone for you." Bosman picked up the phone. It was Charlie Finley, calling from Chicago. Finley was nervously clearing his throat, as was his custom.

"Boz, ahem, ah, we're going to release you this morning," Finley said. "I guess we're going to have to get another player rep to take your place."

"What? I didn't hear that," Bosman said.

"Yeah, we're going to make some moves today. We're giving you your release."

"Wait a minute," Bosman replied. "In two years I've been fifteen and six for you. I've been your starting pitcher for two years, pitched out of the bullpen, and you're going to release me today, on the twenty-eighth of March? You could have traded me all spring. You could have released me earlier and given me a chance to get with another team."

"I'll make some calls for you," Finley replied.

"Charlie, I'm sunk," Bosman said. "Everybody's set. Everybody knows where they're going."

"Well, ah, make sure you take your stuff with you. You might get a chance somewhere."

Bosman hung up the phone.

The A's bus was leaving. His teammates were getting on it. "You coming?" he was asked. Bosman was speechless. He walked back into the clubhouse and cried.

Finley ordered Bosman to clear out of the A's hotel by nightfall. Bosman tried out with the Indians. Frank Robinson wanted him. General manager Phil Segui didn't. Guess who won? The Cubs said that if Bosman went to Triple A for $20,000, he might come up in May. Bosman saw the offer as financial suicide. His wife, Pam, told him, "Keep your pride, babe. Come home."

He got up the next morning, looked at the mirror, and told himself, "It's done, over." He watched the Cubs' bus drive off to Chicago.

Bosman went into the clubhouse, picked up his gear, and stuck it in the car. It was a long drive from Scottsdale, Arizona, to northern Virginia all alone. He had a CB radio in his car. It was just him and the stars above. As he drove, he replayed every year of his career in his mind.

He took the southern route, and his intent was to drive straight through without sleeping. But he was exhausted, and he decided to make one final stop. He would stay overnight in Kingsport, Tennessee. That was where his career began.

Bosman stopped at the Holiday Inn outside the city of Kingsport. The next morning he tried to find the ballpark. He couldn't. Everything had changed. There were no familiar landmarks. This was fifteen years later, but it seemed like a lifetime.

It was a high school field, and Bosman had to ask directions. It was still there, and finally he found it. The gate to the ballpark was ajar. He walked out onto the field, stood on the mound, and looked around. Here it finally sank in that his career in major league baseball was really over.

There were nights when Bosman would lie in bed, crying. It was difficult for him to let go. His wife, Pam, would say, "It's hard, isn't it?"

He'd reply, "Yeah, it's hard. It's very hard."

But in time the bitterness left, and he resumed working with his brother-in-law in the automobile business.

After being out of the game nine years, Bosman was hired by Hawk Harrelson in 1986 to coach in the Chicago White Sox organization. The recommendation came from Syd Thrift, who also lived in northern Virginia. Dick became the pitching coach at Buffalo in Triple A. Two months later Dave Duncan and Tony LaRussa were fired, and Bosman was promoted to the White Sox. Then, as often happens, there was another change in management. Bosman was fired.

Today he is pitching coach with the Baltimore organization, working at the Triple A level in Rochester.

"Looking back," he said, "I'm awfully happy I had a chance to play with Oakland. I had a chance to play with all those winning players, and though my clubs didn't win much before that, now I could say, 'I'm a winner too,' and that has helped me so very, very much. Because that's the way I feel."

9

Bitching and Moaning

After the Pelicans twice defeated St. Lucie, they bused over to Fort Myers, where the Sun Sox won three games. The mood of a team can be as volatile as the swing of the stock market. One day the market can be booming along, and the next day, without warning, it can drop five hundred points. It was the same way with the Pelicans. Everything seemed pleasant and calm. Then all hell broke loose.

The opening game in Fort Myers was held before an appreciative crowd of 1,750 fans, who watched their heroes deliver seventeen hits and score thirteen runs as Bobby Tolan steamed. The Pelicans had begun the series at a disadvantage because third baseman Roy Howell had to fly home to San Luis Obispo, California, while his wife delivered a child. He wouldn't be back for about a week. Injuries also were slowing the offense.

What galled Tolan were mental mistakes and sloppy base running that killed rallies. Steve Henderson, who rarely made errors, was thrown out at third to kill one Pelican rally, and Alan Bannister, who was suffering from muscle pulls, was thrown out at home after making the turn and limping his way toward disaster. Then the next inning Kenny Landreaux decided to test the arm of right fielder Bobby Jones, who threw him out at home by a good five feet. Adding to all that, the Pelican relief pitching stank.

The only player to derive any satisfaction out of this ugly loss was Dick Bosman. With Dave Rajsich, Randy Lerch, and Nardi Contreras hurting, Bosman was needed. He was informed that he would be in uniform for the series.

It had been a rout long before he got to pitch. He didn't get much time to warm up. Finally when he reached the mound the chilly weather made it tough for him to get loose, and Bossie wasn't sharp either. He faced six batters. He allowed two singles, two intentional walks, a sacrifice bunt, and he got a double play. Two runs, three hits.

Bosman had been a starter for most of his pro career. It hurt his pride for him to have to mop up, but at least he finally got to pitch. He wasn't pleased. But he wasn't totally unhappy either.

The next day Bosman and the Pelican players *were* totally unhappy. Though the team's record was a solid 13–5 and the Pelicans had a four-game lead, Bobby Tolan in the morning called the players into the visitors' clubhouse in Fort Myers for a heart-to-heart and berated them individually for mental mistakes and other on-field transgressions. He tore into Hendu—for bad base running—and Banni—for not telling anyone he was hurt—and Landreaux—for bad strategy. Tolan picked out a number of others who he felt were giving less than a total effort.

Tolan, who could wield a Wilkinson-sharp tongue, was no politician. Like Dick Williams, his mentor, he had no trouble dressing down his players publicly. But unlike Williams, Tolan had never managed in the majors. In 1983 Bobby had led San Diego's Double A farm club, the Beaumont Golden Gators, to a pennant. The next year he lost the pennant by half a game. He was then fired. He became a hitting instructor for Seattle. After getting into a feud with outfielder Phil Bradley, he was fired there as well. In 1988 he managed in the minors for the Baltimore Orioles. The rap was that Bobby was too tough on the players. He was again fired.

So Bobby, though he patterned himself after Dick Williams, didn't have the major league experience and the built-in respect Williams had. Some of the Pelican players were furious at the way Tolan treated them. All morning players seethed. "Fucking minor league manager," they grumbled. A couple threatened to quit the team, but their threats seemed to stem more from petulance than resolve.

Tolan knew the players were angry at him, but he didn't care. "I want them to know how I feel," he said. "And I don't care how big a lead we have.

"Crybabies," he said. "A bunch of crybabies."

It isn't necessary that the players like the manager in order to win. It also isn't important that the players like each other to win. What's needed is cohesiveness and talent in the front office. Morley and Tolan were tight, and they had picked a solid group of players. So long as Morley backed Tolan, the players could grumble all they wanted.

Elias "Lee" Sosa, who had played on eight different major league teams during a twelve-year career, was talking about harmony on a team, when it mattered and when it did not. Two of his clubs, the Los Angeles Dodgers and the Atlanta Braves, were steeped in discord, and yet the Dodgers were National League champions and the Braves were floor mats. The difference: On the Dodgers, as with Bosman's Oakland A's, the players didn't get along; on the Braves the men in the front office fought.

Teams like the battling A's, Billy Martin's New York Yankees, and the Dodgers proved that the players didn't have to get along to win ball games. But if the front office is in disarray, a team doesn't have a chance.

Sosa had played for the 1976 Dodgers under Walter Alston and in 1977 under freshman manager Tommy Lasorda. What impressed Sosa was the amount of bickering, especially among the famed Dodger infield of Steve Garvey, Davey Lopes, Bill Russell, and Ron Cey.

According to Sosa, none of the others liked Garvey. The reason he gave was jealousy.

"Garvey got all the attention from the press," Sosa said. "He always gave the right answer, and the press admired him. His picture was in the paper all the time. He always cooperated with the fans, and he was making a lot of money, had his own TV show, and all this creates jealousy.

"Unfortunately, that's the way it is, but to me personally, Steve Garvey was one of the best guys I ever played with. He'd help you with anything you wanted. Right now, if I needed help, I would not be afraid to pick up the phone and call him, which I would not do with the other fellows."

Those "other fellows" meaning Lopes, Russell, and Cey. Lopes, Sosa said, was the ringleader against Garvey.

"Davey Lopes was a very good ballplayer, but he always talked behind people's backs, especially Garvey's. Lopes didn't get the attention he deserved to get, and he wasn't a very pleasant person to be around. He played hard, no doubt about it, but he liked to get into somebody else's business and dictate to people on the field. Garvey would just pat you on the back and say, 'Get 'em next time.'"

According to Sosa, Russell and Cey joined Lopes against Garvey.

Still, the Dodgers won, unlike his Atlanta Braves teams in 1975 and 1976. "Getting traded to Atlanta was the *worst* thing that ever happened to me in baseball," Sosa recalled. In 1976, under manager Dave Bristol, Atlanta finished dead last. According to Sosa, as long as Hank Aaron runs the farm system, the Braves will never be successful, not only because of Aaron's incompetence but also because the other Braves officials dislike him and try to keep important information from him. The biggest loser in this power struggle, Sosa said, is owner Ted Turner. He might have added the Braves' fans as well.

"When I came to Atlanta, Ted Turner got involved with the ball club and made a lot of mistakes," Sosa said. "It's not a secret. He gave players who didn't deserve it a lot of money. The year after I left he went into the dugout to manage. Everybody around the league thought it was a joke.

"He finally gave up and returned the club to the people who handled it before, and those people are a bunch of idiots." Sosa laughed and shook his head.

"Until somebody sits down with Ted and Stan Kasten, the president, and explains to them what is wrong with the Braves organization and what changes have to be made and how to run a minor league system, it doesn't matter how many years they run the front office. Until they get rid of those people and bring in fresh guys, they will never win."

Sosa was asked to be more specific. The heart of the problem, he said, was the legendary home run hitter, Hank Aaron, now the vice president of player development.

"Hank Aaron was not a business guy," Sosa said. "Unfortunately, he was not a minor league director. He had so many public engagements, he didn't care about that. But Turner had him in that position, and Hank Aaron didn't know what was going on behind his back. Hank Aaron didn't even know which players to move from Single A to Double A. Because the other executives wouldn't tell him anything. The manager wouldn't tell him anything. No one did. They hated his guts. But you know who kept Hank Aaron in that spot? Ted Turner. Ted Turner said, 'You are my brother. You are my friend, and you mean a lot to the organization,' which is true. He did. But the people around him didn't want him in that position, and so somebody else was making the

decisions for him, and the organization was running like a wild goat."
Sosa looked disgusted. He shook his head at the memory.

"The Braves sent players who were supposed to be playing in Double A
to the Rookie League. Hank Aaron didn't know that. He didn't know
what was going on. It was terrible. And Ted Turner didn't know these
things. Sometimes the little people in the organization know more about
it than the big guy who owns the whole enchilada. And you can't run a
business that way. I don't care what kind of business it is."

During the second game of the Fort Myers series, a second loss, the
climate worsened on the Pelicans. Second baseman Lenny Randle pulled
a muscle running out a ground ball, and the shortstop, Sergio Ferrer, was
left hurting when fullback-sized Pat Putnam rolled over him at second as
he attempted to make a double play.

Adding to Tolan's woes, his starting pitcher, Pat Zachry, had to come
out of the game in the third inning when a line drive nailed him square in
the foot. After the game Zachry was hobbling badly.

"I think it's broken," the pitcher said.

Fort Myers won the finale, 13–1, sweeping the series. But box scores
do not always reveal the most important aspect of a game, which actually
turned out to be a disaster for the Sun Sox.

Their star pitcher, Rick Waits, the league leader in just about every
pitching category, severely sprained his ankle covering first base on an
infield hit and would not be the same pitcher for the rest of the season.
Still, no one knew that at the time, so there was little solace for anyone.
The Pelicans, their pitching in disarray and their offense anemic, spent
the final two days of November in St. Lucie to play the dreadful Legends.

A night game on the road following another night game results in the
players having to entertain themselves between the time they wake up and
four in the afternoon, when the bus leaves the hotel for the stadium.
Much time is spent watching TV, walking around aimlessly, and reading
the Senior League box scores in whatever local newspapers the players
can find.

At breakfast you read the local paper, then in the lobby pick up *USA
Today,* which has become the daily Bible of baseball players and fans
because it usually includes box scores of even the West Coast games. You
study the box scores, looking for information buried in the agate until
your eyes begin to blur. Then you walk across four lanes of dense traffic

to go to Albertson's to buy a deck of cards. You play hearts, sit around, read *The New York Times,* get your bags, sit around, get on the bus, sit around some more, ride on the bus at a crawl to the ballpark, and get dressed for the game.

The *game.* It's what the players wait for all day. It is the best part of being a ballplayer. Which is why, when a team is losing, the game itself stops being fun, and so does the experience. Players on winning clubs talk about camaraderie and teamwork and speak about how much they love the game. Players on losing clubs talk about batting averages and how many RBIs they have and about how they can't wait for the season to end.

What kept the Pelicans from falling into a depression was the significant fact that they were still in first place. They had been there from the start. And so long as the team remained in first, how many games they won or lost didn't matter. The Pelicans split with St. Lucie. Despite losing five of six, they were still three games ahead of Winter Haven.

The Pelicans began December at home for a week of games. The morning after their return, Pat Zachry came limping into the clubhouse at Al Lang, carrying X-rays. He held them up to the light for all to see. His foot was broken.

"The wheels are coming off," Gary Rajsich said. "We're not the team we were three weeks ago."

The one bright element was the return of Roy Howell and his bubbly presence. His wife had given birth to a baby boy, and he was back with the photos. Everyone came over to his locker and shook his hand. They were glad for him, but they were also happy for themselves. Without Howell, the Pelicans were just another team.

Sergio Ferrer asked him, "Does he have a big peter?"

Roy replied, "Just like his old man."

Everyone within hearing distance chuckled or rejected his statement. It sure was comforting to have Roy back. With him, the players were confident that the bad run would end.

The Pelicans won that December 1 game in the bottom of the eighth, when Sun Sox reliever Dave LaRoche walked Steve Henderson. Gary Rajsich then hit a line drive into the left-field corner, and by the time the ball came back in, Hendu had scored and Gary was standing on third.

Bobby Tolan sent Dock Ellis to the mound to protect the lead. Dock struck out Larry Harlow, but he walked Kim Allen, and with Tim Ireland up, the speedy Allen stole second. Ireland then struck out on hard sliders.

Two out. Dan Driessen was the batter. A dangerous left-hander. Tolan wanted to play it by the book. He needed a left-handed pitcher.

Joe Sambito, his top left-handed reliever, had already been in the game. Dave Rajsich was hurt. Like most good managers, Tolan decided to play the percentages and go with what he had. He picked his one healthy left arm, Mike "Tex" Williams, even though Tex had been struggling. Tolan believed that every player had a role, and regardless of past performance, if it was a player's role and the situation called for him to be used, then into the game he went.

There was a lot of tension in the Pelican dugout. This was real baseball they were playing against real pros. St. Petersburg had been swept by Fort Myers in their last series, and this was a win everyone was pulling for.

Driessen stepped in. Tex stared down, and he threw his best pitch, a hard slider, and Driessen swung. The ball soared into the air—straight up—above first base, where Gary Rajsich waited for it and made the catch to end the game.

The thousand fans at Al Lang stood and cheered, and the exhausted, exhilarated Pelicans rushed the mound to pound Williams on the back.

In the locker room afterward Tex was naked, his belly jiggling as he carried on, babbling, happy to have contributed.

"I'm the Senior League Rolaids Reliever of the Year," he shouted.

Across the aisle Milt Wilcox yelled over to him, "Hey, Tex! In this league it's Pillsbury, not Rolaids!"

Tex feigned anger, but he grabbed his gut and kept laughing.

10

The Case of the Haunted Hurler

Baseball players like to say about themselves, "There's a lot of little boy in all of us." Sure there is. How could there not be? During six months of every year ballplayers have few responsibilities except to stay in shape and be at the ballpark on time. The wife watches the kids. The agent and accountant watch the money. The players spend most of their working moments playing catch or hitting a ball. During their free time, they sit in their room and watch TV or carouse with each other in bars or if they desire search out the best-looking chick in the vicinity for a nightcap. What unadulterated fun.

But being a ballplayer is like making a pact with the devil. Here's the deal: You get to do all of the above until the day you retire. After that you live in hell. You have to work at a job you hate, earn a fraction of what you used to make, lose all your status, and you never again can take advantage of the one skill that made you famous: playing baseball. Living the life of a ballplayer—that's glamorous. It's the other part few ballplayers can bring themselves to talk about.

Glib, entertaining, and intelligent, Pelican pitcher Randy Lerch seemed to be a man in control of his life. The life of any party, he acted assured, even boastful. Before the season Randy told tablemates at a dinner gathering, "I can't wait for people to see me pitch." In the clubhouse Lerch would sometimes put on a T-shirt he reserved especially for occasions when he felt good about himself. On the shirt were the words: BECAUSE I AM THE BLADE. The Blade was the nickname given to him when the then-skinny left-hander first became a ballplayer.

But behind the mask of confidence lie confusion, anger, and a touch of regret. Randy Lerch has been haunted by baseball's and life's vicissitudes.

The game looks easy, but it isn't, and Randy Lerch has been tortured by it. In some games, the harder you try, the better you do, but baseball is not one of those games. As the coaches say, in baseball you have to "stay within yourself"—not try too hard. A pitcher who tries too hard will lose both control and velocity. Other pitchers know this to be true. They develop a credo of emotional balance—not to get too high or too low. They do the best they can and do not get upset no matter what happens because so many variables are out of their control.

Not all pitchers are in control of their emotions. They can go along for a few innings, and them *bam*, something upsets them and they lose concentration and blow up.

Randy Lerch has always *cared* whether he did well, *cared* whether he won, *cared* whether he had control. Randy Lerch was a supremely gifted athlete, but partly because he *cared* so much, he has been a head case on the mound.

Randy Lerch was well aware he had talent. Randy had been a pitching star since high school, when he was named California Athlete of the Year. Throughout his career he had failed to put everything together, to pitch seven innings without blowing sky-high. The problem plagued him during his entire major league career, frustrating him and his managers because being erratic means that if you are bad sometimes, on other days you are also outstanding.

Bobby Tolan became highly impressed by Lerch during training camp. He had expected Lerch to be the ace of the Pelican staff. All Randy needed—what all pitchers need—was confidence, sustained concentration, and consistency. Concentration can be improved with practice. Confidence is more difficult. Psychologists agree that self-esteem is an important component in success. How to improve self-esteem? That's the hard part. Randy is such a terrific guy, has such raw talent, and is so quick to seek answers from fellow pitchers that staff members lined up to advise him how to correct his mechanics and become a winner. It seemed as if anyone on the Pelicans who knew anything about pitching had an idea.

Pelican teammate Dick Bosman, the pitching coach for the Rochester team in the International League, had worked with Lerch until Pelican pitching coach Dock Ellis ordered Bosman to stay away from him. Another teammate, Jon Matlack, a minor league pitching coach with San Diego, began to advise him, and so did pitcher Milt Wilcox, a knowledgeable craftsman who would make a terrific pitching coach for somebody. The problem, of course, was that each "coach" had different views about release points, motions, and follow-throughs. Each had a slightly different idea of what Randy was doing wrong and what he should be doing right. Too much help can be just as dangerous as no help at all.

Also working with Lerch was a professional sports psychologist who had flown at his own expense from the state of Washington to St. Petersburg, hoping he could help the Pelicans and subsequently convince a major league team that what he had to say could benefit the team. The shrink had a monumental task before him, because most ballplayers equate psychiatry with witchcraft. Ballplayers tend to be conservative creatures of habit who fear changing old ways, even if they are destructive. To many ballplayers, anyone who sees a psychiatrist is "crazy."

But on the Pelicans, just as he gave Bobby Tolan his chance to manage and Dock Ellis his opportunity to be pitching coach, the innovative Jim Morley allowed this psychologist to work with his team. There was one Pelican player who would have let the Exorcist work with him if he thought it would do any good: Randy Lerch.

The psychologist, a tall, bearded, ethereal-looking man who wore a jogging outfit, had great confidence in his theories. He was animated and enthusiastic and had a lot of charisma. He would often be seen hovering near Lerch, and they would discuss his theories, including one embraced by many ballplayers: visualization. He wanted Lerch to picture himself throwing a strike before he let fire to the plate. If he succeeded, the Pelicans could visualize an easy pennant.

The psychologist also taught "awareness thinking." Lerch capsulized the theory: "There are two different thought processes, the original thought process and the learning process. What he wants me to do is get back to my original state of thinking rather than what the mind has learned."

He added, "If I can stay in my original state and get hitters out, it would be great." Indeed.

Tom DiPace

Randy Lerch

Randy Lerch had been inconsistent over his entire career, and he stopped getting hitters out in 1982. He was involved in a drug scandal in Philadelphia, became the victim of blood pressure drugs in Milwaukee, and went on to the Giants, where he got hurt. When his career was over, he went back home to discover that his wife was having an affair with a close friend.

Distraught, Lerch turned to the one man whom he could trust, his father, who had coached him throughout his childhood. And when Randy the adult needed his dad, father and son reverted to old roles: The father gave orders, the son had to follow them. After two years of working seven days a week for his father, Randy Lerch walked out on him. At age thirty-something Randy Lerch learned you can't go home again. He sank into a deep depression and even considered suicide. His life seemed to be going nowhere until the Senior League came along.

For many young athletes, Little League baseball can be a blessing. It provides competition and plenty of ego boosting. But one of the major flaws in the Little League system is that fathers are encouraged to coach sons. What can be wrong with that? Plenty. The organized nature of Little League squeezes enough of the fun out of the game by putting pressure on a kid without a supercharged dad pushing his youngster in practice after practice, game after game. When Dad is coach, he is always looking over the kid's shoulder. Criticism is never far away. And when a boy gets involved in an argument on the field, rarely does he get to fight his own battle. The coach—Dad—ends up fighting it for him. The kid doesn't get a chance to grow up.

Another thing that can happen is that fathers who coach tend to make baseball a mission rather than a game and turn their sons into zealots rather than players. When this happens, the boy confuses his performance on the field with how he feels about himself as a person. Some kids are never satisfied with their performances. If they go four-for-five, they consider themselves failures because they didn't get that fifth hit. If they go five-for-five, they take little satisfaction in it because this is what they expect of themselves.

In a game where going three-for-ten is exceptional, the perfectionist is asking for great emotional trauma. And he always gets it. Moreover, the immaturity of perfectionists haunts them all their lives. How is it possible to feel self-confident when on your best day you feel like a failure?

And so it was with Randy Lerch and his dad, who was always hitting pepper to the boy, having him pitch to his target, drilling the fundamentals of the sport into him. Dad Lerch had been a semipro player who had tried out with the Sacramento Solons and who might have made the team, except that before they were married the future Mrs. Lerch told him, "It's either me or baseball." He chose her, and so when Randy came of age, Pop Lerch transferred all his hopes and dreams onto the shoulders of his son. From the age of seven going through Babe Ruth League, which is high school age, Randy Lerch had but one coach, his father.

"He was my coach," Lerch said. "Always."

Randy put constant pressure on himself not to disappoint Dad. He rarely did. From his first year in Little League, Randy was always the best athlete on the field. In his first all-star game the opposing coaches walked him intentionally every time he batted, even when no one was on base. This made Dad Lerch so angry that he instructed his son to try to hit one of the balls thrown in the dirt on one hop. Randy obliged, hitting a bounced pitch over the center fielder's head. "I almost hit a home run to dead center," Lerch said.

The next year Lerch threw a perfect game in the all-star contest. At twelve, he was five-foot-two, 120 pounds, a skinny kid, but he threw hard, and his curve snapped. The contest took place in Fair Oaks, California, the first perfect game ever thrown in that stadium. The next day the boy was brought onto the field and introduced and congratulated and given a standing ovation.

"It didn't mean that much to me at the time," Lerch said. "It was just something that happened."

For most twelve-year-olds, such a feat would have had great significance. But in part because Randy expected to be that good, he never derived much satisfaction from his accomplishments. Another reason was that coach Dad also expected it and, no matter how well he did, never complimented the boy.

"Dad would never tell me how proud he was of me," Lerch said. "Dad was never anybody to tell you he loved you. He showed it in other ways. He would never take me aside and say, 'Great job.' It would be his friends, the other adults, who would say, 'Your dad is so proud of you.'"

Lerch lived in a suburb of Sacramento, California, and went to Rancho Cordova High School, which had one of the best baseball programs in the country. In his high school career Lerch was 35-1. In his senior year he lost, 1-0, on a day when his arm was aching. Lerch had not intended to tell the coach, because he didn't want to miss the start, but against his wishes his father had the coach take Randy out of the game. "I wouldn't talk to him for a couple of weeks," Lerch said.

In 1973 Lerch was chosen among half a dozen candidates as the best amateur athlete in the state of California and inducted into its Hall of Fame.

"I won. I couldn't believe it!" Lerch said.

Right after that he was signed to a professional contract. The Philadelphia Phillies, fearing he had a sore arm, drafted him in the eighth round. They believed that if he failed as a pitcher, he had enough talent to play big league ball in the outfield. He had made the All-American team as a hitter, batting over .400 and hitting 13 home runs.

When Lerch signed the Phils gave him $20,000, plus another $8,000 in incentives bonuses if he were to get to the majors. The Phils told him, "We need pitchers right now, so you be a pitcher until you prove you can't. Then we'll make you a hitter."

When Randy flew to his first minor league team, he was an immature eighteen-year-old. He had never been away from home, never been far from the shelter of his mom's nurturing or his dad's coaching. When he got on the plane and the doors closed, tears ran down his face. He asked himself, *What am I doing?*

The Phils sent Randy to Auburn, New York, in the New York–Penn League, one notch above rookie ball. Usually the high school kids went to rookie ball. Even though Lerch was eighteen, he joined the college kids. It was an experience that scarred him.

He was frightened, and when Randy arrived to play for Auburn, he tried to cover his fear the best way he knew how, by boastfulness. Immediately he alienated the older college players, who sought to make his life miserable by downgrading, ignoring, and taunting him. One time teammates stole his uniform, and he couldn't dress for the game. He was small, insecure, and immature. He avoided his teammates whenever he could.

In sixteen games at Auburn, he was 9–2 with a 2.91 earned-run average. He also pinch-hit often, which infuriated some of the hitters on the team. "There was a lot of jealousy there," Lerch said.

The next year the Phils sent Lerch to Rocky Mount, North Carolina. He played for $850 a month. "It wasn't a whole lot to live on," he said.

That year he had his worst minor league season. It was his first full season, and his arm wasn't used to the strain. One night his elbow popped and he couldn't straighten it. It was like that for about a month. Lerch feared for his career.

In time the elbow healed. He won seven games. He struck out a lot of batters.

During his climb toward the major leagues, Lerch always sought father figures. As a youngster, he had never played the game without Dad hovering in the background. Once he left Dad, he sought to duplicate his childhood.

At Auburn there had been Mark Ammons, who had tried to keep his teammates from bullying Lerch. When Lerch arrived in Reading in the Eastern League in 1975, he was handled gingerly by manager Bob Wellman, the Gentle Giant, and taken under the wing of former major leaguer Tony Gonzalez, who called him Keed and continually sought to boost the youngster's confidence. "Hey, Keed, you can pitch, Keed," said the twelve-year veteran. "I've seen a lot of pitchers in my time, and you peech as good as them."

With Reading in 1975, Lerch finished 16–6, with a 2.69 earned-run average. He spent the 1976 season in Triple A under the tutelage of manager Jim Bunning, once a splendid pitcher. Lerch was both awed and intimidated by Bunning.

"He was like God," Lerch said. "Everybody was scared to death of Jim. 'Cause he's such a hardass. Oh man, he was." But Lerch respected Bunning, and he pitched well under him. He won thirteen games at Oklahoma City, leading the American Association in innings pitched and strikeouts.

In part Lerch became very successful at Oklahoma City because he found one of his most cherished surrogate fathers, ex-major league pitcher Bob Tiefenauer. Tiefenauer, the roving minor league pitching coach, had been a knuckleball pitcher with six different major league teams over his 9–25, ten-year career. He hadn't been a great pitcher, but for Lerch he was a great coach.

"He was my second dad," Lerch said. "Whenever he came to town, I knew everything would be all right. My favorite major league season occurred when Bob was our bullpen coach in the major leagues. I would be in the outfield, and I would ask Tief, 'What am I doing differently?' And he knew. He saw me when I was at my best and when I wasn't."

But on that 1979 Phillies team Tiefenauer wasn't the pitching coach, and Tiefenauer's assistance was not appreciated by Herm Starrette, who *was* the pitching coach.

"Starrette always was trying to undermine him," Lerch said. "It got to the point where they called me into the office and told me I wasn't allowed to talk to Bob any more.

"Starrette finally went to Ozark and told him, 'I'm the pitching coach.

What's Lerch doing ... da, da, da, da.' He was a backstabber. He'd brownnose people and backstab them. And after I had my best year, they fired him. Because Starrette was so insecure. It made me hate the man."

Randy Lerch was twenty-three years old when he made the Philadelphia Phillies in 1977. That season Lerch won five of his first six decisions, finishing the season 10–6 with a 5.06 earned-run-average, helping the Phils to their second straight division title. That year the Phillies averaged six runs a game.

Manager Danny Ozark, though gruff, was wise enough to see that Randy Lerch needed special handling. Kid gloves were needed. No one on the team could wear a beard, except Lerch. Unusually brittle in ego, Lerch was even the subject of a special team meeting called by Phils catcher Tim McCarver. Tim told the others, "Don't talk bad about Randy. Leave him alone, because he's sensitive and everything bothers him."

Lerch said, "They saw great talent there, so they just left me alone. They didn't mess with me."

The Phillie team was a powerhouse led by Mike Schmidt, Larry Bowa, Greg Luzinski, Steve Carlton, Garry Maddox, and Bob Boone. And of course, Tug "Ya Gotta Believe!" McGraw. Add the flaky Randy Lerch, and it was a wild and crazy group, except for Mike Schmidt, the All-Star third baseman, who pretty much kept to himself.

"He really wasn't one of the guys," Lerch said. "Garry Maddox was his best friend. They ran together."

According to Lerch, Phils star shortstop Larry Bowa had such a violent temper that Lerch bought a doll of a Tasmanian devil and placed it in his locker. Bowa threw his most visible tantrums on the field whenever an umpire made what he considered to be a bad call, but Lerch says there were plenty of times Bowa got involved in scraps in the clubhouse as well, usually starting after Bowa's criticism of a teammate.

"If you had a bad game or two, Larry was going to talk about you, not to your face but behind your back," Lerch said. "To the press. To teammates. He had everybody hating him, but he couldn't shut up."

One time Lerch had Bowa down on the ground with his hand around his throat and a finger in his nose, telling him if he ever criticized him again, he would kill him.

Bowa shouted, "Blade, let me go! I swear I won't do it again!" Lerch let him up.

"But as soon as he went around the corner, you could feel the daggers hitting you in the back again," Lerch said. "Hell yeah."

Another time Bowa antagonized star third baseman Mike Schmidt. Schmidt had embraced religion, but during a game he had sworn, and Bowa called him a "fucking hypocrite."

"It took eight guys to keep Schmidt from killing Bowa," Lerch said.

Another time Greg Luzinski struck out with the bases loaded to lose a game. This was during a time when he was being criticized for being overweight. Bowa yelled out, "If it was a fucking cheeseburger, you would have hit it."

Lerch said, "That big motherfucker was chasing Bowa around the clubhouse, trying to kill him. He was always saying shit like that, man. You just loved to hate Larry."

Like most perfectionists, the person Bowa abused most was himself. One time Bowa had a bad series, and on the plane ride to the next city he got drunk and started ripping out the inside panel of the airplane beside his seat.

"All you saw were wires hanging down at thirty-five thousand feet," Lerch said.

The stewardess told Bowa if he didn't knock it off, they were going to land that plane and kick him off the flight. Bowa replied, "I don't give a fuck. Land it in a motherfucking cornfield. Just have the bus waiting for me."

Above all, Bowa was a great competitor. He was psychopathic about winning, according to Lerch. When Randy won his first five games his rookie year, Bowa was so appreciative that he let Lerch borrow his Thunderbird. When Lerch proceeded to pitch ten times in a row without a victory, Bowa took back the car.

"Oh, he was a treat," Lerch said.

Over Lerch's career with the Phils, the team also had a couple of other personalities in pitchers Larry Christenson and Dick Ruthven.

"Larry thought he was God's gift to women," Lerch said. "He called himself the Blond Viking. He loved all the little girls. And he had all these different names for his wiener like the Blue Veiner. He'd say, 'Let's hope the Purple Helmet doesn't come out.' If he didn't have a girl a night on the road, he wasn't happy. He was better off with two. He loved to run. And he made sure everybody knew that the women loved him, that he was The Master. To this day he's single, just a funny human being.

"Dick Ruthven was like from *One Flew over the Cuckoo's Nest*. He was a great guy, but you never knew what was going on inside that brain. You looked in his eyes, and you knew everything wasn't quite right.

"You couldn't intimidate him. He didn't care. He knew how much I hated tobacco, and if I leaned across the dugout steps, he'd spit all over my sanitary socks. You knew you could pound on him. But you also knew it didn't matter, because he was going to do it again tomorrow anyway.

"Ruthven and Tommy Hutton married identical-twin sisters. They met them at a bar in Clearwater, and both of them fell in love, and now they're brothers-in-law."

If Lerch had a soul brother, it was Tug McGraw. They shared certain personality traits. On the mound they were extremely intense, and each was supercritical of himself. When Tug did poorly, his self-denigration could go to the extreme.

"I remember Tug had a series in Pittsburgh where he had three save opportunities and blew them all," Lerch said. "In one game he gave up a grand slam to lose the game.

The next day Tug got on the bus. His hair and clothes were disheveled. "Where have you been?" Lerch asked. "In prison," McGraw replied. "You lying cocksucker." "Yes, I have," Tug McGraw said. "I was a detriment to society, and they locked me up."

Tug told the truth. Apparently, after the game, when everyone else had gone home, Tug stayed and drank all the beer that was left in the clubhouse. He decided to walk back to the team's hotel, and on the way stopped at a local pub, where he drank whiskey. All the while he got madder and madder at himself for his poor performances.

He continued his drunken promenade. Outside on the sidewalk he began kicking trash cans. When he came to downtown Pittsburgh's state penitentiary, he started rattling the gates and screaming and hollering for the guards to let him in.

McGraw hollered, "I'm a detriment to society. You let me in now, because you're going to lock me up now or later. But you're going to lock me up some time tonight."

The guards opened the doors and brought him in and locked him up. Inside, he signed autographs for the inmates. They held him overnight and let him go at six in the morning.

The pitching star of the team was a man who could arguably be said to be *the* pitcher of his generation, Steve Carlton. During that era only Tom Seaver and Jim Palmer could be mentioned in the same breath with the pitcher everyone called Lefty. Carlton in his career won 329 games, ninth-most in baseball history, struck out 4,131 batters, second only to Nolan Ryan, and won the Cy Young Award an astounding four times.

Carlton was one of the handful of athletes who had such contempt for the sporting press that he refused to give interviews. Sports reporters who are snubbed by athletes react like lovers scorned. They turned vindictive, and as a result much of the press Carlton got was negative.

Lerch was with the Phils during two of Carlton's four Cy Young Award seasons. He and Carlton were also extremely close. Lerch respected Lefty's talent and understood his moods and why he shunned the press the way he did.

According to Lerch, Steve Carlton was a man very much misjudged. "The press was frustrated because Steve wouldn't talk to them, and they made Steve out to be such a monster," he said. Carlton had come over to the Phillies from St. Louis. In 1972, his first year in Philadelphia, he was 27–10 with a 1.97 ERA and won the Cy Young Award. That year the Phils only won fifty-nine games.

"After every start, Steve couldn't spend enough time with the press, staying extra for Bill Conlin and those people, telling them everything that ticked inside of him," Lerch said.

The next year Carlton lost twenty. "Here was the same guy, and they tortured him," Lerch said. "I lockered next to him. He was one of my buddies. Steve and I used to love to act stupid and party, just acting goofy. The press wrote that he was running late at night, that kind of stuff, and tortured him any way they could."

Carlton told Lerch, "Here are the same people I spent time with and told them everything inside me, and now these same people are stabbing me like you can't believe. Fuck them. I'll never talk to them again."

Lerch said, "And he used that as a driving force to be better, because he said, 'I can never be bad because the press will be twice as hard on me.'"

Carlton, of course, was right. When he lost his superb skills at the end of his reign, he kicked around from team to team trying to hang on. He had been the best, but since he didn't formally retire he was not accorded the royal treatment bestowed upon teammate Mike Schmidt. In the press, for the most part, it was good riddance.

In 1978 Randy Lerch was a certified South Street hero. That year the Phillies went down to the wire, needing one win over the Pittsburgh Pirates to gain the National League Eastern Division title. After losing two to the Pirates on a Friday night, there were two games left in the season. If the Phils could win Saturday, the title was theirs. If they lost, they would have to play Sunday for all the marbles.

Randy started the Saturday game against Don Robinson and gave up a grand slam home run to Willie Stargell in the first inning. "I remember how pissed off I was," Lerch said. "I hung a slider, and he smoked me over the center-field wall. I said to myself, *I'm going to win this game, and I'm going to get a piece of Don Robinson.*"

After the Phils scored a run, Lerch hit a two-run homer off Robinson, and then he got him again, hitting a solo shot to tie the game that the Phils eventually won. Years later, it's the performance he's remembered for most.

Having won three division titles in a row but no pennant, the Phils faltered in 1979, when over the July Fourth weekend starters Lerch, Christenson, and Ruthven all were injured. As a result, the Phils finished fourth and easy-going Danny Ozark was booted out. In came tough guy Dallas Green, whom Lerch neither admired nor respected.

Lerch began the 1980 season 0–6, losing close ball games every time, and his confidence suffered. Then Green lost faith in him, and his performance fell further. It's hard for any pitcher to do well when a manager is down on you. It was especially difficult for Lerch. He began pressing. He fell apart.

"I started trying to change things," he said, "turning the ball over, doing stupid things a young pitcher would do. Then Dallas started ripping my ass. He skipped me in starts. It was a bad situation. I had no respect for him. I think it's so much bullshit when he says he's a man's man. Dallas just had a big mouth. He comes across like he's a tough son of a bitch, but I don't take him that way. When the team won, it was 'We won,' and when it lost, it was 'They lost.' Dallas intimidated a lot of people, ripped people in the paper, which I didn't agree with."

Lerch said, "Some people like him. Some people don't. He didn't help me any."

Lerch had expected praise when he did well—or at the least no criticism—but during a shutout he pitched against the Mets at Shea Stadium, he was batting with runners on first and second, one out, when he swung and hit the ball off his foot. Lerch stood at home plate as the ball rolled fair, and when the umpire failed to notice the ball had hit his foot, the Mets ended up with a double play.

Lerch completed his shutout. The next morning his wife called him from Philadelphia to read him the headlines in the morning paper: FINE TAKES THE SHINE OUT OF LERCH'S SHUTOUT. Lerch hadn't known he had been fined.

Lerch said, "The next day I walked into the clubhouse, and Dallas called me into his office. He said, "Randy, I've been thinking about it all night long, and I decided I'm going to have to fine you for the good of the team.' I told him I disagreed with his fine, but if he felt it was for the good of the team, well and fine."

All day Lerch thought about it.

"It was just burning my ass," Lerch said, " so I got him the next day at the ballpark. I said, 'Dallas, you said at this big meeting how fair you were going to be with the guys, up-front, and all this shit. All of a sudden, all you are is a liar, because you said you thought about the fine all night, and that night you had told the fucking press you had fined me.' I said, 'What kind of shit is that?'

"Well, he wasn't man enough to say he had fucked up. All it did was piss him off. And later in the papers he said that if some of the minor leaguers had had the same chance I had, they would have pitched better. He ripped me a lot. I just got tired of it."

Green stopped using Lerch. "It was hard for me. I was three and fourteen, and then I had one last start against the Mets, and I won. I knew at that point I wasn't going to start another game for the Phillies."

Loyalty only goes so far in baseball. A player is expected to be loyal to the team, but a manager of that team isn't constrained to be loyal back.

At the end of the season Green was molding his pitching staff for the playoffs. He decided to drop two pitchers and add one. To satisfy the eligibility rules, according to Lerch, he needed to have a pitcher to be declared injured in order to replace him with Marty Bystrom, who had come up in September but too late to be eligible for the playoffs.

Lerch said, "Nino Espinosa, who is now dead, had been having arm problems all year. He was throwing the ball decent but not as hard as he used to. So they needed to find a player who would agree to go on the disabled list so they could put Marty on, and they pressured Nino. When Nino came out of the meeting, he was in tears, because he wanted to be part of a playoff team."

According to Lerch, the Phillie ownership wanted Lerch to remain eligible, if only for his hitting skills. Dallas Green, however, said, "No way." If he wasn't going to pitch, he didn't want Lerch on the team. Lerch became incensed. After four seasons in the service of the Philadelphia Phillies, he couldn't abide being treated so shabbily.

"Basically I told the Phillies to go fuck themselves," Lerch said. "And I stayed home. That's when Tug McGraw, my buddy, went on TV and said, 'The only thing that puts a damper on it is that Randy's not here.'

"There's a lot of crap that goes on. Yup. And I was the same guy who two years before had a lot to do with the Phillies making the playoffs. But it was that backstabbing bullshit that goes on behind closed doors that was hard."

That winter the bullshit became waist-high. Lerch found himself in the middle of an amphetamine-use scandal that rocked the entire Phillie team. During the 1980 season the Phils had played an exhibition game in Reading, Pennsylvania. A doctor in Reading had been a reliable source for their greenies, the pep pills that made the players feel like Supermen before and during ball games.

The cops found out, and the doctor found himself under indictment for selling the amphetamines. The players, covering their asses, said that the doctor had used their names to write prescriptions for pills that he then distributed to buyers on the street. As a result, the players became prosecution witnesses. At the pretrial hearing Phillie players denied that they had known the doctor or that they ever ordered the pills.

Randy Lerch, appalled at the mendacity, refused to go along.

"The guy was getting set up to go away for maybe five years," Lerch said, "and his practice was going to be ruined. I couldn't see it. When it came time for me to go to court, the defense attorney was primed for me to say I didn't know this doctor. When I told the court, 'Yeah, I knew him, and yeah, I had received greenies from him,' they shit their pants and threw the case out of court.

"After that my picture was all over the front pages. I couldn't see an innocent man going to prison. I didn't care what it took. Nobody else ever admitted it, so I took the brunt of that whole thing."

The next spring training, one of his closest friends on the Phillie team stood up and said, "Did anyone thank Blade for what he did?" Lerch wasn't moved.

"Fuck," Lerch said, "it was too late. I told them, 'You know, a lot has happened.' After being dumped off the playoff and World Series team the year before and then this happening, in March of 1981 the Phillies got rid of me. I got traded to Milwaukee for Dick Davis."

Getting traded to Milwaukee was a relief for Lerch, because players in Schlitztown receive relatively little public attention.

"Milwaukee wasn't a media center," Lerch said. "It was just a lot of blue-collar people who would have their tailgate parties. It was a super town to play in, real low-key. Philadelphia had spent a lot of money, had high-tech Nautilus equipment. Milwaukee had a carpet in the clubhouse that was twenty years old. There was no weight equipment. They hardly had any training facilities at all. It was like back to *Bull Durham*. In Milwaukee we put on a uniform and went out and played hardball. We had great talent: Cecil Cooper, Robin Yount, Paul Molitor, Roy Howell, Ted Simmons, and Gorman Thomas, who was a very sensitive athlete. Gorman would drink beer with the fans at tailgate parties. The fans loved him. He was their favorite. He ended up tearing his rotator cuff diving for a ball.

"Rollie Fingers was one of the guys. They called him the Buzzard. He was a tremendous competitor on the mound, with great stuff. He could throw a ninety-mile-an-hour fastball exactly where he wanted it and had an outstanding slider and a good forkball. In tough situations he got better."

Unfortunately for Rollie, during spring training in Arizona he and Randy and Pete Vukovich and Mike Caldwell were involved in a mudball fight. During the childishness, Fingers chased after Lerch, who ducked, picked him up, and slam-dunked him on his head, separating the Cy Young Award winner's shoulder.

"See, I've done so many things," Lerch said sheepishly. "They didn't know what to put in the news release, how to describe the cause of the injury."

At that time the pitchers played a game called flip, in which five or six competitors would stand in a circle and one player would flip the ball at another. The idea is to keep the ball from hitting the ground. Fingers and Lerch decided to blame the injury on their flip game. Reflexively, the manager made the pitchers quit playing the game.

"Everybody hated me because we couldn't play flip any more," Lerch said.

Fingers missed about a month of the season. When a sufficient time passed, Lerch attempted to approach Fingers and affect a reconciliation.

"Are we still friends, pal?" Lerch asked.

"Get away from me, you motherfucker," Fingers replied. "You're crazy. You're dangerous. Stay away from me."

Reflected Lerch years later, "I did a lot of goofy shit. I was in trouble all the time."

The little boy in Randy Lerch never left him.

Lerch enjoyed playing in Milwaukee. He should have remained with the Brew Crew. But once more in his turbulent life he got involved in something not in his control, sending his career spinning in a bitter ending. Again a doctor was involved. This time Randy was the victim.

Lerch suffered from high blood pressure. When he went to see the team doctor about it, according to Lerch, the doctor ordered him to take medication for the condition.

Lerch said, "This doctor, a total asshole, a fucking dick, he said, 'We're going to get you some blood pressure medicine or I will make sure you never play again.' He put me on what I later found out was a huge beta blocker like an elephant tranquilizer."

Lerch says the doctor also put him on a diuretic, and as a result his weight dropped from 204 pounds to 183.

The year was 1982, a time when drug use had become more prevalent in baseball. Cocaine was the drug of choice, and so Randy Lerch, it was being whispered by baseball executives, was a cokehead.

"And I wasn't," Lerch said. "I was on this doctor's blood pressure medicine. So I lost all this weight, and my fastball went from ninety-three to eighty-three, and when I ran sprints, I would double over.

"But my blood pressure was good."

Throughout the rest of his career rumors that he had been on drugs followed him.

Toward the end of the 1982 season Lerch was sold to the Montreal Expos. Lerch believes the rumors of his drug taking led Expos manager Bill Virdon, who came in 1983, to mistreat him.

"Bill Virdon hated me," Lerch said. "He was the general, and I supposedly had a history of drugs, which wasn't the case. I mean, I *had* taken amphetamines. But I was not one of those players who conformed, and if I didn't perform the way he wanted me to, he wouldn't pitch me. He stuck me in the bullpen and wouldn't let me pitch, and so near the end of the next season Montreal asked me if I would go to Triple A, and I told them to go fuck themselves, so they had to release me."

The San Francisco Giants picked him up. In the third month of the 1984 season Lerch popped a groin.

At the end of the 1984 season the Giants fired Frank Robinson, and the team also got rid of Randy Lerch. The Giants didn't offer him a contract. Veterans like Lerch were being tossed aside. Lerch figured he would sit at home, but he became restless. He called his buddy Tug McGraw, who helped get him a contract playing for Portland, the Phillies' Triple A team.

Lerch pitched well for Portland in 1985, poorly for the Phillies in 1986, and when the Phils wanted to send him back to the minors, he refused and was released. He pitched the last month of the season for Louisville and pitched well. But the Cards had a lot of left-handed kids in Triple A, so Lerch wasn't in their major league plans. He retired.

When a ballplayer retires, he has to start all over again. Many players can only seek the comfort of their families. A newly retired player needs familial solace to get through the difficult search for gainful employment, a hard task at best since he takes an emotional beating because of the drop in salary. It's not easy to go from making hundreds of thousands of dollars pitching a baseball to taking a salesman's job for $36,000 a year— if the player is fortunate enough to get the job at all.

Former Oakland pitcher Steve McCatty said, "When they asked me, 'What are your qualifications?' I wrote down, 'Pitching a baseball.'"

Randy Lerch had intended to return home and begin his civilian life, but when he got back to Placerville, California, he discovered that his wife didn't love him any more and wanted a divorce.

Lerch had done what so many young minor leaguers do; he married young. He had been lonely that first year, away from home for the first time, and he desperately missed his high school sweetheart. She visited him for a week, and at the end of the season he went home and married her. He was nineteen. She was eighteen. Then, after the children came, it wasn't so easy to uproot the family every time Randy had to go off to play, so their separations became longer and more frequent. During his final stint with the Phillies and Louisville, Randy was away from his family the entire time. Evidently, it was more loneliness than his wife could bear.

"I had played for fifteen years and never really spent the quality time with my family," Lerch said. "I had been away from them for eight months, and I felt I was going to go back home and start a new life. Little did I know my wife was seeing one of my friends. When I got home, I didn't even have a wife. A lot of it may have been loneliness. This guy was around all the time. I gotta believe if he wasn't ... I don't know. I mean, she got tired of me. I've never been able to put a finger on it. She just said she didn't want to be married any more, and she turned right around and married him. I know it broke me in two. 'Cause I loved her a lot.

"So they are married now and have my kids. Yup."

He discovered something else that devastated him just as badly. Though he was thirty-something, to dear old Dad he was still a kid who couldn't be trusted. It was the ultimate indignity.

Lerch's father had retired. He and Randy had always talked of operating a restaurant with the old man's retirement money, and they opened a beautiful ninety-two-seat restaurant in Placerville called Smokehouse 1898. He worked there seven days a week for two years.

Randy Lerch thought he was going to be a partner, only to discover that his father would not allow him to hire or fire anyone.

"I found out it was okay for him to coach me, but we couldn't be partners," Lerch said with great bitterness.

When he discovered he was a lackey, not a partner, Randy Lerch left Placerville. He was virtually penniless. On the advice of his agent, he had bought an expensive house with a mortgage at 17¾ percent. The payments totaled $3,100 a month. He had to liquidate nearly all his other investments to keep the house long enough to sell it in a down market.

"It ended up knocking me for pretty much everything I ever had," Lerch said.

Lerch moved cross-country from California to Atlantic City to live with Tug McGraw. Tug and Larry Christenson got him a job with a casino so he could earn some money to live.

Lerch became depressed and considered suicide.

"I'm lucky I'm alive," Lerch said. "I'm lucky I didn't flip out and lose my mind. It's a good thing I have a sense of humor. I thought about it—but nah. I thought, *You love yourself too much. Don't do that.*"

While Lerch had lived in California he was a logger. He installed auto glass. He cooked and bartended at the restaurant. He became a carpenter. After he moved in with Tug in Atlantic City, he worked construction as a laborer. He drove a tractor trailer, operated heavy equipment.

"I'm a jack-of-all-horseshit-trades or a horseshit-jack-of-all-trades. I can do anything," Lerch said.

It was only when he learned of the founding of the Senior League that his heart began to beat again. Pitching for the Pelicans, he made more money than from any of his other labors. Most important, during the season he fell in love with a local gal. Much of his loneliness and bitterness have melted away.

"I'm superexcited because I have somebody I love a lot down here. I'm living with her, and she's very, very special, so I have my best buddy now. We talk and we share. My life has gone from being a ditchdigger with no money whatsoever to someone who has an opportunity to live again."

Tears were beginning to well in the eyes of Randy Lerch. He had once been an important ballplayer on one of the best teams in baseball. He had also seen the depths of despair. Because of the Senior Professional Baseball Association, he was climbing back. Jim Morley and his league have something to be proud of.

On that first day in December in 1989, for six innings Randy Lerch was in control. Pitching in Al Lang Stadium against Fort Myers, he gave up but five hits, walked three, and allowed only a single earned run.

Dock Ellis closed out the win by striking out Amos Otis with the winning runs on base. In the clubhouse the team appeared in high spirits. Randy Lerch was giggling, acting like a kid. Hovering near him, the sports psychologist strutted about, acting like he himself had won the game. Because owner Jim Morley had given the psychologist permission to hang around, Dock Ellis kept out of his way. Ellis didn't want to put himself in a position where he would be forced to tell off the "voodoo shrink." No one had to ask Dock how he felt about him. Dick Bosman knew exactly.

"Just wait until Randy loses one," Bosman said ruefully. "The shrink will be ancient history."

In his next game, Lerch got beat up, and magically the sports psychologist disappeared. "Plus he was bugging me," Lerch said.

Despite the aid of his guru and four pitching coaches, Randy Lerch would spend the rest of the season winning big, losing ugly, still partying, and desperately searching for the elusive consistency. At the end of the year he would try out with Baltimore's Triple A club. He wouldn't make it, but this time his life would not come crashing down around him. He had a woman who loved him, and he could look forward to the prospect of pitching one more glorious season in the Senior League.

11

The Color of Money

With five weeks of the season behind them, the Pelicans had settled into a win-one, lose-one mode as they struggled to survive the rash of injuries, big and small. Their division lead hovered at around three games over Winter Haven, Orlando, and Bradenton as the three teams scrambled for second place.

Mark Corey, who had been involved in the Kenny Landreaux trade, sat in the home dugout before the game of December 6 at Al Lang field. Corey was aware that Ron LeFlore had been released and that the Pelicans were looking for right-handed hitters. He drove to St. Petersburg to try to talk Bobby Tolan into taking him back, but he was politely told that his services weren't needed.

Corey sat on the Pelican bench in civilian clothes as the uniformed players wandered in and out, going to and from the clubhouse and the field. There were a few perfunctory hellos, but little real interaction. Corey, who just weeks ago had been a laughing, joking member of the Pelicans, was now a nonperson. He was a reminder of the grim possibilities in baseball—and no one on the team wanted to be reminded.

Just before the game was to begin, Corey vanished. He was never seen at Al Lang field again.

Up in the press box before the game St. Lucie manager Bobby Bonds, a large, imposing man, dressed in his Legends uniform, was on the telephone.

"You can't do that," he said with conviction. "I've been in this game twenty years. You can't *do* that."

At the other end of the phone was the owner of the St. Lucie Legends, Joe Sprung, whose team was drawing flies and losing money fast. Earlier Sprung had traded his manager–first baseman Graig Nettles to the Bradenton Explorers, which already had a manager in Clete Boyer. Nettles, angered because he had lost his chance to prove his managerial ability, called the owner "Joe Sprungbrenner." At least Graig hadn't lost his sense of humor.

Sprung had informed his general manager, Ray Negron, that even though the players were on the road he wasn't going to pay them meal money the next day because no game was scheduled.

Bonds, representing his players, became adamant. The practice was clear. If you're on the road you get paid meal money, game or no game. A player has to eat, regardless.

Before the season began some of the owners figured that all they had to do was throw open the gates to the ballparks, and people would come to watch these former major leaguers play. The owners were wrong. Just when some of them needed to beef up their budgets for advertising and promotion, they began cutting back. In St. Petersburg, for instance, attendance was just over a thousand fans a game, less than expected, and the income was far less than had been anticipated.

Down the hallway a couple of cubicles from where Bonds talked on the phone, the Pelicans' radio play-by-play announcer, Jack Wiers, was informed by owner Jim Morley that the possibility existed that the broadcasts would be discontinued. Because there was so little radio advertising revenue, each game cost the team about $250. Since Morley didn't have deep pockets, he was getting nervous. The team had tried unsuccessfully to obtain sponsors, but the team, the league, and the concept proved too new. Everyone was taking a wait-and-see attitude before committing to sponsorship. Advertisers always want to be associated with a proven winner. No one wanted to chance being caught backing a loser.

The catch-22, of course, is that this attitude could spell the demise of the new league. So could panic, which the league owners were beginning to exhibit.

Exacerbating the situation was the nature of sports reporters, who love a good funeral. The press had been slow to embrace the league, but as soon as the local writers saw that attendance wasn't very good, they were quick to comment. In terms of national coverage, the first reports were about injuries. The follow-ups were about poor attendance.

There were precious few articles about how much fun it was to watch the games, and no one talked about how important the league was to the players. The Tampa paper kept trumpeting how great it would be for the Bay Area to have a major league baseball team.

But in its coverage of the Senior League, it paid a stringer to cover not the Pelican games but the games in Winter Haven. The Pelicans had a solid franchise. The Super Sox were in disarray. What the readers of *The Tampa Tribune* read about all season were the Laurel-and-Hardy Super Sox. The Pelicans got bupkes.

As game time approached, Bonds was still arguing on the phone. Finally he and St. Lucie general manager Ray Negron emerged. Negron was grim.

"We won that one," Negron said.

"And the next one?"

"Who knows?"

It was December 8, a Friday, and Sergio Ferrer and Alan Bannister sat in the dugout at Al Lang, watching the rain fall. They were scheduled to play Earl Weaver and the Gold Coast Suns. However, the torrents of rain made it unlikely the game would take place. The tarp covered the field, but as nightfall drew near, the darkened skies gave no hope that the bad weather would lift.

Sergio felt blue. There were rumors that the Pelicans were looking for stronger defense at shortstop. It appeared they would sign former Phillie star Ivan DeJesus as soon as his winter league team finished playing in Puerto Rico sometime in late December or early January. Sergio heard the talk. The footsteps spooked him. He was not playing well.

Sergio, who is very emotional, said that during his first year in pro ball he would punish himself if he went 0-for-4.

"I couldn't handle the game," he said.

"What did you do?"

"I got married," he said. He was in pain as he said it. Once again the game of baseball was eating him up.

On a rectangular table in the middle of the clubhouse a hearts game was in progress. Hearts is a perfect game for baseball players. It is a macho game, and if you win, you proclaim your skill, and if you lose, you decry your luck. The object is to give the other players points: each heart is a point, the queen of spades is thirteen points. The player with the fewest points wins. They didn't play for money. The prize was bragging rights.

Three pitchers—Milt Wilcox, Jon Matlack, and Dave Rajsich—vied this day with coach Ozzie Virgil. While they sat with their cards, they argued over which player was most often full of shit. Each made cogent arguments as he threatened to discard vengeance on the others. Occasionally the queen of spades would come blasting out of a hand, forcefully slapped onto the table with a shout. The victim would howl as the other three shouted with laughter and derision.

You can learn a lot about a person by observing the way he plays hearts. Ozzie Virgil rarely took chances. Jon Matlack could be sneaky. Milt Wilcox came right at you, and Dave Rajsich took the scientific, play-the-percentage approach. The best cardplayer on the team was manager Bobby Tolan. He was also the most arrogant. He would slap the queen of spades on you and then make fun of your game.

While the card game went on, Randy Lerch sat in his cubicle, chatting animatedly with his personal motivator. The clubhouse manager, David Chavez, whose desk was at the far end of the room, wrestled with a career decision with veterans Roy Howell and Steve Kemp. Last year Chevy, as he is called, was clubhouse manager for Triple A Iowa, a minor league affiliate of the Chicago Cubs.

On this day the manager of the Triple A Buffalo team offered him a job as visiting clubhouse manager, a position he would have taken because Buffalo was one of several cities major league baseball was considering for expansion franchises. Chavez's ultimate goal after toiling in the minors for fifteen years was to land a position with a big league club.

And so Chevy wanted the job... except. The problem: He would receive no salary, only tips. Had it been a major league job, he would have taken it immediately, because the tips in the majors are generous. In the minors a tips-only life becomes problematical at best.

The clubhouse manager is responsible for so many services to the players, providing the spread of food after the game, cleaning uniforms, making certain the gum, coffee, oranges, sunflower seeds, chewing tobacco, peanut butter, baseballs, bats, uniforms, fan mail, and clean cleats are all taken care of. The clubhouse manager does so many things it's hard to imagine a team running without him. It was not unusual for Chevy, a bachelor, to sleep in the clubhouse after a night game. In short, the man did not have much of a life of his own. He was wedded—to baseball.

Chevy's quandary: He had an attractive job dangling in front of him, but it was an offer without a guarantee of income. He shook his head, angry he wasn't getting what he considered to be a fair deal.

Roy Howell was sympathetic. He had experience with baseball's Scylla and Charybdis. It sucked you in. It spit you out.

Howell said, "You have to be able to walk away. If you take it, they've got you."

"I know," Chevy said—and he did know, but he was unhappy about it. "I know," he repeated, "but it doesn't seem fair."

With Ron LeFlore's release the Pelicans had a weakness against left-handed pitching, and so Jim Morley, Bobby Tolan, and Dock Ellis decided to do something about it. In the major leagues a team need only beckon from its minor league system for a new player, but in the Senior League you could only spread the word—and hope for the best. The grapevine would prove crucial.

On one afternoon in early December a large, smiling man with a sizable paunch arrived at Al Lang Stadium. Sight unseen, he was signed to play for the Pelicans. His name was Lamar Johnson, once a cog in the Chicago White Sox hitting machine of the late 1970s. One year he had hit 18 home runs.

Dock Ellis had been on the phone to a childhood girlfriend of his living in Arlington, Texas, a woman who had once been married to Al Oliver, one of Dock's best friends. He had told her his team needed a right-handed hitter or two, and the woman had said, "Lamar Johnson isn't playing, and he'd like to play."

Tolan called Johnson. "You been working out?" Tolan asked him.

"I've been playing racquetball and working out with my son two or three times a week," he replied. "I've been swinging a bat."

But when Lamar Johnson arrived, it was clear he wasn't in good shape. How could he be? He hadn't played since 1982. When he arrived, it looked like he was at least thirty pounds overweight, an irony since the Pelicans had released Ron LeFlore for being overweight.

How could this man *possibly* help the Pelicans?

To cover their bets, the Pelicans also signed the muscular Manuel "Bombo" Rivera. Also right-handed, the former Minnesota Twin and Montreal Expo outfielder seemed intense and proud, yet reticent.

When he was a Little League player in Ponce, Puerto Rico, Manuel would hit towering fly balls. One of his father's friends began to call him *Bombo*, which is Spanish for "fly ball." The nickname—and the player—became so popular in Minnesota that Garrison Keillor, star of "The Prairie Home Companion," even wrote a song about him called "Bombo."

Another new player signed by the Pelicans was a pitcher named David Gershon. With Dave Rajsich, Pat Zachry, and Nardi Contreras all injured, Tolan needed pitching help. Hitters could waltz in and still hit. Pitchers needed time to get ready. Again Tolan and Ellis ignored their color broadcaster, Dick Bosman.

Instead, they signed Gershon, a man from the sandlots of Kansas City, where he had starred in an over-thirty semipro league.

All summer long Dave Gershon had bugged Jim Morley about letting him pitch for the Pelicans. He had a business in Kansas City with an 800 number, and he called often. Gershon kept telling Morley he was the "best pitcher in Kansas City," and later he sent press clippings. Morley finally let him try out. When he arrived, Morley saw that Gershon was only five-foot-seven. "He didn't tell me he was the size of a charm bracelet," Morley said later.

In tryout camp Gershon threw a lot of breaking pitches, and he got some hitters out, but the Pelicans held his size and lack of control against him and cut him.

He had resurfaced in St. Lucie in early December, pitching batting practice to the Legends for their less-than-impressed manager, Bobby Bonds. Gershon had a good slider, but he didn't have control. He had enough stuff to dominate a semipro league, but to major leaguers, hitting against Gershon wasn't much tougher than batting practice. All a pro batter had to do was look for the slider and then whack the hell out of it.

Gershon, if nothing else, had supreme confidence in his ability. Even after the Pelicans cut him before the season, he kept trying. When the Pelicans last were in St. Lucie, there was Gershon, still trying out. Tolan took note of how badly he wanted to play, and finally, in desperation, Tolan signed him. He needed a body.

On December 9 Randy Lerch started against Earl Weaver's Gold Coast Suns and was rocked for fourteen hits and five runs in five innings. In the sixth Bobby Tolan brought in Gershon, the smiling, chunky cherub with the good slider but little control. The league was supposed to be for former pros. Gershon, unlike Hoot Gibson or Tex Williams, had never even played in the minors. The other pitchers couldn't understand why Tolan had signed him.

Commented Jon Matlack, "It had to be a motivational ploy, as if to say to Lerch, 'If you don't hold the lead, I'll bring in Gershon.'"

Gershon got Bert Campaneris to fly out, but then he gave up a single to center. He retired Rafael Landestoy on a rope to shortstop. Dave Gershon was one out from celebrity. He gave up a single to Cesar Cedeno and two consecutive doubles to George Hendrick and Rennie Stennett, and after Bobby Ramos singled, four runs were in and the game was a rout.

Gershon did manage to get through the seventh unscathed, but the damage had been done. When Tolan came out to replace him with Elias Sosa, Gershon surprised the normally unflappable Sosa by greeting him with a smile and an extended hand. Reflexively, Sosa shook hands. Gershon then walked off the mound.

One couldn't help but note the one great irony surrounding Gershon's appearance. He owned a company that manufactured leather tool pouches and nail bags. Here was a man who was making big bucks but who wanted to pitch with the Pelicans more than anything in the world. At the same time most of the players would have loved to be in David Gershon's financial position. He was the president of a thriving company, wealthy enough to blow a few months chasing a pipe dream in Florida. The players could make fun of Gershon's Day-Glo workout suit, his diminutive size, and his lack of ability. They could not, however, say much more, because at the same time they realized that he was far more successful than most of them.

After the game Jim Morley, Tolan, and Dock Ellis called Gershon into an office in the clubhouse and told him he was being released. Gershon graciously understood. "This is a lot different from the league I played in back in Kansas City," he said.

That night Gershon was partying in Wings, the bar in the Hilton Hotel across the street from the St. Pete ball field. In the bar he ran into Cesar Cedeno, who had begun his downfall. Gershon greeted him and shook his hand. Andy Warhol once said that everyone would be famous for fifteen minutes. In Gershon's case, his "fame" lasted for a couple of innings, but nevertheless he had done something no one else had done before—pitched in the Senior League with no minor league experience. Then he was gone.

The next night brought another ugly loss. The Pelicans made six errors, allowing the four unearned runs that beat them. The losing pitcher was Elias Sosa, who in six innings allowed six runs, two earned. His record was 1–5. His ERA was under 2.00. He kept his equanimity, but losing was becoming nettlesome.

Three of the six Pelican errors were made by shortstop Sergio Ferrer. In the eighth George Hendrick hit an easy grounder to him, and he booted it. After two outs Rafael Landestoy hit another easy one, and he kicked that one as well. Earlier in the game he didn't catch a grounder by Cesar Cedeno, and that led to three unearned runs.

After the game one of the pitchers who sat watching from the dugout muttered: "It was *ug-ly*. Sergio, Sergio, what's happened to his hands?"

Twenty minutes after the game, Sergio was still framed in front of his locker, his head in his hands, alone with his thoughts.

With this last loss, the Pelicans were 4–7 after their 12–4 start. The team was still three and a half games in first place, because the other three teams kept losing to the teams in the other division.

Bobby Tolan tried hard to sound upbeat. "I really wouldn't say we were struggling, because we're in first place. But," he conceded, "we haven't played as well as we did in the first couple of weeks."

CHAPTER

12

The Latin Beat

On December 12 the team traveled for four hours across the state by bus from St. Pete to Florida's east coast to play the Gold Coast Suns in Pompano Beach, the start of a week-long road trip. It was several hours before game time. After the players dressed they walked onto the field in the ballpark to warm up.

The Gold Coast players were already there, working out and enjoying the sunshine. The team was called Gold Coast because originally it was scheduled to play in both Miami and Pompano Beach, but atrocious attendance in Miami convinced the owners early in the season to switch all games to Pompano, a hundred miles to the north, where they drew a larger crowd, though not many more than a thousand fans a game.

The Gold Coast players were mostly Latinos, because the owners had figured Latinos would draw in Miami. Despite former big league stars such as Cesar Cedeno, Joaquin Andujar, Bert Campaneris, and Ed Figueroa, Miamians stayed away from Bobby Maduro Stadium. The rap: It was in a bad neighborhood. So much for the "Latinos-will-draw" theory.

It was several hours before game time. The grandstands of the homey Pompano ballpark were empty, and from the field it seemed as though all the Gold Coast players were chattering at once, a Spanish cacophony that prompted Pelican pitcher Dave Rajsich to comment, "Playing these guys makes me feel like I'm back in the winter leagues in Venezuela."

Out on the field Suns outfielder George Hendrick discussed the nonguaranteed million-dollar contract teammate Joaquin Andujar had just signed with the Montreal Expos. For at least one Senior League player, performance had been noticed and rewarded. This "one tough Dominican" was getting another chance at the big time. Hendrick was kidding that Andujar would take his money and quit his Suns teammates.

"He's making a million dollars," Hendrick said, "and now he's going to take the money and go home." He laughed, this man called Silent George with the reputation for being a real grump, one of a small group of ballplayers who had refused to talk to the press during most of his career. In the privacy of his workplace, George Hendrick was showing a delightful, fun-loving side.

"I love to tease him," Hendrick was saying about Andujar. "He hates to be called Jackie. I told him, 'In the Dominican Republic, you're Joaquin. In the United States, you're Jackie.'" Hendrick laughed again, happy for his friend but even happier to be playing again.

Joaquin Andujar had a shot to retire rich. For the Latino players in the Senior League, he was the rare exception. Most were thrilled just to be getting paid so they could make a few mortgage payments.

If American players have a difficult time making it to the majors, Latin players have it harder. Part of the difficulty is learning English so they can get along in their new land. Latin players also have a more difficult time coping with the system. Some of their problems can be attributed to individual prejudice. An American ballplayer who has a quick temper, who throws bats, smashes helmets, and breaks water coolers, is seen as a fierce competitor. If a Latin player exhibits the same type of behavior, he is called "hotheaded" or "unstable."

In addition, Latinos are trapped by an informal quota: Never put more than three Latinos on a team if you don't want to look for trouble. The stigma is that they play for themselves, look out for each other, and don't play hard every day. In their defense the Latinos will tell you that if they go all out and then get hurt, management will get rid of them much quicker than they will a white player. So Latinos are more wary of getting hurt, hence they tend to play with less abandon.

If American players find it hard to adjust to life after baseball, Latin players have it even harder. Baseball is ruled by the good old boy network. To get a coaching job, you have to be buddy-buddy with a general manager. Former teammates hire each other.

Former friends hire each other. Latinos do not run front offices in the major leagues. Few get hired in baseball after their careers as players are over.

For most of the Latinos who played until very recently, when salaries have become astronomical, they began poor and they ended poor. Finding employment back home has been difficult. Finding employment in the U.S.A. after baseball has been just as difficult.

The Pelicans had four Latino players on the team: Sergio Ferrer, who spent parts of four seasons in the major leagues with Minnesota and the New York Mets; Bombo Rivera, who played for four full seasons and parts of two others with Minnesota and Montreal; Elias Sosa, a twelve-year major leaguer, who came from the Dominican Republic; and Nardi Contreras, who pitched in eight games for the White Sox in 1980 and had grown up in Tampa's Latin ghetto. During his climb to the majors, he felt discrimination just as surely as if he had come from his father's native Cuba.

Bombo Rivera, the new Pelican outfielder, spent his childhood in Ponce, Puerto Rico. His father hoped he would finish high school and go to college, because he didn't want his boy working in a construction job as he did. But the Montreal Expos offered Bombo $17,000, and he opted for the immediate opportunity to move his family out of a poor neighborhood. So he signed.

Sensitive, very young, and away from home for the first time in Bradenton, Florida, Bombo felt alone. He knew no one and, like most young Latinos who come to America to play ball, knew no English at all. His manager, Ed Sadowski, constantly yelled at him. Though Rivera desperately wanted to tell his manager that he didn't understand what Sadowski was saying, he couldn't because of the language barrier.

"He would scream at you and call you names," Rivera said. "It was all mixed up, because I didn't know what he was saying. He would say, 'No, no, no, no, no, no, no, not like that...' but I didn't know what he wanted me to do."

The frustration grew so great there were nights when he would go home and cry, wishing he were back in Ponce.

"It was hard, hard for me," Rivera said, "because I don't know no English at all. I tried so hard. I bought myself a dictionary. The man who signed me, Jose Garcia, he was hired to be my interpreter. But when I really needed him, where was he? Every day I was writing letters to my family: 'I want to see you. I want to come home.' My parents would write back: 'You are young and you will learn. Stay there, play as hard as you can, and in no time you'll be home.'

"I never thought it would be like this. I'd think, *I can't get along, because I can't talk the language.*"

Getting yelled at by Sadowski made his life miserable. Not being able to respond made it worse.

Because of the language problem, Rivera was limited in what he could eat in restaurants. "I ordered chicken all the time," he said. "I knew *pollo* was 'chicken.'"

Many American players often criticize Latin players for their clannishness. At the same time those same American players don't try to meet their teammates halfway, to learn some Spanish to help them communicate. The American attitude is: *You're in my country. Speak English.* And so the newly arrived Latinos may be teammates on the field, but off the field they are strangers, seen every day, heard every day speaking to each other in Spanish, but who keep to themselves.

Bombo Rivera was fortunate his first year. He made friends with his roommate, Jerry White, who is black. With the help of Spanish-English dictionaries, Bombo and Jerry taught each other their languages.

"At the end of the year I was surprised," Rivera said. "Because at first I was scared to say something wrong. But he says, 'No, Bombo, no, this way, not that way,' and I began to learn."

After three years in the minors, Rivera knew English well enough to understand it. It took him a few more years to communicate with others.

Rivera, who played the outfield, made the big leagues with Montreal in 1976. Part of why he got there was the faith of Montreal's manager until 1975, Gene Mauch, who was particularly sympathetic to the plight of Latin players.

Rivera remembered his influence:

"Mauch, he talked to me a lot. The first time I talked with him, he said, 'Bombo, do you know how much talent you have? I want to tell you. I've been in this game a long time, and you don't know how good you are. I want you to believe in yourself, because you're a good player. Just go out there and do your best.'

"And when he told me that, oh man, I mean I was over my head, because I had never heard that before. And when he left Montreal and went to Minnesota, he got me back and played me all the time."

Bombo's career lasted four seasons, not counting two years in which he appeared in five games each. After Montreal, he was a Minnesota Twin for two and a half years under Mauch. Then in a game in Seattle he dove for a ball and fractured his kneecap. Mauch was fired, the organization lost confidence in Rivera, and he was released.

Because most Latin players start poor, scouts tend to offer them peanuts to sign, knowing they are grateful for what little money is given them. Once in the major leagues, say Latin players, they are often paid less than white counterparts. It was certainly true for Bombo Rivera.

Rivera had the misfortune to play for the Minnesota Twins under perhaps the cheapest skinflint owner of them all, Calvin Griffith. After Bombo hit .281 in 1979 and led all Twins outfielders in assists, Griffith gave him a $1,500 raise.

"I had three good years in a row," Rivera said, "and the most I ever made was $80,000. Other guys were making $250,000. How was I making $80,000?"

Part of the reason was Rivera's lack of financial sophistication. Bombo admits as much. Another part was fear. Bombo was afraid that if he hired someone to represent him, the Twins would become angry and punish him.

"I didn't have no agent," Rivera said. "I was discussing my contract myself, and they take advantage of me. They were businessmen, and as a player you know you're going to lose. My thinking was I wasn't making good money, and if I had an agent I would have to pay him a percentage. I was going to save that money. Also I thought if I got an agent, they would be angry with me. I wanted to show them I was a team player. That was a bad decision. I was showing good faith. And they took advantage of Bombo."

Only after his knee injury did he hire an agent, Ron Shapiro in Baltimore, but by then it was too late. Shapiro negotiated for Bombo, but the offer the club made was so small that Shapiro refused to take a commission. "I was lucky," Rivera said.

Rivera became a baseball vagabond, playing in Mexico and Japan, but injuries kept knocking him out of the game.

His final team was Tabasco in the Mexican winter league. At the age of thirty-two he tired of the thirty-hour bus rides through the Mexican countryside.

"I figured I would work to make a living. It was easier to stay home." He returned to Ponce, where he joined his dad and worked in a construction job.

Nardi Contreras, the son of a Cubano from Tampa, was one of the finest high school pitching prospects ever to come out of the state of

Florida. Pitching for Tampa Catholic High School, Contreras consistently pitched no-hitters and averaged seventeen strikeouts per seven-inning game.

In 1968 as a junior he pitched and won the semifinal game of the state championship, 1–0. After a teammate faltered in the finals after two and a third innings, Nardi came in and struck out ten and won that game too.

When Contreras was a senior in high school, he was constantly being compared to Palm Beach phenom Pete Broberg, who reportedly was offered $200,000 to sign out of high school. Broberg went to Dartmouth instead and signed for six figures after he graduated. They faced each other in an American Legion game once, and each struck out sixteen batters. Broberg won the game because Nardi's teammates made some crucial errors.

Contrera's father figured his boy was as good as Broberg and had to be worth at least half of what Broberg was worth. Pittsburgh wanted to draft Nardi in the first round and was offering $50,000, and St. Louis offered $75,000, but each time the scouts were told that the price was $100,000 or else the boy would go to college. It was a ruse that didn't work. The scouts backed off.

Cincinnati drafted Contreras in the twelfth round. But, as with Bombo Rivera, here was ready money available to escape the ghetto and buy a fabulous car. Nardi Contreras didn't own a car. Contreras signed—for $30,000. He bought his family a new home and got a sporty new automobile.

In his first game in Sioux Falls, South Dakota, in thirty-two degree weather, the Tampa phenom blew out his arm in the cold. He had tendinitis and calcium deposits. He asked the doctors what he should do. They said, "You ought to forget about baseball."

"For two years I couldn't comb my hair or wipe my butt," Contreras said, "but I kept on pitching." He developed a sidearm motion so he wouldn't have to use his shoulder. He went from ninety-two miles an hour to seventy-five. The Mets drafted him from Cincinnati. After two years of learning to pitch again, he had a great year at Tidewater in 1975. He says the Mets then screwed him, just as they screwed other Latin players on his team. His manager, Joe Frazier, was the culprit.

"I don't like to talk about Joe Frazier, because he wasn't a very good person," Contreras said. "We just didn't get along, but not only me, a lot of Latin and black guys.

"In 1975 we had Benny Ayala, and he didn't want to play Benny Ayala. We had Nino Espinosa, and he tried to take Nino Espinosa out of the starting rotation, and pitching coach Billy Connors came in and said, 'This guy has to be in there to pitch.'"

Unfortunately for Contreras, Frazier became the Mets' manager in 1976. At Tidewater in 1975 Nardi had three wins, four saves, and the lowest earned-run average on the team. In spring training with the Mets he pitched twelve innings and didn't give up a run. But because Frazier was the manager, Contreras couldn't make the team, no matter what his record or how well he performed.

Pete Gabriel, the Mets' minor league director, called Nardi in and said, "You know the problems you had with Joe Frazier? As long as he's the big league manager in this organization, there's no room for you."

"He said they had to release me," Contreras recalled with a pained expression.

Contreras found Christ in 1978 and says that since then he has accepted everything that has happened to him. One look at his face indicates perhaps not quite everything. Perceived discrimination can leave deep scars.

"That's in the past," Contreras said. "That was 1975. We're in 1990 now. It happened. It makes me angry, but I would like to leave it be. I don't like to bring the guy up."

Contreras did make the big leagues in 1980 with the Chicago White Sox, but injuries forced him to retire after that year.

"The Lord has been very good to me," Contreras said. Had Nardi not been a Latino, maybe baseball would have been good to him too.

Elias Lee Sosa is a quiet man. He talks softly, and he comports himself with dignity at all times. Sosa is from the Dominican Republic. Spanish is his native language. To talk to him, you'd hardly know it except for a slight lilt. He gets along. He always does what he's asked. He gives his all.

Elias Sosa is the perfect team player. Blessed with a rubbery arm, Sosa can start, he can pitch long relief, and he can close. All a manager has to do is ask. "I do my job," he says. He never second-guesses. He never makes trouble. He never has a gripe. If you ask him how he's doing, he'll smile. "I can't complain," he says.

During his twelve-year career, Elias Sosa twice finished his season with an earned-run average under 2.00, once with the L.A. Dodgers and once at Montreal. During his career he won 59 games and saved 83 others.

But Sosa was not treated very well by the baseball brass. He played for eight different teams. It is hard to imagine that a team wouldn't want the combination of talent and demeanor embodied by Lee Sosa. Sose, as his teammates call him, is too much a gentleman ever to come out and say it, but when he talks about his career in the big leagues you begin to understand he did not receive the respect due him by certain general managers because he was a Latino.

Sosa may be a gentleman, but he isn't blind. He knows injustice when he sees it, and when asked, his analytical nature and honesty impel him to talk about what he experienced. While blacks are the vocal minority in baseball, Latinos are the silent minority. Compared to the blacks, how many Latinos ever get a chance to manage or coach or work in the front office once they are out of baseball as players? To date, Sosa is not part of this extremely select group.

Sosa has come from his home in Phoenix to St. Petersburg to pitch baseballs because he loves doing it, but he also needs the money. The San Diego Padres had hired him in 1988 to coach pitching in the Gulf Coast League, a one-year stint. He does not know why he was let go. His goal is to become a minor league manager. He wonders whether he'll ever get the chance.

His dignified demeanor belies the hurt he feels over his inability to get hired by a baseball organization. From his experience he has drawn the conclusion that it helps to be a former ballplayer who just happens to be white.

"I write letters," Sosa said. "I am asked, 'What is your experience?' I say, 'I pitched in the major leagues. I know how the game is played.' They write back, 'I am sorry. We are looking for someone with experience.'

"This past November I went to Nashville to the winter meetings. I ran into Chris Speier." Speier was a seventeen-year veteran who had played shortstop for the Giants and four other National League clubs. "He told me, 'The Giants offered me the manager's job in Phoenix, but I told Al Rosen I didn't want it.'" Sosa rolled his eyes.

"Speier doesn't have any experience. Chris said, 'After I said no, Rosen offered me a job as his assistant. I am here watching how trades are made, trying to learn what goes on.'

"Nothing against Chris Speier, but here he is turning down jobs, and try as I might I can't even get a nibble to manage anywhere."

Lee Sosa made a face and shook his head. His hands were upturned, as if to say, "Where is the justice?"

Of course, whether Al Rosen hires Chris Speier or Lee Sosa is strictly up to Al Rosen. But for whatever reasons the general managers of

Tom DiPace

Elias Sosa

baseball choose not to hire him, Sosa's hurt is real. When asked, Sosa will admit he wishes he had a friend in the executive offices. "I just need for someone to give me a chance," he said.

Al Campanis, the longtime L.A. Dodger general manager, has become famous for his appearance on "Nightline" in which he talked about blacks not having the "necessities." Campanis was fired after going on the show, and accused by many of being a racist.

Lee Sosa experienced some of Al Campanis's ill will toward minorities after having perhaps his best season for the Dodgers in 1977. That year Sosa pitched in 44 games, had a 1.97 earned-run average, and helped propel the Dodgers into the World Series against the Yankees.

Sosa was making $55,000 with the Dodgers and after his fine season asked for $85,000. Sosa and his agent had studied what the other top relievers made. Most earned between $140,000 and $150,000 a year.

Sosa said, "We had just come from the World Series. I told my agent, Steve Schneider, 'I don't want to move around. I want to stay with the Dodgers. We have a chance to win again.' I said, 'Do everything you can. I don't want to leave. But I want a fair raise.'"

Schneider explained all that to Campanis, who proceeded to denigrate Sosa, calling him ungrateful. Campanis suggested that Sosa should go back to the Dominican Republic where he came from and try to get a better-paying job there.

Sosa said, "My agent told me, 'After the discussion I had with Campanis last week in regard to you, I want you to hear this conversation yourself, because I don't want you to think I was making this up.'"

Schneider dialed Campanis, and Sosa listened in. "I tell you," Sosa said, "Campanis was throwing gas from that mound. I tell you, it was ignorance. I could not believe a businessman could talk that way.

"He was saying things like 'He doesn't deserve that. He's lucky to be in this country...'—like I should take whatever they offer me, like I was lucky to be playing for the Dodgers' organization. And he even threw in: 'Why doesn't he go back to where he came from?' I mean, real stupid things."

Sosa's eyes turned sad when he remembered the hurt. There are different ways to handle prejudice. You can lash out, like a Dock Ellis. Or you can swallow the hurt, like Lee Sosa.

Sosa said, "I said, 'Just tell him I don't want to play for them, period. Just tell him to find me a place to go. If that's the feeling he has, I don't want to be involved.' It was really stupid, so I ended up being sold to Pittsburgh and then traded to Oakland."

Sergio Ferrer loved being a Pelican. Diminutive, at five-foot-seven, Sergio had had some tough times before making the Pelican team. After leaving the majors in 1979, he sold women's clothing and lottery tickets back home in Puerto Rico. He wanted to go to the United States to find work, but his wife refused to leave the island. The Senior League was his chance to make some money playing ball. If there was one player especially happy to be a Pelican, it was Sergio Ferrer.

Ferrer, from Santurce, was discovered during a tryout in Puerto Rico by the great Roberto Clemente. "He was my idol, and he was the one who gave me my first break."

After playing in Puerto Rico, Ferrer signed with the Los Angeles Dodgers. He played no more than 37 games in any of his four seasons in the big leagues, two with Minnesota as a teammate of Luis Gomez, and two with the New York Mets, where he sat on the bench for Joe Torre while Tim Foli and Frank Taveras played.

"Joe Torre didn't play me. He didn't give me the chance to play, which has been my life in the big leagues. I didn't really get the chance to prove myself. One year, that's all I wanted, one complete year in the big leagues to see if I could play or not. But that's the way it goes."

Ferrer came to the Pelicans as a walk-on and impressed with his effort and his desire. Shy but quick to smile, Ferrer more than anything wanted to be accepted. He didn't tell anyone he was playing with a groin pull and a pinched nerve in his neck, which made fielding difficult. Throughout the month of December he would make errors in crucial situations. Adding to his emotional instability was his knowledge that the former Chicago Cubs and Philadelphia Phillies shortstop Ivan DeJesus would join the team at the end of his winter league season. Ferrer knew that when DeJesus arrived, either he or Luis Gomez would be gone, and he began to press in the field and at bat, trying too hard and performing worse and worse. He was hearing Ivan DeJesus's footsteps.

"I'd like to stay the rest of the season," he said. "I hear they are talking about how St. Lucie needs a shortstop, and I'm thinking I might be going there because they want me. And I don't like that. I would like to stay in one place at least once in my lifetime. I'm thinking too much some times. I hear Ivan DeJesus is coming here to play, and maybe I will be expendable. I wish it's not me. Because I'm having fun here. I know I made my errors. I'm human. But I can make the plays. I can't tell you, 'Oh, I have a bad day.' Every day is a good day for me, because whether I do good or bad I always try hard. I try 110 percent."

Sergio was hoping against hope.

With less than a week left in December, Ferrer went to the trainer's room before a game for treatment. His groin pull and pinched nerve needed treatment. When he got there, the trainer, Brian Ebel, was on the telephone. When Ebel got off the phone, he began attending to one of the other players. Ferrer took the slight personally.

"When I want treatment, you're always busy doing something else," Ferrer complained. "I have to wait and wait and wait. When the other guys want treatment, they get it immediately."

Sergio yelled at Ebel, "Why don't you do your job!"

Angry that Sergio had questioned his competence, Ebel asserted that Sergio was "less than a man."

It was too much for Ferrer to bear. Sergio hit the Pelican trainer with a right to the jaw, loosening a few of Brian's teeth.

Among his teammates, Sergio received little sympathy. In their opinion Ebel hadn't acted improperly. Sergio was being too impatient. Part of their lack of sympathy stemmed from the fact that Sergio was not

Sergio Ferrer

The Pelicans

high enough in the team pecking order to demand better service. If it had been Lenny Randle, Roy Howell, or Steve Henderson, others would have listened and sided with him. For those three, though, Ebel would have been more attentive. Also, Sergio had made crucial errors of late, and everyone knew that Ivan DeJesus was coming.

By coincidence, the very next day Ivan DeJesus arrived in St. Petersburg from the winter leagues. The day that Sergio Ferrer dreaded had arrived. DeJesus, a star in any league, came ready to take over as the starting shortstop on the team. Bobby Tolan hadn't been satisfied with Ferrer's glove or Luis Gomez's bat. With DeJesus's arrival he now had arguably the best shortstop in the Senior League to go with two other infielders who were the best in the league at their positions, Roy Howell at third and Lenny Randle at second.

On January 10, with twenty games left in the season, Sergio was sold to the St. Lucie Legends, just as the rumors—and his fears—had suggested.

The next time the Pelicans met the Legends, Ferrer, wearing his St. Lucie home uniform, was taking batting practice. Before the game he came over to the visitors' side and shook hands with everyone. He missed being a Pelican. When approached, Sergio had a sad smile on his face.

"It could have been worse," Sergio Ferrer said. "I'm getting to play." He brightened. "And I'm still getting a paycheck."

CHAPTER

13

Mr. Normal

Who is the typical major league ballplayer? What's his career like? What happens to him when it ends?

Certainly those who get the most press are the superstars, former players like Mike Schmidt, Brooks Robinson, and Reggie Jackson, players who perform year after year at a superhuman level, Hall of Famers as soon as they are eligible.

But far more common is the ballplayer who comes out of high school or college as a top draft choice, the likelihood of his making the grade excellent. But then, once he makes the majors, something bad happens to him. Sometimes it's a decision by an organization to switch a player from his natural position to some other position to fit a team need. That something can be an injury. Sometimes it's a new manager who decides that someone else is better or who wants to bring in his "own people." Barriers to success go up as immovable as the Great Wall of China.

If he wants to stay in the game, the player then has to make a compromise. More practical goals are substituted for more lofty ones. To be the best utility player in the game. To get in ten years of service to receive the maximum pension. The player hangs on. And if he's lucky, when his career is over, he can coach. If he isn't, he has to scrap for a living.

Alan Bannister, the Pelicans' Mr. Utility, was a typical major league ballplayer. He began with lofty goals, was messed with, got hurt, and settled for a lesser role.

Banni, as his teammates call him, is stocky but not large, talented but not impressive, well spoken but not eloquent, sensitive but not neurotic. His most impressive attributes are inside: character, dedication, and love of the game. He never made excuses, and he never complained, even when he had reason to do so. On the Pelicans early in the season he had reason.

A former Arizona State University star, Alan Bannister set NCAA records in 1972 for hits (101), RBIs (90), and total bases (177), while hitting .380. A year earlier he set a college record with 13 triples.

He had been drafted as the number one pick in the country by the Philadelphia Phillies in 1973. He played twelve years in the major leagues, hit a lifetime .270, and after the 1984 season declared himself to be a free agent, a dreadful mistake in timing because what followed was that no teams were signing anyone but their own free agents. Banni, a valuable utility player, was put out to pasture when no team would pick up his contract.

During his major league career, Banni was used at first, second, short, and third and in left, center, and right. He was also used as a DH when he was in the American League. The only positions Bannister didn't play in the pros were pitcher and catcher. On the Pelicans, Banni knew, if anyone got hurt he would be Bobby Tolan's insurance. And in the Senior League, it was not "if" but "when." Before the season was through Alan Bannister would prove to be a very valuable player indeed.

During the early part of the season, when he was planted on the bench, Banni, in a proud whisper, guaranteed that if he got to play he would bat over .300. He was right too. Bannister knew just what he could do as a ballplayer. By mid-December Banni was getting playing time, and against the Gold Coast Suns on December 13, he stroked out four hits, raising his average to close to .290.

Throughout the entire time he was sitting, Banni never complained. He admitted to being upset about it, but that was as far as he would go. It was one reason managers enjoyed using him in the utility role. Not all players will play intermittently, accept it, and perform. Banni did. Once given the chance, he proved his worth, hitting for average and in the clutch. All his career he had demonstrated patience and self-confidence, and it always held him in good stead.

Alan Bannister grew up in Southern California, spending much of his youth on the ball fields of Buena Park, near Disneyland and Knott's Berry

The Pelicans

Alan　Bannister

Farm. From Little League on, he was a hitting fool, and he played a solid shortstop. By the time he was a junior in high school, the scouts were on his trail.

"It came natural to me," Bannister said. "My skill level surpassed most of my peers, and I realized pro ball might follow."

When he graduated from high school in June 1969, Bannister was the fifth player chosen in the pro draft. Though the California Angels had selected him in round one and offered him $55,000, he spurned the cash to attend college.

"My father had elected to give up a college education to go into the service. He had preached to my two brothers and me the value of that piece of paper," Bannister said.

Nevertheless, his parents encouraged him to make up his own mind. The strong-arm tactics of California general manager Dick Walsh convinced him to go to college first.

"I had had some scholarship offers," Bannister recalled, "and when I hesitated about accepting his offer, he said, 'You're going to have to make up your mind whether you're going to go to work or not someday, young man.' He was very stern, and I thought, *Maybe I'm not ready to go to work for a living.*"

Bannister instead went to Arizona State University under coach Bobby Winkles, whose ASU teams won the College World Series in 1965, 1967, and 1969.

His junior year Bannister hit .380 and led the NCAA in total bases. When Winkles left ASU to manage at California, Bannister sat out the fall semester of his senior year, which made him eligible for the January 1973 draft. He was drafted number one in the country by the Philadelphia Phillies and signed for an $85,000 bonus.

Even before he signed, he had been involved in an international incident. While captaining a college all-star team on a two-week tour of Japan, he killed a Japanese player with a thrown ball. Bannister, playing shortstop, was turning a double play and threw to first, but the base runner coming into second didn't slide. Just as Bannister threw the ball, the runner turned his head and the ball hit him with full force. A few days later he suffered an aneurysm and died.

Bannister felt terrible. He talked to the team manager, Rod Dedeaux, discussing whether he should quit the tour. He wanted to continue if at all possible. It had been a fluke, but neither Dedeaux nor Bannister knew how the Japanese would react. They decided to wait and see.

When Bannister returned to his hotel room, it was filled with flowers and gifts, like fish cakes and candy. Some of the Japanese fans wanted to make it clear that they understood baseball and understood death and realized it had been an accident. The fans were very concerned and hoped that the incident wouldn't affect Bannister's career.

"It knocked me for a loop," Bannister said. "The Japanese people felt so bad for me and were so concerned for my welfare that for the rest of my stay I was swamped with gifts and well wishes. I'd go out on the bus, and there'd be swarms of people outside wanting to hand me things through the window."

Bannister continued to play. In a game at Tokyo Stadium forty thousand fans gave him a standing ovation. Bannister cried.

He attended the boy's funeral, and during the service he sat next to the boy's parents. Behind the dais was a picture of the boy in his uniform bigger than life. Incense pots burned on both sides of the stage, billowing smoke into the air.

"I met the kid's parents and through an interpreter expressed my condolences, and again they told me they were just as concerned about my welfare," Bannister said.

"And so I returned to the States, and I got drafted by the Phillies, and in January I went to a press conference. Dallas Green was in charge. He said, 'There will be TV cameras and microphones. I just wanna take a few minutes to tell you that they'll probably jump on the Japanese situation right away.'

"I said, 'That's okay.'

"I came through the door and there were bright lights, TV cameras, and I took the podium. They introduced me, gave me a Phillies hat, and the first question was from a sportswriter named Bill Conlin. His question was 'How did you feel after you killed that guy in Japan?'

"His second question was, 'What makes you think you can beat out Larry Bowa?' Bowa had just become an All-Star shortstop.

"To the first question I told them about what happened, that I didn't expect it to have any effect on my ability to play the game. I don't believe it ever has. To the second question I responded with some nice-guy attitude, like 'Larry Bowa is a fine player. He deserves All-Star recognition. My goal is not to beat anybody but to try to play to my ability. If I do that, there will be a place for me sometime, somewhere.'"

"But I remember those two questions. Very quickly Conlin got right to the heart of the matter."

When Alan Bannister signed with the Phillies, scouts had hopes he would be a superstar-caliber shortstop. The Phillies thought so much of him that Bannister began his professional career in Triple A, a lofty starting point for any youngster. Bannister struggled, did poorly, and the next year went to Toledo, where he regained his stroke and his confidence.

In May of 1974 Greg Luzinski tore up his knee on the AstroTurf, and to replace him in the outfield, the Phillies decided not to call up one of their minor league outfield prospects but to call up Bannister, who had never played the outfield in his entire life.

"I was a good athlete," Bannister said. "I could run. I could throw. I could see the ball and catch it, and I could play the offensive part of the game. And apparently they saw the same thing. They convinced me without too much problem that I could be an outfielder. I was hitting .300 at the time, and they gave me a ten-day lesson in playing the outfield. So I went up to the big leagues as an outfielder."

Bannister got into twenty-six games and had twenty-five at bats, three hits, and an RBI, but the Phils must have liked what they saw because during the winter they traded their center fielder, Del Unser. Said manager Danny Ozark to Bannister, "Hit .280, and you'll be the center fielder."

Bannister had a good spring, stole some bases, and showed his skill with the bat. But during that spring training Bannister did something to his throwing arm. He doesn't know exactly what happened, but he hurt it badly. Every time he went to throw the ball, he felt a sharp pinprick and the ball would die.

The arm is a funny thing. It only has so many throws in it. The arm is a creature of habit. Throw a thousand times from shortstop, and your arm knows what it has to do from shortstop. But if you take that same arm and move it to the outfield, that arm has to use a different motion and is subject to different tensions. You risk what happened to Alan Bannister.

For the rest of his career Bannister was saddled with a subpar throwing arm. From that point on, he was denied the opportunity to become the superstar everyone thought he would be.

And once the pain was there, the Phillies, who originated the Great Experiment, couldn't let Bannister develop as a shortstop, because All-Star Larry Bowa was entrenched there. They summarily discarded him.

"I was hitting okay, about .260, nothing spectacular, and we were on the bus going from Veterans Stadium to the airport. On the bus the word came through, 'Did you hear? We signed Dick Allen. He's coming out of retirement to play.'

Bannister said to Tommy Hutton, "If Allen plays first, what are they going to do with Willie Montanez, our first baseman?"

"We traded him."

"Who'd we trade him to?"

"The Giants."

"Who'd we get?"

"Garry Maddox, the Giant center fielder."

Bannister thought, *Shall I get off the bus now?*

"We flew to St. Louis," he continued. "When Maddox arrived, he was playing, and I was on the bench. It wasn't long after that I got sent to the minors, and when I was brought back it was as a utility player. I was upset, disheartened, all those things a player feels when he gets demoted. I was mad I couldn't play to my capability, mad I had an arm problem.

"I filled in here and there, played some outfield, some shortstop. The season ended, and in December I was traded to Bill Veeck's Chicago White Sox."

Veeck had just taken over the Sox, and getting Alan was the great promoter's first trade for his new team. "I didn't look forward to going," Bannister said. "I still had arm problems."

Bannister began the 1976 season in Triple A, Des Moines, Iowa. He spent a month there and got called up. The White Sox were a team with defensive liabilities spread around the field. Ralph Garr, the left fielder, and second baseman Jorge Orta could hit, but neither was considered a good fielder, and Chet Lemon was young and erratic. Bannister found himself playing a lot at one of those positions or at third. "I played all over the place."

Just before the start of the 1977 season Bill Veeck traded Bucky Dent to the Yankees, and Bannister became the every-day shortstop. "It was my best and most gratifying season and also my worst year all rolled into one," Bannister said.

The 1977 White Sox were nicknamed the South Side Hitmen. They fielded a tremendous offensive team. The White Sox won 90 ball games. As a leadoff or second hitter Bannister drove in 57 runs. In the middle of the summer the Sox were in first place.

Bannister said, "That year Kansas City won an ungodly amount of games late in the year, something like twenty-eight of thirty-five, and so we lost to Kansas City.

"We scored a lot of runs, and we let in a lot too, and I contributed to that as well. I led the league in errors, made forty that year, and our two announcers, Harry Caray and Jimmy Piersall, never let me or the fans forget it. I was at a particular time of my life where I didn't handle it very well. I couldn't understand why they kept harping on the errors."

Bill Veeck, the White Sox owner, was a man who truly cared about his players. One afternoon he called Bannister into his office. He said, "Don't worry about the errors and what the announcers say." Veeck ripped up his contract and gave him a $5,000 raise.

His manager, Bob Lemon, didn't care either. When Lem was asked, "What are you going to do about the errors at shortstop?" he said, "I'm not going to do anything. They aren't hurting us." Lemon made Bannister feel comfortable about playing. His teammates respected his work ethic. He dove for every ball. He played hard-nosed, never loafed. Eric Soderholm played third and Jorge Orta was at second, so he had a lot of range to cover, and Bannister took a lot of errors.

"There were some depressing days for me," Bannister said. "I made four errors in a doubleheader in Anaheim, which is where my parents always came to see me play. Three of the four were oddball errors. I threw the ball to the cutoff man and hit the runner in the helmet, and the ball bounced into the seats. There was a pickoff play, and I dove to try and make a great catch on a wild throw. I fell across the runner, and he couldn't get up, and they called interference. An error.

"I had a day in Minnesota where I threw a ball away in extra innings and we lost the game. I took it harder on myself than anybody. Bob Lemon came over with a six-pack and said, 'Forget it. So what?' And in my defense, of the forty errors something like thirty-two were throwing errors. I just could not throw the ball like I once could. I kept telling myself, *I can handle this heat.*"

A more seasoned vet would have told the reporters, "I'm proud to be leading the league in errors, because we're winning." Instead, since it was his first season, Bannister brooded. He tried to ignore the criticism. He would kid. Reflecting on it now, he laments, "When Gary Templeton made forty errors, he got his picture on the cover of *The Sporting News*. I made forty errors in the American League, and the White Sox went out and signed six new shortstops," which they did, including Harry Chappas and Greg Pryor. But behind the kidding, pressure built in Bannister, and he tried harder, which caused him to make more errors.

Despite the criticism about his errors, Bannister thrived in Chicago while playing for the White Sox. Every night was memorable, as Bill Veeck entertained his fans with his exploding scoreboard and different "nights" during the season.

For Bannister and the other White Sox players, Veeck's "nights" were a distraction, because they rarely got to take batting practice. If it was belly dancer night, the ladies would be out on the field, gyrating away, which made taking batting practice impossible. Still, looking back, Bannister says he is glad he was there when Veeck ran the White Sox.

Bannister said, "It's kinda like the best stories you tell later in life were all the terrible things that happened to you when they were going on: like the night you got a flat tire in a driving rainstorm on vacation. It was miserable then, but a funny thing to tell ten years later."

The most memorable was "Disco Demolition Night." That promotion was the idea of Mike Veeck, Bill's son. Mike loved rock 'n' roll music and hated disco. He arranged with a local disc jockey to have an anti-disco night at the ballpark. If you brought a disco record to the park, you got in for a heavily discounted price. The plan was to burn all the disco records in center field in a huge bonfire between ball games of a doubleheader against Detroit. Forty thousand plus fans packed Comiskey Park on a wild summer night.

Bannister remembered, "Sometime around the middle part of the first game we started hearing what came to be a familiar humming of records being thrown from the stands down across the field like Frisbees.

"Comiskey Park is built on a garbage dump. All the years I was there the outfield grass was damp, wet, and mushy. This night the records would come down, *Fffffffffttt*, and stick on their edges right into the turf, and more than a few of them would hit on the infield dirt and explode. As time went on, more and more started flying around.

"Finally we got the first game over with, and now the fans were inebriated, excited. They've got their albums. A wild bunch of rock 'n' rollers. They're going to bury disco, right?"

Bannister went into the clubhouse between games. From their vantage point under the stadium, the players could hear what sounded like a stampede. The fans, many of them drunk, rushed out of the stands and flowed onto the field, throwing their disco records. Cops were dragging fans through the Chicago clubhouse. There was a rumor, which turned out to be true, that there was a riot in the parking lot.

"The fans were chaotic, partying everywhere, stealing bases, tearing up the turf," Bannister said.

The Sox forfeited the second game. The cops spent the rest of the night trying to keep the stadium from being decimated. The White Sox players, meanwhile, were trapped inside.

"We were told to stay in the clubhouse," Bannister said. "They locked the doors. They took our wives into the parking lot and told them to get in their cars and lock the doors and not get out. You couldn't drive your car without being rocked and rolled. It was a pretty scary situation.

"In the clubhouse we were asking each other, 'What's next? This is a joke.' We said, 'I wanna be traded to a real big league team.'"

Finally time went by, and the crowd petered out. The police finally let the players go home.

"It was a night to talk about," Bannister recalled.

When the 1977 season ended, Bannister was determined to do something about his bad arm. Unfortunately, when it comes to injuries, character traits such as determination and desire become irrelevant. It can happen that once you hurt your arm, you can go to extremes to rectify the situation, but nothing works. Bannister discovered this truth the hard way.

During the offseason he lifted weights, performed prescribed exercises, and continued to see doctors who kept telling him the X-rays were clean. Despite those assurances, when he arrived for spring training, he could barely lift his arm. "I was half the player I was capable of being," Bannister recalled. "I told myself, *I'm not going to go out there and embarrass myself. I'm going to take care of this problem.*" Bannister wanted his arm operated on by Dr. Robert Kerlan, the world-renowned surgeon.

But Veeck refused to let him go. Instead, Bannister agreed to see a hypnotist. The hypnotist, who had an effeminate voice, talked in long-drawn-out syllables. His initial greeting to Alan was "Heelllllllloooohhh."

"It was too much for me," Bannister said. "I broke out laughing. I thought, *Mentally I'm not ready for this to work.*"

Bannister ran out of patience. He left the team for L.A. to see Dr. Kurland and Dr. Jobe. "I'm just going to take a couple days," he told Veeck. "I'll be back."

Bannister got an examination the likes of which he had never experienced before. The doctors discovered what the problem was: In the joint of his arm there was heavy calcification, which they described as being like "very old toothpaste." The calcification was making little holes in his rotator cuff area. Surgery was recommended. Dr. Kurland said it was really the only way to repair Bannister's arm.

"It was the happiest day of my life," Bannister said.

His joy was premature. When Bannister returned to the White Sox' spring training camp, he had to face the continued criticism.

"Harry Chappas, Greg Pryor, and Don Kessinger were getting playing time at shortstop, while I was the deadbeat guy with the sore arm," Bannister said. "Jimmy Piersall, one of our announcers, was trying to convince all the pitchers not to let me play shortstop. There was a lot of negative crap going on. But I was happy. I said to Bill Veeck, 'I have a problem. Let's take care of it so I can come back and be the player I know I can be.'"

Veeck refused to let him have the operation. He needed Bannister's batting skills too badly.

Bannister did as he was told. He didn't have a very good season. He wanted to be an every-day player, but his arm prevented that. By August the White Sox were out of the pennant race, and Veeck finally let him go. He had surgery August 8 and missed the rest of the season.

When he returned the next year, he discovered that though the operation had been labeled "a success," Bannister had a dead arm. He never could make the throw from shortstop again.

"I could throw the ball with all the effort I ever did, but the ball wouldn't go anywhere. It never came back. Never."

Had Bannister not hurt his arm, he might have been the regular White Sox shortstop for fifteen years. Once he lost his ability to play shortstop, he allowed himself to be used as a utility player, shifting to the outfield. It was the beginning of Bannister's slide out of baseball.

"Part of my problem," Bannister said, "was that I never knew when to say no."

It seemed that every six months Bannister played for a new manager, and each manager had a different idea of where to play him. When you play for enough managers, eventually one of them will decide you can't play at all.

Bannister said, "I started with the Phillies and Danny Ozark, and with the White Sox there was Paul Richards, replaced by Bob Lemon, who was replaced by Larry Doby, who was replaced by Don Kessinger, who was replaced by Tony LaRussa. Each one of them saw me as a different guy. I had managers who would say, 'You're the best outfielder on the team, and that's where you play.' He'd get fired, and the next one would say, 'No, I want you in the infield.' Kessinger saw me as a second baseman."

When Tony LaRussa, a young law school grad with no prior big league experience, was named manager, he wanted Bannister to play third base and platoon.

Bannister thought, *How can I hit if I don't play every day?*

Bannister recalled, "I was only hitting against lefties, even though in my career I'd hit over .300 against right-handers and .250 against left-handers. I had all the arguments on my side. *Why is he doing this? It doesn't make sense.* Of course, I was the one who got hurt. I didn't hit very well. I started the season hitting about .180.

"Finally I talked to Tony. He said, 'That's the way it's going to be. You better get your act together.' So I talked it over with Bill Veeck. He said that if I wanted, he would try to trade me.

"I said, 'Yes, trade me,' and on June 13, 1980, right before the trading deadline, I got traded to the Cleveland Indians for catcher Ron Pruitt."

During his four years with the Cleveland Indians, Alan Bannister became Mr. Utility. Look up those Cleveland seasons in *The Baseball Encyclopedia*, and you'll discover for positions the notations OF, 2B, 1B, SS, DH, 3B. Translated, that means Bannister played the outfield, second base, first base, shortstop, designated hitter, and third base during his seasons there. One season he played in 117 games, despite his limited utility role. He wasn't a regular in Cleveland, but most of the time he made manager Dave Garcia's lineup card.

"I had four good years in Cleveland, from 1980 through 1983, and that's where I learned to take a great deal of pride in being a quality utility player," Bannister said. "And that was Dave Garcia's doing. I liked the hell out of Dave Garcia. Those years in Cleveland I never got five hundred at bats in a season, but I got close to four hundred, and I played a different position almost every night. Dave would tell people, 'Banni is one of the more valuable guys on the team.'"

After Dave Garcia was fired as manager, Mike Ferraro came in and batted him only against left-handed pitchers. And then Ferraro got fired. His replacement was Pat Corrales, who wanted Bannister gone.

Bannister said, "He was going to change the world with his strong-arm tactics. He said to everybody, 'You gotta take pride in being a Cleveland Indian. You gotta want to play here.' *He* was the outsider.

"At that time I was adopting a little girl, and we had to declare residency. I had just signed a long-term contract, and so I decided to buy a home in Cleveland. I went to spring training, and the last day of spring training Pat Corrales took me into his office. He said, 'We've sold you to the Houston Astros.'"

From that day on Bannister had daily thoughts of retirement. When he got to Houston, he discovered that no one in the Astros organization was aware of what he had to offer.

"On the last day of spring training I met the Astros team," Bannister recalled. "I met manager Bob Lillis, who asked me if I was left-handed or right-handed. This was coming off four years of believing I was the best utility guy in baseball.

"I said, 'Well, I'm right-handed.'

"'Are you serious?' he said."

Bannister spent two months with Houston, and he got twenty-five at-bats, and that was only when they didn't have anybody else and were desperate. Lillis had no idea of his value or how to use him.

"One day we were in Dodger Stadium, and all their shortstops were hurt, and Lillis told me I was going to play shortstop," Bannister said. "Fine. I played four games, did a respectable job, and when we got back to the Astrodome, the general manager, Al Rosen, asked me why I never threw the ball hard. I made a joke about how I was throwing hard, only the ball just wasn't going fast, and I said, 'That's the way it's been since

1978. I'm not going to impress you with my arm strength. I gotta play with my brain.' They had no idea I had arm surgery."

The Astros had no respect for his off-the-field work or for his being as good a utility player as he was.

Bannister said, "In my baseball career there have been only a couple of people I couldn't get along with. Al Rosen was one of them. He did his best to make me feel as inadequate as possible."

When Rosen wondered aloud if Bannister could even play, the player told him, "Hey, do what you have to do."

Bannister was disgusted. He knew he had a guaranteed contract. At the time his second child was about to be born in Florida, and he told Rosen, "I'm going to be with my wife for forty-eight hours. I'll be back."

Rosen said, "I think this is a negative thing to do."

Bannister said, "Well, I'm going to go." And he did.

When Bannister returned he never got another at-bat. A short while later he was traded to the Texas Rangers.

The day of the trade Rosen called Bannister into his office. He said, "We traded you for Mike Richardt," a minor league player. "We needed a little more versatility."

Bannister replied, "I'm happy to go to the Texas Rangers. But I have to tell you, you have no idea who's sitting in front of you right now. You have Denny Walling, Craig Reynolds, Bill Doran, but I am telling you, I can play with any of those guys. I can do what they do. But you don't know that, and it's too late to try and convince you."

Bannister added, "I'm happy to go, and good luck to you."

Bannister didn't play much at Texas either. He became a free agent at the end of the 1985 season.

"Like some thirty-odd other free agents, I never got a phone call. At that time the major league teams were cutting their rosters from twenty-five to twenty-four, and I got polite no's from everybody. My agent said he called all the teams, and I believe him. 'We're going with youth,' they all said."

Bannister had prepared himself for retirement. He had an opportunity to go into the real estate and the financial planning business. He took it. He didn't have a choice. No team wanted him.

"I would have loved to have somebody want me," Bannister said, "but I had two new little children. When March came and I got to stay home, I didn't have to drag my family all around, live out of suitcases, travel around a lot. I was excited about my new career.

"I wasn't a guy who was willing to say, 'Yeah, I'll go down to the minor leagues.' And maybe if I had a couple good months, they might have brought me back up. But I never got a call.

"I'm not bitter about it. I do have my pension, and I was a good player. I had some very good times, some great, some not so great, some real trying. I don't harbor any bad feelings. I still have a big place in my heart for the game. I still love it."

Bannister was out of the game completely in 1986 and 1987. At a golf tournament he ran into his old coach, Bobby Winkles, who was with the Montreal Expos at that time. He asked if Banni was interested in coaching. Banni replied, 'You know, they only pay minor league people fifteen to eighteen thousand a year.' Winkles said, "If you're ever interested, give me a call."

Like many other ballplayers, Bannister played the real estate game. About three years ago the market collapsed and real estate as an investment went down the tubes. Coaching suddenly became a viable, though chancy, alternative.

"I saw a lot of former teammates who were coaches," Bannister said. "I thought, *I'll give it a try. I can handle the money for a while. Let's see where it goes.*"

Bannister called Winkles, and twenty-four hours later he had a job as manager in A ball in the Midwest League. His team won the Western Division of that league. The Expos made him a Double A manager in 1989. He managed Jacksonville in the Southern League. The team had a very good first half and a very poor second half, because management moved up his best players.

Like so many other minor league managers, he was fired for no reason in particular.

The Expos then said they were going to offer him a job as hitting director. That job later became hitting instructor.

Bannister said, "All the Expos staff people went to the World Series in San Francisco, and when they came back, they told me, 'We're going in a different direction in our hitting program.'"

He asked, "What would you like me to do?"

They said, "We're going in a different direction."

"Oh, I get it."

Bannister is quick to point out that the farm director who fired him is no longer there. He says he is happy being a civilian again. Making a living in baseball was too problematical. Jobs were not handed out on skill or ability but rather on politics. And Banni was no politician. He hated to leave baseball, but he vowed he had been fired for the last time.

"I'm anxious to do what I'm supposed to do, which is get back to my life away from baseball," he said.

"I don't mind working for eighteen, twenty, twenty-five thousand a year—if it's on the road to something. But I didn't see the light at the end of the tunnel. I'm not committed to spending ten years in the minor leagues to get a big league job. I'm not even sure I want to go back to the big leagues.

"I'm going to go back home when the Senior League season is over. So baseball, for me, is coming to an end. I really hope the Senior League withstands the test of time and survives. We'll see how it all pans out."

CHAPTER

14

Staying the Course

Certain games stick out in one's memory. On a chilly night in mid-December in Pompano Beach, the Pelicans and the Gold Coast Suns played one such game. The score was 2–1. The Pelicans won. Then in a flash it became 1–0, and the Pelicans lost. The winner was Suns manager Earl Weaver. The Mouth That Roared, the Earl of Baltimore, stole the game away from the Pelicans.

The victorious pitcher should have been Elias Sosa in relief. But the way his season was progressing, it was only fitting that he failed to win. Hoot Gibson pitched six and two-thirds innings of one-run ball, proving to everyone he could compete in the league. The run itself had been a cheap one. A seeing-eye bouncer, hit inches between Roy Howell at third and Luis Gomez at short, went for a double. After a wild pitch and a sacrifice fly, the Suns had their puny run.

But against former Yankee Stan Bahnsen, the Pelicans could do nothing—until the eighth.

With two outs and Roy Howell on first, Dwight Lowry came up for the Pelicans. The left-handed-hitting Lowry stood in against Bahnsen, the former Yankee flamethrower. The Pelicans were down by a run.

Lowry hadn't hit a home run all year, despite his early promise. During the two weeks of preseason training, Lowry had hit five towering home runs against semipro pitching. Pelican owner Jim Morley had convinced himself that the tall catcher would be one of the team's power hitters.

But Lowry soon showed a flaw in his swing. He tried to pull the ball, no matter where it was pitched. The pitchers in the league quickly learned that if you pitched him outside, the end result would usually be a ground ball to the infield.

This time he swung at a pitch over the middle of the plate, and rocketed a projectile that headed for the moon, rising high and passing many feet above the short foul pole in right field. The ball was hooking, and it appeared to be fair as it passed the pole. The first-base umpire, Billy Williams, seemed to confirm that call when he signaled by raising his arms. Howell and Lowry circled the bases. The numeral "2" was lit on the scoreboard for the Pelicans. Dwight received a hero's welcome.

Large, gentle Dwight Lowry grew up in Pembroke, North Carolina, the son of a Korean War POW. In high school he caught and played quarterback and was offered a full scholarship to Clemson to play football. He turned it down. He didn't want to ruin his knees.

Lowry went to the University of North Carolina to play baseball. His coach was Walter Raab, for thirty-four years the baseball professor at UNC. Raab once asked Lowry, "Son, you ever had the tisma?"

"The tisma?" said Lowry. "I don't know what that is."

Raab told him, "Well, the tisma is when all the iron in your blood turns to lead and settles in your ass and you can't move." He said, "I got the tisma today."

In 1978 Raab led North Carolina to third place in the NCAA tournament. Lowry, whose timing was never good, didn't play. He had a pain in his chest one night, and the doctors wouldn't let him play that year. He played four other seasons. Carolina didn't go those other years.

Lowry was a respectable but not great college player. At six-foot-four he had good size for a catcher. He had a good arm and blocked the ball well. He was a left-handed-hitting catcher, a highly sought commodity. He was drafted by the Detroit Tigers in the eleventh round in 1980. He got a $7,000 bonus and $600 a month to play. After taxes, he cleared $480 a month.

He began in the minors platooning. His first year at Lakeland he didn't even hit .200.

"I played every other day, every third day, and you don't know when you're going to play sometimes. My career has been like that, one year good, the next year terrible," Lowry said.

When the season was over, he went home and got a job as a substitute teacher. He did that for six years in the off-season.

Lowry said, "You can't come home and expect to get an entry-level position with a company, because you have to leave again in four months. But substitute teaching didn't get you a whole lot, especially when you have a family and a couple of kids."

Each spring Lowry waited to find out if he was going to get invited to camp or get released. His whole career was marked by uncertainty. After an unproductive year in Macon in the Sally League, he was sent to the Florida State League. He was twenty-four years old, playing in the lower minor leagues. He was at a crossroads and was worried that he would be released.

"I talked to the Savior about it," Lowry said. " 'If the door is open, continue to play,' the Lord told me."

Lowry stopped worrying about getting cut. He made the ball club, and he had his best year. In 1982 he made the all-star team.

He moved up to Double A Birmingham, and he helped defeat the Kansas City farm club with Bret Saberhagen and Mark Gubizca in the Southern League championship. Lowry was placed on the Tigers' forty-man roster, and in the spring of 1984, as Lowry put it, "Lo and behold, I made the big league club."

He was backup to Detroit's outstanding catcher, Lance Parrish, with the 1984 Detroit Tigers, who won the World Series that year. Parrish was the cornerstone.

"I was part of the ball club," Lowry said, "but not an integral part. I don't know—I got to the big leagues so fast, it was almost like I wasn't there. Because it didn't sink in. I look back, and I can hardly believe I was there."

The first game he started as a catcher was against the Chicago White Sox. The Tigers' starting pitcher, Juan Berenguer, threw a three-hitter. It was Easter Sunday, a snowy, freezing day. One time when thirty-six-year old Carlton Fisk came up to bat for the White Sox, the veteran catcher told Lowry, "The next major league contract I sign is going to have a clause in it that I don't play when the temperature is below my age."

He returned to the minors in June, splitting time (ironically) with Butch Benton in Triple A. Though he didn't hit well, the Tigers called him back up. When the Tigers beat the Padres in the Series, Lowry got a check for $26,000. He got married and bought a mobile home and a car.

Tom DiPace

Dwight Lowry

The next year the Tigers kept Marty Castillo and sent Lowry back to Triple A. He hit .220. He began to wonder, *Can I still play? What's happening to me?*

The Tigers took Lowry off their forty-man roster. He had become a suspect, rather than a prospect. Lowry started the season at Nashville as the starting catcher. He hit the ball hard, driving it, making good contact. In mid-May he was called back to the Tigers.

"It was the last thing on my mind," Lowry said.

He started against Mark Langston, got a couple of hits, and by the All-Star break was hitting .360 in about fifty at-bats. Then Lance Parrish's back went out on him, and Lowry played every day. His average dropped to .307.

The last week of the season Lowry's knee buckled under the strain. The Tigers called up young Matt Nokes, who hit very well.

The next year Parrish became a free agent and left Detroit. Sparky Anderson touted Lowry as his starting catcher. But the Tigers had traded for Mike Heath toward the end of the 1986 season. They decided Matt Nokes had more potential than Lowry. When the Tigers started the season poorly, they sent Lowry down. Nokes took his job.

At Nashville he tore something in his arm and couldn't throw. He missed three-quarters of the season. Though the Tigers called him up in September, he didn't play. After the season the Tigers released him.

"They didn't need me any more," Lowry said.

On the way to his home in North Carolina from Detroit Lowry was stretched out in the back seat to ease the pain in his knee. His wife drove. He got out his Bible and began reading. He prayed about his future.

"A peace came to me that told me everything was going to be all right," he said. "After that I didn't worry about it any more."

Two days after he got home, the Minnesota Twins called. In 1988 he made the Twins team. He was up for three weeks before the Twins sent him down to Triple A Portland. Then the Twins released him.

In January he was asked if he wanted to play professionally in Italy. The Lowrys flew to Grosseto, Italy, a little town between Rome and Florence, and Dwight helped Grosseto to the championship. The team had needed a strong catcher, a team leader, and Lowry had filled that role. After Italy, Dwight's next stop was the Senior League.

Lowry still had hopes of returning to the majors. He was only thirty-two years old. He was hoping the Senior League would be his ticket back.

Lowry had barely crossed home plate and returned to the dugout when Gold Coast manager Earl Weaver, short, fiery, and crazed, ran out onto the field. Weaver had been berating the umps all season long, so often that the league finally had to tell him to put a sock in it. Earl, an umpire-baiter since he was a child, didn't pay any attention. On this night he raced out of the dugout, hat in hand, gesturing to the home plate umpire, spitting saliva. He was even more apoplectic than he had been two innings earlier on a line drive by Cesar Cedeno that an umpire called foul.

The home plate umpire listened to what Weaver had to say, then he looked into the Pelicans' dugout. It turned out that when umpire Billy Williams threw his arms up, he wasn't signaling a home run. Rather he was indicating that he hadn't seen the ball go out. Now it became the home umpire's call. The home umpire ruled Lowry's drive a foul ball.

Now it was Bobby Tolan's turn to get excited. Toland began screaming as loud as he could, "The guy intimidated you! The guy intimidated you!" But this time the umps held their ground. Howell had to go back to first, and poor Lowry had to bat again.

Tolan, meanwhile, refused to let up. "You didn't get one goddamned call right all night!" he shouted.

The home plate ump shouted back, "I won't throw you out! I won't give you the satisfaction. It's too late in the game." Which only served to make Tolan angrier.

Powerless, Tolan finally returned to the dugout. Lowry reappeared at home plate, grounding weakly to second base. Poor Dwight. Hitting under .200, his season had started with such promise, but his penchant for trying to pull everything had begun to take its toll. And when he did hit the ball hard, most of the time it was right at somebody. He hadn't had a single extra-base hit, and here when he finally hit one to win a ball game, he had the home run taken away from him by Earl Weaver and some gutless umpiring.

After the infuriating loss, the Pelicans tramped onto the bus. They were angry, emotional, feeling they had deserved to win. Though they had lost, they weren't despondent. The players sensed the team was playing well again. Their record was 19–13, still three and a half games in front.

As the bus backed out of its parking place to leave Pompano for West Palm Beach, the bus driver failed to notice that he was scraping the front of a brand-new gray sedan. The car's left fender was bashed in, and the hubcap on the front left tire was missing.

The players yelled out. The bus stopped. The players sitting in the back noticed that the gentleman standing next to the car wore a Pelicans cap. It was owner Jim Morley's dad, Herb, who was affectionately called the Grandfather of the Senior League. The car belonged to his son.

When asked about the missing hubcap, Jim Morley said, "Somebody stole it while I was playing golf this afternoon."

He added, "I've had better days."

The banged-up bus drove south to West Palm Beach, where the Pelicans were scheduled to play a three-game weekend series against Dick Williams's Tropics.

The Pelicans were getting consistent pitching from Milt Wilcox and Jon Matlack. Elias Sosa pitched well but was losing. They needed some consistency from Randy Lerch, who started the three-game opener against West Palm Beach, Dick Williams's Southern Division leaders. The Pelicans had to play at the top of their game to beat them.

Randy Lerch was ahead of Pete Broberg, 3–0, going into the West Palm Beach third. With one out Randy loaded the bases, but he struck out the free-swinging Dave Kingman on some outstanding pitches. Then he got Tito Landrum to hit a ground ball to shortstop.

Sergio Ferrer, who was still with the Pelicans at the time and was still having his problems in the field, glided to his left, but not fast enough. The ball hit his glove and continued into the outfield. Two runs scored. Lerch tried to contain his emotions, but he was angry. He knew he should have been out of the inning. He went back to pitching, but his concentration deserted him. Four runs later the Pelicans were out of the ball game.

The final score was 13–4. In the clubhouse after the game there was little talk. Players dressed purposefully. None of them seemed particularly upset by the loss. It was just baseball. West Palm Beach had played better.

Bobby Tolan was stoically philosophical. "We got our asses kicked. We'll get them tomorrow." Through the run of bad play and injuries, Bobby Tolan hadn't panicked. In fact, he had done just the opposite, releasing LeFlore and going about his business replacing him, all the while aware that the Pelicans were in first place, and no first-place team should ever panic. Tolan stayed the course. The Pelican ship remained upright.

Bobby Tolan had been right not to panic. The Pelicans rebounded. In the second game of the West Palm Beach series, Milt Wilcox pitched seven innings of overpowering baseball, allowing just two singles and not walking a single batter.

The rubber match was pivotal, in that it would determine early who would have bragging rights to say they were the best team in the league. The game shaped up as a pitchers' battle between the Pelicans' Jon Matlack and West Palm Beach's human oak tree, Tim Stoddard, at six-foot-seven one of the tallest men ever to play.

Stoddard had been a star basketball player at North Carolina State University. He threw a heavy, hard ball.

The Pelican players were aware that West Palm Beach was viewed as the best team. Their recent run of .500 baseball made them appear vulnerable, but they still led the division by three games. As a result, the players certainly wanted to beat West Palm Beach, but because winning their division was paramount, they cared more about what their division rivals were doing.

Team spirit had never been higher. On the dugout wall before the game one prankster stole one of Bobby Tolan's blank lineup cards and listed the All-Attack-the-Spread Team. The spread is what the players call the meal after the game. The clubhouse manager "spreads" the food out before them.

There were some big-time trenchermen on the Pelicans, players who would leave the field after a game, enter the locker room, and, without pausing to piss, attack the mound of food set out on the table for them by the clubhouse manager.

The players individually and in groups sidled over to the "lineup card" to see whether they made the "team." The ones who made it laughed and grumbled at the same time. The honor was a dubious one. No one wanted to be perceived as a glutton. Even the gluttons.

Eating in the first position was pitcher Nardi Contreras. Next came large Lamar Johnson. Elias Sosa, the gentle pitcher who usually hit the spread first and fastest and, with rapid hand movements, could shovel great quantities of food before the rest of the team even reached the table, Sosa was slotted in the third spot. Fourth and clean-up was Mike "Tex" Williams. Mike's ample belly gave silent testimony to his prowess. Tex feigned great anger at his placement. No one was sympathetic, not even Steve Kemp, who was listed as number five. When it came to fried chicken, Steve Kemp always had a drumstick in each hand, and never mind the mashed potatoes.

Though the rubber match with West Palm Beach was supposed to be a pitcher's duel, it wasn't. Tim Stoddard, unable to control his breaking ball, came in with fastballs against a team that devoured fastballs. The

Pelicans jumped ahead, 14–3. Stoddard hated what was happening, and in the fourth, with two outs and runners on first and third, he reared back and hit Gary Rajsich in the middle of his back. No one doubted that Stoddard had done it on purpose.

When the umpire warned Stoddard rather than expelling him, Bobby Tolan argued vehemently. Tolan then went up to bat against Stoddard. On this day, in the lineup as the Pelicans' designated hitter, Tolan banged out four hits and drove in five runs. It takes guts to be a playing manager, because if you do poorly, you lose face with the players. This time up, after having asked the ump to toss Stoddard out of the game, Tolan *had* to hit against him. Tolan stared back at the mean pitcher, who quickly threw two fastballs past him. Stoddard tried it again, and Tolan lined a hard one through the middle into the outfield as the runs kept coming in to score.

Even though Tex Williams had given up five runs in two innings the day before, Tolan went back to him again, hoping he would regain his confidence. On this day Tex came into the game and immediately threw high-octane fuel on the fire, allowing a double, a single, and a walk before Tolan had seen enough.

Nardi Contreras replaced him. The first batter bounced to Sergio Ferrer at third. Sergio butchered the play, and more runs scored, and then Dave Kingman hit a scorcher through poor Sergio's legs for more runs. By the end of the seventh, West Palm Beach trailed by three, 14–11.

By the eighth inning, the mood of fifty or so Pelican fans had changed from one of arrogant joy to one of panic, but Contreras, despite a rocky beginning, finished strong. After a leadoff double in the eighth by Harrah, he got a pop out and two impressive strikeouts against Dave Kingman and Tito Landrum. Nardi Contreras had finally contributed.

When Dock Ellis came in to face West Palm Beach in the ninth, everyone relaxed. In a crucial situation, Dock became virtually unhittable. So it was on this day as he shut down the Tropics to win the rubber match by a field goal, 15–12.

Dock, stalking the mound like an animal, gritted his teeth and made a fist. Out there, he was the King of the Jungle. The Tropics submitted meekly.

CHAPTER

15

I Am Family

Before Dock Ellis arrived on the Pittsburgh scene in 1968, the Pirates were an aging team. Some of the players, like Roy Face, Bill Mazeroski, and Roberto Clemente, had played in the 1960 World Series against the Yankees. When Dock arrived, some of the older vets didn't quite know what to make of Ellis, who was already under the pernicious influence of alcohol and drugs. Dock admits that coach Bob Skinner was the only person on the team Doc might have sought out to help him conquer his problem. "He was the only one I could relate to." Unfortunately, Skinner wasn't aware of the extent of Dock's problem, or of how much respect Ellis had for him.

Thus, no one stopped Dock Ellis from pitching his entire career on drugs. Even so, he was a great one, and off the field he had a big hand in making Pittsburgh a "family," not because of any song but because Dock Ellis knew how to party. He also knew the importance of black-white harmony, and Ellis fought hard for that too.

Ellis made it to the Pirates in 1968 because of his Triple A manager, Johnny Pesky. "Pesky saw the coming of a new era," Ellis said. "He knew the kind of players these kids were. Johnny said, 'We're going to kick ass and take names.' And that's what we did."

Early in the season Pesky asked Dock, "Would you be my dog every day?"

"What do you mean?" Dock said.

"Be ready to pitch every day."

"All right."

The season began, and after nineteen games Dock had a couple of wins and twelve saves, and *whammo*, he was in the big leagues.

"Within two years the Pirates called up Johnny's whole team," Ellis said. "Everybody was in the big leagues. But the Pirates never brought him up to manage. I don't think he fit the Pirate mold. And he couldn't have them, because Danny Murtaugh wanted them. Murtaugh saw a world championship, and he wanted to be part of it. He had been a special assistant who had said, 'Send Dock here, send Gene Clines here, Dave Parker there, Freddie Patek here.' He had a lot of input. Now he was saying, 'I want to manage.'

"The Pirates were an old clique-fucking team when I came up. I told them, 'You motherfuckers ain't gonna be around here. You are gone.' Because I knew the talent behind me. I knew who was coming. And I said this to anybody in the clubhouse, guys like Donn Clendenon with his intellectuality. Donn would say, 'Well, yeah, the kid seems to know what he's talking about. But he's still a motherfucking asshole.' I said, 'Yeah. You better hope you're going to be around, because I'll be here.'

"I don't know what guys like Elroy Face were saying, but I know they were looking. Jim Bunning too. When I met him, he said, 'You can't make the club in a tub.' I said, 'Man, fuck you. Who are you anyway?' I didn't know who he was, and I didn't care.

"Bunning was still a good pitcher, but he was hardheaded. He refused to change his style. He thought he could still get by mostly on his fastball. He still thought he was nineteen.

"I told him, 'Man, when I get to be your age, I'm not going to be pitching like I'm nineteen.'

"Bill Mazeroski sat on the fence. Maz didn't say much, but whatever he had to say he would tell you straight out. He wasn't one to be talking behind your back.

"I knew what was going on because I used to date some white women who would tell me what the other players were saying about me. I'd send them over to find out. I said, 'Let them think they're going to get some pussy. Get 'em talking. Find out what's going on.'"

Dock Ellis seemed to be angry at something all the time. He was angry that the vets were resentful of the new players. He was angry that the Pirates had wasted two years of his career in the minors. He was angry, angry, angry.

"I really got pissed when they brought Bob Moose up. He was twenty. When I was nineteen, they said to me, 'You're too young. We don't do that.' And then, several years later, here was Moose."

Because Ellis was talented, some of the Pirate veterans tried to counsel him and keep him cooled off.

"Maury Wills and Willie Stargell used to try to key me down, but it was useless. Roberto Clemente would cuss me out. He used to try to explain to me that the way to get things done was through the Galbraiths, who owned the team. But I used to tell him, "My name isn't Roberto Clemente, and I'm not going to talk to them like you, and I'm not going to listen to them like you.' And he'd say, 'Fuck you, stupid rookie motherfucker.'

"I'd say, 'Yeah, but I'm not going to do it.'

"Clendenon was another one who tried to key me down. He said, 'You can do what you do, Dock, but you have to be diplomatic about it.' I'd say, 'Man, get away from me.'"

As it turned out, the Pittsburgh Pirates were the perfect team for Dock Ellis. The Pirates, under general manager Joe Brown, tried hard to make the black players feel comfortable. It is doubtful Dock would have been as successful on a team like Boston, where the white players were lionized and the black players filled out the roster. But on the Pirates there *was* true racial harmony. Dock thrived.

"The Pirates were one team that made a sincere effort to find out how the blacks were being treated," Ellis said. "Joe Brown wanted to know who was doing what and who was saying what, and who was making things comfortable for us, who was all right. He made a sincere effort. I can remember him calling all the brothers together. That's when he started humming those old-timers out of there. Because he knew that these kids had a camaraderie and a togetherness that they had never seen."

Coming through the Pirate system were Ellis, slugging first baseman Al Oliver, catcher Manny Sanguillen, another first baseman, Bob Robertson, infielders Dave Cash, Richie Hebner, Gene Clines, and Rennie Stennett, and outfielder Richie Zisk. And these guys were tight.

"And yet," Ellis said, "there were still people in the Pirate organization trying to undercut all that. One guy they wanted to stop was Bob Robertson, because he was a white guy who was sitting on the bus pounding to the beat of Aretha Franklin. 'Why is this big ole white dude beating on drums to Aretha Franklin?' That was unheard of. So Bob

Tom DiPace

Dock Ellis

Robertson, I don't know if he will admit it, was compromised. He stopped acting that way, and then they created animosity between him and Al Oliver. Ask Al how he became an outfielder. Al Oliver was a hell of a first baseman. That's why they called him Scoop. Al didn't want to go to the outfield. But he did so Robertson could play first base.

"The next one they got to was Richie Zisk. Richie Zisk was supposed to be in the big leagues two years before he got there. But he had those little rabbits in front of him. Gene Clines was one, and Dave Parker was on his heels, and I used to tell Richie, 'The writing is on the wall. You've got to get out of here.' Because Richie could play ball. But Richie couldn't outrun them brothers, and they wanted rabbits in the outfield. He could hit, but they didn't have the DH. I said, 'Richie, you're supposed to be in the big leagues, but they're not going to bring you. Make them give you $25,000.' He said, 'What do you mean?' He was so competitive, he still felt he would make it. I'd say, 'No, man. Uh-uh.' Back he'd go to Triple A, but at least he got more than he would have—just to be quiet. They tried to hold onto him just in case somebody got hurt, but nobody did. The Pirates had a lot of talent, man. They had so much talent it was ridiculous.

"And the reason why was their scout Howie Haak. And later on they got rid of him. Howie told a newspaper the Pirates had too many blacks, and then they got rid of him. Howie was old. He had been saying that every year since I was in baseball. Now all of a sudden they can him.

"I called the press and told them, 'Why do they want to do that to Howie Haak?' I said it, and it was headlines too. What's wrong with that? It was the truth. But Joe Brown didn't give a damn how many blacks the Pirates had. He didn't give a damn how many of us were out there. He wanted to kick ass and take names."

In his eight seasons with the Pirates, Dock Ellis's team won four division championships, a pennant, and a world championship. The skipper for the team during its run of three straight division championships beginning in 1970 was the legendary Danny Murtaugh, who looked like a kindly smiling Irishman, but who was a tough, hard-bitten competitor. Dock Ellis admired him greatly.

"Murtaugh was cool," Ellis said. "His thing also was 'Kick ass and take names.' At all costs. He was 'Go git 'em.' Murtaugh loved to win. If we were winning, he wasn't even walking on the ground. He would be walking with that bowlegged ass on Cloud Zero with that big cigar.

"And when we were walking through the airport, none of the players would pass him. We let him lead his troops. We all wore these little suits, black pants, gray blazers, black-and-gold ties, and the Pirate logo. That was him. 'There go Danny Murtaugh and the Pirates.' That was all you heard people say. He had them white patent-leather shoes on. Oh, he was styling. Oh yeah."

Murtaugh was a stickler for fundamentals. He taught the game. During spring training he walked the players through the drills. Coaches would walk from the outfield to where the ball was supposed to go to the cutoff man. When the season began, they were prepared.

Danny Murtaugh was also one of those managers who realized that his players were human and that they made errors. If a player made a mistake, Murtaugh didn't get all over him. He also knew from long experience that players cannot be mentally prepared every day of the season. He taught his players that a season is a long one, with its ups and downs, and he insisted that his players maintain their cool at all times. A Pirate never kicked dirt or gave a teammate a dirty look if he made an error. A Pirate never argued with an umpire.

For Dock Ellis there was only one way of doing things, the Danny Murtaugh way, the Pirate Way. It would bother him when players from other teams would do things he considered to be "bush." Dock, naturally, would let the players know it too.

"I remember one time doing an article with the press," Ellis recalled. "I was talking about the players on the Pirates who had come from other organizations. I called them 'orphans.' I said, 'These orphans coming over here are starting all this shit.' For instance, you'll hear Milt Wilcox in our clubhouse saying, 'Save me some runs for tomorrow.' With the Pirates he couldn't have said that. I'd have been all over him. There was a pitcher named Nelson Briles, who used to try saying stuff like that, and I'd eat his ass up. One time he made a statement about Dave Parker leaping at the ball and missing, criticizing him because he was a young outfielder.

"I said, 'Okay, motherfucker, from now on Parker's not going to be in the lineup when you pitch. You going to like that?' See, he was an older guy coming to that team. That's when the Pirates started watching who they'd bring into the clubhouse from other teams.

"One time I overheard Jim Rooker talking about John Candelaria, saying he was a 'stupid ass.' I said, 'You're calling him a stupid ass, and he's going to take your job. That's why you don't like him.' Because we weren't used to that kind of talk.

"I didn't really dislike these guys. I just disliked their ways. They were all right. They were just full of crap, that's all. Pitcher Dave Giusti was from another organization, but he was intelligent enough to know he had to mix. He knew all the groups—black, Latin, and white—and he knew how it was supposed to go. He knew there was supposed to be camaraderie all the way around.

"You have to make a concentrated effort to try to understand the other groups. If you don't, you can't have camaraderie. No matter how false it sounds."

Most years the Pirates had it. Perhaps too much of it, because these Pirates were a hard-living, hard-drinking bunch of guys, with Dock the man who lived the hardest life of them all. It took everything Danny Murtaugh could do to slow them down.

"We had some sneaky dudes on the Pirates," Ellis said. "They would drink, but they would be sneaky. I was in the open doing my thing, but them guys..." He shook his head, smiling.

"Sometimes Murtaugh would tell the bus driver to get lost on purpose so that we would not sit at the airport bar too long. One time we were in Los Angeles, and I said, 'Bussy, where do you live? This is L.A. You don't take this freeway to get to the airport at this time. We've been in traffic for an hour.' And Murtaugh would be sitting there, chomping on that cigar. He knew that on the bus the only thing the players could drink was the little tiny pints of whiskey they snuck with them. And he knew they weren't going to share it. 'Get away from me. You can't have any. We're going to be on this bus another hour? I'll be drunk by the time I get to the airport, and I'll sleep all the way to Pittsburgh.'"

Murtaugh knew all the tricks. He'd give the elevator operator a ball and ask him to get all the players who came in after three in the morning to sign it. Then Murtaugh would have a team meeting the next day.

"How many guys were out last night?" Nobody would raise his hand. Then he'd say, "I'm going to give you one more chance. I got an autographed ball from the elevator operator. Anybody's name on here is going to be fined $1,000 if they don't raise their hand now."

Ellis said, "Them hands shot up."

When Murtaugh stepped down in 1972, his lieutenant, Bill Virdon, took over. Virdon was a disciplinarian. Ellis insisted on playing by his own rules. But by this time Dock's drug problem had become so acute and his behavior so disruptive that his days with the Pirates were numbered.

Ellis said, "He wanted to treat everyone the same, and I told him, 'You can't do that, especially with me. I'm not like these other guys. I'm different.' He said, 'Oh no.' I said, 'Oh yes.' And he found out I was not lying. He had to fine me a lot, because I did what I wanted to do.

"They say I got him fired. I didn't get him fired. Richie Hebner got him fired. Richie was going to beat his ass. They were arguing about something, and I said, 'Richie, don't fight Virdon, man. Fuck that. Let's go.' And I kept going.

"But Virdon would challenge the players. If I'm not mistaken, he got hurt in Houston when Cesar Cedeno tried to kill him. That didn't make sense. And he wanted to fight Hebner. Hebner was the type of guy you leave alone."

In the middle of 1973, Murtaugh apparently saw what was happening, and Virdon lost his job. The Pirates asked their old manager to come back. In 1974 the Pirates won the pennant again.

That September a line drive smashed the back of Dock's pitching hand and broke it.

"If they'd have let me pitch, we would have gone to the World Series," Ellis said, "but when I said I could pitch they figured I was full of it, that I just wanted to go get them." The bone was, after all, still cracked, but Ellis didn't really feel too much pain, despite the serious injury.

"See," Ellis said, "I was doing a lot of dope at this time, and I was so high, I couldn't feel it."

Dock was certain the Pirate organization was aware of his heavy drug use. "We had another white dude on the team," he said. "This white dude and I were heavy into acid and mescaline. They wouldn't let us room together. I remember one night in Montreal, the airplanes couldn't leave Canada, and we had to stay the night. They saw this guy and me put in for the same room. They stopped us, because they knew we were getting ready to get loaded."

This was 1974, at the height of baseball's and the nation's first drug problem. In those days, cocaine use was not stigmatized by society the way it is now. It was illegal, of course, but cocaine use was glamorized. Supposedly, it got you high safely. Its addictive qualities were not fully understood. It was before the "Just Say No" campaign. It was also before crack.

Drugs apparently were messing up baseball as badly as they were messing up society. Dock remembered one Pirate who missed a doubleheader because of his drug use.

"We were in the heat of the race, and one of the players got so loaded he couldn't play a doubleheader, and we needed his bat. He didn't come to the park because he was scared. But that was the last time that happened, because we told him he didn't have to be afraid, that the other guys would pick up the slack. We told him, 'Be scared, but be there.' And after that, he was.'"

After the 1975 season Dock became an ex-Pirate, not because of his drug use, but because Danny Murtaugh sought to make him a relief pitcher.

"I got traded because I refused to go to the bullpen," Ellis said. "Murtaugh tried to get me to go, and I told him, 'I'm not going nowhere.'

"He told me, 'Get off the team.'

"I said, 'Bye.'"

The Pirates fined Ellis $25,000.

When the Pirates went into the playoffs against Cincinnati in 1975, they pitched Ellis exactly two innings in the opening game, when they were way behind.

Maury Wills was broadcasting, and he mentioned that "Dock Ellis is being showcased." Wills said, "He wants to play someplace next year, and he wants to mention to Billy Martin that he wants to play for him." Dock had told that to Wills.

In every case when Dock Ellis takes a stand, he does it for a reason. You may not like the reason, but Dock is not an arbitrary person, and so it was with his refusal to go into the bullpen. History had been his guide.

"I didn't believe in that loyalty crap, no way," Ellis said, "but the thing that the Pirates were overlooking was the fact that I was a black pitcher. I had seen what they had done to black pitchers in the past, like Bob Veale. He went to the bullpen, and that was it. He was gone. I started looking into the record books. I said, 'Veale, if you could have stayed here, man, you could have broken all these motherfucking records.' He was gone. And that wasn't going to happen to me."

In December 1975, Dock, Willie Randolph, and Ken Brett were traded to the New York Yankees for pitcher George "Doc" Medich. Ellis couldn't wait to taste the Big Apple. As everyone knows, the Yankees ooze tradition. One tradition concerns winning pennants and world championships. Another longtime tradition boasts star athletes who loved to party, beginning with the legendary Babe Ruth, and extending through outfielder Bob Meusel, relief pitcher Joe Page, manager Casey Stengel, relief pitcher Ryne Duren, and the triumvirate of Mickey Mantle, Whitey Ford, and Billy Martin.

Martin was back in New York, managing the Yankees. Free from any constraints, Dock Ellis would be in his glory.

CHAPTER

16

Target

In the clubhouse after the tense 15–12 victory over West Palm Beach, the Pelicans were in a happy but surprisingly unemotional mood. After playing one game short of half the season's seventy-two scheduled games, they were 21–14, leading Orlando by a fat four games and Winter Haven and Bradenton by four and a half.

Players wandered to the middle of the narrow clubhouse for the fried chicken and mashed potatoes, eating heartily. Roy Howell, who had gotten three hits against the Tropics that day, was sitting in front of his locker, wearing shorts and an undershirt. His uniform, sweaty and crusted with dirt, sat in disarray in front of him.

On the field Howell was tough and combative. At bat he was selective but his bat had pop. In baseball there are two kinds of third basemen. There are the home-run hitters, the RBI men in the mold of Brooksie and Schmitty. And then there are the Ping-Pong hitters who specialize in defense like Tom Brookens, Randy Velarde, and Wally Backman. Teams desire the former, settle for the latter.

Look what the Mets went through before they finally found a third baseman with pop in Howard Johnson. Since their inception in 1962, they tried scores of candidates ranging alphabetically from Bob Aspromonte to Don Zimmer. Few succeeded. Some came at a high cost. They traded pitcher Nolan Ryan to get third baseman Jim Fregosi. They traded Amos

Otis to get Joey Foy. Ryan and Otis became stars. Fregosi and Foy were busts.

With Howell the Pelicans had pop at the hot corner.

As Howell sat in front of his locker, you could see a ragged path of stitch marks on his left arm.

"How'd you get those?" he was asked.

He smiled. "I got shot," he said.

You have to be tough to play the game. You have to have extra-big ones to stand at third base eighty-five feet from the batter when you're playing in on the grass, risking a whistling line drive at your body or a one-hopper at a hundred and twenty miles an hour that you have to dive into the dust to stab. It isn't easy to face a ninety-mile-an-hour fastball, protected only by a protective helmet covering your head. You have to be tough to survive getting shot.

Before the start of a game Howell would yell out, "Let's play hardball!" When he ran out onto the field, his teammates knew that "hardball" was just what Howell was going to play.

Roy Howell, a tall, blond, mobile chunk of granite, became the embodiment of the Pelican team, a blue-collar performer whose motto was "Strap 'em on. Let's go get 'em!" Howell played mostly for the love of the game, and he prided himself on playing for the team, not for himself, and between the lines he burned with an intensity that was palpable.

Howell was alternately quiet, brash, and contemplative. While you watched him, at the same time you knew he was watching you. He was an observer. He led by doing, not by talking about it.

A fierce competitor, Howell had learned to play hardball as a boy growing up in Lompoc, California, and then refined that ability under one of the masters of that art, Billy Martin, his first major league manager. While they were together at Texas, Billy gave him a Ph.D. course in toughness, intimidation, and mental acuity. If Billy thought a player was weak, Billy would try to destroy him. The tougher you were, the more Billy respected you. Few players had Billy's respect as much as Roy Howell did.

Howell had been a hard-nosed kid all his life. He grew up on a farm about 120 miles northwest of Los Angeles in a rural part of California, where playing sports and hunting became the lifestyle for many youngsters. He got to be 200 pounds in high school, not by lifting weights but by farming and ranching. He was a star in baseball—scouts had followed

The Pelicans

Roy Howell

him since the seventh grade—and he was a bruising fullback, an All-American his junior year at Lompoc High.

He had baseball and football scholarship offers from all the big western jock schools—UCLA, USC, Arizona, Arizona State—but he became a professional baseball player when the Texas Rangers drafted him as their number one pick in 1972. After Dave Roberts, Rick Manning, and Larry Christenson, he was the fourth player picked in the entire draft.

Howell, however, almost missed playing pro ball. A man in a pickup truck tried to murder him on a back road after he had finished hunting one evening.

Howell's nickname is Target. Without knowing the story, one might think it's because he makes such a good target at third. The scar on Howell's left arm says otherwise, and the story says something about the toughness of the man.

After being drafted by the Texas Rangers in 1972 and playing two months of Double A ball, he returned home to Lompoc for some deer hunting. It was the last day of the deer season. Howell and a buddy named Eddie trekked across the high mountains and down into some rough terrain on the other side to hunt. When the day was done, they waited by the side of Highway 1 for friends to pick them up. They were in a cutout in the mountain, just above the highway, their guns unloaded.

A pickup truck passed by. Then it turned around and came back past them. Howell figured it was just another hunter in the area. But the truck returned again, and then again. Finally the driver stopped the truck about fifty yards from where they stood, his headlights marking them. Howell tried to recognize the driver, because he knew almost everyone in the area, but the driver was a stranger. The driver turned the lights off. Then he turned them on again. Then he went to his brights, blinding Howell and his friend Eddie. Then the driver began shooting.

"The first shot hit me in the left arm and flipped me up over backward," Howell said. He and Eddie scrambled for safety into a ditch while the man continued shooting. As the truck started to pull away, Howell sighted his own gun—until he remembered that it was unloaded.

When Roy returned his attention to Eddie, his friend was screaming and hollering. Eddie thought he had been shot in the head. "So," Howell said, "I punched him, threw him over my shoulder, picked up my guns, and I started walking down the white line to find help."

Try to imagine giving a lift to two hitchhikers in camouflage outfits who are covered with blood and carrying guns. Finally a Toyota station wagon stopped, and Howell asked for a ride to a nearby hospital. They were ten miles from Lompoc, fifteen miles from Santa Barbara. The driver agreed to take them to Lompoc.

Howell dragged Eddie into the car, and when Eddie began moaning and groaning, the woman in the car started screaming in terror. There was blood all over the place.

The driver, perhaps in confusion, drove in the wrong direction. Meanwhile, Howell, who had been shot, was tearing Eddie's clothes off, trying to see where he had been hit. Eddie had said he had been hit in the head, and Howell was poking his head, looking for holes. But there were no holes.

The driver offered a flashlight, and when Howell made an inspection, he discovered a gob of his own flesh was on Eddie's head. The shooter had used a deer rifle with hollow-point bullets. On contact Roy's arm had exploded, hitting Eddie in the face with his flesh and blood, blinding him. So Eddie thought he was dying, but he really hadn't been hit at all.

As they rode toward Santa Barbara, Howell suddenly spotted the guy in the truck. He grabbed his gun, but the driver's wife became hysterical. She didn't want a gun battle.

The driver stopped at a gas station. Howell knew the owner. He said, "Call the ambulance and the highway patrol, and report a shooting." Howell gently put Eddie, who was in shock, on the concrete floor, then he went into the bathroom and cut off his jacket. When Howell finally got to look at his arm, he saw that his watch and the bottom part of the arm were in the palm of his hand, and the other part was behind his elbow. There was a seven-inch gap.

Howell somehow sensed he was okay, despite the carnage. "There was no way I could have done what I did, grab Eddie and all," he said. "The shot had hit me on top of the forearm, so it didn't hit any bone. If it had hit my arm underneath the tendons, my baseball career would have been history."

Howell tied himself off and went back to the garage and lay down on the floor, waiting for the ambulance.

When the police came, they rolled Howell on his back and put handcuffs on him. The cop said, "How do I know you guys weren't the ones doing the shooting?"

The police took Howell to a hospital in a little town called Santa Ynez. There was a doctor there by the name of Van Baylen, a master surgeon who had operated all over the world.

"He had just come back from Europe that day," Howell said, "and he was on call. He took a look at my arm, and he said, 'I'm going to put it back together.' With no anesthesia, no nothing, he threw about four hundred stitches into it. He said, 'The tendons are in shock. Everything's all over the place. You have to tell me how you're feeling.'"

Dr. Van Baylen would stitch, and Howell would pick up a finger and it would wiggle. There were hundreds of strings tying everything together.

"When he took all the strings and pulled it straight up, everything in my arm came back together," Howell said. "He sewed me up and put a cast on it and said, 'I'll see ya in the morning.' Howell didn't know it at the time, but his aunt had once stuck her hand through a window, and the broken pane of glass came down and cut much of her nose off, and Dr. Van Baylen had put it back on. "You couldn't even tell," Howell said.

The next day Howell left the hospital. Three weeks later he took off the cast. Howell wiggled his hand, and he went off to spring training.

"About two weeks after I took the cast off," Howell said, "I went duck hunting in Mendota County, and some guy shot me in the back. But that's another story."

Roy Howell has always believed in integrity. Spike Lee and he would have gotten along famously. Howell always did the right thing.

Whatever he's doing, there is a right way and a wrong way. If you play ball with Howell, you had better play it the right way. You'd better hit the cutoff man, better cover your base, move the runner, and run the bases intelligently. Fundamental baseball to Roy Howell has always been the key to playing the game right. It was that way for Howell since childhood, when he realized he had talent for the game.

In the three years he played for Lompoc High School, the team's record was 91–12. Seven of those losses came his first year. Each year Lompoc High played in the Southern California finals. Among his teammates were Roy Thomas, who later pitched for Houston, St. Louis, and the Seattle Mariners; Dave Stegman, an All-American at Arizona who made it to the majors with Detroit, the Yankees, and the White Sox; Monte Bolinger, who played in the minors for the St. Louis Cardinals; and his younger brother Russ, who played with the Detroit Lions. Mike Brotz, who became a professional basketball player, was also on the team.

"We had great teams—baseball, basketball, football. We all played together," Howell said.

In the June 1972 major league baseball draft, San Diego had the first pick and chose another third baseman, Dave Roberts, who went directly to the major leagues. Before the draft San Diego had asked Howell whether he would be interested in doing the same.

A young man who evidenced maturity beyond his years, Howell told the San Diego scouts, "I'm eighteen years old. I love playing the game. But you would be doing me a big disservice to take me out of high school and give me a few weeks in the minors and take me to the big leagues." He said, "I don't think that would work." Howell didn't think it was fair to him or to them.

"I was no dummy," Howell said. "I had been around enough to know that the game isn't that easy. I didn't want to put that kind of pressure on myself."

When it was Texas's turn, the team chose Howell. The Rangers had just moved from Washington, D.C., and the Lompoc native didn't even know who the hell the Texas Rangers were.

"Being very honest," Howell said, "I couldn't have named all the teams in the majors then. I grew up in a part of California where my dad listened to the Dodgers. We were too busy playing, and I didn't pay that much attention. I was not a baseball fan. I didn't collect autographs or baseball cards."

Instead, Howell was a *player*. His attitude was "You want to play hardball? Let's go."

The Texas Rangers offered Howell $40,000, and he accepted. The signing took place on a Wednesday. The scouts told him, "We'll see you Friday." Howell was being sent to A ball.

Most ballplayers, young and old, do as they are told, believing that a reputation for insubordination can hamper or damage a career. From the start Roy Howell didn't worry about the politics. He stuck up for himself.

Howell informed them, "Before I put my signature on this, I want you to know that I won't be there for two weeks." His father and uncles had planned a hunting expedition into the High Sierras on horseback, and Roy intended to join them.

He told the scouts, "We're heading for the mountains, man."

They said, "Oh no, no, no."

Roy said, "And besides that, I'm starting in Double A, not Single A." After all, the Padres had wanted him to begin in Triple A.

The Rangers didn't think he was ready to play at the Double A level. They told him, "You can't do that."

"That's what I want to do," Howell insisted.

They said, "You can't."

"That's what I want to do," Howell replied. "I'm not going to waste your time, and I'm not going to waste my time. Either I can play or I can't. The question is whether I can make the adjustment. That's what the game is all about."

Finally the Rangers agreed. Roy went to the mountains. Two weeks later he reported to the Rangers' Double A Pittsfield, Massachusetts, team.

Howell's home in Lompoc was near Vandenberg Air Force Base. Planes flew overhead all the time. But when it came time for Roy to fly to join the team, it was the first time he had ever been on an airplane.

Howell arrived in the middle of a game against Elmira. About the fourth inning he was sitting by the water cooler in the dugout when his manager, Joe Klein, kicked the water cooler, broke the glass, and dumped water all over Howell.

Later in the game, Klein barked, "Grab a bat." Howell hadn't had a bat in his hands in over two weeks. The bat was marked "R-43." Roy had never seen a bat designated that way before. His whole life the bats had players' names on them. *Where's the Mickey Mantle model?* he wondered. Howell went up to hit with his R-43, and on the first pitch he got a base hit up the middle. The lesson in humility would follow.

Howell said, "We were still wearing wool at the time, and the uniform I got was so big my number was tucked into my pants and the crotch in my pants was hanging down to my knees. On the next pitch, the batter hit a ground ball. I started to run. My pants were down so low I got hung up and fell down. All the guys were just busting out, laughing their asses off."

This was the first test for Roy Howell. How would he react to the ribbing?

Howell said, "I laughed about it, and the guys saw I was laughing, that it wasn't that serious to me. The game was never that serious to me. It was something I enjoyed doing. That's the only reason I play it."

His biggest adjustment in the minor leagues was learning to hit the slider, a pitch he rarely saw in high school. In his two months in Pittsfield, he got his feet wet.

The next year Howell went to spring training and made the Double A Pittsfield club on merit. He hit 15 home runs and had 47 RBIs. He was improving.

He learned the importance of not getting too high, not getting too low. He saw how unjust the game could be, when several of the players seemed talented enough to make the big leagues but never got a chance. Howell was particularly disappointed when the team's first baseman, Tommy Robinson, who had good numbers, was never called up to the big leagues.

"I suspect it was because he didn't *look* like a ballplayer," Howell said. He thought, *There is so much injustice here that you can't worry about anyone else but yourself as far as what happens on the field.* But Howell thought the injustices to be "horrendous." It upset him greatly because his dad had taught him that if you do your best job on a daily basis, no matter whether you're digging a ditch or hitting a fastball, and you are the best, you will win the job. He learned that his father was wrong when that standard is applied to professional baseball—and to many other arenas of professional life as well.

"That was the single hardest thing for me to adjust to," Howell said, "watching guys who could play, watching how well they played, and then watching them not get the chance."

After the 1973 season, Howell went to the Instructional League in Plant City, Florida, with Mike Hargrove, Jim Sundberg, and Mike Cubbage. Only the best of the team's prospects got invited to this special teaching session. The manager of the Texas Rangers, Billy Martin, was down there watching pitcher Bruce Kison, who was trying to come back after an injury. Kison pitched against Howell and the others.

After the game Billy walked up to Howell and his fellow players. "I'll see you guys in the big league camp," Martin said.

In 1974 everyone stayed with Billy and the Rangers except Howell. He was the last guy cut. That year Howell played Triple A ball for Spokane, where he hit 22 home runs, drove in 80 runs, and hit .281. Howell came to the majors for the first time at the end of that season. He played some and hit a little, impressing Martin enough that he was given the Texas third-base job the next season.

"He realized I was a hardball player," Howell said.

Martin had a reputation for being tough on young kids. But Howell, only twenty-one, says he had no trouble at all.

"I had played for Spokane in 1974, and we won the Pacific Coast League. We had a bathtub full of beer when it was over. We went after it pretty hard. Hadn't been in bed for two days. In Albuquerque I was told, 'Meet us in Texas.' I flew to Arlington, Texas, to wait for the team to return from the road.

"But after I walked into my hotel room at the Roadway Inn the phone rang. 'We want you in Anaheim tonight.' I packed my bags, got on the plane, and flew to Anaheim. I walked in, hadn't slept in two days, set my bags down, and I was told, 'Billy wants to see you in his office.'"

Howell met Martin in his cubicle under the stadium. Martin handed the youngster the lineup card. Billy said, "We're playing a doubleheader, and you're playing both of them."

Howell was not fazed. He thought, *All right, let's go!*

Howell recalled, "That was Billy instilling confidence in me. He wanted to see what I was made of."

"I had heard that Billy Martin was tough on young players, that he preferred experience and knowledge. I heard he expected the game to be played the way he had played it. Which I had no problem with. I'm a dirtbag, and I enjoy playing the game."

Martin saw that Howell knew how to play the game, that he wasn't going to have to teach him the fundamentals.

"That took away the little bit of the youth bullshit that Billy always had trouble with," Howell said.

Even though the Rangers had a veteran-oriented ballclub, Billy gave his kids, including Howell, Mike Cubbage, Jim Sundberg, and Mike Hargrove, the opportunity to play.

Howell sought to gain the respect of the veterans by busting his ass on the field and enjoying himself off it. When they played pranks on him, such as the times he found his spikes nailed to the locker room floor or his glove filled with shaving cream, he laughed. One day the vets cut the stitches in the crotch of his pants. He stepped onto the bus, and his pants ripped all the way up his crotch. He had to take off his coat and tie it around his waist. He laughed. Another time Fergie Jenkins put a black bullsnake in his locker. Howell reached in to grab his glove and felt the head of the snake. He nearly tore his locker in half, trying to get out of there.

If the veterans were tough, Howell's greatest challenge was to anticipate the moods and moves of his quixotic manager, Billy Martin.

"Billy always had a love-hate relationship with his players," Howell said. "You love him or you hate him. He would build you up to the biggest thing since bubble gum and then tear you down and see how you'd react. Today you're the greatest, tomorrow you're the lowest piece of shit on earth. How do you handle that? By doing your job on a daily basis."

What bothered his players most was Billy's unpredictability.

"He would test you tremendously," Howell said. "There would be no explanation for what he did, and you'd be hot.

"You'd be playing every day, and suddenly you wouldn't be playing for a week. The next time you went out and played, maybe you'd be facing

Sparky Lyle in the ninth. Billy wanted to know: 'What kind of balls you got, kid?'"

But Billy was tough on you only if you let him be. Roy Howell knew how to deal with Billy Martin. He only let Billy go so far. If Billy stepped over the line, Howell would go face-to-face. That's why Martin respected his young third baseman. Billy always wanted to know about a player: "Will you stand and fight or turn and run?"

When Howell came up to the Rangers, he wore number twenty-seven, but he had been wearing number thirteen in the minor leagues and nobody was wearing thirteen at Texas, so he walked up to Billy at the batting cage and asked to switch uniforms.

Billy said, "Nobody wears thirteen on my ball club."

Howell looked him right straight in the eye and said, "Why, are you scared?"

Everyone turned around and looked at Howell, and Billy just looked back and started laughing. Martin replied, "Go get the fucking number. I don't give a shit." So Howell wore number thirteen.

Billy Martin motivated the team by fear. He let his players know: "Either you do it my way, or I have the ability and the power to get rid of you."

Some of the veterans were intimidated by Billy as much as the youngsters, but a player who has been around long enough is usually hard to manipulate. He knows the ropes. Howell had a course in watching the Texas vets handle Billy.

"They shut Billy off," Howell said. "Just like you do your mom and dad. In one ear and out the other. What a player wants from a manager is for him to make the appropriate move, to do what he needs to do, and most of the time Billy made the moves when he was supposed to. He was a good tactician. He knew what to do. But when he made the right move, and we still gave it up, then he snapped, and *nobody* would be safe. He would start at one end of the bench and go to the other end and talk about anything that he thought the players should have been doing during the last month. He would start on anybody about anything and just go down the line. And when we came off the field, he'd go up and down on us. It's like a mom or dad, an uncle or an aunt, constantly hooting on you. You get to the point that you just don't listen to it."

If you could do that, you'd be okay. If you took it personally, Billy would get to you. Catcher Jim Sundberg, a young player, let Billy get to him. Sundberg had come from Double A and began playing when catcher

Bill Fahey broke his nose. Sundberg was impressionable, and Billy abused him badly.

"If the pitcher made a bad pitch, it was the pitcher's fault *and* Sunny's fault," Howell said. "If there was an 0–2 base hit, the pitcher got fined $500 and so did Sunny."

Even when the pitcher did exactly what Billy wanted him to do, Sundberg was blamed. One day Jackie Brown, a curveball pitcher, came into the game, and Billy said, "Don't throw anything but curveballs." And in the seventh Willie Horton hit a curveball out of the park. Billy was furious at Brown and Sundberg.

"That was the hardest thing for the guys, but you couldn't let it get to you," Howell said. "It did, of course, if you were human. So Sunny turned gray real quick and began drinking scotch."

Ownership is the reason a franchise fails to win year after year. To win, an owner must hire a smart baseball executive, who then hires an effective field manager. An owner's got to keep his nose out of the baseball executive's business. In Texas, ownership always meddled. In Texas, owners always sabotaged success.

Billy Martin took the Texas Rangers to a second-place finish in 1974, finishing five games behind a powerful Oakland A's team. It was an extraordinary achievement for the fiery manager, taking the perennial loser, formerly in Washington and then in Texas, to heights never before attained by the franchise.

In 1975 the club faltered. At the same time, the Rangers management began trading away some of their best young kids for veteran players with name recognition.

"We didn't know if it was Billy's thing for veterans or whether it was the front office, but when you walked into the clubhouse the first thing you did was look at your locker to see if your stuff was packed," Howell said.

In midseason Billy was fired.

"When Billy left, it was traumatic," Howell said. "Baseball can be a cruel, cruel game. The way Billy got fired—the backstabbing by coach Frank Lucchesi—that's all history. Lucchesi was the type of guy who would go around the back door of a thing, and that's what he'd been doing, chirping on Billy. 'Billy's been doing this. Billy's been doing that.'

"Danny O'Brien was the general manager. Lucchesi would tell him,

'Billy's the whole problem' . . . and this and that, and so what are they going to do? They can't fire the whole ball club, so you fire the manager. Billy went to the Yankees after that.

"And when Billy left, the reaction of the ball club was 'We're in trouble.' Guys didn't have the confidence in Frank. He was a good third-base coach. He knew his business over there, but Frank managed with his feelings, instead of with knowledge. Billy did both. Billy would say, 'I believe this is going to happen,' but it was an educated risk.

"Frank would say, 'This is gonna happen. I just know it is,' and he'd make a move that way."

Ballplayers aren't comfortable with managers who make decisions arbitrarily or emotionally. Lucchesi did both.

"Baseball is its own monster," Howell said. "If you do it in the right form and fashion, everything is predictable. If the count is two-and-one, three-and-one, you know you've got to hit-and-run. You know when to pitch out. But Frank would manage away from that."

One day after Howell had gotten three hits and driven in all the runs against a left-handed pitcher, he came up in the ninth with the score tied and two outs. On the first pitch he took a good swing and fouled the pitch off. Another pitch, another foul.

Lucchesi called time out and sent up Gene Clines to pinch-hit for Howell. Clines chopped a ball that landed behind the pitcher and drove in the winning run, but to Howell that was irrelevant. Lucchesi had shown him up, and he was furious.

Howell stormed into his office and told him how he felt. And Howell was not the only one who was angry. Lucchesi's managing didn't set well with the other players, especially with those men who were loyal to Billy Martin and who couldn't forgive Lucchesi for being the catalyst to Martin's ouster.

Lucchesi, who apparently held grudges, in the spring of 1977 made it clear to two of Billy's biggest supporters, Howell and Lenny Randle, that no matter how well they played, he was not going to play them.

Howell said, "Frank came up to Lenny Randle and me, and he said, 'I don't care if you guys hit a thousand in spring training and make every play, you're not gonna play.'"

How can you say that in spring training? There was only one explanation: vindictiveness.

"Lenny and I were both gamers, like Billy, and Frank didn't like us *because* we were gamers," Howell said. "We played the way the game was supposed to be played, and Frank managed by feelings. We didn't like that. Frank felt he didn't have any control over us, and our contracts were up, and they wouldn't even negotiate with us.

"Frank got into it on a personal basis, let his personal feelings get in the way of his professionalism. Lenny's wife was helping to negotiate his contract at that point, and Frank was making racial comments on the bench and in the papers."

Lucchesi didn't flat-out say, "I don't like black people." What he did was continually call Lenny "a punk."

"Lenny is not a punk," Howell said. "And where Lenny grew up on his side of L.A., it's not said in a good sense."

Randle told Lucchesi, "It's nothing personal. Keep the personal bullshit out of this, and let's just do what we need to do." But Lucchesi just kept needling him all the time. He'd say, "Hey, punk, go do this," or "Hey punk, go do that.'"

Lenny, who resented being called a punk and felt Lucchesi was using the term because he was black, finally told him to knock it off or he would do something about it.

"He pushed Lenny too far," Howell said.

In Orlando during spring training, a reporter and radio broadcaster were interviewing Lucchesi. Howell and Randle were standing on the field nearby, getting ready to play catch. During the interview, Frank again called Lenny a punk.

Howell recalled, "Lenny just turned and hit him one shot right to the cheekbone, and that was all. One punch. That was it. Lenny took off running toward the outfield. He was caged, and he just started running."

Lucchesi went down hard. The manager sued Randle in court in Florida. The case went to trial. When Billy Martin came in to testify, the case was dropped.

"Frank was a little man with a little man's complex," Howell said. "He just pushed a man too far. He's lucky he didn't get hurt worse. Lenny's mistake was doing it in public. If he was in Frank's office, it would have been a black eye and see you later. No witnesses. But it went to trial, and then Billy arrived, and now you're coming back to how Frank got the job in the first place. So the shit would have hit the fan, and that was it."

In 1977 the Texas Rangers brought in Bert Campaneris to play shortstop and moved Toby Harrah to third base. Howell found himself on Frank Lucchesi's bench, as promised. He was twenty-four years old. Howell, who got seventeen at-bats that year in Texas, told the Rangers, "I won't sit here. I'm history. I've got to play."

Howell gave Dan O'Brien fifteen days to trade him or else he threatened to quit.

"I promised Dan O'Brien that I would bust my ass and do whatever I was asked. He promised he'd trade me by the end of the first month," Howell said. "When the month was up, I was heading out the door. O'Brien stopped me."

Howell said, "Have I kept my end?"

"Yeah."

"Well, a deal's a deal."

"You can't walk out on a three-year contract," O'Brien said.

"Oh, sure I can, because my word is what it is. Your word isn't. And I don't want to play for anyone who can't keep his word."

The game ended, and Howell returned to Texas, where he was called into the office of Ranger owner Brad Corbett. Howell had just signed a three-year contract with the Rangers, but the reason he signed it was the promise on the part of the Rangers that if he did so, the team would trade him.

Corbett showed him the contract. "Is this your contract?" he asked. Howell looked at it and said it was.

Corbett pulled out another one and handed it to Howell. All the numbers were doubled.

"Would that make you stay?" Corbett asked.

Howell tore it up and handed it back to him. Two days later Howell was traded.

For Roy Howell principle comes first, everything else second.

Some players just sit back and take it when a manager does them wrong. Not Roy Howell. When he saw Texas manager Frank Lucchesi wasn't going to play him, he acted. He told his former Texas teammate, Bill Singer, who was by then in Toronto, that he was available. Howell knew that Toronto needed a third baseman who could hit. In May of 1977 Howell was traded to Toronto, where he hit in his first fifteen games and finished the season with a .316 average.

One might have thought Howell would have been happy in his new situation. He played every day. Just the opposite was true. Howell always had been a player who cared much more about the success of his team than any personal feats. He found himself on a team that lost around a hundred games year after year, and what he found most frustrating was that his manager, Roy Hartsfield, was the diametric opposite of Lucchesi. Hartsfield *always* went by the book. He managed in such a conservative way that he was totally predictable in his moves and never did anything that might creatively generate some runs. Hartsfield's lack of imagination or spark drove Howell crazy.

"God, the other team just knew everything we were going to do," Howell said. "My wife would sit in the stands and knew when we were going to hit-and-run and when we were going to steal and pitch out. It was automatic, and we never varied from it.

"I came in dirty and bloody every single day, knowing that tomorrow I was going out there with an 85 percent chance of losing. And after four years of that, it takes a tremendous strain on you mentally. Especially when the guys I was playing with on Toronto were outstanding athletes, competitors to the hilt, and all we wanted was a little help. We never got it."

For the next three years the Blue Jays lost more than a hundred games a season. Howell says he remembers every one of them.

"Over that period we lost something like 50 percent of them by a run or two. Just give us ten of those games a year and we'd have been competitive."

Howell, unable to stand it any longer, went to talk to Hartsfield about his strategy. Players discover that suggestions are seen as criticisms or second-guesses. Managers do not like suggestions. They take them personally. Howell went anyway.

He said, "Roy, we're losing a hundred games a year. Can we hit-and-run once today maybe? Who cares? Let's do something different. We're gonna lose anyway."

Of course, Hartsfield didn't like that. The Blue Jays kept doing what they were doing, and the losses mounted.

Toronto, an expansion franchise, was so thin in players that in spring training of 1978 Howell played every inning of every exhibition game at third base, getting over 120 at-bats.

At the end of the season the Blue Jays regulars would wear out. The team would nosedive. Having to play the strong Eastern Division clubs— New York, Boston, Milwaukee, and Baltimore—the last month also contributed to the end-of-year swoon.

To battle the pressures brought on by losing so much, the Blue Jays sought to make the best of it through jokes and levity.

Most teams have a highlight film. Because the Jays lost so often, the players thought it appropriate that they stress the lowlights. Every time a photo of a Blue Jay doing something stupid appeared in the paper, it got hung in Tim Johnson's locker. It became known as the "Wall of Shame."

One day General Manager Peter Bavasi came into the clubhouse and ripped it down. Howell thought that the move was pathetic.

"Management doesn't understand the mental capacity it takes to go out there on a daily basis and get your ass kicked, and so you have to have releases," he said. "You have to have things to laugh about."

After Howell's third year at Toronto, the Jays fired Roy Hartsfield and brought in Bobby Mattick. It didn't help.

"Bobby had never managed a game in his life until he took over that job. That was not pretty either," Howell said.

Nevertheless, Howell says he wouldn't trade his experience in Toronto "for anything."

"It was like raising a new child. My regret is not being there when it grew up."

The reason Howell wasn't there had to do with a contract renegotiation and extension requested not by Howell but by Peter Bavasi. Howell had signed a three-year contract, and when Bavasi asked him to renegotiate, offering him more money, Howell wanted to know why.

"Because you had a good year," Bavasi said.

Howell said, "Thank you, I appreciate it, but I'll live up to my contract. I'll wait till after the third year, and then we can negotiate the option."

Howell had no ulterior motives for rejecting Bavasi's advances. But once Howell refused to capitulate, the Toronto general manager evidently held it against Howell. Roy Howell became Peter Bavasi's whipping boy.

In 1979 Roy Howell was the Blue Jay Player of the Year. Usually the Blue Jays have a big ceremony. That year Howell had to ask for his trophy, and they sent it in the mail.

And after his contract expired, Howell wasn't offered another one by Toronto. He went to arbitration, won it, and after 1980 was a free agent. Roy was the first Toronto player to go to arbitration and the first one to be declared a free agent.

Toronto permitted Howell to leave, even though management didn't have anyone to replace him at third. "It was a matter of principle between myself and Bavasi. Peter told me, 'We're going to lose with you or without you.'"

Howell was selected by five teams, including the Milwaukee Brewers. Some of the Brewer players called him to tout the benefits of playing with the Brew Crew. They said that with him, the Brewers had a chance to be winners, which was all Roy Howell had to hear.

Brewers officials promised Howell the opportunity to play every day at third base. Unfortunately for ballplayers, promises like that mean nothing. Once a player signs his contract and accepts his salary, a team has license to screw around with him any way it sees fit. Howell never did play every day in Milwaukee.

"It's called baseball—to the max," Howell said. "What they say and what they do are two different things."

The Brewers had intended to move Paul Molitor from third base to the outfield to open up the position. They wanted to put the talented Molitor out there so he wouldn't get hurt, but it turned out he was in greater jeopardy in the outfield. Brewer management looked around the infield, and since Howell was the new kid on the block, Molitor returned to third. Howell then found himself platooning, and after that sat on the bench as insurance for indestructibles. Roy Howell had outsmarted himself. For the rest of his career he would either platoon or languish on the Brewer bench, dying a ballplayer's slow death when the Brewers refused to trade him.

In 1981 the Brewers had the best record in baseball. Then came the strike. At the end they still had the best record but lost the miniseries to New York. The next year the Brewers won the playoffs and lost the World Series in the seventh game.

In postseason play Howell played little. In the World Series he was the Brewer's designated hitter. He would have preferred to have been out in the field as well. The World Series had been his goal for his entire career, and when he finally got there in 1982 against the St. Louis Cardinals, he didn't get a single hit in eleven at-bats.

In 1983 Roy Howell was a bench fixture. He was ready if needed, but Molitor was a fixture at third. At age thirty, when most players are in their prime, Howell that year played exactly two games in the field. He provided insurance again in 1984, a role he filled in the Philadelphia farm system in 1985 and in the Pittsburgh farm system in 1986. With the Pirates he was supposed to be a backup for a phenom, but Howell proved more talented than the phenom.

"This time," Howell said, "the Pirates released me because I was clearly better than the kid."

Howell swore he was through.

Until the offer from the St. Petersburg Pelicans came along. He would play again—one more time.

"It's baseball like it ought to be," Howell said. "There's no politics in this league," he said. "It's just pure baseball. Strap 'em on. Let's go get 'em!"

CHAPTER

17

Kangaroo Court

While the bus traveled back to St. Pete from West Palm Beach, Chief Judge Lenny Randle convened the one Pelican Kangaroo Court of the season. To be a judge on a team's Kangaroo Court is a high honor for a player. Kangaroo Court serves as a vehicle for humor and playfulness, but only the most respected teammates get to be judges. On the Pittsburgh Pirates of the 1970s, for instance, Pop Stargell became the judge. On the San Francisco Giants, it was Willie McCovey. Don Baylor served as the judge for the Oakland A's.

For the last two weeks Randle and his assistant judges, Jon Matlack and Steve Kemp, had been collecting a list of sins perpetrated by players, primarily obtained from teammates who had ratted on them. With the two-out-of-three mastery of powerful West Palm Beach under their belts, the time and mood were right for "court" to be called in session.

The procedure was simple. The Chief Judge read the charges. The accused player could find someone to defend him or stand up and defend himself. The rest of the players served as the jury. Guilt or innocence was declared by voice vote. The fine for each transgression was one dollar. The money would go toward a team party at a later date. The object was not the money, but rather to embarrass the player in front of the whole team. This was silly time, a chance for a group of semi-adults to act like kids again.

Kangaroo Court wasn't much more sophisticated than child's play. But for two hours, everyone laughed as the miles melted away on the roads back toward St. Petersburg.

Lenny Randle called the meeting to order. "All right, we got court in session." The players sat up in their seats, took off the Walkmans, put away their books.

"We might as well start at the top," Randle said. "We got Sosa for being the first guy diving into the spread."

There was a titter of laughter. It was not a new allegation. If you recall, Sosa led the all-star list of players who attack the table of food put out after the game.

Randle continued, "Every day for five days in a row." There was a roar of laughter.

Sitting toward the front, Elias Sosa turned around to face Randle. He had a hurt expression. He was gesticulating, as if to say the charges were grossly overexaggerated.

"Sosa, do you have a lawyer?"

From the front of the bus Lee Sosa rose to stand in the aisle.

"I'm going to defend myself," Sosa said. There was more laughter. To defend yourself is to invite added abuse. Slowly Sosa began his defense. "That's...not...true," he said. More laughter. "Yesterday I was third at the spread." Laughter. "Today I wasn't the first either."

"What about at home before we left—twice?" Randle asked.

Sosa replied, "No, I was not the first. I may have looked the first, I don't know why, but Mr. Randy Lerch was first."

A roar. Everyone looked to the back of the bus for Lerch. Lerch was vigorously shaking his head.

"Lerch beat you to the spread?" Randle asked. "You trying to reverse these charges, or what?"

"He is always ahead of me," Sosa said.

"Randy Lerch to the floor," Randle said. "Randy Lerch, defend yourself."

Lerch tried to be judicial. "There has to be a charge," he said. "Who wrote me up?"

Lenny said, "Wilcox wrote you up. And Sambito got you today, and Ferrer got you for yesterday."

Sosa had successfully taken the spotlight off himself and put it on Lerch. The lefty pitcher attempted the same ruse.

"Sergio," yelled Lerch, "is it true that you took seven pieces of chicken off the first fucking helping today?"

Lerch had sinned. He had usurped Randle's assigned role as accuser. It didn't get past Jon Matlack, who piped up, "That's a dollar on you, Lerch, for stepping in."

"A dollar on Lerch," repeated Randle, who wasn't going to let the focus of the investigation shift again. Lerch clearly was the preferred target.

A chorus voted to fine Lerch a dollar. After their verdict of "Him! Him! Fuck him!" there was great laughter. It was time to get back to Sosa.

Randle asked, "Hey, Matlack, what do you think about Sosa?"

Matlack replied, "Who wrote him up?"

"We have Wilcox, Sambito, Ferrer."

Steve Kemp jumped in. "Do you have a witness, Sose, who says you weren't the first one at the spread? We need to have a witness."

Roy Howell shouted from the back, "There was no one up there besides Sose!" Again there was laughter.

Lenny said, "He denies it three times, but that leaves two other times."

The chorus rang out: "Him! Him! Fuck him!"

Randle decreed, "Sosa, that will cost you a buck . . . and another buck for wasting court time."

Sosa paid the two dollars.

The next target was David Chavez, the clubhouse manager. A clubhouse manager is always a convenient target. He has a million things to do every day. Once in a blue moon Chevy would come up short in the players' eyes.

Randle said, "We got Chevy for having weak Gatorade. Guys were sweating like pigs. And no towels in the clubhouse."

Chevy asked, "At home or on the road?"

A chorus of voices shouted, "Doesn't matter!"

Chevy, who knew it was best to pay the dollar and keep his mouth shut, said, "I plead guilty." To let them know his guilty plea lacked conviction, he added, "I'll be the convenient scapegoat."

Randle wanted more. "That's two bucks, a dollar per crime."

"I'm guilty." Chevy knew the quicker he pleaded guilty, the quicker they would go on to someone else. To escape the heat, Chevy gladly coughed up the money.

Relief pitcher Joe Sambito was the next target.

Randle said, "Matlack has Sambito spilling coffee on Kemp during a game and talking too much with fans in the bullpen. They said you were doing a radio show down there with the fans during the game."

Chevy yelled out, "Joe, you want to run for office some day. Don't be grandstanding!"

Lenny: "We'll take them one at a time. First one, spilling coffee on Kemp."

Sambito: "I am guilty of that."

Lenny: "They are accusing you of grandstanding with the fans in the bullpen during the game."

Sambito: "Who brought it up?"

Lenny: "Tex."

Sambito: "Where is Tex?"

"He's not here." Tex was driving his van and wasn't on the bus.

Sambito: "If my accuser isn't here..." If the accuser was not present, the charge would be thrown out.

David Chavez didn't want Sambito to get off just because his chief accuser wasn't on the bus. Chevy shouted, "I'll stand in for Tex!"

"Whoa, whoa, whoa, whoa, whoa," Sambito protested.

Steve Kemp said to Chavez, "You are going to take Tex's spot?"

Chavez said, "I saw Joe propped up against the wall of the dugout, rapping to the fans, signing shit, talking. I don't know exactly what he was doing, but he wasn't watching the game."

Sambito explained: "I was spreading goodwill."

There was great laughter. The players were impressed with Sambito's quick thinking.

"That's a good one," Lamar Johnson said with a smile.

Sambito, buoyed by their reaction, added, "I was giving away free baseballs, hoping they will be repeat customers."

Lenny said, "Due to your good public relations and Tex not being here and Chavez coming out of 'Star Search' with nothing to do with it, Chevy is fined a dollar. A 'Him!' on Chevy."

"Him! Him! Fuck him!" rang the chorus.

Lenny moved on. "We got Hendu?"

Outfielder Steve Henderson shot up from his seat like he had been ejected. "Hendu for what?" he asked gruffly.

Lenny looked at the sheet of paper. Sheepishly, he realized that he was reading a charge made by Henderson that he, Lenny, had forgotten how many outs there were during one of the recent games and had begun to run off the field when first baseman Gary Rajsich stopped him.

Randle skipped to the defense. He said, "Hendu, I knew how many outs there were. There were two outs. I was telling Gary to make sure there wasn't a bunt, because Rodney Scott might bunt."

That too was quick thinking, but Henderson wasn't buying the rationale. He knew Randle had forgotten. "Don't give me that shit," he said. "You ran off. You were all the way over to the first-base line. But Gary stopped you. Gary said, 'Whoa, wait a minute.'"

Kemp tried to stick up for his fellow judge. "Hendu, let him have his say."

Lenny pressed his defense. "I went over to say, 'Watch out, this guy will definitely lay one down, and he doesn't care how many outs there are with a man on third.'"

The explanation was blatantly absurd, and the rest of the players howled in disbelief. They hooted, laughed, and finally chanted the guilty verdict: "Him! Him! Fuck him!" And more laughter followed.

The next target was a team favorite, trainer Brian Ebel. Even though Ebes, as he was called, was in his midtwenties, he was going bald, something the players reminded him about every day. He would take the few hairs he had left and try to arrange them on his head, and the players would always muss up his handiwork. Ebes was a lousy golfer, and they gave him grief about that too. He was very sensitive and defensive, so he made the perfect foil.

Lenny read off the charges. "We got a fine on Brian Ebel for sending Tex out to get the red-hot during a game. We got Brian for weak therapy for Bombo Rivera. We got Brian for no hat and then not wanting to go out on the field. We got him for hotdogging, suntanning, no hustle, and then shaving and looking for puss during the game." He paused. "We'll take them one at a time."

"What happened, Ebes?" yelled one player.

"You don't have a chance," said another.

"Ebes, what happened, Ebes?"

"One at a time."

Lenny said, "You sent Tex out to the mall to get the red-hot because you didn't feel like getting it."

Ebes: "I'm pleading not guilty on that."

Matlack: "You didn't send him out? He went on his own?"

Ebes: "The night before, when he left the game, he said he would pick some up."

Lenny: "Is that Tex's duty to do that?"

"It was strictly volunteer," Ebel said. "No one asked him to. Come

Saturday, when I asked him, he said, 'No, I forgot.' And all of a sudden he left. I didn't ask him. He went on his own."

The players couldn't figure out which of the two was less responsible, Ebel or Tex, so they went on to the next "charge," knowing eventually they'd get him.

Lenny: "We're back to the weak therapy for Bombo. Bombo said he's been getting weak therapy, no ice, no treatment, that you're just here on a vacation, checking puss, not being responsible..."

Ebes said with a serious face: "Not guilty on that one."

Someone called out, "Hey, Bombo!" Bombo was wearing a little round beanie on his head.

Randle asked him, "Hey, Bombo, were you an extra in *The Golden Child?*" The reference was to Eddie Murphy's dreadful movie in which Murphy wore a beanie similar to Bombo's. The bus erupted in laughter.

Bombo wasn't laughing. His legs were hurting him, and he was annoyed with Ebel, just as Sergio had been. Bombo tried to explain, "He got the ma-cheen. I be looking for you. I on time, and after he finished with the ma-cheen..."

"The what?"

"The ma-cheen."

Bombo continued. "I was supposed to get some heat on my leg to get it warm for the game. But he didn't do nothing. He said, 'That's it, Bombo,' so I just go out on the field, and you know..."

Ebes: "Not guilty on that. Due to the physiological injury to Bombo's left hamstring, the injury to his biceps where he had minute microchips. I noticed Bombo had a grade-two strain of that muscle." Ebel was rambling on, using medical terms. The players couldn't stand it any longer.

"That's enough," Kemp shouted. "The court's heard enough."

Matlack warned, "The fine's going to be triple. It's going to be triple."

Ebes refused to be cowed. "Let me finish," he pleaded.

Jon Matlack refused to let him say another word. "Ebes, we got you for contempt for faking intellectuality." The laughter built. Everyone began talking at once. There was a cacophony of sounds like crickets. It was impossible to understand a single word the players were saying, except to know it was all directed derisively at Ebes.

Ebes, meanwhile, fended off the charges and accusations with his hands, as though they were mosquitoes. "Whoa, whoa, whoa, whoa," he kept saying.

Matlack ordered, "Double the fine. Let's vote."

Led by Lenny, all the players found Brian Ebel guilty with a chorus of "Him! Him! Fuck him!" There was great laughter.

Lenny stayed on Ebes's case. He said, "The next charge is, Ebes, a guy gets hurt on the field. You don't even make an attempt to take two steps to go out onto the field to check the guy. Everybody's going, 'Where's Brian!' Brian is in the clubhouse, having coffee, listening to the Top Twenty from Kasey Kasem. Okay, you want to defend yourself?"

Everyone laughed. They knew Brian wasn't glib enough to keep the vultures off his back.

Ebel replied, "Yeah, not guilty on that." His answer brought raucous laughter. Of course, he ended up being found guilty. Reluctantly, Ebel paid his fine.

Lenny's next target was pitcher Milt Wilcox, who wasn't on the bus. Milt was driving his van to his condo in Lakeland. Milt took his cocker spaniel with him wherever he went. Some of the players were getting tired of having the pooch around.

Lenny said, "Randy, you have Wilcox for having a dog in the clubhouse, a dog on the field, a dog in his room for a roommate, and you're baby-sitting his kids."

Lamar yelled out, "Randy is used to having dogs for roommates!" The bus rocked with laughter.

Kemp: "The court will save this one so we can hear what Milt has to say."

Lenny said, "Wilcox got Tex and his girl for impersonating seals in a whirlpool at the hotel."

Lenny: "We'll save that one. Okay." Pause. "Hendu."

Roy Howell, knowing the answer, shouted: "Where's Hendu?" As usual, Hendu was listening to music on his Walkman. Someone yelled, "He's holding his own court, man!"

Hendu took off his headset. Randle said to him, "Hendu, I understand when we said we were going to have Kangaroo Court, you said, 'Fuck all the judges.'"

Hendu, who was even more sensitive than Ebes, quickly sprang to his own defense. "No, you ain't hearing it right."

The chorus sang out: "Him! Him! Fuck him!" Guilty as charged.

Hendu pridefully asked for a continuance. "Oh man, shit. Let me explain the motherfucking shit to you. Give me a chance."

Matlack: "Did you or did you not say, 'Fuck the judges'?"

Hendu: "No, that's boolshit, because you have that big-nosed mother-fucker back there"—he pointed in the direction of Randy Lerch—

"saying that I said that." Hendu stood up and glared at Lerch, one of his close friends on the team. "You're a goddamn liar." Hendu knew he had them entertained, and he was loving it as laughter filled the bus.

Randy said, "Let me explain."

Hendu wouldn't let Lerch say a word. "No, this is what happened. I was getting my ankles taped, all right, and Wilcox was pitching that night. So Wilcox came in first and said, 'Let me get some heat on my arm.' In front of me, so I said, 'Shit, okay.' So he got some heat on his arm. So I was taping my ankles, and this ugly motherfucker came in to talk about that court and shit. I had tape already on my ankles, and Wilcox said, 'Don't worry about it. They're just discussing court.' And I'm already taped up, and so I said..."

Hendu paused and thought about it. "I don't want to say what I said," he said. There was a roar of laughter.

He continued, "No, but I was already in the process of getting taped up, man. I couldn't jump off the goddamn table to get..." Hindu stopped. He knew his explanation wasn't getting him anywhere.

"Fuck that," he said as the laughter continued. "No. But that's what it was. You asked me to be there, and I couldn't come there."

Matlack still hadn't gotten an answer to his question. "Hendu, but what did you *say*?"

Hendu: "I said, 'I can't come because he is taping my ankles.' This was the loudest eruption of laughter of the bus ride yet as Hendu imaginatively recreated the conversation.

Lenny asked: "What did you say about the judges?"

Hendu said defensively, "I didn't even know who the judges were at the time. I didn't know you all were the judges."

Matlack: "But you said something about 'Fuck...'"

Hendu: "No, no, I don't curse." The laughter rose. Hendu said, "I'm serious."

Kemp: "That's a fine." For even pretending he was serious.

Hendu replied, "That's booool-shit." Everyone laughed. Hendu said, "Aw, man." There was another burst of laughter. He turned to the back of the bus. "Fuck you, Lerch, man." Then he realized he had indeed cursed. "No, no, aw, aw. Lenny..."

Lenny looked up smiling.

Hendu said, "Kiss my ass." This response brought laughter that even surpassed the response to his last repartee. Hendu fought on.

"Wait a minute, man. I didn't say that. Hey, Kemper, wait, let me explain."

Laughter rang out.

"For me to be there, that's all you wanted, and I had to get ready for the motherfucking game. To be there, that's what it was. Oh, Lenny..." Hendu was seeking assistance. Lenny provided some in that Henderson was one of the star players of the team. Status has its rewards.

"Hendu," Randle said, "first of all, you pleaded your case real good. A high-five for that. I'm proud of you for that."

Steve Kemp agreed. "That will save you a buck."

But Randle was not going to let Hendu get off free of charge. Randle said, "You owe the court two bucks for wasting precious time of the court and for disrespect. You threw out four 'motherfuckers.'"

Hendu rationalized. "I was talking to the guys, and the guys don't mind."

Lenny compromised. "That'll cost you a quarter a 'motherfucker.' That's a dollar."

Kemp added, "And you got fined a dollar for lying."

Hendu shrieked, *"What?* For what?"

Kemp reminded him, "You said you didn't curse."

Hendu: "I was talking to them guys back there."

Kemp: "You said you didn't curse."

Hendu feigned anger. He paused. "Kiss my ass," he said. "I was talking to the people back there. No, I didn't say that. I'm talking back here."

Lenny closed the hearing. He said, "We have to take a team vote. For two dollars. Is this a 'Him!'?"

Hendu tried a last-minute plea. *"Him* this, goddamn it. I didn't do nothing." There was more laughter. Hendu pleaded, "Don't give me no 'Him!'"

He paused and tried the feigned anger approach. "Goddamn. You have a lot of goddamn nerve." He brightened.

"I'm going to write Lerch up." There was a lot of laughter and raucousness.

They never did vote.

Roy Howell asked, "Does anyone else have a charge against Kemp? I want to write him up for eating up all the mashed potatoes today."

Lenny: "Is that a charge?"

Roy: "Yeah."

Howell said, "Sosa didn't get any, Rajsich didn't get any, I didn't get any. Fucking animal ate all the mashed potatoes."

Matlack asked, "Hendu, did you get any mashed potatoes?"

Hendu shook his head and said, "I didn't get any." Everyone was laughing.

Kemp, knowing he was guilty, was not the sort to bullshit his way out. "I'll take the fine on that one," he said as everyone laughed at his honesty. He paused. "I pulled a Sose." There was great laughter. Kemp told his teammates the unvarnished truth. He said, "I hadn't eaten all day, and I said, 'Fuck, I'm going to eat this shit quick.'"

Roy Howell yelled, "That's another dollar for not spending your meal money to eat."

Kemp replied, "It was all gone from buying drinks." Laughing so hard so long was beginning to make everyone physically uncomfortable. No one cared.

Whatever had gone on in their lives before this bus ride was forgotten. Lenny Randle, a standup comic in the offseason, often said that his favorite activity was making people laugh. He was leading an entire bus filled with laughter. He was having a blast.

CHAPTER

18

The Chief Judge

Chief Judge Lenny Randle grew up in Southern California, not far from Bobby Tolan and Dock Ellis. Since he was old enough to lift a baseball glove he had always been a star player. But Lenny was different from the other athletes. He had a vision of life that extended beyond the foul lines. Talented enough to have been either a professional baseball or football player, Randle decided that sports would be a means, not an end. He wanted to travel and see the world. He wanted to experience life. And he wanted to be rich.

His parents had a primary goal for their son. They wanted him to be educated. "When I was born, the first thing my father gave me in my crib was a bat, a glove, and a diploma. My mom threw in a football. She said, 'I want you to be rough-and-ready.' But all of us had to get good grades before we could go out onto the field. Without good grades, we couldn't go out to the park."

The park became Lenny Randle's second home. He began Little League at the age of seven. When he was ten, he played against high school players, semipros, and ex-major leaguers.

"I was a catcher and a right fielder," Randle said. "I was not afraid of the ball. I wore a large cup. I remember in 1959 [he was born in 1949] I played against a team of old pros. Albie Pearson was on the other team and so was Chuck Connors. To me it was no big deal. I just felt like I belonged. I was just a young kid playing with a bunch of guys."

During Randle's freshman year at Centennial High School, he was a regular on the varsity. Two of his teammates were Wayne Simpson, who could throw the ball ninety-five miles an hour, and Mickey Cureton, who was being compared to Willie Mays and who could run the hundred-yard dash in 9.4 seconds. Simpson and Cureton also started as freshmen.

The year Randle became a senior, his class had seven players drafted by the major leagues, fourteen football players offered full scholarships to college, and five for basketball.

Randle, who was all-state in both football and basketball, received two hundred scholarship offers. In football he had led the entire state of California in kickoff and punt returns and in pass receptions. Simpson, his quarterback, had a cannon of an arm and could throw the ball sixty yards on the run. Their coach, Larry Todd, had been a former running back with the Oakland Raiders.

True to his parents, Randle went to Arizona State University along with his teammates Simpson and Cureton. He played baseball, but he also played varsity football under controversial coach Frank Kush. Randle held eight school records. He ran one kickoff back ninety-seven yards and another for ninety-eight, the latter against the University of Arizona, Arizona State's archrival. "The UA fans wanted to kill me," Randle said.

In baseball Randle played three years and was named an All-American. A switch hitter, he hit .340 and helped lead a powerful, awesome team to an NCAA national championship.

In addition to Randle, Arizona State featured Larry Gura, Craig Swan, Lerrin LaGrow, Alan Bannister, Floyd Bannister, Paul Ray Powell, a number one pick of the Minnesota Twins, Kenny Landreaux, Bump Wills, Hubie Brooks, and Jim Umbarger. There was also J. D. Hill, a great baseball player who ended up starring in the NFL, and Danny White, who became the quarterback of the Dallas Cowboys football team. Mickey Cureton became a track star. And Wayne Simpson decided he didn't need college. In 1967 he was the number one draft choice of the Cincinnati Reds and signed for $88,000. With the Reds in 1970 Simpson was a top rookie. He finished with a 14–3 record and a 3.02 ERA. A year later Simpson injured his arm and was never the same again, although he managed to pitch in the majors, on and off, through 1977. His lifetime record for four teams was 36–31.

Randle almost failed to return to college after his sophomore year, lured then by the big money.

"Reggie Jackson had left ASU early and signed, and Sal Bando, Gary Gentry, and Rick Monday all signed. It was *Do I take the money or do I want to get an insurance policy? Choose.*"

Randle waited a year and signed after his junior year. It was the way the system was set up. To graduate and then sign hurt a player's bargaining power.

"You had bargaining power after your junior year," Randle said, "because you could say, 'If you don't give me what I want, I'll go back to school for another year' and the draft pick would be wasted.

"If you waited until your senior year, you only had bargaining power if you had an electronics or business degree and there was a job waiting for you to make an automatic $30,000 to $50,000, rather than a minor league contract worth $500 a month."

In 1970 Randle was drafted number one by the Washington Senators, a year before the team became the Texas Rangers. He was the first choice in the first round of the draft's secondary phase, one of the best-rated prospects in the entire country. "To me it didn't seem like a big deal," Randle said. "Everyone else got more excited than I did. I knew I was going to play baseball or football."

Intelligent and analytical, Randle talked to pros he knew from both sports before making up his mind as to which he should play. In chatting with Ben Hawkins, Art Malone, and John Spagnola, all of whom had fine professional football careers, he discovered how easy it was to suffer a career-ending injury in football. In baseball, as he put it, "I could play until I dropped."

"I knew a baseball injury would lay you up for fourteen days," Randle said. "Football injuries were kind of permanent."

In his negotiations with the Senators, Randle made it clear he intended to finish college and get a degree. "I knew if I didn't, my father and mother would be very upset," Randle said. "So I didn't look at it as a need and a greed. I just looked at it as another vehicle to pursue."

Which is just the kind of attitude that puts panic in the hearts of the team officials trying to sign a player like Lenny Randle.

Randle got an $80,000 bonus to sign and a ticket directly to the Senators' Triple A Denver team.

The night he landed in Denver, he arrived at the park during the game. A couple of innings later Denver pitcher Art Fowler hit an opponent. Randle found himself in the middle of a brawl.

"Art was still throwing smoke at the age of forty-eight," Randle said. "He had a little pot gut, but he was quick. A guy bunted on Art, and Art brushed the next guy back. There was a bench-clearing brawl. I was in street clothes, but I joined in. I was part of the team, and if you didn't leave the bench, it was a $100 fine."

The Pelicans

Lenny   Randle

The game was suspended and had to be played later.

Randle struggled at bat in 1970, but the next year he hit .288 and halfway through the year he played for the Washington Senators. He was twenty-two years old.

Ted Williams, the Splendid Splinter, was his manager. Ted wanted Randle, as he did so many other hitters, to pull the ball and hit home runs. But Randle was smart enough to realize he didn't have Ted's power. "I knew what worked for me, rather than what worked for Ted," Randle said.

Instead he chose to emulate Ranger coach Nellie Fox, who had been the sparkplug of the Chicago White Sox Go-Go years in the late 1950s. Fox convinced Randle to return to switch hitting, something he dropped in Denver, and he worked with him on bunting and slapping the ball to the opposite field. Fox taught Randle bat control.

"My need was to be a situation and fundamental ballplayer, to switch hit and play every day," he said.

Under Williams's tutelage, Lenny Randle struggled to become a Texas Rangers regular. It took a few years, but all the while he was there, Williams never lacked encouragement. Randle appreciated the Splendid Splinter. Williams, in fact, may well have kept Randle from quitting baseball entirely at an early age.

When Randle injured his shoulder sliding into third base with three weeks to go in the season, Ted advised him and Pete Broberg to return to college to get their degrees.

"I respected Ted for that," Randle said, "and it made me look at baseball in a different light."

Randle, like so many players, hated playing for the Texas Rangers. Few teams were run as poorly. Randle saw friends traded unfairly. He was crushed when he understood what Howell had learned, that even if you busted your butt and were better than the next guy, you didn't necessarily get the promotion.

"I couldn't understand some of the things I saw going on," he said. "I felt baseball wasn't a fair business. There was no loyalty, no love."

When the Rangers sent Randle back to Triple A at Spokane in 1973, he was glad. He enjoyed playing for Del Wilber, who told his players, "Relax and enjoy the game." The team won it all.

At Spokane Randle became friendly with teammate Steve Greenberg, the son of Hank, the legendary slugger. Steve was into investments and real estate, and so was Lenny, who bought condominiums and land with his bonus money. Randle's goal was to have an income that freed him from needing baseball to survive. If he succeeded, he could be himself and not worry about the game's politics. For Lenny baseball was important, not the money, and so Lenny preferred playing at Spokane rather than Texas.

"We were having more fun at Spokane," Randle said, "winning it all, enjoying life, playing as human beings. I got more value out of it than if I would have gone up to Texas."

Everything changed when the Rangers fired Whitey Herzog and hired Billy Martin. Like Howell, Randle loved playing for Martin more than for any other manager.

"Oh man, Billy Martin knew talent," Randle said. "He respected players. He knew how to get the most ability out of each guy, and if a guy played for him, he'd back you up contractually, moneywise, go to bat for you. That was Billy. Give him 100 percent and he'd stand behind you. And there was no one that didn't want to play for him. He kept fifteen guys happy, maybe ten, the rest were up in the air, and maybe a couple hated him, but we won. At the end of the year everybody was happy with the checks they got then or the next time they negotiated their contracts."

When Martin came to Texas, the team was disorganized and lacked talent. After Martin chose a group of young players from the farm system and promoted them to the big club, he announced that the team would contend for the pennant. The experts scoffed when he said, "I see a pennant." But in 1974 the Rangers finished just five games behind Oakland.

"Billy and I got along great," Randle said. "To me he was like a godfather. He was the kind of guy, if you needed help, or if you needed to talk about something, he was there."

Randle was also a help to Billy. Martin's teenage son, Billy Jr., loved football and wanted to be a wide receiver, and Randle would teach him the proper techniques.

"Sometimes in baseball it's hard to relate to your son," Randle said. "So some other person can work better with your son than you can. I used to do that with Billy Jr. Billy wasn't tough on him. There was just a gap there. And he was into football, and we would talk football."

Billy knew Randle had studied psychology and sociology in college and that he was mature. "He knew I could relate to his son on a human level."

The relationship between Martin and Randle thus contained a dimension beyond that of player and manager. Randle genuinely loved both Martin the person and Martin the manager.

"Playing for Billy was the most fun I ever had in baseball," he said. "I remember in college bunting, executing the squeeze, having fun and winning. And I did that with Billy and the Rangers. I remember executing the squeeze bunt in three games: man on third, get him in. Billyball. He knew that I could bunt. I would bunt for a hit almost at will. You would do the little things to win ball games. Steal a base, hit-and-run, or you'd steal a sign from the catcher while you were on base and pass it on to the batter. If you know a fastball's coming inside, *boom*, there it goes. And Billy taught us how to do all that. It's the difference between managing and showing up. And that's why so many of the guys who played for him had long careers.

"Billy was like Al Davis of the Raiders, a guy who built winners. And Billy could get one of these guys and get him to play his best. He could make a good player a great player."

Martin, says Randle, gave him the self-confidence he needed to be a major leaguer.

"He made me believe in myself. He made me believe I could play third, short, second, center field every day of the week or even catch if I had to. I played those positions and still got up 520 times a season, and it wouldn't faze me."

Mickey Mantle once told Randle, "Gawddang, Lenny, Billy told me he didn't know what he'd do if it wasn't for you. You got multiple personalities."

And so in 1974 Billy Martin and Lenny Randle had great success. Lenny played at his peak. He hit .302 and stole 26 bases and was an integral member of a team that nearly upset the pennant express of the powerful Oakland A's. Unfortunately, as happens too often in baseball, the Rangers started slowly in 1975, and management panicked.

Owner Brad Corbett, who had just bought the team and thought he knew something about baseball, began to interfere with Billy, who resented his interference.

"Corbett was a pipeline magnate, owned a company called Robintech, and all of a sudden after one year of owning a baseball team, he became an expert," Randle said. "It was like Toys 'R' Us, 'This is my toy now, and I want to play with it. I want the PR, and I want to be *the* guy.'"

Martin would say to Corbett, "I'm a baseball man, and I know baseball, and I don't try to tell you how to run your pipe business, so don't tell me how to run my baseball business. I'm trying to help you win so you can have the champagne and get all the glory, but at least let me run the club."

At the same time coach Frank Lucchesi began telling the front office that Billy was the cause of the problems. Randle was contemptuous.

"We weren't into that," he said. "We just wanted to play and win. And then the team broke in two. The nucleus of the club stuck with Billy, but the players who thought they would maybe get a better deal if Billy got the gate went with the guy who was backstabbing Billy." That "guy," as Roy Howell noted earlier, was Frank Lucchesi.

Randle continued, "During the summer Billy got fired, and Frank took over. It was kind of strange, because the morale had been good.

"I remember being in Kansas City, and one night we all went frog hunting, Billy, Mickey Mantle, and about fifteen of the players. You go out at night into the swamp with a flashlight, and when you see the eyes of the frog, you grab it and make frogs' legs the next day.

"Maybe they thought we were *too* loose. But we were still playing good ball. And they fired him, just let him go, and we were shocked. A very morbid feeling, because we had so much going for us. The year before we almost won the pennant, and you don't lose it over a season.

"I don't know what went on in the front office. I just know that Billy's third-base coach ended up being the manager." That third-base coach was Frank Lucchesi.

"And it was bizarre. And everybody started remembering, 'Well, Frank was always up there talking to the front office.' I never said anything publicly. I would say, 'I don't remember nothing.' But I knew he was backstabbing Billy."

When Lucchesi took over, Roy Howell and Randle didn't play as much. The club's chemistry changed. Something was missing. When the losing continued, management's panic increased, and it began trading the young players.

Randle also hated the way he and some of the other players were treated by Lucchesi.

Randle said, "When you use people to either motivate or degrade or humiliate them, use them as whipping boys in order to enhance discipline, to take an Edward G. Robinson type of approach—'I'm gonna be a tough guy, and this is how it's gonna be...'" Randle's smile was gone. The experience had been a painful one. What made it worse was the irrationality of letting go one of the finest managers and bringing in one of the least effective.

"We had won without the tough-guy approach," he said. "It didn't need to be that drastic a change. We were mature enough to know what we had to do. We had learned what our roles were.

"And then, under Frank, we didn't know. Frank wasn't wise enough to know the roles we should have had...it was like he had amnesia or something. He just wanted to do something different, and it changed the morale of the team. Why he picked on me I have no idea."

But pick on Randle he did. He continually called Lenny a "punk." Randle warned him not to call him that again. And then in front of members of the media, Lucchesi said it one more time. Lenny decked him with one punch. Because of that one punch, Lenny Randle is remembered for his fists, not his baseball skills, and it's a shame.

Since then, whenever Randle has stepped out onto a baseball field, fans rarely fail to call out, "Hey, Lenny, how's Frank?" He's used to it. One would have thought such a wanton act would have been detrimental to his career. Randle, for his part, never saw the incident as an obstacle. He is a man whose philosophy in life is to look ahead and go forward. He never worried about the consequences.

"I wasn't a negative person, never have been, never will be," Randle said. "To me I was in America, and there were two million other jobs I could do."

He stayed in baseball. Afterward Randle signed a lucrative five-year contract with the New York Mets. But he landed in New York during a time when the Mets were run poorly and the best players were being traded because New York management didn't want to pay them competitive wages.

Randle said, "I remember coming into the clubhouse the first day, and Tom Seaver said, 'You're going to be needing a bigger cup, kid.' So I knew right away we had a good rapport. He said, 'I'm glad we got somebody who will dive for a ball.' I said, 'Yeah, I'll dive.' He said, 'I like your hustle and your effort. That's all we need to win some ball games.' If only he had still been there. But he ended up getting traded the next year. I had no idea a player could have that much impact on a city."

Randle played for the Mets for two years. The second year he pulled a groin muscle and a hamstring. Management asked him to play hurt. He tried, but he should have refused. Randle was the sort of player who would do whatever he could to help his team win. Unfortunately, with his injuries Lenny couldn't bunt because he couldn't run fast enough to beat out the ball. According to Lenny, that failing took thirty points off his average. He couldn't steal. He couldn't play his game.

To this day Randle doesn't understand why he was asked to play hurt. Had the Mets been pennant contenders, he would feel less bitter about it.

"Sometimes you don't know the details of why," he said. But after he hit only .233 in 1978, on Opening Day of 1979 he was released by the Mets.

Randle asked manager Joe Torre why the club had released him. Torre replied that he didn't know. In fact, Torre said, he had intended to name him the team captain. Randle felt betrayed.

"It was the pits," he said. "I felt, *Why are you doing this to me?* I couldn't figure it. Then I felt, *Baseball doesn't owe you a thing. There's no justice. No fairness. They don't care.*"

After a stint in the minors in Portland and then Phoenix, Randle went back to Billy Martin, who was managing the New York Yankees, where Lenny had a backup utility role and was rarely played.

With the Yankees, Randle was witness to one of baseball's great tragedies, the death of catcher Thurman Munson in an airplane crash.

"That took priority over everything," Randle said. "It blew everybody away. Everybody's perspective on life changed at that moment for the rest of our careers, the value of life, of giving and doing over baseball.

"The team was contending when that happened, and it really damaged us. Thurman had been a catalyst and an influence on that team. He was a great, great one, a psychologist behind the plate.

"Thurman was the kind of guy who would talk to you while you were hitting. You'd complain to the umpire, Nestor Chylak, 'Nestor, could you get the guy to talk to me at a club or a bar? I want to concentrate now.'"

" 'Oh, am I bothering you?' Thurman would say."

Thurman Munson was a psychologist with the umpires. If a pitch was outside, he'd say to the batter, "God, just missed, huh? How much did it miss by? Oh, by a cunt hair."

The next pitch would be in the same place, and the umpire would call it a strike.

He'd say to the hitter. "A cunt hair, but it depends on whose hair."

The batter would become irate. He'd say to the umpire, "Are you calling this game or is he?"

Thurman would say to the batter, "Do you want that pitch? Do you want it?" Then, to the umpire, he'd say, "What do you think, man? You think we ought to give it to him?"

The batter would look down at both Thurman and the umpire and complain, "What do we got here? Are we going to play the game or is this 'Rowan and Martin's Laugh-In'?"

Munson would say, "Why don't we use the honor system?"

The next pitch would be a ball. Thurman would say, "Golly, that was a good call." Now he had the umpire on his side. Thurman would say, "Good call, good call, good call." The umpire would say, "Yeah, I know it's a good call."

The next pitch would be in the same place, and the umpire would call it a strike. The batter would be mumbling to himself, *I'm swinging. Anything close, and I'm swinging.*

After 1979, Randle left the Yankees. They didn't want him any more.

"The Yankees didn't know what they wanted at that point," Randle said. "They were getting a whole new bunch of guys, so I had to look out for Lenny." He became a free agent.

Lenny again had his choice of teams. Bob Kennedy, the general manager of the Chicago Cubs, had wanted to draft Randle out of college. Lenny knew and liked manager Preston Gomez, and so in 1980 he chose to play for the Cubs.

"Chicago was the most fun playing in any city in America," Randle said. "All day games. You got to watch the six o'clock news, got to do things with the family, a normal American way of life.

"As long as you dove and gave an effort, that's all the Cubs fans asked for," Randle said.

The Cubs would have been a contender had everyone been healthy, but injuries to Dave Kingman, Bruce Sutter, and infielder Mike Tyson hurt, and then in August the team suffered from burnout.

"Some said it was the day games," Randle said. "I thought it was the night life. I knew from talking to Billy Williams, Fergie Jenkins, and Jose Cardenal that if you're going to play in Chicago, you have to be in bed by twelve o'clock. That way you can get your nine hours sleep, get up, have breakfast, and go to the ballpark. If the clock struck three . . . to me, you can't play under those conditions.

"But I had enough discipline not to do that. I would pass the word along, 'Hey, guys, if you want to win, let's get our rest.' Some guys did. Some guys didn't."

At the end of the year Randle again became a free agent. This time he made the mistake of going to the Seattle Mariners. Lenny didn't realize at the time the consequences of heading to the beautiful, scenic Northwest.

Randle went because he wanted the peace and tranquillity. Also he had never lived in the Pacific Northwest before. This was part of his see-America philosophy. Unfortunately, Seattle was a graveyard for players.

"Playing at Seattle was like playing for Mr. Rogers in the beautiful neighborhood, very low-key, tranquil," Randle said. "The fans were polite and applauded. But Seattle was not a contending team, and only after I got there did it dawn on me that if you play at Seattle, that was pretty much it.

"Everyone who played there either retired or had one more year. I don't know why. It was as though Seattle didn't register with the rest of America as a major league franchise."

Randle played two years in Seattle, languishing on the bench that second year. His career in America was over. When he was offered an opportunity to play ball in Italy, the worldly Randle immediately agreed to go. He was thirty-four years old. He learned Italian, played for five years, and became an Italian cult hero. Lenny Randle was doing what he loved most. He was playing baseball, and he was getting to globetrot the world.

It was past midnight when the bus with the dents in it arrived at Al Lang Stadium. Many of the players were asleep and didn't see the thick mist that shrouded the city until the vehicle came to a halt.

For some, the entire experience had an air of unreality. In their early middle age they were playing baseball on December 17 in towns all over Florida against strange-sounding teams like Suns, Sun Sox, Super Sox, Juice, and Tropics. But they were playing for a winner, and they were enjoying the sensation of laughing again.

The players found rides back to their apartments. They couldn't wait for tomorrow.

Tomorrow came four days later. On the day of their return the field at Al Lang Stadium was too wet. The next evening the fog hung so thickly that the big red "H" atop the nearby Hilton Hotel was obscured, and then came a scheduled day off. On December 21, game thirty-six, the midway point of the regular season, the Pelicans bused across the new Skyway Bridge to Bradenton to play Clete Boyer's Explorers.

Press coverage of the Senior League initially had been slanted toward stories about old players getting hurt. But none had given the dishonestly false impression that *Time* magazine offered when it ran a photo of Tropic bullpen coach Joe Bonfiglia and captioned it as player Joe Minceberg. Poor Joe. Aside from David Gershon, he was the one player in the league who had actually made the Senior League with no prior pro experience. When he got his name in a national magazine, it was attached to the body of the paunchy, out-of-shape Bonfiglia.

For a lot of people the story of the league was about players who had been able to come back from inactivity and perform amazingly well. *Time* instead chose to write about the "cunning humiliations" of age. The author wrote that "the players rarely dirty their uniforms" and quoted a Tougaloo, Mississippi, college professor, who decreed, "These guys don't have the speed or the hunger," as though this authority was an authority on anything.

The owner of Joe Minceberg and the Tropics threatened to sue for libel. He would have had a good case.

The talk in the newspapers about the poor attendance had increased. *USA Today* had stopped running the daily box scores. Even in the local papers coverage shrank from ten-inch stories plus a box score to three-inchers plus a box. No one considered the league's history, that it had been conceived in April and hastily thrown together, that there had been precious little time for the owners to advertise and promote, that too many owners started with way-over-the-hill players and couldn't compete with the younger teams like the Pelicans and the West Palm Beach Tropics.

Bradenton was one of those cities to receive poor support from the local chamber of commerce and the local paper. One wondered why a town would sabotage a team like that. Bradenton had Al Oliver, Graig Nettles, Jim Morrison, Omar Moreno, Tippy Martinez, Rick Lysander, John D'Acquisto, not exactly marquee names, but solid, talented major leaguers. Before the season would end, the Explorers would challenge the Pelicans for the top spot.

The ho-hum media failed to note the very high level of performance that could be seen at any Senior League game on any given day or evening. The Pelicans reminded the 656 fans in Bradenton of that fact in the very first inning.

Al Oliver, who had 2,743 hits over an eighteen-year career, smacked a hard ground ball to the right of second base. Second baseman Lenny Randle took a cross step and ran toward the ball, his arm outstretched. He reached down and gloved it and, while he was in midair about to fall, like an acrobat he flipped the ball with his gloved hand to shortstop Luis Gomez, who caught the ball with his bare hand and threw the ball to first to beat the chugging Oliver for an out.

All season long Lenny Randle had been making plays like that, and so had Gomez, whose skill in the field had always been overshadowed by an anemic bat.

That play and others like it were reason enough for the Senior League to exist.

19

The Man Who
Loved God

The Pelicans lost the December 21 game to Bradenton, 1–0, when relief pitcher Joe Sambito threw the game away in the tenth inning.

Sambito started off on the wrong foot, walking Graig Nettles. Under orders from manager Clete Boyer, a Billy Martin disciple, the Explorers' Wayne Garrett bunted to get him to second. The ball was dumped in front of the mound. Sambito picked it up and threw it over Gary Rajsich's head at first for a two-base error. Nettles stood at third. Garrett went to second.

The next batter, Jim Morrison, squared, and he too bunted in front of Sambito. The Pelican reliever pounced on the ball, straightened up to throw to third, and off-balance fired the ball past Howell and into left field. After releasing the ball, Sambito ran from the mound into left field and then into the clubhouse as the winning run scored.

In the clubhouse after the game, Sambito felt "horrible." He went over to Bobby Tolan. Joe said, "Bobby, I feel so bad. I'm sorry."

Tolan replied, "Hey, don't worry about it. That's baseball."

As he stood in front of his locker, Sambito thought to himself, *If I can't throw the ball forty feet on two consecutive plays, what am I doing out there?* Later he thought, *Maybe I shouldn't be on the field.*

Sambito said afterward, "I felt I let my teammates down. It was a tough game, so long, and nobody scores, a good game, the fans are excited, and to lose a game so sloppily. Not only do I walk the guy to start the inning, but I throw two more balls away, so how ironic is that? A guy who gets paid for throwing a baseball can't throw a ball forty feet."

One wondered what the Tougaloo professor who was quoted in the *Time* magazine article would think if he had heard Joe Sambito talk about his feelings.

After the 1–0 loss to Bradenton, there were two days of rain and fog and two added days off for Christmas vacation. Bradenton had won eight games in a row, making a run at the Pelicans, who had played but one game all week because of the bad weather. But at the Christmas break, halfway through the schedule, the Pelicans were still in first place, three games ahead of Bradenton, three and a half ahead of Orlando, and four and a half in front of Winter Haven.

Christmas interfered with Bobby Tolan's plans. When the team resumed action on December 26, Lenny Randle had returned to Texas to take care of some private business. Kenny Landreaux was still away, and so was Dwight Lowry. Tolan inserted Sergio Ferrer at second, Bombo Rivera in center, and Butch Benton behind the plate.

Benton, who continued working at his day job as a building contractor during the season, habitually arose at 5:30 A.M. every morning, went to the job site until early afternoon, and then reported to the ballpark for his second job. Because Lowry was away, Benton was pressed into service despite his having removed a fingernail with a staple gun. Every time the ball crashed into the mitt, the purplish finger must have screamed. If so, Benton would not admit it.

Butch Benton is one of those names remembered in New York Mets history for what he didn't do. He had been picked the number one athlete in the state of Florida in 1975, and that June the Tallahassee native was the Mets' number one choice in the free agent draft. When Mets fans talk about draft choices like Butch Benton and Steve Chilcott, players who never fulfilled their early promise, they invariably wonder, "What happened? Why didn't he make it?" Always there is a story.

When you watch Benton play baseball, it's only natural to ponder the question. Behind the plate, he's quick and alert. He fields in the style of Johnny Bench, one-handed. His arm is a gun. He has the right combination of bravura and steadiness. He can hit. And on the bases, it's hard to predict what he will do, except that you can be assured the play will end in a cloud of dirt and dust. It's hard to miss the reality that the Pelicans are a more exciting team when Butch Benton is in the game.

The Pelicans got lucky. The big reason they signed him is that he's now a Tampa resident, and they were looking for local players to draw fans. What they never envisioned was that he would turn out to be the finest catcher in the entire Senior League.

Benton, considered by Met fanatics as one of the great draft pick failures, proved to himself and everyone on the St. Pete team that he richly deserved his number one draft status out of high school. He hit in twenty-four straight games, tying Sun Sox shortstop Tim Ireland for the record. He finished his year in the Senior League hitting .374, highest in the league.

But because he had platooned, he was thirty-five at-bats short of getting the official recognition he deserved.

Movie-star handsome, Butch Benton was the team heartthrob. At many of the games a young woman would sashay down to the Pelican dugout and attempt to pass her telephone number to Benton. Benton would be flattered, but regardless of how beautiful the girl, he would politely inform the woman that he was happily married with six children. What the young women didn't know was that Butch Benton is a born-again Christian. He isn't blind, so he'll look, but he doesn't touch. His attraction to his faith is strong. Nothing, not even the charms of young women, can break it.

The day after Christmas Benton sat in the dugout. He was asked, "What did you give your kids for Christmas?"

"Nothing," he said firmly. Benton went on to explain that to him Christmas was the celebration of Jesus' birthday and was not meant to be an orgy of giftgiving and boozing. He was clearly unhappy with the idea of how society had diluted the message of Christmas into a bonanza for Toys 'R' Us and Hallmark.

Throughout his major league career Benton had made a number of baseball executives uncomfortable with his strict adherence to the teachings in the Bible. Moreover, Benton would very effectively spread the word of the Gospel. On his major league teams he would hold prayer meetings and discuss the Bible with any teammate who would listen.

Traditionally, baseball executives have usually not thought too highly of religious ballplayers. Bobby Richardson of the New York Yankees was one of the first to declare his love for the Lord. When he was a rookie, his

Tom DiPace

Butch   Benton

manager, Casey Stengel, who drank with the best of them, sometimes would make fun of Richardson and his equally Simon-pure sidekick Tony Kubek, calling them "milk drinkers" and wishing they could hit as well as a booze drinker who was the best hitter on the team, Mickey Mantle. When Billy Martin, Casey's pet, later became manager, he didn't have much patience for the milk drinkers either.

It may well have been that Butch Benton's conversion to Christianity ended his chance of playing regularly in the big leagues.

Butch Benton was a poor kid with a world of natural talent. He grew up on thirty acres on the Florida Panhandle with four siblings, a horse, and twenty-one cats, down the road from Tallahassee. His father abandoned the family before Butch was two. Though his mother remarried, they were so poor that some winters they didn't have enough money to heat their home. If it wasn't for the help of friends and family members, there were times the Bentons might have gone hungry.

Butch Benton grew up rebellious. He was very bitter and angry and felt the world to be cruel. If a teacher gave him a hard time, he would lash out. "I was mouthy," Benton says.

When Benton got to high school, he came under the influence of baseball and football coach Rick Smith. Smith, impressed with Benton's potential, took him home to live with him.

"I owe him everything," Benton said. "Rick doesn't know this, but he was instrumental in me going into the ministry. I played ball eleven years, and when I got out of ball I pastored, because he cared about people."

In his senior year Benton was voted by the state of Florida as its athlete of the year. In football he was a linebacker. In baseball he caught. Scouts viewed him as another Johnny Bench.

Benton was naive and parochial. He knew nothing of the world around him. He didn't read the newspapers, didn't even follow major league baseball.

"Playing major league baseball was the farthest thing from my mind," Benton said. "I wanted to get married and be a father and carry a job."

He noticed the scouts, knew that they were looking at him. Benton said, "It would never sink in, never penetrate what that meant." One thing it meant was that Butch Benton was a prime target to get fleeced by a major league organization.

In June 1975, the New York Mets selected Benton in the first round.

When a friend called to tell him about it, Butch replied, "What's the number one round?" He didn't know.

The friend said correctly, "That means you're supposed to get a lot of money."

Benton said, "That's good."

The friend told him, "And not only that, you were the sixth guy in the nation to be drafted."

Butch said, "Well, that's good."

Met scout Julian Morgan offered him $17,000 to sign. During a period when other first rounders were commanding six figures, the offer to Benton was low. But to a poor kid from the sticks of Florida, $17,000 seemed like fabulous riches.

"My God," Benton thought, "where do I sign?"

But his American Legion coach, Mike Easum, who had played pro ball and gotten to Double A, knew Benton was getting fleeced. He took Benton outside the Motel 6 where they were meeting with the Met scouts. Easum told Benton, "There is no way you can sign for that."

Benton replied, "What are you talking about? I'll never make that much money in my whole life."

Easum said, "We're going to walk in there and ask for $150,000."

When Easum made his request, the Met scouts turned him down and left. Benton began crying, convinced he had blown his chance.

"I was a big kid. I weighed 220 pounds, but I was in tears," Benton said. Benton figured that he was never going to play.

The Mets, of course, called back. But Benton was at a tremendous disadvantage in his negotiations. Major league teams know how badly kids want to play, especially those from poor backgrounds. Benton ended up with a bonus of $30,000 guaranteed and another $15,000 in performance bonuses, which, Benton said, "looking back on it now was a joke." The same year Danny Goodwin got $150,000 and Clint Hurdle received $100,000.

"Boy, if I knew then what I know now, those guys would be paying out the kazoo," Benton said. If Benton knew then many things he knows now, his life and career might have turned out differently.

Quickly he found out how little he was getting in comparison to the other bonus babies. When he reported to Marion in the Appalachian League, everyone would ask him how much he got. He lied. Sometimes he said he got $100,000. Other times it was $200,000. He was too embarrassed to tell the truth.

Despite being drafted number one by the Mets, Butch Benton had no aspirations about making the big club. Unlike more sophisticated candidates, he didn't resent the minors, with the small salaries and long bus rides. It was all an adventure. Butch Benton enjoyed every moment of it.

At Marion, Virginia, he and five teammates lived in a woman's home. For entertainment, the players had shaving cream fights.

"Things eleven-year-old kids would do," Benton said.

Marion was so small it boasted one hamburger joint, and it wasn't McDonald's. There were eight thousand people in the town, and according to Benton, it was rumored that most of them were crazy, because there was a mental institution there.

One time Benton returned to his room to find his window open, a cigarette burning in an ashtray on his bed, and a butcher knife stuck in his dresser.

Another time he and his roommates picked up a couple of girls. When one girl was asked her name, she said, "Mother Nature." Benton freaked out.

"I didn't even stick around to hear what the other girl's name was," he said.

If life off the field was an adventure, life on it became a nightmare. When the Mets drafted Benton, he was the number one high school catcher in the nation. He could throw runners out at second from his knees. He used a break mitt, which was made like a first baseman's glove. It had a crease and could be closed around the ball with one hand.

"I could really pick it with one hand," Benton said.

When Benton arrived in Marion, the first thing the Mets did was take away his break mitt and replace it with a Ray Fosse model mitt with no break in it. The new glove had padding all the way around with a hole in the middle. The Mets told Benton, "This is going to make you a better catcher."

He was seventeen years old. The pitcher would throw the ball, and it would hit the mitt and bounce past him. He'd have to wait for it to quit rolling to pick it up.

Benton said, "I couldn't catch a cold. The guys on the team were calling me the Human Sieve. I really think that shattered my confidence. I would go a couple of games and miss everything. Then I'd have a good game, and there would be a ray of hope. I'd think, *Maybe they're right.* This went on for two years, but the good games were far apart.

"Finally they said, 'Evidently this is not working. You are our number one pick, and we have to do something.' They gave me back my break glove."

In 1977 at Lynchburg, Benton was the all-star catcher. He made it again in 1978 at Jackson. Shortly thereafter, Butch Benton would find religion. His devotion to the Lord would hurt him in the eyes of baseball executives even worse than his Ray Fosse catcher's mitt.

Discrimination comes in many forms. The common element is that the person being discriminated against is different from the person doing the discriminating. In America there are obvious minority candidates targeted for discrimination: blacks, Latins, Jews. There are also less obvious targets: fat women, short men, and the religious.

Hell-raising managers like their players to raise hell. They do not like players who keep their hell-raisers from their appointed rounds and turn them into Milquetoasts. Benton went from being a hell-raiser to a disciple of the Lord. The new Benton made management nervous. They liked him better the old way.

"I was pretty wild my first couple years in ball," Benton said. "I fell into drinking a lot and carousing, but the fulfillment wasn't there. And then on January 7, 1977, I had been drinking. I was driving my Corvette over a hundred miles an hour in St. Lucie County on a bridge and ran into another car."

After the impact his car traveled over a hundred yards, but it never went off the bridge. It was totaled. The other car was also totaled. Benton escaped with a cut. The other driver was also okay.

"It just wasn't humanly possible," Benton said.

The police put Benton in a holding tank when he refused to take a Breathalyzer test.

Benton said, "I was in the tank with two winos and a prostitute. It was like it happened yesterday. I'm not trying to make this spooky, but I had always been taught that if you're going to get something out of life, you have to do it for yourself. But as I sat in there, I heard a small, inaudible voice say, 'You know, Butch, I don't love you any more or less than the two winos and the prostitute.' I knew it was God. Everybody knows when they come to that experience that it's the Almighty. My attitude was *What do you mean? I've made something out of my life. What are they?* Because this was how I had been programmed, that if you're going to get anywhere in life, you're going to have to do it for yourself."

Benton called upon God. "God, if you're out there, and if this is you, I need help."

He did not hear bands play or see stars shine. Contrary to what people may think, his life did not change overnight.

Benton explained, "People have this idea that when you become a Christian, you suddenly become a saint. I'm going to tell you, that's not the way it is."

After the accident and his arrest, Benton had to go to trial. His driver's license was revoked for a year.

"Everything I had sown, I had to reap," he said.

The experience changed him dramatically.

"I had determined in my heart to change," Benton said, "and that's the key to any relationship with Jesus Christ. I didn't know it at the time, but the Bible says, 'Those that call upon the name of the Lord shall be saved.' When I read that for the first time, I thought, *Wow, that's what I did.*"

He developed a strong urge to go into the ministry. As a result he began attending Bible study classes.

"I started getting into the Word," he said. "The Bible says in Romans 12:1, 'Renew your mind daily.'" At one of those Bible study meetings he met his wife, April.

Benton said, "It was all coming together now that God really had a purpose for my life."

He quit drinking. He no longer cursed, no longer threw helmets or bats when he made an out. He began a chapel program for his teammates. As a result, management labeled him as "too religious."

Benton said, "I had all the tools to make it, but the Butch they signed was no longer there. The intensity was there, but the violent outbursts were gone. Management felt I had lost my desire to play the game. I would strike out in a crucial situation and just sit down without losing my temper. They would feel, *What happened to Butch? Doesn't he care any more?*"

The Mets released him. He signed with the Cubs. Benton began Bible studies there.

"Guys were changing, really giving their lives to Christ, and it was a neat thing," Benton said.

Management called him in for a talk. They said, "We want you to keep that religious stuff at home."

Benton told him, "Baseball is here today and gone tomorrow. Eternity is forever."

That winter the Cubs sent him to Montreal, who sent him to Triple A. He had a great season, hitting .330 with 11 homers and 57 RBIs. The next season he was traded to Detroit, where he hit .298 at Wichita. Then in 1985 he signed with Cleveland and made the ball club. Pat Corrales was the manager, and the two didn't get along. On Father's Day the Indians sent Benton back to the minors.

"Great Father's Day present, huh?" Benton went to Old Orchard Beach, where he finished his career.

At the end of the 1985 season, Butch Benton felt a call to the ministry and dropped out of baseball. He pastored for two years in Tarpon Springs, Florida, then in Largo. Because of the financial pressure brought on by having to feed six kids, he also worked construction to make ends meet.

Benton worked in the field, learning his trade, making five dollars an hour toting lumber. Today he owns his own construction firm, getting up at 5:30 A.M. and working through the afternoon, building homes in the Tampa area.

Though Benton had to quit being a pastor because he couldn't afford to continue, he still believes God has a purpose for him.

"My ministry isn't through the pulpit, but it might be through construction or through ball," Benton said. "I try to touch people's lives whenever I can."

Butch Benton shakes his head at his bad luck. In the minors he had four understanding managers who didn't resent his religious bent—Bob Wellman, Jack Aker, Gordie McKenzie, and Felipe Alou. In the majors it was a different story.

"Joe Torre, Lee Elia, Pat Corrales, they didn't understand my position and the stand I took for the Lord," Benton said.

He still ponders what might have happened if one of the minor league managers who cared about him had managed him in the big time.

"There's no doubt in my mind I would have been a successful major league player," Benton said.

Nevertheless, though Benton feels he was treated unfairly, he also believes what happened to him was in God's hands.

"He was directing my path," Benton said, "so if you look at the overall picture, what happened to me was trivial. Do I believe my trust is in Man or in God?

"If it's God, what do I care what Man does to me?"

CHAPTER

20

Too Smart for the Game

In any season there is often one team that is tough to beat. For the Pelicans it was the Bradenton Explorers. Bradenton had excellent pitching, solid defense, and not much hitting. But it was the nature of the Explorers' pitching, off-speed, breaking-ball pitchers, that consistently frustrated the Pelican bats.

Milt Wilcox, who beat almost everyone, won his eighth game on December 26, but the next day the Explorers' Dan Boone, a bright college star at California Fullerton, matched zeros with the Pelicans' Jon Matlack inning for inning. Both pitchers left after nine. Then Explorer relief star Rick Lysander, sporting an excellent sinkerball, and Ken Kravec shut out St. Pete through the fourteenth inning.

The Pelicans finally lost in the bottom of the fourteenth when Dock Ellis gave up three runs. A pop-up by Danny Meyer over a pulled-in infield turned out to be the key blow.

The next day Bradenton beat the Pelicans in eleven innings. Before the game Ken Landreaux's shiny uniform hung in his locker while everyone else was out on the field warming up. The other players noticed. They weren't happy about it.

"That's why he's no longer in the big leagues," Roy Howell said, grimacing.

Landreaux eventually showed and played, going 0-for-5. Some teammates wondered aloud whether the trade of their buddy, Jerry Martin, and the three others had been worth it.

Dick Bosman lost the game in the eleventh. Things had not been looking up for Bosman. Ten days earlier Jim Morley informed him that the radio broadcasts were being discontinued. He wasn't allowed to pitch batting practice (on orders from Dock Ellis), and when he found out the radio gig had ended, he stayed home.

"I don't need this," Bosman said.

But Morley assured him that he would get his chance to pitch, and Bosman returned. Against Bradenton Bossie got the first man out, but Graig Nettles, who annoyed the Pelicans all season long, legged out an infield hit. After a second out, Stan Cliburn doubled, but still no run had scored. Bossie should have been out of the inning unscathed. But Wayne Krenchicki hit a grounder that Luis Gomez was able to flag down. However, the long throw flew past the first baseman. The Explorers had two runs and the ball game. It should have been an error. But true to Bossie's luck, the scorer gave Krenchicki a hit and so the runs became earned. The Pelican lead was shrinking. Orlando, in second place, was only a game and a half back, and Bradenton trailed by two.

The Orlando Juice came to town, and in the locker room before the game Tex Williams seemed unconcerned that the Pelican lead had dropped.

"Don't worry," he said, "when Zack and Razor come back, we'll start winning again. We're just starting to get healthy."

St. Pete badly needed a win.

In the middle game of three, it looked like another extra-inning marathon as the score stood at 0–0 going into the bottom of the eleventh. The Pelicans had lost three straight extra-inning games, and winning or losing this one meant the difference between a half-game and a two-and-a-half game lead over Orlando.

In the bottom of the eleventh, Dwight Lowry fought off a Jamie Easterly fastball and blooped a single to center. After an out, Luis Gomez elated everyone with an infield single. Leadoff hitter Lenny Randle, one player the Pelicans counted on all season long, hit a ball toward the outfield that center fielder Ike Blessitt raced in and dove for, but couldn't get. Randle had a single and an RBI, and the Pelicans had their win.

One of the marvelous things about baseball is that when you go to a game, no matter how many games you have seen in the past, there exists the possibility that you will see something you never saw before. On the day before the new year, under sunny skies in St. Petersburg, the 668 fans saw something remarkable though not uplifting. It came with two outs in the ninth inning.

The game never would have reached such a climax had Bombo Rivera, who was playing center field for the Pelicans, been healthy. In the second inning Orlando's Ike Blessitt hit a line drive up the middle toward Rivera. He should have caught it waist-high, but Bombo was running on legs with badly pulled muscles. Either he didn't tell Bobby Tolan because he didn't want to go on the disabled list and lose half his pay or else his fierce pride kept him in the lineup. In any event Bombo's bad wheels looked like they were going in slow motion. As the ball went past him, it rolled to the back wall for an inside-the-park home run.

Despite the gaffe, the Pelicans still led by two going into the ninth. Bobby Tolan sent in Pat Zachry, back from his broken ankle, to pitch.

Zack gave up a single and got the first out. He worked Larvell Blanks to 2–2 and threw a slider over the outside corner of the plate. Zack knew he had a punchout, except the umpire called it a ball. His next pitch also missed. Runners were on first and second.

After a pop out to Butch Benton behind the plate, two were out. Zack should have been out of the inning. Instead U. L. Washington was up. Washington had been a slap hitter in the majors but turned into an all-star performer in the Senior League.

Zack threw Washington one pitch. It was a fastball, up. U. L., batting lefty, swung up. No one on the Pelican bench could believe it, but the ball arched high in the air toward the right-field foul pole. When it cleared the wooden fence, it was about five feet to the fair side of the pole. As the ball landed in the middle of the street and bounded toward the Hilton Hotel, the Orlando players were cascading out of the dugout and showering U. L. Washington with great affection.

In the Pelican dugout no one moved. They were numb. Had the team won, the lead over Orlando would have been significant. With the loss, the lead was back to only one and a half games.

In the dugout pitcher Hoot Gibson tried to put it in perspective. "The more you pitch," he said, "the more shit happens. It doesn't matter who you are. If you go out often enough, you experience it."

For his part, Zachry remained admirably calm. He crinkled his nose, made a face, and shook his head. "He'll never do that again," he said about Washington. Knowing Zack, the next time he faced U. L., the Juice second baseman would find himself lying in the dust on his back.

Everyone felt bad for Zachry, but no one was angry or even upset. It was just part of what happens in the crazy game of baseball.

If no one was upset by U. L. Washington's home run, Bobby Tolan *was* distressed because Bombo Rivera had played without telling anyone how badly his legs were hurting. In the very first game he had played, he had injured his leg, trying to run from home to first on a ground ball. He was never healthy. His failure to catch the Blessitt line drive was Bombo's last act as a Pelican. He had feared going onto the disabled list. It turned out worse than that. That afternoon, soulful, optimistic Bombo Rivera, Garrison Keillor's hometown hero, was released.

Bombo disappeared from the Pelicans. The other players didn't seem to notice. Bombo Rivera had heart and zest, and he was a decent guy. But his legs were gone, and even a big heart couldn't make up for that.

Players going and players coming is a ritual on all ball clubs. It's one reason some players refuse to form friendships with teammates. It hurts too much when friends depart. As Bombo left, relief pitcher Dave Rajsich returned to the Pelicans after sitting out for two weeks. Dave's pinky finger on his left hand, his pitching hand, had been hit by a ground ball the first week of the season. For several weeks Rajsich had pitched with the pain, in part because the doctors said there wasn't much they could do for it. He also did not want to go on the disabled list and lose half his salary, as was the rule in the Senior League.

"I can't afford that," Rajsich said. Before pitcher Gerry Pirtle was traded away, he had been aware that Dave had a broken pinky. "Why would he continue to pitch with a broken finger?" Pirtle was asked.

"Because you go out there, or you go home," he said.

But it wasn't the only reason. This was Dave's first opportunity to play on the same team with younger brother Gary, and he didn't want to leave. Since Dave was three years older than Gary, they didn't get to play Little League together. Both had short major league careers, and they were never on the same team. On the Pelicans, both Dave and Gary were quiet men who kept to themselves. They were not carousers or hell-raisers, but both loved the game and the camaraderie. It was clear they also loved and admired each other.

Before the season Dave, whom his teammates called Razor, had spent hours back home in Phoenix, throwing a baseball against a brick wall under the intense Arizona sun until his neighbors thought he was crazy.

After all that work to get ready, Razor wasn't going to let something like a broken finger bring an end to his first Senior League season.

His doctors had told him he had a couple of alternatives: rebreak it and set it again, which would force him to miss the rest of the season, or grit his teeth and pitch with it, which is what Razor chose to do.

Dave Rajsich had had an odd career. He had not been a college superstar, so he was surprised when he ended up as a professional ballplayer. His interests were biology and physics. He was an intellectual who was spending his life throwing a ball.

As he developed, he performed well enough in the minor leagues that one could predict great things for him in the majors. He had a hard, biting slider that was tough to hit, and he had composure. What he never had was the confidence of management. Like Benton, who was religious, Rajsich had characteristics that scared management to death. He was insightful and aware.

Because he was smart, he was always aware of what was going on around him. Rajsich knew when management messed with him and his friends. And management knew he knew, and that bothered them.

Rajsich played primarily with two organizations, the New York Yankees and the Texas Rangers. Both were incredibly political in their own ways. Rajsich, who hated the politics, knew exactly what was screwy about each of them.

Dave Rajsich will admit that he is a bad politician. He does not suffer fools lightly. He speaks his mind. A baseball executive once told him that he was too smart to be a baseball player.

But in the Senior League it was different. "There aren't any politics here," Rajsich said. "It's like the good old days of high school and college. You play for the fun, the camaraderie, the enjoyment of knowing you can go out and play. That's great. I still love the game. I just don't like the politics."

Dave Rajsich began his pro career with the New York Yankees in A ball at Fort Lauderdale in 1975. It was an era in which being a minor leaguer in the Yankees chain was like being an understudy to Yul Brynner in *The King and I*. In part because owner George Steinbrenner preferred to man each position on the Yankees with All-Stars, and in part because manager Billy Martin preferred vets to younger players, it was rare for a Yankee minor leaguer to make it to the big club and remain. The kids in the minors, meanwhile, were blocked—actually and emotionally.

"The Yankee farm system in the late 1970s was dynamite," Rajsich said.

In the three years that Rajsich toiled in the minor leagues for the Yankees, he witnessed some great talent stagnate and wither. At Fort Lauderdale, some of his teammates included Damaso Garcia, Domingo Ramos, Jerry Narron, Dennis Werth, and Mike Heath, who began his career as a shortstop.

In the ensuing years Rajsich watched teammates such as LaMarr Hoyt and Jim Beattie prepare for careers in other organizations.

"LaMarr won sixteen games for us in Double A," Rajsich said. "The White Sox got him in the Bucky Dent trade. He could hit the spots, work the curveball, go in and out. He was talented, and we knew it."

He also saw some young pitching prospects who injured themselves and never really made it for anyone. Among those were Kenny Clay, Eddie Ricks, and Gil Patterson.

"I saw Gil pitch a no-hitter at West Haven," Rajsich said. "Most dominating game I ever saw a guy pitch. He was absolutely awesome."

Willie McGee was one player who was languishing in the Yankees system. Rajsich remembered, "He was stuck in Double A, for crying out loud. *Boom,* the Cardinals find him, he goes to the big leagues, and he never sees the minors again."

Part of the reason the Yankees bought vets and shunned the kids, Rajsich felt, was manager Billy Martin.

"Billy wasn't known as a manager who worked for young kids," he said. "He was a veteran manager, and if you made a rookie mistake, you're done. 'That's it, the guy can't play. Get him out of here.' And that's the way he approached things. When he went to Oakland, where he had nothing but young kids, he made men out of them.

"When I was with the Yankees, we didn't get the opportunity. Beattie didn't get a chance, Damaso Garcia didn't, and Billy was the key reason he got traded. In the fifth or sixth game, he didn't cover first base on a bunt and we ended up losing the game. That was the end of Damaso Garcia as far as Billy was concerned. I thought he was going to be a great, great infielder. A year later he was traded. But, of course, Willie Randolph was there."

Rajsich played for Syracuse in 1977. He was a spot starter and pitched in relief for the first time. He wasn't used to warming up in the pen. Coming from Arizona, he also wasn't used to the cold weather in Syracuse. One day he pitched in forty-degree, damp, rainy, dreary weather. He strained his elbow and struggled with his control.

The Yankees decided to send Rajsich back to Double A. Rajsich didn't want to go. At Syracuse there was an ultrasound machine and a whirlpool. West Haven had neither.

"I felt it was like signing my death warrant," Rajsich said. "I told them I was leaving. I said, 'When the paycheck comes on the fifteenth, I am going home. My truck is packed.'"

Only after Rajsich got the Yankees to allow him to use the equipment of the Double A Waterbury team did he agree to report. After a week of treatment, his arm came back. And he never had trouble after that.

Mike Ferraro, Rajsich's manager at West Haven, gave his new pitcher ten days off to rest the arm. Rajsich told him, "There are days I can't throw." Ferraro took heed.

Pitching in short relief Rajsich compiled an 8–2 record after only thirty innings of work.

At West Haven Rajsich loved manager Ferraro, and Hoyt Wilhelm was the finest pitching coach he ever encountered. Wilhelm taught him a great deal about the art of pitching.

Wilhelm was a fundamentalist when it came to watching form. In five minutes he could spot what a pitcher was doing wrong and tell him how to correct it. And if the pitcher wanted to go along, fine, and if he didn't, that was fine too.

"More than anything else, he taught situation pitching," Rajsich said.

Wilhelm taught Rajsich to use whatever was working best in the bullpen before coming into the game as his "out" pitch. He taught him to force the catcher to call what he wanted to throw in key situations. He taught him to pitch around hot hitters. He taught him that some batters like to bat in the clutch and others do not. "Pitch to the ones who don't," Rajsich was told by Wilhelm. "And the ones who do, make them wait and don't worry about walking them."

Dave Rajsich came up to the Yankees in July of 1978. He had been pitching short relief in Triple A for Syracuse. The team was in Hawaii when the phone rang at seven in the morning. His roommate, Bob Kammeyer, was sitting in bed reading *The Wall Street Journal.* Kammeyer picked up the phone. His manager, Mike Ferraro, was on the other end. Kammayer said, "It's for you. It's Mike." Rajsich went, "Uh-oh." He couldn't imagine it was anything good. The voice said, "You're starting in New York against the Tigers the day after tomorrow."

Rajsich was a short reliever, and Kammeyer as a starter was 11–0. To Rajsich, his call to the majors didn't make any sense. Rajsich said, "Kammy, are you sure this isn't for you?"

Two days later Rajsich started the second game of a double-header. Rajsich hadn't worked five innings even once for Syracuse.

"And Kammy," Rajsich said, "he never got a chance. He never once started a game for the Yankees."

Dave Rajsich joined the 1978 Yankees, the team that trailed the Boston Red Sox by fourteen and a half games in August and came to win the division title and eventually the pennant. Rajsich was on the team early and on the team late, pitching in four games. In the middle he got hit on his pitching hand with a ground ball, shelving him the same way he had been put out of action with the Pelicans.

The first game Rajsich pitched in the major leagues was in front of fifty-five thousand fans in Yankee Stadium. The Yankees were playing a doubleheader against the Tigers. Nineteen seventy-eight was the year Ron Guidry won 25. Guidry pitched the first game and won. Rajsich started the second.

Before Dave left Syracuse, Hoyt Wilhelm told him, "Go down to the bullpen a little early and get your work in. You need ten minutes. Don't leave it all in the bullpen. Go out there, and pitch as long as you can and hold them close."

Rajsich remembered, "The first batter I faced was Ron LeFlore, and I struck him out. Mike Heath was catching, because Thurman Munson caught Guidry in the first game. It was awesome. I left the game in the fifth inning, leading 3–2, and they tied it up, and we won, 5–3. I didn't get the win. It was eerie, because I was nervous. But I was totally concentrated. I never took my eyes off the glove. Maybe I was afraid to look elsewhere, but I never again felt that type of serenity on the mound. Never. It was like I had total control of everything."

During his initial stay with those 1978 Yankees, Rajsich noted their professionalism and confidence. The 1978 Yankees were a special baseball club.

"What impressed me most about the Yankees was the relaxed attitude the veterans had when it came to winning ball games," Rajsich said. "Because I was in the rotation, I sat in the dugout. I was looking at Lou Piniella, Roy White, Chris Chambliss, Graig Nettles, Thurman Munson, Reggie. It would be the eighth inning, and they'd go, 'All right, time to turn it on. We need to get two.' And they'd get it. Very professional. Very intense. While Billy, Reggie, and George did the sideshow, the rest of them went about their business."

Quickly, Rajsich developed a rapport with his catcher, the late

The Pelicans

Dave Rajsich

Thurman Munson, who impressed him with his knowledge and head for the game.

"Thurman took time to talk to me," he said. "He would come over and say, 'Do you want to know what you did right and what you did wrong?' 'Yeah, let's go.' And he would tell me about how I was pitching. He said, 'In the first inning you don't need to throw a 3–2 slider. You might need that pitch in the seventh or eighth inning. Why did you throw it?'

"I said, 'I knew I could throw it for a strike. It was my best pitch.'

"He said, 'When I catch you, go with what I call. There will be a reason for it.' And the next time I pitched, he caught me, and we talked about that. I learned so much. In the minor leagues everyone was feeling themselves out, but these guys were proven veterans and took the time to take you under their wing."

Rajsich cracked his hand in his second start. A ground ball almost took his finger off. The hand started swelling. In the third inning he could no longer feel his hand. He told the assistant trainer, Herman Schneider, not to tell Billy Martin.

"Because I was going for my first win," Rajsich said. "But in the fourth inning I gave up four runs. It got to where I couldn't feel anything." Goose Gossage came in, and the Yankees eventually lost the game.

Rajsich became one more victim of Yankee shenaniganism when he was sent back to Syracuse, instead of being put on the disabled list. Rajsich was a kid. He didn't know there was a rule against sending down a player who was hurt.

He was brought back in September. The day Rajsich returned to New York, Andy Messersmith and Ken Clay were sent down. The Yankees were fourteen and a half games back. Owner George Steinbrenner called a meeting.

Rajsich recalled, "George came into the clubhouse and said, 'If there is anybody here who is going to give up, you can leave now.' He said, 'We still have a chance. Fourteen and a half is a long way, but this ball club is good enough to win.' And he walked out.

"The ball club had so many veterans and had gone through so much adversity in the first half of the season that nobody was concerned. They knew they were going to win. Boston was walking away with it, but they *knew* Boston couldn't maintain that kind of intensity the whole year. Then the Red Sox started having their injuries, started losing ball games, and the Yankees slowly started catching up."

When Rajsich returned, he discovered that his locker was situated adjacent to that of Reggie Jackson, Mr. October. Rajsich was perplexed as to why a young kid would have his locker next to one of the biggest stars in the game. After his first game, thirty reporters stood in front of Jackson's locker, making it impossible for Rajsich to dress.

He thought, *Now I know why.*

Rajsich had mixed feelings about Jax.

"Reggie was a little too hyped for me," Rajsich said. "But he produced when he had to. But I don't think he was the leader of that ball club. There is no doubt in my mind that he wasn't. Thurman was, and so were Nettles, Chambliss, and Catfish Hunter."

On Rajsich's first road trip, the Yankees went to Boston. Catfish Hunter said to him, "I'll take you out and show you the places to eat." Rajsich was grateful that a seasoned pro like Hunter would take the time to make him feel part of the team.

When he returned from the minors in September, relief star Sparky Lyle tutored him in the art of pitching in relief. Lyle taught Rajsich how to get ready. "You have to go out and throw five minutes every day," Lyle said. He added, "Don't baby your arm. Don't ice it. Once you baby it, you'll be more susceptible to getting hurt."

Lyle also impressed on him the importance of eliminating the highs and the lows and taught him what to look for in hitters, what to do in certain situations.

After Lyle's tutoring, Rajsich admits, "All of a sudden I became more consistent. Sparky made me a much better pitcher."

Rajsich got a front-row seat to one of the most dramatic games in the history of baseball. He was in the bullpen for the Yankees–Red Sox playoff game in 1978.

"The veterans on our ball club knew they could beat them," Rajsich said. "They *knew* Boston starter Mike Torrez wasn't going to hold us."

Rajsich's most vivid memory in that game was the absence of reaction when Yankee shortstop Bucky Dent hit the game-winning home run off Torrez.

"It got unbelievably quiet," Rajsich said. "It was as though somebody had turned off thirty-five thousand fans *boom* right now. Then when Graig Nettles caught the pop-up for the last out, you could have heard a pin drop in the ballpark. The Boston fans were stunned."

Rajsich was impressed with the professionalism of his Yankee teammates.

"It was quiet and crowded in the Yankee clubhouse after the game. There weren't any corks being popped or guys jumping up and down and going crazy. They knew what we had to do."

They had to fly to Kansas City and meet the Royals in the League Championship Series.

Rajsich said, "One of the greatest things the Yankees did—I'll never forget this—when we were on the plane going to Boston, they gave everybody their meal money. They said, 'Here is your money for Boston, *and* here is your meal money for Kansas City.' I can't think of another organization that would have done that. They *knew* they would win. What a psych job that was on everybody."

The Yankees defeated the Royals and then went on to beat the L.A. Dodgers in the World Series.

"We lost the first two games in the World Series in Los Angeles and were flying back," Rajsich recalled. "I was thinking, *We have to fly all the way back to New York.* I was a rookie, not even on the active roster, but I'm looking around, and the guys are happy, laughing—you'd have thought we had *won* two games. They knew they were going to win. They had that kind of confidence in themselves. And they went out and won four straight."

Those were heady days for Dave Rajsich. "It was incredible to be a part of that and also be outside looking in and getting that kind of an education."

At the end of the 1978 season, after the Yankees trained him for the big leagues, they traded him to Texas, along with Sparky Lyle. It was a bitter disappointment for Rajsich, who knew that Lyle was on his way out. Rajsich was hoping he would be Lyle's left-handed replacement in the Yankee bullpen. Going to Texas was difficult for him to accept.

Texas at the time was one of the worst franchises in baseball. During his first year in Texas, Rajsich suffered emotionally.

"I was in the big leagues with an organization I didn't know, playing with teammates who were hard for me to relate to, in a situation where I was competing at a level I had never been at. If I had stayed with the Yankees, I wouldn't have been so stressed out. Texas was just no fun for me."

One of his early problems was that he had difficulty communicating with manager Pat Corrales. Then when he saw the moves pulled by general manager Eddie Robinson, he became disenchanted entirely.

"They'd call a guy up, and you'd look at his stats, and you'd ask yourself, *Why?* I mean, they made moves you wouldn't believe."

The crowning blow came when Rajsich was sent down to Tucson on the first of July. Dave had a 2.10 ERA, second on the team behind Jim Kern.

"It was just devastating," Rajsich said.

Rajsich was sent to the minors for exactly four days. The reason he went, he believed, was not because there was a pitcher Texas liked better, but because the four days in the minors could save the club money. By making sure he wasn't on the Texas roster 127 days, Texas could postpone his eligibility for both salary arbitration and free agency. If he was on the team 171 days or fewer, he would not be eligible for either until a full year later. Texas thought it had made a smart business move. Instead, it ended up alienating one of its players. When Rajsich returned from Tucson, he was no longer the same player he had once been. Rajsich became so upset that he stopped working. "I saw what the incentives were."

For the first time in his life, Rajsich became disenchanted with the game. Baseball was no longer a sport. It had become a business.

Rajsich said, "Texas shuffled people around with what appeared to be no rhyme or reason, started messing with your contracts, refused to negotiate fairly. You lost your motivation."

According to Rajsich, the Rangers also took the nucleus of a young ball club and destroyed it.

"They had a possibility of having a great ball club there," he said. "They had Billy Sample, Pat Putnam, Nelson Norman, myself, Gary Gray, and Danny Darwin. All these guys were coming.

"And Texas in essence didn't want to negotiate with anybody. They just renewed everybody's contract. And the thing was, they were blatant about the way they did it. They couldn't care less.

"They took the heart out of the entire ball club."

By midseason Rajsich wanted nothing more than to leave Texas.

"I failed myself, and that's what upsets me more than anything," he said. "But it was the only way I could think of to get out of that organization."

In 1980, Rajsich told the Rangers he wanted to be traded by the fifteenth of July. "If you don't, I'll just quit. I'll go home. I've had enough," he told general manager Eddie Robinson. When the fifteenth came, Rajsich walked out.

Rajsich returned to Triple A. With the Rangers he had pitched so poorly that he was no longer desired by any other big league organizations. Rajsich self-destructed himself right out of the majors.

"I lost market value. By then they couldn't even trade me. By then I was dead, as far as major league baseball was concerned."

In the minors, he began having fun again. After pulling a hamstring, he was traded to the Phillies organization, only to discover that the Phils had ten pitchers with large guaranteed contracts, including Steve Carlton, Dick Ruthven, Mike Krukow, Sid Monge, Ed Farmer.

When he arrived in spring training, the general manager said to him, "I've heard a lot about you." Eddie Robinson had spread the word that Rajsich was an agitator.

"It was the first thing out of his mouth," Rajsich said. "I knew I was in trouble." The Phils released him.

No one else would pick him up. With nowhere else to go, Rajsich re-signed from the Texas organization and went to Triple A at Denver as a starter. He was happy playing Triple A ball. He was having fun again.

The following year he pitched at Texas's Triple A club in Oklahoma City. That year he had a 2.30 earned-run average, managed eight saves, and didn't give up a home run the whole season. Texas didn't have a left-hander in its bullpen. Nevertheless, the new general manager, Tom

Grieve, made it clear that Rajsich wasn't going to get called up if he had an earned-run average of 0.00.

His roommate, Dave Tobic, told him, "Man, you're throwing the ball absolutely great. If you go up in September, you'll be my roomie."

Rajsich said, "I guarantee you I won't go up."

Rajsich knew. He understood that he had been ostracized.

At the end of the season he became a minor league free agent. In 1984 he played in Japan, where he fell in love with the game all over again.

Dave Rajsich, like many ballplayers, is a nomad. Each year he moves somewhere. He's played in fourteen cities in fifteen years.

"My older brothers live sports through me," Rajsich said. "I'm single, and I live through my brothers, their roots and family."

Razor made more money in one year playing for the Hiroshima Carp than he made in his cumulative three years in the big leagues. Also for the first time he felt what it was like to be a baseball star.

"I flew to Osaka, and when I got off the plane, there were fifty reporters and photographers," Rajsich said. "I thought, *What the heck is this?* They said, 'Welcome to major league baseball in Japan.'"

In Japan, Rajsich felt discrimination. Rajsich and his other American teammate, Tim Ireland, were not allowed to stay with their Japanese teammates. During his one season, he only had limited success, because he wasn't allowed to pitch very much. After the Hiroshima Carp won the championship, management decided it could be competitive without any Americans.

Razor returned to the States and went to Baltimore. He had a great spring. The Orioles wanted to send him to Triple A. His heart wasn't in it, and he pitched poorly. After three weeks the Orioles released him.

He signed with Louisville in 1985 and helped the team to the championship. Halfway through the 1986 season he was traded to Kansas City. After 1987 his brother Gary invited him to live in his house while he played in Japan, so Rajsich called the Louisville Cardinals and asked for a job. He played in 1988 for Louisville. It would be, he knew, his last year.

In the past, when he pitched in Triple A, Rajsich made certain his earned-run average wasn't too *low*. He knew no major league team wanted him. To keep from embarrassing anyone, every once in a while when he had a big lead he would give up a few runs just so his numbers wouldn't seem too gaudy.

"I figured if I have a 1.85 ERA and I don't get called up, it's embarrassing for everybody," he said. "It was better to just melt into the woodwork."

But in 1988 he thought, *I'm going to go out and have the best year I can and show these guys I can play.* He knew he was retiring, so he stopped caring about the politics. *All I want is the respect of my teammates,* he told himself.

Dave Rajsich had a great year pitching in relief. His final numbers read 2.70, but they don't tell the real story. Going into the last two weeks, he was 1.80. Then he had to start two games. He gave up five runs against Denver and four against Nashville, and his ERA jumped a whole point.

Rajsich said, "But what's important, I got the respect of my teammates."

Razor left the game with his head held high.

The Pelicans headed down the west coast to Fort Myers. Pelican pitcher Hoot Gibson matched one of the league's stars, Rick Waits, for five innings. Elias Sosa, relieving again, threw two shutout innings. After Sosa allowed a leadoff double in the eighth, he struck out Marty Castillo.

Sun Sox manager Pat Dobson sent a pinch hitter, Larry Harlow, up to bat. Bobby Tolan called time and brought in his lefty middle man, Dave Rajsich.

Harlow took a third strike looking. Jerry Terrell batted, and he grounded out. In the ninth Razor was one, two, three, and with both Pat Zachry and Razor back, as Tex Williams had predicted, the Pelicans were threatening to break the race wide open again.

CHAPTER

21

Mental Mistakes

New Year's Eve for the Pelicans seemed tame. In the North the festivities break up the unrelenting monotony of winter. In Florida, the swimming, boating, and fishing continue unabated, so that when New Year's Eve comes, it's welcome. But no one crowds the main square of St. Petersburg to mark the occasion. You break out the Brut, kiss your significant other, and go to bed.

After beating Fort Myers the day after the new year, it was on to Winter Haven to resume the feud with Bill Lee and the Super Sox. Pitching for the Super Sox was Mike Marshall, whom the Pelicans had tried to sign but who had left for some reason or other—nobody knew for sure. The Super Sox, who desperately needed pitching, hired him.

In the dugout before the game, Roy Howell described the time in Texas when Marshall told Roy that he wasn't intellectual enough to locker next to him. Dock Ellis had been listening, and in the second inning when pitching coach Fergie Jenkins went out to the mound to confer with Marshall, Dock yelled out at Fergie, "You need a 175 IQ to talk to him, Home Boy!" Dock paused. "Get the shovel, Fergie!" he shouted.

Marshall didn't even blink. He had no reason to, because on this day the kinesiologist was perfect, allowing no runs and no hits in his four innings of work. Dock Ellis wasn't impressed.

"He's a crazy motherfucker, that one is," Dock said.

Randy Lerch matched Marshall zip for zip and pitched five innings of shutout ball. But home runs by the Super Sox's Tony Scott and Butch Hobson off Tex Williams beat the Pelicans, 2–1.

A rare mental mistake cost them the game. With one out and catcher Dwight Lowry on third base, Ozzie Virgil, Sr., the Pelicans' third-base coach, gave the sign for the safety squeeze. For the runner to get the message, first there was a visual signal, the rubbing of the hand across a part of the uniform, and then there was a verbal sign. Ozzie shouted out the key word to Lowry, but Dwight didn't know the day's verbal signal. Now he was in a quandary. He figured that if he called time and conferred with his third-base coach, the Super Sox would know something was up. So he did nothing.

Luis Gomez got the bunt down perfectly, and if Lowry had been alert for the bunt, he would have scored easily. But without foreknowledge, Lowry held his base, and the attempt, perfectly executed, went for naught.

After the game the usually unflappable Ozzie Virgil, Sr., was furious. "You can't do that," he told a contrite Lowry. "You can't afford to do that."

Ozzie Virgil began his career as a shortstop with the New York Giants in 1956. At the age of fifty-six, he has forgotten more baseball than most players know. Baseball on the surface is a simple game. See the ball, hit the ball. See the ball, field the ball. But it can be as complicated as mastering chess. Heady teams can beat you with special plays, the hit-and-run, good base stealing, intelligent defense. Ozzie Virgil brings to a team his knowledge of all these aspects of the game, imparting it to the players whenever he can. In a sport that is described as a "game of inches," any advantage can win you a ball game. Ozzie Virgil provides a big advantage.

Virgil coaches at third, a difficult task requiring nerves of steel and impeccable judgment. He faces public scrutiny every time he decides whether to send a runner home. Ozzie also pitches batting practice, hits fungoes, and during his spare time sits with the players and discusses philosophy and strategy—in either English or Spanish. When Ozzie talks, the players listen.

Throughout his career he has preached one important truth about the game of baseball: The team that executes best wins.

"You can have a good club on paper, but the bottom line is, winning clubs execute," Virgil said. "You can have a good club statwise, but the stats don't win games, execution wins games. You may not have a real

The Pelicans

Ozzie Virgil, Sr.

good club, but if you execute well, you'll win. A good example was the New York Giants back in the 1950s.

"I think we had a much better club than the Brooklyn Dodgers did. The nine men on the Giants were better than the nine on the Dodgers, but the Dodgers executed much better than the Giants. The Dodgers played hit-and-run, get them over, bring them in. The Giants played three-run homers. They would come to a situation in the ninth inning with a man on first and Willie Mays up. They were not going to bunt Willie Mays. And it's difficult to win that way. Take the Red Sox in the 1940s. They had a great team, Ted Williams and Gene Stephens, but couldn't win either because of the same thing. They didn't execute. And you have to have guys who can catch the ball to win."

"Why were the Giants able to beat the Dodgers in 1951?" he was asked. That was the year Bobby Thomson hit a home run off Ralph Branca in the bottom of the ninth in a playoff game to win the pennant. Virgil's answer proved surprising.

"I know this for a fact," Virgil said. "The only reason the Giants were able to beat the Dodgers in 1951 is that the Giants were relaying the signs to the hitters. For sure. Joey Amalfitano played with me in Minneapolis in 1956 and 1957, and that was Joey's job.

"Joe was behind the screen in center field in the Polo Grounds. He had spyglasses. It was like watching the game on a TV camera. He would be looking in to the catcher, get the sign, and he would telephone the bullpen. The guy in the bullpen would sit with a towel. If it was going to be a curveball, he would put the towel inside the leg. If it was a fastball, he'd put it outside, or vice versa, I don't know which, but they were getting it. I used to do the same thing in Venezuela. I would take one of the players and set him in center field. Once we established the signs, we'd relay that to the hitter. They do that today in baseball. In fact, the 1985 Minnesota team was doing that.

"Today, believe it or not, players don't like it too much, because they are afraid of getting hit. But when you gave signs to Mays, McCovey, and those Giant clubs, they would tear your head off. It would be like batting practice."

By standing in the third-base coaching box Virgil can divine whether a pitcher will throw a fastball or a breaking ball just from watching his delivery.

"I can get the pitches from 85 percent of the pitchers," Virgil said. "And if the batter wants it, I will relay that information to him.

"Watch a pitcher long enough, and there is something he does different every time he throws the ball, such as between the fastball and the breaking ball. The Giants had every pitch Sandy Koufax was going to throw, and they couldn't hit him, because he had such good stuff. But he was very obvious. You could see it from his windup. Koufax's hands would be higher for the fastball and in closer to his body for the curve.

"If a pitcher has a fault in his windup, I can pick it up. I had a real good teacher. Wes Westrum, the Giant catcher, taught me. He taught me to take my cap, put it over my face, and look through one of the eyelets. It becomes just like a TV camera. Especially in the pitcher's stretch. In a stretch, a pitcher will come a little lower or a little higher when he throws the curve.

"It's easy to relay signs to the hitter. If I start walking toward him from the third-base coaching box, and if he can see me walking, he knows it's a fastball. If I stay still, it's a curveball.

"I did it so often. I can remember in 1971 the Giants won the division on a home run that Dave Kingman hit. I gave him that sign."

After a nine-year playing career with the New York Giants, Detroit, Kansas City, Baltimore, Pittsburgh, and back to the Giants, relocated in San Francisco, Virgil coached with the Giants ten years, then spent one year in Montreal when he joined up with manager Dick Williams. Each discovered the other was a stickler for fundamentals. For the next thirteen years, wherever Williams managed, Virgil was there as his third-base coach. It was a precarious existence for Virgil, because his survival depended on Williams. When Williams finally left the game in 1988, Virgil was out of baseball. He has no regrets.

He said, "I was with one of the greatest managers in baseball. How many guys get lucky enough to run into a job like that? Very few. Unless you were Frank Crosetti coaching under Casey Stengel during his era, or coached for the Sparky Anderson era. Sparky always took Alex Grammas, his third-base coach, with him. One year Alex left to manage Milwaukee, and after he got fired, he came back to Sparky."

Virgil was proud he lasted as long as he did.

"Dick knew I was a very sound baseball person. I was on top of the game. He liked my work. To be a third-base coach is a lot harder than a lot of people think it is."

The day after the Winter Haven game when Dwight Lowry missed the squeeze sign, Ozzie Virgil was lecturing the big catcher. Ozzie told Dwight, "I will only accept one excuse: 'I fucked up.' If you say that, I will respect you. Anything else, no."

Ozzie took this opportunity to discuss something else that bothered him, Dwight's penchant for trying to pull everything. The opposing pitchers continued to throw the large catcher balls on the outside part of the plate, and Lowry consistently tried to pull the ball, usually directly to the second baseman. Lowry, who had hit five home runs during training camp, had a batting average that teetered just above .200.

"They know what your weakness is," Ozzie said. "You're going to have to take the outside pitch the other way. I'd rather have two bloop singles than four line outs."

Lowry nodded to indicate he had heard.

In the second inning against Winter Haven, for the first time in the season the left-handed-hitting Lowry blooped a single the opposite way, to left-center. In the fourth, he went the other way with an outside pitch and singled just to the left of second base. Ozzie Virgil always said that there was a difference between hearing and listening. Finally, it appeared, Dwight Lowry was listening.

CHAPTER

22

Kemp Goes
to Disney World

After their split with Winter Haven, the Pelican lead was reduced to two
and a half measly games as Orlando and Bradenton kept winning. The
post-New Year's blues set in. The season began to drag. Morale was at a
low point. Injuries had reduced the effectiveness of a number of the
players. The spark seemed to be missing. This season, like all seasons,
had ebbs and flows. Now it was ebbing.

Manager Bobby Tolan's spirits were roiled. He was angry, not only
with the way some of the players performed, but also with their attitude.
Steve Kemp took off to Disney World with his two kids, who live with his
ex-wife in California. Although Jim Morley granted Kemp a two-day
sabbatical, Tolan and the other players didn't like it. They questioned
where Kemp was coming from.

Kemp, like Ron LeFlore earlier, had started to grate on Tolan. A
perfectionist, Kemp was dour, intense, and judgmental, a constant critic
of everything and anything. He easily became upset whether it was over
the time the team got to a game, or the batting order, or the fact that the
uniforms were damp before a game.

All season long Kemp had been an enigma. He was the highest-paid
player, one of the marquee names, and he had been hitting around .300

throughout the season. But it was an unproductive .300. He had only batted in seventeen runs and had not hit a single home run. He had left baseball in 1988 at the age of thirty-four, five years after injuring his shoulder in an outfield collision and after being struck in the eye by a batted ball during batting practice. Maybe he was having trouble seeing the ball.

A leg injury, moreover, had kept him from playing in left regularly. Tolan had to make him the designated hitter. So this marquee player wasn't even visible when the Pelicans were in the field.

As long as Kemp drove in runs, no one minded his niggling comments. But with a lack of productivity, Tolan had begun to wonder whether the Pelicans would be better off trading him. Kemp, hearing the tradewinds, told owner Jim Morley he would quit rather than be traded. Morley knew he would do just that. Kemp, who in December 1982 signed a five-year, $5.5 million-dollar deal with the Yankees, was one of the few players who had managed to keep some significant baseball money. He hadn't signed with the Pelicans for the money, though his $9,000 a month salary was hardly peanuts. Rather, he had come to Florida to play ball again and to get away from the bad feelings left by a recent divorce.

Morley informed Tolan he had to keep Kemp.

Tolan wondered aloud how Kemp could leave the team and go off to the Magic Kingdom with his kids. It was an act antithetical to everything Kemp had believed in. Baseball had always been his whole life. But Tolan knew exactly what he was going to do with Kemp upon his return.

"As soon as he gets back," Tolan said, "I'm going to put him in left field and play him every day. If he complains of being hurt, I'm going to put him on the disabled list."

For Steve Kemp, baseball was his life. From childhood on, it was all that mattered to him.

"I'm fortunate enough to do something God gave me the ability to play—baseball," Kemp said. "But there are plenty of kids who had the ability, but they didn't take advantage of it. They got caught up in other things—cars, girls, drugs, alcohol, getting bored with the game. Once I made it, a lot of people would say to me, 'I used to play with you, and I was just as good as you. How come you made it?'

"It was because we would have a game, and my friends on the team would go to the beach and have a good time. I would stay home and relax to get ready for that game. And it wasn't a case of forcing myself. It was what I wanted to do. I wanted to feel like I was as ready as I could possibly be. No one had to tell me to stay home.

"Baseball caused me a lot of problems in my life down the road, but it also helped me to excel. Maybe if I had been different, I wouldn't have had the drive to help me make it to the big leagues. Maybe my being that way helped me become the player I was."

Steve Kemp always believed in himself, even when others didn't. In high school he had been all-California Interscholastic Federation, but at five-feet-nine and 150 pounds he was thought to be on the small side. Not only did the pros fail to draft him, but he didn't get a scholarship from a major college—not even a nibble.

As a result Kemp enrolled at Pasadena Junior College. Ron Dedeaux, the coach at the University of Southern California, saw Kemp play in the North-South All-Star Game for California high schoolers. He had been impressed, but he had no more scholarships available. While Kemp worked out at Pasadena Junior College, Dedeaux asked him if he was interested in playing at USC, which was one of the finest colleges for baseball in the country.

"We can't give you financial help," Dedeaux said, "but if you prove yourself, we'll give you a scholarship next year."

Kemp had to gamble. He told his parents, "I'll prove myself." The first year his parents paid, and he commuted.

As a freshman at USC, Kemp was one of the best players on the junior varsity and at the end of the season got called up to the varsity. He was 4-for-10. That summer he played for Liberal, Kansas, a top semipro team, though he had only been a JV player. He ended up a summer all-American. When he enrolled for his sophomore year, Steve Kemp had a full scholarship.

"Now that I look back on it," Kemp said, "baseball has always been a security blanket for me. Baseball gave me a confidence about myself. I could walk around campus at Arcadia High or at USC and know I had accomplished something and I was somebody. It made me feel good about myself, to where I didn't feel intimidated by people. I relied on that a lot."

In college Kemp found that by excelling in baseball he got special treatment. He learned that if he selfishly, myopically concentrated on his own needs—excelling at the game—he would succeed in life.

"We're brought up to think of ourselves," he said. "Basically I think a lot of the great athletes are selfish, think about themselves. I'm not saying that's bad. It's part of being a great athlete, but again, too, maybe that's not good for life." It was a lesson Kemp wouldn't learn until much later.

At USC Kemp became a star, and he became the number one choice in the entire country when he was drafted by the Detroit Tigers in 1976. He signed for $50,000 and a guaranteed salary for three years. He began his career at Double A Montgomery, Alabama, taking the endless bus trips around the Southern League. At the time Kemp felt his pro life had taken him a step down from his college days at USC.

"I was thinking, *God, I gotta get out of here*, because I wasn't used to the long bus rides," Kemp said. "At USC everything was first-class. We flew. We had ten trainers, a nice ballpark."

By summer Kemp was promoted to Triple A Evanston, and he tore up the American Association. He hit .386 and 11 home runs in half a season. Two days before he was to go up to the Tigers, he tore ligaments in an ankle. While he recuperated in a hospital in Detroit, Tiger manager Ralph Houk told him, "Get yourself ready. I don't care what you do in spring training. You're my left fielder."

In 1977 Kemp played and struggled. Houk traded Willie Horton to Texas to prove to Kemp he intended to have Kemp play left field. Houk told him, "Did I have to trade Horton to prove it to you? Go out and relax and have fun."

That day he hit a home run off Bill Singer in Toronto. Kemp caught fire. As a rookie he hit 18 home runs and had 88 RBIs. Under Ralph Houk, whom he loved, Kemp learned about life in the majors, its ups and downs and how to handle stress. He learned how hard the game can be on you emotionally.

At a team party in front of some of his teammates, outfielder Rusty Staub told Kemp, "They are so disappointed in you." Kemp was crushed. The next day he went into Ralph Houk's office, and he said to the manager, "Ralph, if you guys are that disappointed in me, then you don't have to play me. I feel bad for you, because I'd do anything for you."

Houk had no idea what Kemp was talking about. "Where did you hear that we're disappointed in you?" Houk asked.

"Rusty said that."

Houk said, "That damn Staub. He thinks he can manage this damn club. I'd love to let him manage for a fucking day and see how he likes it."

Kemp said, "You have to remember that players are human beings and they are going to make physical mistakes. They're going to strike out and

Tom DiPace

Steve Kemp

have bad days and good days, bad years and good years. That's the bad things about this game. I was always told by Willie Horton and Mickey Stanley, 'Stay on an even keel. Don't take the roller coaster.' And I've lived by that for so long.

"But it's hard to be up for 162 games. You get tired, playing every day. And other things are happening in your life. You're going out and drinking, and again, the one part of your life that seems to get cut out is family. It's wrong, totally wrong.

"You're on the road, and your family wants to come, and you say, 'Fine, but I'm not going to go out with you. You get up on your own and go. I have to sleep in.' And I looked at myself as being very selfish. I look back, and I see it caused a lot of problems for me. I learned it, but too late. Baseball was the most important thing."

It seemed Steve Kemp would eventually become a superstar. In 1979 he batted .318, hit twenty-six home runs, and drove in 105 runs. In 1980 he drove in 101 runs. After 1981, a season in which he only played 105 games and had only nine home runs, Kemp demanded a free-agent-type million-dollar contract. The tightfisted Tigers didn't feel he was worth the money. They traded him to the Chicago White Sox.

"I was the first player who was going to command a big free-agent-type contract," Kemp said. "The Tigers weren't ready for that. They signed Alan Trammell to the deal they had offered me. I said, 'Just because Alan is happy with that deal doesn't mean it's what I'm worth.' Alan had fewer years and wasn't the player he is now."

Once Kemp turned down the million dollars over three years deal, the local reporters started writing about the ingrate who turned down the million dollars, and his popularity in Detroit plummeted.

"Understandably, it's hard for a fan to understand that a player is turning down a million dollars," Kemp said. "When I wouldn't sign, the best thing for them to do was to trade me. They got a good player, Chet Lemon, from the White Sox."

Kemp had an excellent year for the White Sox in 1982. He hit .286, smacked nineteen homers, and drove in ninety-eight runs. He wanted to stay, but Kemp's agent told the White Sox he had to be signed before the free agent draft. It didn't happen.

Kemp said, "I felt I had produced for them, that I had had consistent years and proven what I was capable of doing. I didn't want to have to get into the free agent market to see how the teams would react to me and then treat me accordingly. The White Sox knew what I could do. Make a decision."

Co-owner Jerry Reinsdorf told Kemp he would be signed before the day of the draft.

"We never reached an agreement," Kemp said. "The day of the draft I was drafted by nine teams. The other owner, Eddie Einhorn, called and said, 'We'll give Steve what he wants.'"

Kemp told him it was too late.

"In my position I had to think of not only myself but the other players," Kemp said. "One of the things owners were doing at the time was stringing players along. I had said what I was going to do. They didn't sign me by the deadline. I felt I had to stand behind what I said. So I became a free agent and signed with New York."

George Steinbrenner paid him $5.5 million over five years, angering the other owners. Baltimore owner Edward Bennett Williams, a close friend of Steinbrenner's, was the angriest, accusing the Yankee owner of stockpiling players.

In 1983 Kemp went to spring training and led the Yankees in home runs, RBIs, and batting average. In the fourth game of the season he severely injured his shoulder in a collision with Jerry Mumphrey and Willie Randolph. The injury prevented Kemp from swinging the bat. Kemp continued playing anyway. It hurt his batting average and his confidence.

Then during batting practice in Milwaukee, Omar Moreno hit a line drive that struck Kemp in the left eye. He had retina surgery and spent a week in the hospital.

"My pupil would no longer contract, but fortunately I was still able to play."

The next January Kemp began taking batting practice. He discovered his eyesight would never be as good as before. But Kemp convinced himself that he could continue as a major league player despite the handicap. For the next five years he fought against all those who believed otherwise and concentrated on his game in his battle to return to his former status as a star player.

With Kemp having to play under the handicap of both shoulder and eye injuries, the Yankees gave up on him after 1984. They were able to unload him and his large salary only because the Pittsburgh Pirates wanted to get rid of Dale Berra and his big salary. Dale returned to his dad, Yogi, who was managing the Yankees, along with minor league outfielder Jay Buhner. Kemp went to the Pirates, along with Tim Foli and $400,000.

In 1985 Kemp hit only .250 with two home runs in ninety-four games. That year he was 9-for-27 as a pinch hitter.

A doctor informed Kemp that he would never see out of the eye as he once did. The eye specialist told the same thing to Pirate general manager Syd Thrift, who, says Kemp, spread the information around the league. His manager, Jim Leyland, started Kemp on Opening Day against Dwight Gooden in 1986. He went 0-for-4, striking out three times. Kemp didn't play again for two weeks. He went 2-for-4 with a home run against Dennis Eckersley and sat another two weeks. Pinch-hitting duty followed.

"I don't think I had thirty at-bats. Then they released me. No one wanted to have anything to do with me," Kemp said. "It was because Syd Thrift talked to that eye specialist. Even in Japan, the response was 'He can't see.'"

Kemp says he can hit at the major league level despite his eye troubles. His only drawback, he says, is that because his pupil will not contract, it is harder for him to see the ball in the daylight. But he says he has compensated by becoming a better fundamental hitter.

Kemp said, "Before I would go out and swing the bat, and even if I wasn't right mechanically, I could still put the ball in play. But with my bad eye if I did that, I would miss, and so I worked on my mechanics until they were right."

Kemp feels his eye injury has left him persona non grata with baseball's executives.

Once the Pirates released him, Steve Kemp, the perfectionist who had dedicated his life to baseball, had to make a decision. *Do I get out of baseball permanently, or do I work my way back?* Kemp decided to work his way back.

Kemp said with pride, "I didn't want someone in the front office telling me, 'You can't play any more.'"

Whether he wanted it or not, that's exactly what happened. Kemp had been labeled "permanently injured," and no matter how well he performed in the minor leagues, he wasn't going to get another chance.

Kemp quit the game at the end of the 1988 season. He was thirty-four years old. He returned to his home in California. His wife told him she wanted a divorce. He had devoted all his time and energy to the game, leaving little for his wife and kids. Baseball had been everything to Steve Kemp, but in the end it had cost him his family.

In January of 1989 he and his wife split up. After it was over, Steve

Kemp forced himself to look in the mirror and ask himself, *Why?* He concluded that if blame had to be assigned, he would accept most of it. Part of the problem, he believed, lay in his being on the road so much. Another part lay in his self-absorption.

"I think a lot of people who perform really well think about themselves and what is important to them more than they think about other things in life," Kemp said.

"There is also no question that I expect a lot of myself. And when you play baseball, people expect a lot out of you too, and you're always open to criticism—someone is always telling you, 'You're doing this wrong or that wrong.' We learn as players to deal with a lot of abuse, even in the clubhouse every day when the guys are getting on you. A lot of people can't handle that kind of criticism. They say, 'God, why is he so hard on me?' Well, that's the type of environment we're around all the time at the ballpark. We're just taking it home with us."

Kemp also recognizes the danger of being a perfectionist. For Steve Kemp, everything has to be in its place and be clean and neat.

"I expect things to always be the way they are supposed to be," he said. "I am probably very difficult to live with."

Kemp suffers with his guilt.

"We were the American family, with two beautiful, very intelligent children," he said. "It was a very good situation that was thrown out the door. A lot of people were saddened when our family split up. Now I'm saying to myself, *I realize there are more important things in life than baseball.*"

He added, "You can be bitter and negative, or you can try to get the most out of a situation, to learn from your mistakes. I'm trying to change myself so that I can enjoy life. I know I have a long way to go, but before I never gave. Now I'm *trying* to give. That's the important thing."

And so Steve Kemp, mindful of how much he lost, took his kids to Disney World for two days instead of insisting that baseball come first. He knew that Bobby Tolan would be angry, that his teammates wouldn't understand, but it didn't matter any more. The happiness of his kids, that's what counted most. The Pelicans would be there when he got back.

As Tolan vowed, upon his return Kemp was playing in left field. From then on he was in left every day.

At Pompano Beach against the Gold Coast Suns in the very first inning of his first game back with one runner on base, Kemp, rested, hit a long fly ball down the left-field line, an opposite field hit that carried over the high green fence and on into the adjoining tennis courts. It was Steve Kemp's first home run of the season.

It has often been said that some of the best trades are the ones that don't get made. For the Pelicans, it was certainly true in the case of Steve Kemp.

In the next two weeks Kemp raised his average to .327. In the field, no one would mistake him for The Natural, but he got to most balls, always threw to the right base, in short, made the plays. Steve Kemp's steady play turned him into a major catalyst for the Pelicans as they made their run for the pennant.

23

Tolan Is Teed Off

Besides Steve Kemp's absence, Tolan was angry because center fielder Kenny Landreaux didn't seem to be hustling in the field. His batting average had fallen, and on ground balls he barely ran to first. Constantly complaining of being tired, Kenny seemed to have been sleepwalking through the season. On this day Landreaux complained of having a cold.

Tolan was saddled, moreover, with various player ailments. Pitcher Jon Matlack and outfielder Steve Henderson suffered from the flu. Shortstop Sergio Ferrer still had a leg pull and a pinched nerve in his neck. Catcher Butch Benton had an ankle sprain.

During batting practice before the January 4 Winter Haven game at Chain O'Lakes Park, Lamar Johnson squared to bunt. He missed the ball and then hunched forward as though paralyzed, gritting his teeth in pain, waiting for back spasms to pass. After a few minutes he walked, very slowly, to the clubhouse, scratched for the day. Steve Henderson had not expected to play, but with Lamar out, he had to go in as the designated hitter.

"You're running out of players," a fan kidded him.

"And some of them don't give a shit," Tolan barked, walking away.

Bobby Tolan *always* gave a shit. His intense nature and his strong ego would not have allowed otherwise. He had signed with the Pittsburgh

Pirates in 1963, was drafted by the St. Louis Cardinals when the Pirates didn't protect him for the draft, and at the age of nineteen got to sit on the Cardinals' bench as St. Louis won the National League pennant and the 1964 World Series against the Yankees.

The Cardinals had anticipated an outfield of Lou Brock, Curt Flood, and Bobby Tolan, but when Roger Maris postponed his retirement for two years, in October 1968 the Cards traded Tolan and Wayne Granger to the Cincinnati Reds for Vada Pinson.

Reds manager Dave Bristol gave Tolan two months to prove his worth. "All I need is a month," Tolan told himself. He got off to a great start, won an outfield job, and became an important cog in the Cincinnati hitting machine. In 1969 the Reds hit 171 home runs and led the league in runs scored. Lee May had 38 homers, Tony Perez 37, Johnny Bench 26, Tolan 21, Alex Johnson 17, and Pete Rose 16.

In the last week of the season the Reds were eliminated and finished third to the surprising Atlanta Braves. Bristol was fired. His replacement in 1970 was Sparky Anderson.

This time it was a runaway. The Reds won 70 of their first 100 ball games. That year Tolan became a National League star, hitting .316, with 16 homers, 80 RBIs, and 57 stolen bases. He was twenty-four years old, in his prime and in his glory. But in baseball, stardom can end quickly.

In 1970 he was a supernova, burning up the base paths that one golden year. Then, in January 1971, while playing basketball on a team composed of Cincinnati Reds players, Tolan's Achilles tendon snapped. Like so many injuries, it was sudden, and was serious. It signaled the beginning of the end for his career.

It was predicted that Bobby Tolan would never play again. After two straight .300 seasons, writers were penning his obit. "He would have been a superstar," they wrote. At one point Bobby Tolan believed that his career was over.

Tolan was living in Cincinnati. He went out to a sporting goods store and bought some big old combat boots. At one in the morning in the snow Tolan would go out running. Bobby Tolan could not live with himself if he could no longer be a productive player. He had always seen himself as a star. In his dreams he was being inducted into the Hall of Fame. All his life, with the Millie Tigers, the Thompson Tigers, the Little Pirates, Bobby Tolan was the best of the best. For the rest of his life, he would become good, then fair, then no longer adequate. But one thing would never change: his belief that baseball executives, owners and managers, should continue to treat him like a star. His downfall would be swift, and with the loss of stature, Bobby would find himself standing on principle and tilting at windmills wherever he went—and getting slapped down for it.

After missing the entire 1971 season, he came back in 1972 and helped the Cincinnati Reds win the pennant. With him in the lineup in 1970, the Reds won. Without him in 1971, they didn't win.

"I can't help but think we didn't win in 1971 because I had hurt myself," he said.

At the end of the 1972 season Bobby Tolan was named Comeback Player of the Year, an award he didn't feel he deserved. To many players, the award would have signified an achievement: coming back from adversity. To Tolan, it was a put-down.

"It wasn't like I hit .220 all my life and suddenly hit .300. Yeah, I'd be excited as a big dog then. But, in fact, I was disappointed because I hit .283 and didn't feel I had a good year. There were a lot of pitchers who had come into the league who I had not seen or who had developed a new pitch. And about halfway through the season I was dead tired from not playing the year before. But I refused to rest. I didn't want to miss any games. I had already missed 162 the year before, and when the season finally ended, I was exhausted, completely drained."

They gave Tolan the Comeback Player of the Year Award because no one expected he would come back at all. "My career was supposed to have been over with," he said.

The Reds had started the 1972 season sluggishly. Part of the reason involved Tolan, who, afraid to test his Achilles tendon, was reluctant to steal bases.

Three weeks into the 1972 season Tolan was concerned that the team wasn't winning. He was determined to play with his old intensity and ignore his injury. He told himself, *If the heel is going to go, it's going to go. I have to help the team win.*

He began stealing bases. And then Joe Morgan, the fleet second baseman, started hitting and started stealing bases, and the Cincinnati Reds began to win.

Tolan credits Joe Morgan with making a big difference on the team. "Now we were two threats. Joe and I were like wide receivers who are long-ball threats. If I didn't get on, they still had to worry about Morgan. Johnny Bench got fastballs to hit. The pitcher couldn't let up."

It turned out that Joe Morgan would have a long and productive career with the Reds and that Bobby Tolan soon would be an ex-Red. Halfway through the 1973 season, Tolan injured his back. He couldn't swing the bat right, and his average started slipping. The doctors could not diagnose the injury, however, and the Reds management began accusing Tolan of manufacturing an excuse for his poor performance.

Tolan kept playing hard, diving into walls, running the bases with his old abandon, but because of his injury, he didn't get on base much. Tolan ended up hitting .206 that year. Through he still hit nine homers and drove in 51 runs, the Reds gave his job to Cesar Geronimo.

A player hitting .206 isn't supposed to argue. He is supposed to go along. It was not in Bobby Tolan's nature to do that.

When Tolan's average slipped, his pride took a major beating. The Reds sought to put him on the disabled list without first sending him to a doctor. Tolan fought the move. He called the players' union chief, Marvin Miller, who told him the Reds were in violation of the rules. While Miller fought to keep him on the team, Tolan felt the terrible pressure of no longer being wanted. He drove to St. Louis for a few days to stay with a friend and former teammate, Ted Savage.

Tolan was in St. Louis when Savage called to tell him he had heard on the radio that the Reds had taken him off the disabled list.

Tolan called Cincinnati to find out if it was true. Dick Wagner, the general manager, confirmed that it was.

"Yes," Wagner said, "you've been taken off the disabled list. The team leaves today on a road trip for San Diego, and you better be on the plane. The flight is in three hours."

Tolan had driven to St. Louis, about seven hours away from Cincinnati. Tolan said, "Dick, there is no way I can get back in time."

Wagner told him, "You'd better be here, or you will face further disciplinary action."

Tolan called the airport and lied to get on a flight to Cincinnati. "They bumped people off to get me and my family on," he said. He had told his wife to go home, pack a suitcase, and send it to San Diego. Tolan stayed at the airport and met the team.

Everything would have been fine, except that while he was in St. Louis, Tolan's rebellious nature got the best of him. He began growing a mustache, which on the Reds was strictly forbidden.

When the team arrived at the airport, Tolan told manager Sparky Anderson, "I'm here. I made it. I want to get the whole situation over with. Let's play some ball."

Sparky said, "You have a mustache."

Tom DiPace

Bobby   Tolan

Tolan told him, "I'm going to wear it."

Sparky replied, "No, you're not. We'll deal with that tomorrow at game time."

When the team arrived in San Diego, team president Bob Howsam called Tolan for a meeting. Howsam said, "Bobby, you've been gone for a couple of days and you're not in shape."

Tolan thought to himself, *Away two days and I'm not in shape?*

Howsam said, "We're going to give Cesar Geronimo your job until you get back into shape."

"I was ready to play," Tolan said, "but I never got my job back."

With four games left in the season Sparky asked Tolan if he could pinch-hit. Tolan said, "Sure," and he made an out. Sparky told him afterward, "If you want to take off, go home."

Tolan returned to the locker room, took off his clothes, and listened to the game on the radio. Chief Bender, the head of player personnel, walked in, and when he saw Tolan sitting there, he said, "Who in the hell do you think you are?"

Tolan said, "I'm Bobby Tolan."

Bender replied, "What's that supposed to mean?"

The two men got into a shouting match. Bender called Tolan a prima donna and said, "You only care about yourself. You're a no-good bastard."

Tolan hit him. It was one punch, Tolan's punch, and three or four people who were in the clubhouse pulled them apart.

Tolan said, "The guys who were in the clubhouse and saw what happened all lied."

After the melee Bender shouted, "You're off the ball club!"

The next day, when Tolan came to play, his locker was empty. The clubhouse manager told him, "Sparky wants to see you."

Tolan went to talk to Sparky, bringing Pete Rose and Ted Kluszewski with him so he'd have witnesses.

Sparky said, "You're suspended because of the mustache."

Tolan felt trapped, that everyone on the Reds had ganged up on him. He continued his defiance.

After Sparky informed him of his suspension, Tolan sneaked into the storage room and got one of his uniforms. He put it on and went out to right field. When Sparky saw him, he came out and said, "You may have won the battle, but you're not going to win the war."

The next day the Reds made sure there was no uniform with his name on it. Tolan could not work out. He was fined and suspended for the remaining three games and was ineligible for the playoffs.

Tolan went home. He had intended to stay there, until he read in the papers that the Reds had hired a special security guard to keep him from the ballpark. He wouldn't even be allowed to buy a ticket.

Tolan said, "I called Brooks Lawrence, who was working for the Reds. He was an old black pitcher who won nineteen games one year for the Reds. I asked Brooks if they had really hired someone to keep me out, and he told me it wasn't true. Because if it *was* true, I was coming. But Brooks said, 'If I were you, I wouldn't come to the park for a few days.'

"The next year I was with San Diego, and I returned to play the Reds, and one of the security guards said to me, 'Hey, Bobby, I'm the one.' I said, 'You're the one. The one what?' He said, 'I'm the one who was supposed to keep you out of here last year.' So it was true."

When the Reds suspended him, Tolan compounded their aggravation by taking them to arbitration. Three days before the hearing was to take place in Detroit, Dick Wagner called and told Tolan he didn't want to go to arbitration. Tolan said he didn't either.

Wagner said, "Why don't we just forget about everything and let it go?"

Tolan said, "You fined me, and I want my money back."

Wagner said no. The next day Wagner called and said, "Look, we will reinstate you in the pension plan for the three days."

Tolan said, "Great. What about the fine?"

"We're keeping it," Wagner replied.

"Do this. Take the money and give it to a charity in Cincinnati in my name," Tolan said.

"No, we're keeping the money."

Tolan went to Detroit and had the hearing. At the hearing the Reds said they had offered to give the money to charity and that Tolan had refused. Bob Howsam said Tolan was suspended for being "a detriment to the ball club," even though his manager, Sparky Anderson, had said the suspension was for wearing the mustache.

In 1974, when he was with the Padres, Tolan found out he had won the arbitration hearing. The arbitrator had asked him, "If you win, what do you want?"

Tolan told him, "The main thing I would like is to have a public apology from the Reds, because I had been slandered in the papers throughout Ohio, and the word around the National League was that I was a jerk."

The arbitrator refused to give him that wish.

"So I won," Tolan said, "but I still lost."

Tolan explained, "It shows I was right in challenging the Reds, but that's been hanging over my head since. It's part of the reason it's been tough for me to get jobs in baseball. On several occasions I've tried to rejoin the Reds' organization. To me, I've forgotten about it. But apparently it's still being held against me that I challenged the Reds in court."

Tolan thought hard about the events that he had been caught up in and his reaction to them. It had been a Pyrrhic victory. He won in arbitration but lost in life. Nevertheless, Tolan does not seem to regret his actions. He felt he had done what was right, even though it had cost him dearly.

For the next six years Tolan bounced from San Diego to Philadelphia to Pittsburgh to Japan and finally back to San Diego, where he began his coaching career. But the beginning of the end came from his defiance in Cincinnati. Tolan, nevertheless, does not feel contrite. It is not in his nature.

"If I had to do it over again." he said, "I think I'd still do the same thing."

24

The Treadmill

The Pelicans on January 5 traveled from Winter Haven to Pompano Beach for three games against the Suns. The Pelican lead was still two and a half games. There was optimism in the clubhouse with the arrival of Ozzie Virgil, Jr., Ozzie's son, a major league catcher and power hitter who had been playing in Puerto Rico, and also with the return of Steve Kemp after his trip to Disney World.

In the opener Milt Wilcox won his ninth game with the help of Dave Rajsich and Dock Ellis. Gary Rajsich, Alan Bannister, and Steve Kemp each drove in two runs.

The next day the linescore of the Saturday St. Pete–Gold Coast game read as follows:

	1	2	3	4	5	6	7	8	9	R	H	E
St. Petersburg	4	2	1	0	0	1	5	1	3	17	27	0
Gold Coast	2	0	0	1	1	2	1	2	4	13	17	2

On a sunny Saturday afternoon in Pompano Beach, first baseman Gary Rajsich had the most productive day of his thirteen-year professional career. In the first inning, with Howell, Kemp, and Ozzie Jr. on the bases and two outs, the younger Rajsich batted against pitcher Mike

Kekich. Rajsich got the bat head out in front of a fastball and pulled a viciously hit ball down the right-field line that cleared everyone off the bases.

In the sixth, he drove in his fourth run with a groundout, and in the seventh with Kemp and Ozzie Jr. on base, Rajsich made a ball disappear over the right-center-field fence for three more runs. Still not finished, in the eighth he singled to right-center to drive in his eighth run of the day.

In just one game he had propelled himself among the league RBI leaders. Had Gary not had to leave the Pelicans with two weeks left in the season to take a scouting job, he surely would have finished in the top ten. Not bad for a guy who spent most of his career in the minors.

Among the words of wisdom coaches tell young ballplayers are: "If you keep your nose clean, hustle, work hard, apply yourself and keep plugging, and if you have the talent, eventually you will make it."

However, you can do all of those things and spend year after year honing your game, and even if you do have the talent, you may discover that you won't get the chance anyway. It's the nature of baseball. Talent is purely subjective. And whether you get the chance may well hinge on luck. Your minor league director may simply not like your game. A manager may not like your personality. You might be playing behind a superstar. How many shortstops haven't made the Orioles because Cal Ripken, Jr., is there? How many catchers were blocked behind Carlton Fisk? How many third basemen rotted behind Mike Schmidt?

Gary Rajsich ended up on a baseball treadmill. The irony was that Rajsich as a youth had no intention of being a ballplayer. Rather, his childhood hobby was astronomy. He wanted to be an astronaut. He would have gone to the Air Force Academy, except that he fell in love with a hometown girl. So the choice was either the academy and flying or the hometown girl and playing football and baseball in front of his family at nearby Arizona State.

Rajsich picked sports and the girl, who later became his wife. He enrolled in engineering at Arizona State University, and after a month and a half of scrimmaging the varsity and getting beat up, he quit. He was afraid of dislocating his shoulder and hurting his throwing ability.

Rajsich made the ASU baseball team as a freshman. Under coach Jim Brock, Rajsich worked hard on conditioning and fundamentals. For three years he played. He never started. Ahead of him were Ken Phelps and Clay Westlake at first. He also was unable to crack an outfield of future major leaguers.

His career in college, as it was to be in the pros, was marked by frustration. Rajsich could not have known it at the time, but once he was bitten by the baseball bug, he was hooked. It became an obsession, an addiction. He has never been able to let go. As Jim Bouton wrote in *Ball Four,* "You see, you spend a good piece of your life gripping a baseball and in the end it turns out that it was the other way around all the time." No matter what obstacles were put in the way of Gary Rajsich, he kept going. For a decade he was the Little Engine That Could, repeating over and over, "I think I can, I think I can." Only that chance just never seemed to come.

Rajsich said, "At one point in the fall of my junior year at ASU, Coach Brock made assurances that if I had a good fall I would start the next spring. I hit .392, second on the team, but come spring I wasn't a starter. It was a grin-and-bear it, get-through-it type of thing. I had switched to business, a finance major, and I was hitting the books, studying hard. After three years of college, I knew professional baseball was a possibility, but there was no way I was planning on it."

Rajsich was drafted because in an intrasquad scrimmage he had hit a home run and a double against ASU teammate Floyd Bannister, a lefty pitcher who was to be the number one draft pick in the country. A Houston Astros scout called him over and asked him if he would be interested in signing if he were drafted.

"Naturally, I didn't even have to think," Rajsich said.

This was in June 1976. Rajsich was drafted by the Astros in the eleventh round, ahead of some of the starters on the ASU team. His long trek to the big leagues had begun.

"That made me feel real good," Rajsich recalled. "I didn't care what kind of money they came up with as a signing bonus. I was going."

The Astros sent him to Covington, Virginia, in the Appalachian League. For Rajsich, who hadn't even started much in college, his introduction to the pro game was a grueling experience.

"I learned quickly that the way to move up through the system was to play well consistently every day," he said.

The core of the Covington ball club consisted of college draftees. When Rajsich compared himself to his new teammates, he was optimistic but cautious.

"One of the first days we were there our manager, Julio Menares, told us, 'Only 2 percent of you guys will ever make it to the majors.' That was a shock. I hadn't realized the percentages were so against us. But I was determined that I would be one of those 2 percent."

Tom DiPace

Gary Rajsich

When he went to Covington, Rajsich wrote to his girlfriend, "I will know if this is what I want to do for my career in a few weeks."

It became a personal joke between them. Each year, year after year, it was "We'll play another year." After six years in the minors, she was still asking, "Gary, do you know yet?"

When Rajsich began his career, he had a plan. Most minor leaguers have the same plan. "Every year I tried to improve some aspect of my game so I could move up to the next level," Rajsich said. "I never wanted to stay at the same level. I wanted to keep improving."

In 1978 he went to Columbus, Georgia, the Southern League. "I remember long bus rides, eight hours to Atlanta, thirteen hours to Memphis, a lot of mosquitoes in the summertime. You just grind it out." He was twenty-three years old. Halfway through the season, he was called up to Triple A Charleston, West Virginia.

For Rajsich, his toughest hurdle was becoming proficient at the Triple A level.

"In Triple A most of the players have a good idea how to play," he said. His first season at that level was hard. He platooned, hitting only against right-handed pitching, and in half a season he hit but .230.

"There I was, sitting on the bench again, as I was in college," Rajsich recalled. Personally Rajsich felt it to be a step back, though he enjoyed the experience because the team won the pennant. Also for the first time he got to watch some players who had been in the major leagues.

It's interesting what ballplayers remember about their careers. Gary Rajsich's most vivid memory in Triple A was his awe of the pitching skills of Mike Scott.

"That was the first time I had seen a major league fastball, an overpowering fastball," Rajsich said. "I thought, *Wow, I better keep improving or I'm stuck here.*"

But Rajsich didn't know *how* to keep improving, and he had no one to give him advice. In 1979 Houston sent him back down to Double A.

"I was very disappointed. It was very difficult for me. You can either throw your arms up and give up, which had crossed my mind: *I don't need this. I deserve to be in Triple A.* Or on the other hand, *Why give up now? Go back down and do great, tear it up, show them, and get back up there.* And that's what I did."

Rajsich helped lead Columbus, Georgia, to the first half of the season championship. He hit .293 with 14 home runs, and halfway through the season he went back up to Charleston. He was more relaxed and more comfortable but found no communication with manager Jim Beauchamp, who preferred veteran players.

"I couldn't talk to him," Rajsich said. "I was platooned. I hit .206."

Whenever Rajsich got stuck, his solution was simple: Work harder. During the winter of 1979, he bought a pitching machine.

Rajsich had heard the scouting reports. His arm was too weak and he ran too slowly. He was informed his legs were too short.

Rajsich said, "I came to realize that I was going to have to hit my way to the major leagues, that I wasn't going to make it with my fielding, even though I was a good fielder."

Rajsich lived in Phoenix. He took four to five hundred swings a day five days a week. He took his pitching machine to the local Phoenix Junior College and used their cages to hit. His wife fed the machine.

His work paid off. In 1980 Rajsich had a great year and got over his Triple A "wall." Finally Rajsich was playing every day at the Triple A level and succeeding. The next step was the major leagues.

That year everything broke right for Rajsich. The Triple A team moved from Charleston to Tucson, two hours from his home. His manager was Jimmy Johnson, with whom he got along well. Johnson put him out in the field every day. Tucson finished the season with the best record in the Coast League.

"Productively and playing-wise, I had my best year," Rajsich said. "I hit .321, with 99 ribbies, and I had a triple-double, 22 doubles, 14 triples, and 21 home runs. It was a fun season."

After a year like that, one would have expected that the Astros would have called Rajsich to the big club for the customary end-of-the-season look-see.

Houston was in a dogfight for the Western Division title with the Dodgers, and they called up several players, but not Gary Rajsich. He was disappointed. He had every right to be.

Players always like to know where they stand. Minor leaguers don't always know. They have to look for clues. One positive sign for Rajsich was that over the winter he was included on the Astros' forty-man roster. Then in the spring of 1981, at the age of twenty-six, he went to his first major league spring training.

"It was a dream come true," Rajsich said. If he could just make the Astros' team, he stood to earn big money. During spring training he could hear the vets talk about the money to be made.

Rajsich said, "Cesar Cedeno had just signed the first million-dollar contract, ten years for a million dollars, and everybody said. 'Wow, that's a lot of money.' I wondered, *What can I do to get there?"*

Rajsich never did come up with a good answer. That spring manager Bill Virdon allowed him twenty at-bats, barely a look-see, and never started him in a game. Rajsich didn't have to be a seer to know he wasn't going to make the ball club. On the final day he was cut.

Rajsich approached Virdon and asked him what he had to do in Triple A to come back to Houston. Rajsich said, "In so many words he told me that as long as he was manager, I wasn't going to play for Houston.

"That really woke me up," Rajsich said. "Again I was at the point where I was saying to myself *I don't need this. I'm going home."*

Rajsich went to the Houston front office and told them he had hit a wall and was going home. He said, "If I can't make it to the Astros' big league club, there's no point going back to Tucson."

The next day Houston traded Rajsich to Tidewater, the New York Mets' Triple A club.

"It was like a breath of life," Rajsich said.

But it was also a slap in the face, a dose of reality about the true nature of his profession. During his five years in the Houston organization, the Astros were the only team he had ever wanted to play for. With his trade, his thinking changed.

"Houston was the team that drafted me," Rajsich said. "All my loyalties were there. I never really thought about getting traded. *Why trade me? I love you guys.* But once I was traded to the Mets, I learned a lesson. By going back to the minors and showing what I could do, I had impressed somebody else. *Somebody else wants you.* So that was a new life."

Under manager Jack Aker, a quiet man like Rajsich, Gary thrived at Tidewater. Every day his name was on that lineup card in an outfield slot. Aker was rewarded with Rajsich's finest season, including 22 home runs in only 66 games. Because 1981 was the strike year, ESPN, a cable channel, broadcast some of the Tidewater games. Rajsich made his mark on national television.

Rajsich said, "Everybody told me, 'You're having a great year, you can hit with power, and as soon as there is major league baseball again, the Mets are going to call you up.'"

Fate intervened, as it does for so many ballplayers. You have to be good, and you have to be lucky. Bad luck comes randomly and suddenly.

Playing in Richmond, Rajsich slid home headfirst, and his right hand got caught in a hole. He rolled over on top of his hand and broke his right wrist. It was a small fracture of a small bone, and for a while the doctors couldn't find it, so he played with pain. For three weeks he struggled. Finally he went to the Mets' team doctor, who put the hand in a cast. Rajsich was finished for the season.

Though disappointed at his bad luck, Rajsich was encouraged by the Mets' enthusiasm about his play. If you want to play badly enough, you look for positives. The next spring he hit a home run against Ron Davis of the Yankees, and he made the Met ball club.

Gary Rajsich had started in the minors in 1976, and this was 1982, a long time to work toward any goal. To celebrate Rajsich's personal triumph, on that first plane ride the Mets sat him in first-class.

"I was flying higher than the plane going to New York," Rajsich said, "Finally I was in the major leagues. It had been a goal, and I was elated."

That elation didn't last very long. Rajsich had waited six years to make it to the major leagues, and when he got there, he found himself playing on one of the worst teams in baseball. Moreover, he was one of those players who needed to play every day to stay sharp at the bat. Even though he hit .315 as a starter in 1982, mostly what he did was pinch-hit, something Rajsich did poorly.

"Primarily George Bamberger used me, a twenty-seven-year-old rookie, as a pinch hitter," Rajsich said. "I was two-for-thirty-five as a pinch hitter. It was difficult for me to relax pinch-hitting. The only reason I stayed was that when I started, I did well. We were a last-place club, and that was very difficult. We were only two games out in May, but a couple pitchers got hurt, and it became a job by July when we were fifteen games out."

The frustrations were great, the rewards few. Try as he might to learn how to be a productive pinch hitter, much of the skill comes from experience. Rajsich had none. But Gary Rajsich kept plugging, kept hoping, kept waiting for his big break. Rajsich, hanging on by his thumbs, knew that as soon as the Mets could find a better pinch hitter, he would be gone.

The next year, 1983, he made the club out of spring training. But Danny Heep, whom the Mets had recently acquired for pitcher Mike Scott, was a more successful pinch hitter.

Rajsich was despondent. He called Tidewater manager Davey Johnson, who told him, "If you come, you'll be at first every day."

"That was good enough for me," Rajsich recalled. "Davey said, 'There are twenty-five other teams out there. Go out and show them.'"

Rajsich said, "I don't know if I was committed to that thought, but that's what I wanted, because I did hit when I started. I relaxed more when I got my at-bats, and I would get a hit or two every game."

Again, when given the chance to play every day, Rajsich had a great year. At Tidewater he smashed 28 homers, had 83 RBIs, hit .270, and led the league in assists and in fielding. Tidewater won the International League, and went to the Triple A World Series, the only year they had it, and won that. And Gary Rajsich was the MVP of the tournament. He was called up by the Mets and played the last ten days of the season when Keith Hernandez pulled a hamstring.

He recalled, "I hit .333, twelve-for-thirty-six, but I was at the point where I felt *If the Mets don't want me, somebody else will. I've been traded before. If I get traded again, it's not going to break my heart.*"

There was no room for him on the Mets. Keith Hernandez would be a fixture at first, and Darryl Strawberry would become one in right. Rajsich asked Met manager Davey Johnson, who had been promoted to the big club, to trade or sell him to another organization. Johnson granted his wish, but little came of it. A day later he was sold to Triple A Louisville. Then he was traded to the San Francisco Giants, where he stayed three months, pinch-hitting and sitting on the bench. He was sold back to Louisville when A. Ray Smith, the owner, wanted him back, and so in 1983, 1984, and 1985 Louisville, led by Gary Rajsich, won the Triple A championship.

By this point Rajsich had to face a problem that career minor leaguers eventually run up against. It's damn hard to raise a family on a minor leaguer's salary.

What rescued Rajsich from his financial situation was a common savior in other segments of American business in the 1980s: the Japanese.

"I was making the major league minimum, $60,000 a year, which is not enough to get ahead when you have to pay mortgage *and* rent," Rajsich said. "My wife and I had two children, and now I had a family to think about. We had bought a home, and I was looking for financial security. When the Chunichi Dragons called to ask if I was interested in playing in Japan, I said, 'I'm at a point where I have to make things happen,' and I went. It was great money, more money than I ever would have made playing in the majors unless I was playing every day. It was like a windfall."

Rajsich was the only American on the team, but he had such an even disposition that nothing bothered him during his three-year stay.

"My brother Dave, who had played for Hiroshima, told me, 'Don't forget. You are a minority.' As an American, I had to produce. I hit 36 home runs, drove in 82 runs the first year. It was like being a superstar here. I would walk down the streets of Nagoya, and everyone knew who I was. But you couldn't talk to the fans or read the newspapers. All your information came from an interpreter.

"The Japanese seem tied to their culture. They work to the point where they can't work any more. They are drained at the end of the day—even if it's contradictory to performing well in the game. The fight—the practice—is the most important thing. They are good competitors. That's not just baseball and business, it's their culture."

Rajsich missed the final month of the 1988 season when he tore a cartilage in his rib cage and then fouled a ball off his shin. It swelled up and he couldn't walk.

Americans playing in Japan can't afford to get hurt. It's like the Latins who play here. If an American gets hurt, the Japanese club doesn't want him any more. When Rajsich injured himself, even though he had played well, it was time to part. Rajsich's children were now school age, and in Nagoya there was no English-language school.

"So it was mutual," Rajsich said.

When Rajsich returned home to Louisville, he had made up his mind that his career was over. Letting go was easy.

He had a little financial security, so he was in no hurry to find another job. He let his body heal. Then when he heard about the Senior League, he came to Florida to play for the Pelicans. He wasn't coming to try to get back to the major leagues. It was just going to be fun.

After he had spent nine months at home, Gary's wife was ready to kick him out. He figured the Senior League would give him a chance to "re-Americanize" his baseball thinking. Perhaps it would enable him to find a coaching job so he could stay in baseball. After thirteen years of playing, that's what he knew most.

What's truly remarkable about Gary Rajsich is his lack of bitterness. Looked at objectively, it's hard to say Rajsich's ordeal was worth the effort. But after spending three years in Japan, Rajsich has adopted an Eastern view of his life. He has become a fatalist. What was meant to be was meant to be. He feels indebted to those who helped him along the way.

Rajsich said, "As I look back on my career, I owe a lot to my parents for making it possible, encouraging me and helping me grow to love baseball. I also owe my wife a lot for being behind me, pushing me, and enduring with me. So due to those three people, I am where I am today.

I've done what a lot of people only dream they can do. For that I am thankful."

With the 17–13 victory over Gold Coast, the mood of the team lightened markedly. Against four Suns pitchers the nine Pelican starting batters each made at least two hits for a grand total of twenty-seven hits on the day. It's hard not to feel a little lightheaded after such success. Lenny Randle was hitting .361, Butch Benton .355, Steve Henderson .352, and Steve Kemp, playing every day, was at .333. With the team hitting again, confidence in themselves seemed to have returned.

The next day the Pelicans banged out sixteen more hits, with Roy Howell going 5-for-5 and Kenny Landreaux hitting a double and a home run. On this day Howell had a single to right, a double to right, a single to center, a single to left, and a single to right. It was a hitting clinic by the productive hard-nosed third baseman.

In the clubhouse after the 9–4 victory over the Suns, the jubilant players did not ignore the complete game thrown by Hoot Gibson. Lenny Randle, rarely at a loss for words, stood in the middle of the locker room and pretended to be interviewing Hoot, who stood there with a quizzical, embarrassed look.

"You're Hoot Gibson," said Randle, imitating the commercials for Disneyland that are played after the World Series and the Super Bowl. "You just defeated the Gold Coast Suns, 9–4. Where are you going after the game?"

In the commercial the response is "I'm going to Disneyland."

From the other side of the locker room, Randy Lerch piped up, "I'm going back to the YMCA." Which was where Hoot was living in St. Pete.

The room erupted with laughter. The diffident Hoot laughed as hard as anyone.

The evening bus ride from Pompano Beach back to St. Petersburg seemed interminable. Dick Bosman, the movie maven, played two antiwar movies on the bus's VCR system, one about a crazy survivalist who ends up shooting his friends, and the other a buddy flick—with one of the buddies an amphibian from another planet. Bosman was getting some ribbing for his choice of films, but they did pass the time. Since there was another hour to travel after the two movies, Bosman put on the movie *Big,* starring Tom Hanks, about a twelve-year-old who gets his wish to be an adult. The players were enthralled with the movie, and why not, here were adults who had gotten their wish to be young again.

When the bus finally pulled into St. Petersburg in the middle of the night, the movie still had fifteen minutes to run. Someone suggested that the driver circle Al Lang Stadium a few times so they could watch the end of the movie. They wanted to see how it came out.

I had seen the movie five times and didn't have the heart to tell them that at the end Hanks reverts to being a child, just as I knew that at the end of the month they would have to once again become adults.

CHAPTER

25

Culture Shock

During the course of a baseball season, things rarely stay the same. Players get hurt or get traded. In the Senior League, sometimes players have to leave to go work for a living.

A day after the Pelicans shellacked West Palm Beach, the team suffered two losses, one to the Tropics, who roughed up Pat Zachry for eight hits and nine runs in five innings. Orlando defeated Winter Haven twice and again closed the lead to two and a half with twenty-four games left in the season.

The second loss was first baseman Gary Rajsich. Rajsich had missed a couple of games with a hamstring pull. When he came to the park, he told manager Bobby Tolan he would have to leave the team immediately.

His new employer was the Central Scouting Bureau, a company that is hired by a number of teams to aid in its scouting of high school and college prospects. At first the firm told him he could finish the season and then report. But then he received new marching orders. So Gary Rajsich, who loved playing baseball more than anything in the world, had to face reality and return home to Louisville, put his house on the market, and fly himself to the Pacific Northwest to begin his scouting duties. For Gary, baseball was still leading him by the nose.

The first baseman's job would fall on the broad shoulders of Lamar Johnson. Lamar, who had come to the team out of shape, had injured himself at the outset. Tolan and Morley had considered trading him. Even with Rajsich hurt, Tolan platooned him, using him against left-handers and batting another right-handed batter, Alan Bannister, against righties. Johnson, a man with great pride, burned inside.

Unlike Dock Ellis, who would have made waves of tidal proportions, Lamar kept it to himself and waited for his chance. Lamar, who is black, had learned the hard way that making trouble gets you in trouble. Sometimes your pride takes a beating, but swallowing hard can be the best remedy.

And so before one game Lamar checked the lineup card. When he saw he wasn't playing, he disgustedly rammed his bat into the bat rack. He flashed anger, but then just as suddenly he returned to his placid demeanor, sitting without emotion on the bench.

On this day he said, "I'm not going to have the red ass any more. I had it for a day, and that's enough. I've made up my mind to go along."

Johnson kept working out, continuing to lose weight, gaining mobility. Toward the end of the season he would launch drives of superhuman proportion.

In one game against Gold Coast at Al Lang Stadium, Lamar hit a towering, awe-inspiring moonshot way, way over the fence in left field and into the palm trees beyond. It was, by far, the longest Pelican home run of the year. As Lamar slowly circled the bases, glowering outside but smiling inside, his teammates met him at the edge of the dugout with a flurry of high-fives.

Before the season was over he would become one of the four or five best home run hitters in the Senior League.

Lamar grew up in Bessemer, Alabama. There were no paved roads where he lived, only dirt. When he was a boy his dad would take him and his brothers to see the Birmingham Black Barons. At home he would take a peach pit, wrap it with cotton, get some tape and cloth, and make a baseball to play with. He and his friends would take broken bats from a local schoolyard and tape them.

In high school Lamar played both defensive end and tight end, making the second-team all-state squad in football. He was going to go to Tuskegee Institute if baseball didn't claim him. He was a catcher, and during his last year in high school he hit .714. In May 1968, the Chicago White Sox drafted Johnson on the third round and sent him to Sarasota, Florida. Like teammate Steve Henderson, Lamar Johnson had grown up in an all-black society. He had gone to an all-black Birmingham high

school, had all black friends. For the very first time in his life Lamar
Johnson would mix culturally with whites. It would be an experience as
strange to him as if he were traveling to a foreign country.

"They looked at me funny," Johnson said. "I was from the South. I
talked with the language I grew up with. It was a dialect used by the
slaves, words they used mixed with English, and they made words a little
shorter. So we would say 'axed,' rather than 'asked.' The whites on the
team who were from the North had never dealt with blacks before either.
So they took it for granted that if I didn't speak or act the way they did,
well, they looked at you like you were dumb or stupid, like there was
something wrong with me up here."

Johnson pointed to his head. He was solemn as he spoke. The topic
was painful to talk about.

"You could feel it," he said, "the way they talked to you and the things
they said. The whites used a lot of words I didn't understand, but then I
got a dictionary and started looking words up, seeing what they were
saying, and when I found out, I would get really upset and let them know.
Kids can be real mean when they feel like it."

Johnson, who was large then, would become incensed and let his white
teammates know that he was offended.

"They just raised their eyebrows a little bit and said, 'I don't think you
should get upset about that.' I said, 'How would you feel if I said that
about you? I don't go around making fun of guys just because they're a
little different.'

"And they even treated the Latin players worse. They would walk up to
them and call them, 'You old asshole.' Curse them out, figuring they
didn't understand the language. I'd think, *I wonder what this guy says
about me when he gets behind my back.*"

Johnson responded by becoming an introvert. On the field he had no
trouble adjusting. He could play the game. Off the field he had a terrible
time. He discovered he was living in a different culture. Until he arrived
in Sarasota, he had never eaten in a restaurant before. At home he lived
on his grandmother's farm, where his family grew their own vegetables
and slaughtered their own animals for meat.

In the minors he ran into rednecks. "There were still a lot of places a
black couldn't stay," Johnson said. "There were just a few places where I
could stay."

He learned to deal with bigots. "If people feel that way, they are the
ones with the problem. I don't have a problem. You see guys come in and
play, and you see white guys who don't have the ability of the black and

The Pelicans

Lamar   Johnson

Latin players, and they would go right by—because it was a white culture. You'd see it all the time. And it irked me."

Lamar Johnson got by because he had a coach, Sam Hairston, whom he could talk things over with. Hairston, who used to play in the Negro Leagues, had scouted Johnson for the White Sox, and helped him get through his rookie season. Johnson hated his rookie-year manager, Tom Saffell, who wanted Johnson to lose ten pounds and who fined Lamar a dollar a day until he lost the weight. Johnson thought Saffell's treatment humiliating. One day Johnson decided that he had had enough. *I'm not giving this guy any more money,* Johnson thought. He packed his clothes in his suitcase and was heading down the back stairs when Hairston happened by.

"Where are you going?" Hairston asked.

Johnson said, "I can't put up with none of this any more. I'm going home."

Hairston told Lamar to take his suitcase upstairs, and then they talked. Hairston told him, "I know what you're seeing now, but all people in baseball are not like this. If you're going to make it in this game, you will run into a lot of people you will not like. You're going to have to put that aside and do it on the field." He said, "They can say what they want about you, but if you put the numbers up, they can't take that away from you."

Johnson continued in the game, and eventually he made the major leagues. The next year Johnson had a new manager, Bruce Andrews, someone he respected. But if Hairston hadn't been there that day, it's doubtful Johnson ever would have made it. One has to wonder how many other young black players never make the majors because they can't cope with a new culture and a new environment and with the racism of ignorant people.

As Johnson moved up the minor league ladder, he learned how to deal with two cultures. He learned what the white culture expected of him, how it wanted him to act, what it wanted him to do. He saw that the whites had no interest in understanding the black culture.

"They say the black kids are lazy and slow," Johnson said. "That's just the way they are in their culture. The black and Latin players are alike in that when they play the game, they look a little nonchalant. Watch an all-black team play and you see that all the time. Hank Aaron—all those great players—they always were called lazy. The blacks don't believe in false hustle, in running hard just because it *looks* good. But the whites don't understand. It's really hard to teach someone if you don't understand their culture. And the whites don't even try. The whites are a society of people who say, 'We don't care about your culture. In order to make it, you have to adapt to *our* culture.' And that's what we had to do."

Johnson saw the way many white coaches would deal with black players—by emphasizing the negative. White coaches would joke with the white players. But the only time they said something to the black players was when a black player did something wrong.

"They'd yell and scream, and that's all they'd get," Johnson said. "And the coaches would wonder why the black players didn't like them. But if all they get is negative, all you're going to get back is negative. And then the coaches say the guy has an attitude."

Today Johnson is a coach with the Milwaukee Brewers. "You have to get to *know* these guys," Lamar tells his fellow coaches. "You can't just give them negative feedback."

Johnson also had to learn to deal with the press. He saw that the white reporters found the black players intimidating. Because Johnson is a large black man, he learned that when he told a joke or made a cutting comment, he had to laugh out loud to make the whites understand he was kidding. Otherwise they would take his comments the wrong way. His wife told him, "When you're joking, you don't smile and everyone thinks you're really talking about them instead of just having fun."

He said, "Really?"

She said, "Yeah, you have to loosen up a little."

And he started doing that, and as a result the reporters became less intimidated.

In his third year of professional ball, Lamar Johnson went to Appleton, Wisconsin, for spring training. Lamar, his wife, and his infant son were the only black faces in town, except for a couple of teammates. "I met some really fantastic people in Appleton," Johnson said. "They showed me a different side of the white culture that I had never seen before. I had a great time."

Johnson's climb to the majors still proved painful. In the minors one time a player called him a "pickaninny," and Johnson decked him. But Johnson had a manager, Joe Sparks, who respected Lamar and encouraged him. Because of Sparks, Johnson stayed the course. In 1974 at Triple A Des Moines, Johnson hit .301, with 20 homers and 96 RBIs. In 1975 at Denver he hit .338 and led the American Association in hitting. The next year Johnson became a member of Chicago's South Side Hitmen.

All because Johnson learned to fit into white society. Lamar Johnson decided to learn the system rather than fight it.

Three weeks remained in the season. The Pelicans led Orlando by three and a half games in the division. Bradenton was seven back, Winter Haven a distant ten games behind. In the other division West Palm Beach was in first, a full eight games ahead of Fort Myers, fifteen and a half ahead of Gold Coast, and twenty-four and a half games in front of the St. Lucie Legends.

St. Lucie earlier had been a laughingstock. The team had signed former Yankees and Mets, but many of the players were too old—even for the Senior League.

Then, for one week in December, the Legends acquired a new owner with capital. During that one week, general manager Ray Negron signed young outfielder Bernardo Leonard, Von Joshua, and Sergio Ferrer and traded Vida Blue to Orlando for Bill Madlock, Roy Branch, and "a player to be named later."

The new owner for the week was named Lenny Wolf, from Detroit, a friend of Orlando owner Philip Breen. But when Breen was accused of embezzling $10 million from his mortgage company, he disappeared from sight. According to Negron, after only a week as St. Lucie owner, so did Lenny Wolf.

"It gave me a week to go shopping," Negron said. So the old owner, Joe Sprung, was back, with a stronger team. Against the Legends the Pelicans played as fine a game as they had all season long. They got timely hitting and excellent defense.

On the mound, starter Jon Matlack and reliever Dave Rajsich were superb. Matlack pitched seven and a third innings, allowing nine hits and only a single run, as the Pelicans defeated Roy Thomas, 4–1. Orlando lost to West Palm Beach. The lead stood at a comfortable four and a half games. Pitchers Jon Matlack and Milt Wilcox won almost every time out. With just twenty games left in the season, it was going to be very difficult to catch the Pelicans.

The Pelicans began the Saturday game against St. Lucie the same way as they had the night before. Lenny Randle started the inning with a walk from pitcher Roy Branch, followed by Roy Howell's long ground-rule double that rolled under the chain-link fence in right field. Steve Kemp hit a high chopper that scored Randle. Then Steve Henderson measured the first pitch thrown by Branch and sent it over the wall in left-center. Henderson had two other hits on the day, including a double and a single.

Every day, it seemed, in the field and at bat Henderson contributed something. Off the field he provided leadership and friendship, counseling and a smile when everyone around him was pissed off. He was a player Bobby Tolan could count on. He was appreciated greatly by his teammates, who felt that Henderson, last year the MVP of the American Association, was in line this year to be named Most Valuable Player in the Senior League.

Henderson, called Hendu by his teammates, like almost every other Henderson in the game, was a man who seemed hard to get to know. Large, black, and capable of looking fierce and unapproachable, he usually jived and bopped and was full of laughter and fun among his teammates. On the bus the other players could hear him sing off-key above the Walkman in his ears about women and love and whatever was playing on the endless tape that amused him as the miles of highway droned by. If you didn't know Hendu, you would think he hadn't a care in this world or a thought in his head. You would be very wrong.

Like Lamar Johnson, Steve Henderson has learned to live in two cultures, black and white. He grew up in the black section of Houston, where he never saw a white person until he went to play pro ball. Understandably, he admits to being more comfortable in the black culture. But he has learned to handle himself among whites without becoming bitter.

To hear him throw the "m-f's" around with the best of them, you wouldn't know that he attended Prairie View A&M College. When you talk about serious matters, it is clear that the persona he fronts to the world is merely a device to maintain his privacy in a public vocation in which so many others want a piece of you. At the same time it also masks his intelligence. For blacks and whites to get along a team needs players like Lamar Johnson and Steve Henderson, and the Pelicans were fortunate to have them—and their skills.

Steve Henderson served as batboy for his father's semipro team when he was barely big enough to carry the wood. Hendu's dad, who worked in the steel mills of Houston, came from Mobile, Alabama, the home of Willie Mays and Billy Williams. The reason the elder Henderson didn't get his chance to go pro was that he had to take care of his family.

"I remember when I was growing up, I caught one of his games," Henderson said. "He could pitch. I wouldn't want to face him."

Because of his experiences hanging around his father's team, Steve

Henderson developed more quickly than other boys. By the time he was sixteen, he was playing regularly on the team.

"I always thought I could hit anybody," Henderson said. "I never faced anyone I was scared of. This one day, the team was short a player at shortstop, and I kept begging them to let me play. I told the manager, a guy by the name of Cleo, 'I can play short.'"

Usually when Steve Henderson asked to play he was told he was too young. On this occasion Cleo said okay, and Henderson became the regular shortstop on the team.

"I was sixteen, playing against men, and I was kind of nervous, but I hit the ball hard. In my second or third at-bat, I hit a home run to right field. I hit it way back into the pasture. They cheered, and I was very excited, because I got the opportunity to play with older guys. After the game they had a beer, and it was awesome. I really enjoyed it. I matured quick by playing with those guys. All the way through high school and college I played shortstop."

Henderson graduated from the all-black Jack Yates High School in 1970. At that time integration had yet to come to schools in Houston.

"It didn't bother me going to an all-black school," Henderson said. "To be truthful, I had made up my mind when I began playing ball with my father that nothing was going to stop me from getting to where I was going to get—the major leagues. But I never did encounter whites on a day-to-day basis. If you've ever been to Houston, you see blacks most everywhere, and certain areas were all-black. The only way I saw a white was if I went downtown somewhere. I never did do that, except for the Boys' Club, where I met a lot of Spanish guys and some whites. It wasn't no problem. It's like this. 'If you don't bother Hendu, Hendu won't bother you.'"

After Henderson graduated he went to all-black Prairie View A&M College, about forty-five miles from Houston. His baseball coach from Jack Yates High School went with him. All four years he made All-Southwest Athletic Conference. In his senior year he led the nation in hitting with a .488 average.

In 1974 Henderson was drafted in the fifth round by the Cincinnati Reds.

"I left Prairie View with sixteen hours of credit needed to graduate. When I left, I was thinking about the finances. My parents had separated, and I was taking the burden. So the money I got went to my mom. I got $2,500. That was it."

When Henderson left, his mother took him to the airport. As he waited

Tom DiPace

Steve   Henderson

in line to board the plane, his mother began to cry. Her oldest, her baby, was leaving. When Henderson arrived in Billings, Montana, he was surprised. After growing up in an all-black milieu his entire life, Cincinnati was sending him to a town without another black face, except for several teammates.

Henderson said, "I got to Billings, and I was sitting around and looking. I was thinking, *I haven't seen a black person yet.* I kept looking, and I still didn't see none. I thought, *Shit, there are none.* It was scary. But I was born on the streets. I had street sense, and I knew when people were trying to take advantage of me."

There were four black players on the team from California. One day they went to a restaurant to eat. One of the other players, Donnie Law, ordered a rare hamburger. When it came back too well done, the player told the waitress to bring him another one. Henderson was appalled.

Henderson told Law, "Man, don't do that." But Law did it anyway, and the waitress brought him another one, this time the way he wanted it.

Henderson said, "In Texas I never would have done that. In the South, if you ordered something and it came halfway right, you ate it."

Henderson learned that the strict segregation of the South didn't apply in other parts of the country. He saw that California blacks weren't afraid of the whites. California blacks hadn't faced lynchings and being tarred and feathered by the Ku Klux Klan. California blacks had not been forced to keep their place like Southern blacks, he discovered.

"When you meet different people, you learn a lot of things," Henderson said. In his two and a half months in Billings, there was one taboo Henderson couldn't bring himself to break: He wouldn't go out with white women. In Billings, there were only white women.

Imagine the loneliness of a youngster playing miles from home in a strange culture without female companionship. This happens to many blacks in the minor leagues in many towns across America. Only the toughest ones make it past the loneliness and anomie.

Steve Henderson was one of those ballplayers unlucky enough to always play on bad ball clubs. He was an excellent hitter. But because he was an outfielder who didn't have twenty-homer-a-year power, no matter how well he played, the general manager always wanted to replace him with someone with greater power. As a result, Hendu went from Cincinnati to the Mets to the Cubs to Seattle to Oakland and finally to his hometown of Houston, a twelve-year career during which he hit a lifetime .280 but received little recognition. There were teams on which Hendu was one of the better players, and he was still traded. Hendu sometimes found himself wondering about the fairness of it all.

The beginning had held so much promise. When he was traded by the Reds to the New York Mets in June 1977 in the big Tom Seaver deal, Hendu was being hailed as one of the finest young talents in the game. He had hit .326 at Indianapolis that year. When he arrived to play for the Mets, the cameras and reporters were waiting for him. Henderson was overwhelmed.

Later the Mets assigned the legendary Willie Mays to tutor him personally. When the Mets insisted that Henderson change his style of hitting and become a power hitter, he balked. When he was traded away in February 1981, he couldn't figure out what had gone awry.

Even though the Mets fielded bad ball clubs, Henderson always played hard, because he figured if he could motivate his teammates, they'd say, "Hendu is still playing hard, even though we're out of it, so we ought to play hard too."

Hendu loved playing in New York. The fans were appreciative of his skills and treated him well, and he loved them back. One of his teammates was Dock Ellis. At the time Dock was on drugs, and Henderson stayed away from him.

"I had heard about this crazy dude, and when we passed, we said hi. Dock always looked like he was spaced out. The other guys would just stay away from him. 'Hi, Dock. 'Bye, Dock.' Nothing else. Now it's different. You can hold a conversation with him."

Henderson played with the Mets from mid-1977 to the end of the 1980 season. He hit .297, .266, .306, and .290. He was always around .300, but the criticism continued. He didn't hit enough home runs. It bothered him.

"I was a line drive hitter when they got me," he said, "but they wanted me to alter my swing and go for home runs. I tried to do that my second year. I struck out a lot, 109 times. I wouldn't drive in runs in situations like I wanted to. So I said, 'No, I'm not doing it no more.'"

In February 1981, New York traded Henderson to the Cubs for Dave Kingman to try to get more home run power. Henderson has always felt manager Joe Torre and the Mets made a mistake.

After he departed the Mets, the rest of his career left him feeling frustrated. Like so many hitters, he needed to play every day in order to be at his peak. Some batters can jump out of bed at midnight and get a base hit. They are the minority. Most hitters must play often to stay sharp.

When Steve Henderson was traded by the Mets to the Chicago Cubs for Dave Kingman in 1981, Henderson found himself on the Cub bench. Once that happened, Hendu was labeled a platoon player. He never again played full-time, not once in the next eight years.

In 1986 Henderson was released and played Triple A ball for the White Sox and then went back to Seattle, who released him. Oakland picked him up again, and in 1987 he was back in the major leagues. That year the A's finished second to the Minnesota Twins when they lost their final four games.

In 1988 Hendu got to play for his hometown, for the Houston Astros. He accomplished his final goal with Houston when he got in his full ten years toward his pension.

After playing in Venezuela, Hendu was asked by Chuck Lamar, director of minor league personnel of the Pirates, if he wanted to play in Buffalo. Lamar told him, "If you do good, fine, but sooner or later I want you to be a coach for me."

Henderson went to Buffalo—to play. According to Henderson, the Pirates were hoping he would fail as a player so he could begin his coaching duties. Instead, Henderson hit .294 and at the age of thirty-four was the oldest member of the American Association All-Star team. He would have been back in the majors had he not gotten hurt.

"Pittsburgh was getting ready to call me up when I broke my wrist," Henderson said. "I came back in three weeks, and I wound up getting all the awards." But Pittsburgh never called him up.

Henderson was angry, but he didn't say anything. It wasn't his way.

At the end of the year Hendu agreed to be a coach at Buffalo. During the offseason there was a meeting of the Pirate brass. During the meeting the executives went down the roster of the minor league teams, reciting the names of the MVPs of each team. When they got to Steve Henderson's name, there was an embarrassed silence. One of the coaches asked, "How can a guy who was MVP on a Triple A team wind up being a coach now?"

Henderson said, "I was better than anybody else they had, but they didn't bring me up. I made up my mind to play in the Senior League and begin my coaching career."

Another person might have fought to stay on as a player. Letting go is always hard, but Steve Henderson was never one to seek out trouble.

It was his way in baseball, and it was his way in life.

Tex

For the week beginning January 12 the St. Pete Pelicans were like the old barnstormers, playing in one town one night, another town the next. After playing two games in St. Lucie, they bused south to West Palm Beach to play a solo against the Tropics. After the game they were to board the bus for a makeup game in Bradenton, followed by two regularly scheduled games in Winter Haven.

Nothing seemed to daunt the players. Bobby Tolan, short of pitching with the sore arms of Pat Zachry and Hoot Gibson, chose left-hander Mike Williams, a career minor leaguer, to face the Southern Division leaders. Tex, whose record was 1–1, seemed no match for Juan Eichelberger, at 9–3 the ace of Dick Williams's staff. But baseball is a funny game.

No one would have predicted the carefree left-hander would shut out the most powerful team in the league through six innings. But that's just what he did before tiring.

Tex threw a hard slider and a good curve. When the Tropic hitters looked for the breaking ball, Tex broke the bats in their hands with a lively fastball. Up to the seventh, when he walked the first two batters, Tex had allowed just five singles.

In the clubhouse after the victory, he was jubilant.

"I sawed off bats today," he crowed. "I couldn't believe it."

It's hard to know when to take Tex Williams seriously. To look at him, you know that when he was eight years old he loved to dip the pigtails of his little girl classmates into inkwells. And you know that when the teacher would accuse him of it, he would look her right in the eye and deny it.

In civilian life Tex Williams sells used cars. The name of Tex's company is Guarantee Auto. "I guarantee you," Tex said, "that if the car I sell you quits, I'll get you into another one." Tex laughed heartily. His entire body shook.

Every time he explains the origin of the name of the company, Tex laughs uproariously. Tex loves to talk about the used-car business.

"Let me tell you something about selling cars," he said. "Car salesmen don't have to lie to sell a car. You just can't tell the whole truth. Okay?

"There's an old saying, 'How do you know when a car salesman is lying? Watch his lips. If they're moving, he's lying.'"

Tex roared with glee. But he's such an endearing rogue that you'd probably buy a car from him anyway. He's counting on it.

Tex is bitter that he never made it to the major leagues. He got as far as Triple A in the Dodgers chain, but manager Tommy Lasorda didn't bring him up from Albuquerque, even when he was the top left-hander in the minor leagues.

There's often a reason, something in a player's makeup, why a prospect doesn't make it to the majors. With Tex Williams, during his career "things" just kind of happened. First, there was the time he injured himself severely while racing a guy he met in a bar over drinks. Another time he told the Dodger management what he thought of them. Then there was the arrest in Mexico for gunrunning. Baseball is a game for conventional people. Williams never was conventional. He wasn't even conventional by St. Pete Pelicans standards.

Williams didn't sign with a major league team until the *third* time he was drafted.

After starring in baseball for Brassaswood (Texas) High School, he was drafted by the Pittsburgh Pirates and offered $100. Insulted, he turned it down.

Williams stayed in Texas and enrolled at Temple Junior College. His girlfriend, later his wife, did his homework for him. At Temple he learned to throw a good slider to go with his curve that he could get over on a 3–2 count. He beat the number one junior college team in the nation,

San Jacinto Junior College, 2–1, and he pitched a no-hitter against Blinn Junior College.

When the secondary phase of the baseball draft came up in January 1973, Williams was drafted in the first round by the Atlanta Braves. They offered him $7,500. Again he turned it down. He went back to Temple.

At the end of his second collegiate season, Williams had led the nation's junior college pitchers in strikeouts and was number two in earned-run average.

The Kansas City Royals selected Tex Williams first in the secondary phase of the 1974 draft. Williams expected great riches. He was disappointed. The offer was $10,000, plus another $7,500 in incentives if he climbed his way to the majors.

This time he signed. He knew that if he had turned down three straight contracts, no one would have looked at him.

"I took the chumpchange they offered me," Williams said.

Williams was 7–4 in rookie ball. The next year he went to Waterloo, Iowa, in the Midwest League. Willie Wilson, Charlie Beamon, Doug Corbett, and Joe Gates were teammates. The team set a record for winning percentage. Williams was 11–6.

After his stellar season, Tex again was invited to the Instructional League, and again he was sent to Single A to play.

There are junctures in every person's life. In some cases, all a person need do is one foolish thing. Tex Williams got tapped by the fickle finger of fate often enough to indicate that success wasn't meant to be. Perhaps he wasn't serious enough. Perhaps he was too carefree or careless to be successful at the top level of the game. Or maybe he was just unlucky. Whatever that missing magic ingredient, it kept him from the major leagues.

The incident that first labeled him began with two guys sitting at a bar, drinking. One of those guys was Tex. The other was a braggart who claimed he could really run. Tex, not to be outdone, gave the opinion that the guy was full of it.

"I can outrun you," Tex said.

"Want to bet?" Tex was asked.

"Sure." Tex had everything to lose and nothing to gain. There are adjectives for such a bet: stupid, reckless, idiotic.

The two measured a course across the parking lot of the bar. As the two raced across the tarmac, Tex failed to see a heavy string of cable running about knee-high in front of him.

Peter Golenbock

Tex Williams

When he hit that cable at full speed, he flipped up in the air and landed on his face and head. He also hyperextended his knee—his push-off knee. The next day he could hardly walk. That day he limped out to the mound, pitched five innings, and had to leave.

Tex's reputation was made.

"In my life I've been in the wrong spots at the wrong times," Williams said.

In 1977 the Royals traded him to the Los Angeles Dodger organization. His leg healed, and he was in good shape. The Dodgers kept him in A ball. Pitching for Lodi, California, he was 11–6, with nine saves and a 2.91 earned-run average.

He pitched winter ball for Mazatlán, Mexico, came back to spring training, and made the Triple A Albuquerque team.

During spring training Tex Williams beat the Atlanta Braves on national television. It was the closest he would get to the majors.

"I felt I should have made the Dodgers' big club," he said. He was upset because that year left-handed reliever Terry Forster was hurt, and the Dodgers won the league championship without a single left-hander in their bullpen.

At the end of spring training Dodger manager Tommy Lasorda told him, "Go to Triple A, have a good season, and I'll try to bring you up."

Tex went to Albuquerque, was 6–0 with nine saves, but had a 6-something ERA, not unusual for the hard-hitting Pacific Coast League. Williams never got to bleed Dodger blue.

"They never called me up," he said. "They promised me, but they didn't do it."

Tex Williams again took the less traveled road. And like the guy in Robert Frost's poem, doing so made all the difference. But unlike Frost's narrator, it was because of something stupid Tex did, not something heroic.

"I said some things I shouldn't have said," Tex said sheepishly. He also had his agent call the Dodgers and order them to get rid of him if they didn't have any plans for him.

Minor leaguers are not ordinarily in any position to dictate to major league executives. That sort of attitude usually results in wish fulfillment.

The next year Williams was demoted to Double A, and he was drafted by the San Francisco Giants, who had no plans for him either. The Giants released him.

He went home to Houston and opened up a paint-and-body shop.

Tex is one of those people who loves the excitement of life. He loves competition. He loves thrills. Running a paint-and-body shop offered neither. He needed an outlet. He started betting on cockfights in Vinton, Louisiana.

Then, as happens in gambling, he started losing more money than he made. He lost his body shop and returned to baseball. He went to play in Mexico for the Nuevo Laredo Techalotes. He kissed his wife and kids goodbye and headed for the border.

"I had to go and play," he said. "It was still in the blood." The Techalotes were playing well. Then on a trip to Vera Cruz, Tex Williams was arrested by the *federales*. The charge was gunrunning. Tex ended up in Mexican jails for thirty-nine days and nights.

According to Tex, on a beach in Vera Cruz one of the other players tried to sell a pistol to a woman who turned out to be the wife of a federal agent.

The next day he pitched and beat Vera Cruz. His picture was in the paper for winning the game. The team got on the bus to go to Mexico City to play the Diablos, but the *federales* stopped it from leaving.

When they searched the bus, they said the pistol seller was a white guy with brown hair and blue eyes. Tex has white skin, brown hair, blue eyes. Tex also owned a nine-millimeter pistol. He had stuffed it in a pillow in the overhead rack. The *federales* found it and arrested him.

"I was the closest *gringo* to the gun on the bus," Tex said, shaking his head.

"Hey, all the Spanish guys carried guns. There were six or seven guns on that bus. I had been carrying my pistol back and forth across the border every day, never even thinking about it. I carried large sums of money with me all the time. At this time I had $2,800 on me to buy Christmas presents in Mexico City. And I had my pistol because Vera Cruz is known for robbing people, you know.

"A lot of people go down there and end up dead in a hotel room, so I was carrying my protection with me."

The Mexican police threw Tex into jail in Vera Cruz and tried to make him sign a confession that he had been running guns. He refused. They refused to let him out. Not even his manager could spring him.

"The bus left," he said. "The team went back home. I was in jail, and it didn't look like I was getting out. They wanted me to sign a paper saying I had all the guns, and I wouldn't do it."

Finally Williams admitted to the one gun, and he was let out of jail after eighteen days. He was sent to immigration in Mexico City and jailed prior to release. While he waited to go home, Mexico City was struck by a devastating earthquake. While officials concentrated on digging out, Tex Williams spent another twenty-one days in the immigration jail before he could get back to the States.

"It cost me $6,000 to get out of everything," Williams said. "They flew me to San Antonio."

According to Williams, if it hadn't been for his arrest, he might have gotten his chance at the big leagues.

"I had been doing really well," he said. "Three or four major league teams were looking at me."

The publicity killed his chances.

"It was in *The Sporting News*. 'Mike Williams Running Guns in Mexico,' " he said. "The article blew the story way out of proportion. It was not the truth. I did not do that. That was the farthest thing from my mind.

"I did have a pistol," he said. "Hey, I won't bullshit you. I carry it now. The way this world is right now, you need protection. I'm not going to get rolled without somebody going down with me. But after the Mexico deal, my baseball career was finished."

Williams went to work for a construction company, then was hired by Dow Chemical, working the day shift, the night shift, and the graveyard shift. His marriage suffered.

"We steadily grew farther and farther apart," he said. Depression set in. "Being away from baseball, the pleasures I had, getting to travel, being with the guys, they weren't there any more. I became bitter. It was hard."

The car game saved him. He found he had a real knack for the used-car business. He specialized in selling cars to customers with bad credit. At his peak he was making two grand a week.

And then the Senior League came along. He padlocked his business and ran to Flordia. His pay: three grand a month.

After he defeated the mighty West Palm Beach Tropics, Tex Williams talked about his future. Hope springs eternal. Selling used cars was his vocation, but pitching baseballs turned out to be his life.

"This is my Field of Dreams," Williams said. "I hope to pitch in the Senior League until I'm fifty."

If he survives his adolescence first.

At the end of the Senior League season, Tex went barnstorming across Europe with a group of players from the league. He was pitching in Italy when he was struck on the side of the head by a line drive. Tex lay in a coma for several days. When he finally awoke, he was left with an indentation in his head.

He wants to keep pitching, but it's not certain that he will get the chance. Owners don't like to see their players killed on the ballfield.

27

Dock Ellis's Courage

After Tex Williams pitched his brilliant six shutout innings against the West Palm Beach Tropics, he tired. The Pelicans led 5–0, but Palm Beach retaliated with four runs in the seventh. With runners on first and second and two outs, Bobby Tolan brought in Dock Ellis to relieve Dave Rajsich, who had come in to start the inning. Ellis struck out Lee Lacy to end the threat.

It was still a one-run game in the ninth, and the tension built because it was an important game for both teams. It was their last confrontation of the regular season, and each wanted bragging rights until their expected meeting in the playoffs. The players on each team believed themselves to be the best team in the league.

Dock made it exciting by walking Toby Harrah to lead off the inning. But Mike Easler grounded into a double play, and the dangerous Tito Landrum flied out to center to end it. It was Dock's sixth save of the season, not bad for a guy who, at the age of forty-four, had to face younger, tough opponents and a daily fight against his own alcohol and drug addiction. The man had raw courage. He displayed it every day.

One of the most dramatic moments of the season occurred early in the season in Dock Ellis's first game. As he had against West Palm Beach, he had come into the game in the ninth inning against the Orlando Juice to try to save it.

Dock Ellis alone was aware of the drama. For the first time in his entire professional pitching career going back to 1964, Dock was pitching straight, without the influence of alcohol or drugs. Mortals don't scare Dock Ellis. But the possibility of using drugs or alcohol again scares him to the bone.

To the fans who came to the games, Ellis had appeared to be the old Dock. He pitched deliberately, taking his time between pitches, glaring like Malcolm X, acting as though he hated the world. He would turn and stare out toward the outfield, holding the ball, making the batters wait on him.

After getting two outs, Ellis temporarily lost control, walking two batters, but he threw a nasty slider past the next batter to end the inning. In his first drug-free inning, his first opportunity to pitch in anger since 1979, he had been a success.

Afterward Ellis talked about his emotions.

"When I first went into the game, I didn't know what was going on. The thought was there: *I'm going in, and I'm* not *going to be high.* The adrenaline was flowing, and my mouth was dry like when I *was* high. My whole body was like that. I'd wipe my head and my lips, because when I was high my lips were dry, and I used to have to rub my lips on my arm because I got a dry mouth. So my body was reacting like I *was* high, but I knew I wasn't high. So I acted like I was high. I was walking around the mound, not doing nothing. I was looking over here, looking over there, which is what I used to do. It was strange."

After the game Ellis went to a Narcotics Anonymous meeting in the Tampa–St. Pete area. He said, "It doesn't look like anybody here knows anything about baseball, but I play baseball. I used to, and now I'm back at it again," and he started talking about what was bothering him. He told the gathering, "I'm afraid."

Dock said later, "In the meeting that fear is okay. But that fear was only because I was remembering the old times. It's like saying, 'I'm going to go into a room where they're doing cocaine.' Sure, I can go in, but I'm going to be frightened."

The old times included a one-year stint of drinking and drugging on the baddest team of them all, the 1976 New York Yankees. At the time it was the perfect place for him because his manager, Billy Martin, was another man who liked the bottle. Martin not only failed to discourage drinkers, he preferred them on his team. One of Billy's pet put-downs was to label a player a "milkshake drinker." The term was first coined by

The Pelicans

Dock Ellis

Billy's mentor, Casey Stengel, who didn't like these men either. Casey once had said about Bobby Richardson, "He doesn't swear, doesn't drink, and doesn't hit .200."

And so Dock Ellis fit in on the Yankees. He also belonged because under Billy Martin there was no difference between white and black. Billy had often said, "I don't care if he's white, black, green, or striped, so long as he can play." Under Billy black players who played Billy's game thrived.

"I was talking with Al Oliver," Ellis said, "and he asked me, 'Which team was better as far as camaraderie goes, the Pirates or the Yankees?' I said, 'Al, in all my years with the Pirates there never was a team that had the camaraderie of that Yankee team the one year I was there.'

"See, when I was with the Yankees in 1976, the Yankees had it. White and black together, we all partied. We did everything together. I mean everything. You name it, partying, dissing, they didn't give a damn. It was take names and kick ass, led by Billy Martin. Billy said, 'Do whatever the fuck you want to do, but give me 125 percent.' "

When Ellis first came to the team, his mind told him that this was a partying bunch, but at first he was cautious. He didn't want to get high in front of men he didn't know.

But the night after the first game, the team was in Milwaukee, and the veterans came and got him. The partying was on.

So was the fighting.

"The first day in the clubhouse when the season opened Lou Piniella and Rick Dempsey were going at it," Ellis said. "Who knows what they were fighting about? I said, 'What is wrong with these crazy mother-fuckers? What are they doing? Why are they fighting?'

"Guys were always arguing: 'You should have caught the ball.' 'You shouldn't have called that pitch.' But they talked baseball all the time."

Fighting, arguing, talking baseball were Billy Martin's favorite pastimes. Intimidation was something else Billy enjoyed.

"I saw Billy win five games the year I was there just by intimidating umpires," Ellis said. "Where they owed him a call. Even if the ball was down the cock, they would call it a ball. On the next pitch our batter would hit a home run, and we'd win the game. A lot of times he would say, 'You owe me.' Even after he got kicked out of the game, he'd be screaming, 'You owe me, motherfucker.' And they remembered. You could tell.

"I'd think to myself, *Why would an umpire call a pitch down the middle a ball? Damn.* Then the umpire would look over into our dugout, and Billy would go, 'See that, he-he-he-he-he-he-he-he-he-he. See that, he-he-he-he-he-he-he-he-he-he.'

"You could see it work, especially with umpires and other managers. Billy didn't give a shit. He'd fuck with other managers. He'd be out there arguing with the managers when they brought out the lineup card, talking shit. One time he got into it with Earl Weaver. Earl was as crazy as Billy."

Ellis went on. "Billy believed in intimidation. That's what he wanted to do to his players, and that's what he wanted his players to do to the other team. 'Here come the fucking bad-ass Yankees. They're coming to kick your ass.'

"Billy wanted to be in charge. I remember at the start of the season Billy wanted us to do things his way, but we had a lot of veterans, especially on the pitching staff, and finally we said, 'All right, we'll do it your way.' We broke out into the lead because the Yankees were playing the way Billy wanted to play. Mickey Rivers took bases at will—run, run, run, run, run, run, run. Thurman Munson was hitting-and-running. He never stopped at first. He just kept going, and if he ducked his head at second, he'd go to third. That's the way we played. You might as well call it Billyball."

Ellis used to tease Billy Martin all the time. He'd say: "You don't run this fucking team. Catfish Hunter runs the fucking team."

Billy would say: "What do you mean?"

Dock would reply: "Everyone respects Catfish. Everyone don't respect you."

Dock recalled, "I used to fuck with him all the time. We'd get drunk and talk about it. He'd say, 'I run this fucking team.' Billy was cool.

"That was the name of Billy's game: intimidation. He didn't give a shit who it was, but he couldn't intimidate me. Just about everyone else he could get going. See, he couldn't get me going."

Dock exaggerates slightly. Billy could get anyone "going," even Dock.

One time Dock and Billy were drunk in the back of a limousine. Billy, Dock, and pitcher Ken Holtzman all resided in New Jersey. It was after a game, late, and Yankee owner George Steinbrenner had sent the limo to take them home. He wanted his boys home so they could get some sleep.

Inside the limo Billy announced, "I'm getting rid of that gutless motherfucker Rudy May." Ellis was offended. He didn't think Rudy was gutless at all.

Dock said: "Man, why do you talk about Rudy like that?"

Billy said: "He's a gutless motherfucker, and you know it."

Dock said: "What the fuck are you talking about?"

Bill said: "And you can go with him."

Dock replied: "Send me to Mexico. They play ball in Mexico, don't they?" Then Dock said: "I'll whoop your little ass. Get away from me with that shit. You're not going to slip up and hit me in the back of the head. I'll kill you, motherfucker."

Ken Holtzman stopped them before blood was shed.

Billy Martin loved the way Dock Ellis played the game. In his own way, he became Ellis's protector against management and the adversarial press.

Dock began the season 10–4, and when he wasn't picked for the All-Star team, a pack of reporters went to Ellis to get his reaction. Ellis went straight to Billy.

"Billy, those motherfuckers are trying to fire me up," Dock said, and Billy made the writers leave his pitcher alone. The next day the headlines read: ELLIS HAS NOTHING TO SAY.

"Billy and I had an agreement that he would keep the press away from me so there wouldn't be any controversy," Ellis said. "Because controversy surrounds me, and New York was a prime area for it. Billy knew New York would be a playground for me. All I had to do was smoke a joint and stand on a stool and start talking shit, and it would be headlines. I'd have had the back page, the front page, and everywhere else.

"I told him, 'Man, I don't want that shit. I just want to play ball.'"

Billy told Dock: "I want the press."

Dock said: "You can have the press."

Dock recalled, "Billy loved it, and I could understand why. He wanted to be the Little General. I told him, 'Be the Little General, but keep the motherfuckers away from me.'"

There was one New York writer in particular Dock Ellis despised: the late Dick Young. The reason: Dock Ellis felt Young was a dangerous hypocrite.

"He always talked about the players who used drugs, saying baseball should put them out of the game," Ellis said. "And he was a drunk.

"I never saw him write about the owners who were drunks. If the players who used drugs were supposed to be banned from the game and never brought back, the writers who were drunks shouldn't have been writing about the fucking game. That's one man who's dead, and I'd spit on his grave today."

Ellis only lasted on the Yankees for one year. His drug use and drinking had become noticeable. Yankee owner George Steinbrenner, moreover, thought Ellis had wished him to die. Most important, Dock wanted more money than general manager Gabe Paul was willing to pay.

Ellis said, "The next spring I came to camp, and I was so drunk I was puking while I was doing calisthenics. Billy said, 'Dock, Dock, go in the clubhouse. Go to sleep. Go back home. Go back to the hotel.'

"And that spring Graig Nettles made the statement: 'It might be good if we keep losing, because it's more likely Steinbrenner will fly in, and that increases the possibility the plane will crash.' And Steinbrenner thought I said that. I never denied saying it. And that had a lot to do with me getting traded. Plus they didn't want to give me the money I wanted, though it was not a lot of money.

"Gabe Paul told me, 'Well, Dock, we don't look at just the hole in the donut, we have to look at the whole donut.' I said, 'Fuck you and the donut too. Get me out of here.'

"And they traded me."

After eight years as a star with the Pittsburgh Pirates and a 1976 season with the Yankees in which he won seventeen games, Dock Ellis's career came to a crashing end in 1979. He bounced from the Yankees to Oakland to Texas to the Mets and finally back to the Pirates, where he appeared in three final games. Dock Ellis, a drug addict and an alcoholic, was no longer able to perform adequately.

Ellis went to spring training with the Texas Rangers in 1980 because of his close relationship with owner Brad Corbett. When Corbett sold the team, Dock knew no one else would have him, and he retired. Shortly thereafter he saw that if he didn't stop his drug and alcohol use, he would die, and he went straight. He has been that way ever since.

Corbett hired Ellis in 1980 to be a sales promotion manager for his company, which sold plastic pipe.

Ellis was in Corbett's office when he made the discovery he was alcoholic.

"It sounds sort of silly, but it isn't," he said. "I had sworn I would never drink scotch. But I would go into Corbett's office and drink his Chivas Regal out of the top shelf and tell myself I was drinking brandy. Brad was trying to figure out where all his scotch was going. I'd say I had given it away or that someone was stealing it. So he'd lock the cupboard, and I'd get the key. I would drink Chivas Regal in the morning with orange juice or coffee, and for lunch I was eating the olives from the martinis. I'd come back to the office and slip out to the local bar to drink vodka.

"Finally, I said, 'Wow, I'm killing myself.' And I was still doing cocaine, even though not as much as when I was a ballplayer, when people were always giving me stuff."

Ellis called Don Newcombe, who is in charge of drug rehabilitation for major league baseball. Newcombe, who was a star pitcher for the Brooklyn Dodgers, once had a bad drinking problem. He has dedicated his life to helping today's ballplayers.

Ellis asked Newcombe about the rehabilitation center.

Newcombe told him, "I don't know if they have a bed. Hold on."

Dock replied, "I'm not holding on to shit. Fuck you."

Newcombe said, "No, man, I'll call you back in a couple of hours."

"I went to my sister's house around ten," Ellis said. "She said she was going to take the kids to McDonald's, and I went with her. I saw a liquor store down the street, and I said, 'Wait a minute. I'm going down to get me a bottle.' I got me some Chivas Regal, and that's when I said, 'I know I have to go now,' because that's when I finally admitted, 'This really *is* scotch.'

"I drove to my mother's, and by the time I got there I had drunk almost all of that scotch. I went to a guy's house down the street to drink some rum. She sent one of my nieces down to tell me Don Newcombe had called to say he had a bed for me in Arizona. I said, 'I'm gone,' and I went."

Ellis stayed a little over a month, two weeks more than the insurance covered. The center kept telling him: "Your insurance is up." Dock would say, "I don't give a fuck. I ain't going out of here." Because he was afraid.

"I was in a protected community, and I knew I wasn't ready to deal with getting out," Ellis said. "I knew I would start using drugs again. It was something I was missing, like I didn't have six bullets in my gun. I had five. I needed the sixth."

It turned out that what he needed was his counselor's permission to go. Ellis had to know what to do once he got out. The key came when his counselor told him to drink Catalpa Pink, which sounded like whiskey but is nothing but grape juice. Dock has been off drugs and alcohol for nine years. He is now trying to locate his counselor, the man who helped save him, because someone told Dock that his counselor is back on drugs.

Dock Ellis shook his head. In his short lifetime he has seen so much, and it often makes him angry. He could have been adored. Maybe he could have been in the Hall of Fame. Today none of that matters. All that counts is that he is straight.

CHAPTER

28

Downs and Ups

After feeling so pumped up about defeating West Palm Beach, the Pelicans played the Explorers at the old William McKechnie Field in Bradenton. William McKechnie had managed the Pirates to a pennant in 1925, the Cardinals in 1928, and the Reds to pennants in 1939 and 1940. The old wooden structure looked like some of the stadiums from the turn of the century. It was charming and intimate and had a short left-field fence. The Explorers, and Jim Morrison in particular, loved pumping balls over that fence.

Pat Zachry started and took a five-run lead in the first inning. He pitched five innings and allowed two runs. But four relievers let the Explorers come back, and the Pelicans lost a heartbreaker in the eleventh.

After the game Zachry was standing in the cramped visitor's locker room, half-dressed. Amid the silence, someone said within earshot, "Incredible game."

"Yeah," Zachry said, "incredibly horseshit."

The locker room turned silent. There was little conversation among the players, except for whispers and a few disparate "fucks."

"It just fucking burns me up when these fucking guys beat us," Lamar Johnson said. Lamar then berated himself for cursing. A few lockers down, the ordinarily bright and cheery Lenny Randle seemed distraught. The final run had scored on a hit by Stan Cliburn that had skipped past his glove. Lenny was mad that he hadn't stopped the ball and kept the runner from scoring.

Steve Kemp was annoyed. The Pelicans were scheduled to take the bus to Winter Haven for an afternoon game the next day. The schedule called for the team to leave Bradenton and go directly to Winter Haven, spend the night there, and play the next day.

After the players boarded the bus, Kemp wondered aloud whether everyone would prefer to spend the night in St. Pete and then begin the trip in the morning.

Dock Ellis stood in the front of the bus. He grabbed the intercom and said, "We will return to St. Petersburg if you want, but you will have to get to Winter Haven on your own." That ended the discussion.

After about an hour of riding, the anger melted away. On the VCR there was laughter at Steve Martin in a movie called *The Jerk*, about a very white man who is raised by a black family and doesn't know he's white. Martin was funny, but the biggest impression was made by Bernadette Peters's cleavage. Several players made remarks about getting their noses in a certain cozy spot and nuzzling themselves in a certain friendly way.

Said one player, "If women didn't have them things, there'd be a bounty out on 'em."

Sitting in his seat, waiting for the ride to end, Steve Henderson commented, "I eat, I sleep, I go to the ballpark."

The next day didn't prove any more merry. The new shortstop, Ivan DeJesus, pounded a ball down off his left foot, and trainer Brian Ebel drained out four cc's of blood to ease the pressure. Quiet Luis Gomez was back in business.

When DeJesus arrived in the Pelican clubhouse, everyone was impressed that he was in such good shape. DeJesus's thighs, like two oak trees, became the topic of conversation among some of the players.

Said Pat Zachry in admiration, "If I had his legs, and he had ball bearings up his ass, we'd be rolling."

Despite his great gams, DeJesus was hurting like everyone else.

The ballplayers, it turned out, were not the only ones reliving their youths through the Senior League. Sitting in a box seat right behind the Pelican dugout was a blond woman in her early forties.

"I understand you're covering the Senior League," she said, adding, "I'm covering the Senior League too, but I'm doing it in a different way." She smiled. "You could write my story."

The woman had gone to one of the Seven Sisters colleges and before that had had a repressed childhood. Her rebirth began, she said, during the last spring training when she quit her job and drove to Fort Lauderdale to pursue a liaison with the man of her dreams, a certain Yankee outfielder whose baseball card she withdrew from her purse.

After luring him with her charms, she said, she decided she would stay in Florida and try to meet as many ballplayers as she could. The Senior League was the perfect vehicle.

"I have close friends on all the Senior League teams," she said.

She then took out a stack of Topps baseball cards. "These are all my friends," she said. She fanned the cards. All the ballplayers were Latino and black.

"I only like to date black guys," she said.

As the season went on, periodically she would show up at the various ballparks, and when she'd see me, she'd wave.

If the ballplayers were fulfilling their dreams, she was living hers too.

"I should have done this long ago," she said.

On January 17, a sunny Wednesday, Jon Matlack beat Winter Haven. He allowed no earned runs in five innings of work. Bill Lee gave up fifteen hits and nine runs, seven earned. Dick Bosman relieved and responded with a beautiful performance, gaining his first save of the year. Orlando hung three games behind. Bradenton and Winter Haven were out of it.

With a playoff berth virtually assured, humor returned to the Pelicans' locker room. In baseball one day everyone can seem to be down, and the next day everyone can seem to be up.

In his cubicle after the game Pat Zachry reminisced about the New York Mets' late clubhouse manager, Herbie Norman.

"If Herbie didn't like you," Zachry said, "he would do nothing short of making you miserable to put you in your place.

"I can remember Eddie Glynn, a pitcher, showed up the very first day, and he wanted everything about his uniform just so. Eddie had hair down to his shoulders and a black leather jacket and skin-tight designer jeans. He had a real high voice—something only a dog can hear—and when he came in the very first day, Eddie asked for pants, size thirty-two. Herbie gave him thirty-eights. They looked like they would fit Lamar Johnson and were long enough for George Hendrick. Herbie gave him a hat too large. Nothing fit right.

"Eddie's voice kept getting higher and higher, and Herbie was laughing harder and harder. Eventually Eddie threw his hands up and went marching into Joe Torre's office. Torre came out and said, 'Herbie, why don't we try to fit this guy a little bit better than we're doing.' Only at Torre's intervention was Eddie able to suit up that first day."

Another time Herbie Norman and some of the Met players decided to teach Fred Wilpon's fifteen-year-old son a lesson. The boy would come into the clubhouse wearing khaki pants, Topsiders, club tie, light blue shirt, and navy blazer with emblem buttons. He made comments and walked around as though he owned the place. To the ballplayers the kid was showing off on his old man's dough.

This day young Wilpon came into the clubhouse. Herbie had an old piece of quarter-inch copper tubing shaped like a horn that he bent to resemble a bugle. He filled the inside of the copper tubing with talcum powder.

The players told the boy that nobody in the world had been able to blow this horn and emit a sound out of it. They knew the kid was cocky enough to take the bait.

The players pretended to blow the horn with all their might, turning red in the face. All they were doing was holding their breath. They faked passing out on the floor, heaving.

The players dared him. He said he thought he could make the horn blow. When he blew, he got talcum powder all over his clothes and into his eyes. The players laughed hard, until they realized he had gotten powder in his eyes. For a couple of minutes he was blinded.

Later that day the boy's father went to Herbie to complain. Herbie told him, "If he can't stand the heat, keep the kid the hell out of the clubhouse."

Herbie loved to gross out people. He'd go to amusement shops and buy "morning breeze" that smelled like rotten eggs. He'd get on a bus smelling like a skunk, just to watch the other passengers move away from him.

On airplanes Herbie would hold a newspaper in front of his face. The stewardess would come over and ask him to put on his seat belt. He'd have a dildo hanging out of his pants.

"He had the eyeglass set with a Groucho Marx-looking mustache, but instead of a regular nose, it would have a five-inch-long penis attached," Zachry said. "He'd drop his newspaper and look up at the stewardess and wiggle his eyebrows.

"Ah, Herbie," Zachry said, remembering his late friend.

CHAPTER

29

The Victims

The good feeling of the day before was dampened when centerfielder Kenny Landreaux failed to show up at Al Lang Stadium for a doubleheader against Winter Haven. Landreaux never called to say he wasn't coming, and some of the players worried about him. It was especially curious because the day before Kenny had had his best day as a Pelican. He went 3-for-4, scored twice, drove in a run, and hustled on the field. On other days Kenny looked half-asleep. But yesterday he seemed wired and ready for bear. Bobby Tolan was angry. "I ought to suspend his ass," he barked. But if he suspended Landreaux, Tolan would have to play in the field every day. His forty-four-year-old legs weren't up to doing that.

At ten of seven, before the start of the second game, Kenny still had not arrived. His uniform hung in his locker. Tolan called everywhere, but his center fielder was nowhere to be found.

"Where is he?"

"I don't know," said Tolan, "but it can't be good."

The next day the AWOL Kenny Landreaux reappeared. Landreaux, clearly embarrassed, would not explain where he had been and why he had disappeared.

"I didn't want anyone to find me," he said. "It was nothing serious, but they could have put me in jail."

Manager Bobby Tolan and owner Jim Morley fined Landreaux $250 for each game missed and another $250 for not calling to say he would be absent. Later Landreaux went to Morley for help.

When he finally did talk about it, it turned out that Landreaux had been victimized, like many ballplayers are, by bad or fraudulent investments, in this case including a tax-shelter scheme to lease boats to a fishing company. The come-on to the ballplayer is that by making such an investment, he will derive huge savings on federal taxes.

When Landreaux's investments turned sour, he was unable to pay back the money he had borrowed from banks. After eleven years as a major league ballplayer, Kenny Landreaux faced the loss of his home and his car. Burdened with a debt he couldn't meet, he panicked. He became scared and disappeared.

It turned out that Landreaux had not been facing a situation where he could have been jailed. He just thought so. It was one more example of life overwhelming a former ballplayer not used to dealing with its demands.

That Landreaux had been lured into making bad investments was not uncommon. No one is immune except those who take their earnings and put them in the bank. It's been said that making the money is the easy part. Figuring out what to do with it is the hard part.

A ballplayer hires a business manager, whose expertise is business and finance, and he places implicit trust in his judgment. You have to. If you don't, you shouldn't hire him in the first place. Unfortunately, as in every profession, some advisers are experts and others are charlatans. If the player hires a charlatan, he stands to lose everything. Casey Stengel and John McGraw were led to invest in oil wells in Texas and became rich. Babe Ruth hired Christy Walsh, and Walsh helped the free-spending Babe keep his money. Mickey Mantle was lured by a string of advisers to invest in a series of get-rich schemes, including hotels and bowling alleys. Mickey ended up losing time and time again. Ron Guidry lost a pile of dough by trusting a close friend.

Some of the biggest names in the Senior League had lost money in similar fashion: George Foster, Rick Wise, Bill Campbell, and Rollie Fingers.

Before a game against West Palm Beach, Pelican pitcher Joe Sambito, who works for an agency that represents pro ballplayers, had been talking to Fingers, who pitched for the Tropics. Sambito that morning had read an article in the Palm Beach newspaper describing how Fingers had lost his savings when his agent, LaRue Harcourte, turned out to be a con artist. Harcourte had taken money from other players as well, causing some of them to lose all their assets, including their homes.

Sambito said, "Gee, Rollie, I'm really sorry to hear you have financial problems. I had no idea. That's a shame."

"That's old," Fingers said. "They just keep digging it up and writing about it." Fingers was matter-of-fact. He had always been a happy-go-lucky guy who never wanted to be bothered with details. He hadn't known what Harcourte was doing to him, and when he found out, it was too late.

Sambito, who was intelligent, sophisticated, and wise, had also been taken. Sambito was lucky. He *only* lost $100,000. And he kept playing, so his hefty salary protected him from any hardship. The man who took him was Peter Lemongello, the singer and the cousin of a Houston Astros teammate, Mark Lemongello.

Sambito got revenge. He ended up sending Peter Lemongello to jail.

Sambito's story began when he and pitcher Mark Lemongello became good friends on the Astros. In 1978 they roomed together on the road.

"Mark was very high-strung but very likable," Sambito said. "He put so much pressure on himself that he was self-destructive. If he wasn't perfect, he would even inflict harm upon himself. He'd also trash clubhouses. He would punch out the jacket hooks. Or concrete. Once he went right down a long tunnel with a bat, hitting all the light bulbs."

Sambito thought Mark a "strange character but a likable guy." One time, when the Astros were playing in Montreal, Mark, a hard-luck pitcher, lost a tough game, and when Joe came back to the room Mark wasn't there. When Lemongello returned the next morning at eight, Sambito asked, "Where have you been?"

Lemongello said, "You know the big cross atop Mount Royal? I slept under it."

Mark Lemongello couldn't handle the pressure he put on himself. He was traded to Toronto, where he was 1–9 in 1979.

Peter Bavasi was the Toronto general manager, and when Bavasi told Mark he was being sent down to Triple A, Mark trashed Bavasi's office, throwing Bavasi's pictures and ashtrays against the walls.

Mark Lemongello left baseball, and Sambito lost track of him. In 1980 Mark called Sambito to tell him he was in St. Petersburg, Florida, Sambito's hometown. Mark said, "My cousin Peter is building homes in St. Pete."

Timing can make all the difference. At the time Sambito was in the market for a house. Sambito asked to meet his roomie's cousin.

Peter Lemongello had been a singer who convinced some big-money local New York investors to underwrite a record, *Love '76,* which he sold via mail order through TV ads. Peter played at Lincoln Center and Carnegie Hall. He even was on the Johnny Carson show.

According to news accounts, Peter Lemongello allegedly kept the money but never delivered the records.

"He never paid back his investors either, so they were after him," Sambito said. "Turns out he was so in debt in New York that he had to get out. Otherwise, they were going to kill him."

Sambito didn't know at the time that Peter Lemongello had never paid back his investors in the record offering and that to keep from being found by them, Lemongello became known as John Ligori, the name of his stepfather, even though his stepfather was still living. With the money he made in New York, Lemongello bought lots at the Feathersound country club in Clearwater, Florida, and began building homes under his new name.

Lemongello then declared bankruptcy in Florida under his own name.

Joe Sambito didn't know any of this at the time he first met Peter Lemongello. He contracted with Lemongello to build him a home. Sambito told Lemongello, "I'll pay you top dollar to do things right."

"Right from day one he started ripping me off," Sambito said. Lemongello was cutting corners, putting in inferior products.

"He heard the 'top dollar' part and forgot the rest," Sambito said.

Sambito was being taken and didn't know it. The only reason he didn't lose more than the $100,000 it ultimately cost him was that Peter Lemongello had promised his cousin Mark a finder's fee on any house Mark got him and then reneged on his promise. When Peter refused to pay Mark, there occurred a series of events that led to the downfall of Peter Lemongello.

Mark knew Peter Lemongello had a safety deposit box with about $70,000 in it. He decided to go after the money.

With Joe Sambito standing right there, Mark pulled up in a van in front of Peter Lemongello's house. Mark got out and at gunpoint ordered Peter into the van.

When Peter said he wouldn't go, Mark hit Peter over the back of his head with a pistol and opened a gash that started bleeding all over Peter's expensive camel hair coat. Mark put the gun to Peter's head and said, "Get in the van."

Sambito said, "I couldn't believe what I was seeing." Mark barked at him, "Joe, mind your own business."

The Pelicans

Joe Sambito

Mark took Peter Lemongello to the bank and emptied the safe deposit box. He dropped Peter off, threw the gun in the bay, and got on an airplane and flew to Ohio.

The police investigated. They put out a warrant for Mark. When Mark called Sambito, Joe had to tell him that he had told the police what he had witnessed. Sambito said, "There's a warrant out for your arrest. Don't do anything foolish." Sambito feared that the high-strung Mark Lemongello might kill himself or get killed while trying to resist arrest.

During that conversation Sambito learned for the first time that Peter Lemongello's home-building enterprise had been a scam all along. Mark proceeded to tell Sambito the details, that Peter had sold him the house with the express intention of milking him for as much money as possible. Joe was stunned.

Around this time Peter Lemongello was arrested for arson, solicitation to commit arson, and insurance fraud. He pleaded no contest.

Lemongello was fined $10,000 and told he couldn't build in Florida anymore. It was a lenient punishment, considering that one woman lost everything she had when Lemongello intentionally burned down the house he was building for her after she fired him for his shoddy work.

When Mark told Sambito about what Peter had been trying to do to him, Sambito began his own investigation. Sambito, feeling pretty stupid, decided he would sue Peter Lemongello for breach of contract. Sambito went to the courthouse and checked the public records. He did title searches, and it was Sambito who discovered the bankruptcy petition under the name of Peter Lemongello and the new start under the name of John Ligori.

Sambito called the judge who signed the bankruptcy petition. It turned out the judge was married to Sambito's mother's first cousin!

He told the bankruptcy judge, "Alex, do I have a story for you," and he proceeded to inform him about the fraud perpetrated on his court.

Sambito told him, "He lied to you." Then he showed him the documents to prove it.

The next day Sambito got a call from the FBI. The avenging Sambito had all his notes and told the investigators exactly where to look.

As a result of Sambito's legwork, Lemongello was indicted for bankruptcy fraud just thirty days before the statute of limitations was to expire. Lemongello pleaded guilty.

Subsequently, Sambito was able to get a judgment of $440,000 against Lemongello, but Lemongello was judgment-proof.

As Sambito likes to say, what goes around, comes around. Lemongello had been put on ten years' probation on the arson charge. But after Sambito contacted the bankruptcy judge with his information, leading to the FBI investigation, Lemongello was tried and convicted in Florida for bankruptcy fraud, and he ended up serving twenty-two months in federal prison.

Joe Sambito hasn't forgiven Peter Lemongello, and recently he's been able to thwart his ambitions.

After he was released from jail in January 1987, Lemongello's wife left him. In 1989 billboard signs began to appear, announcing that Peter Lemongello was going to be singing at the Showboat in Atlantic City. For two dates he drew only a thousand people. Joe Sambito attached the $8,000 in proceeds from the concerts. Lemongello didn't see a penny from his performances.

Sambito promises to haunt Lemongello for the rest of his life.

"Ballplayers are such easy victims," Sambito said. "You gotta figure, here's a guy who makes several hundred thousand dollars a year, more money than most people can imagine. Take Mark Davis. He's going to make over $3 million a year. He gets paid over six months. We're talking two hundred and fifty grand twice a month. Think about that!

"I remember I'd look at my paychecks and think, *This is unbelievable*. I had Jumbo CDs. A Jumbo CD is $100,000. I'd go through a season and have four or five of them floating around. You think you can never run out of money."

Sambito had close friends who lost everything. He remembered a man named Howard Golub, who approached him several times to get involved in his business deals. His agents, however, advised him not to invest. Other Astro teammates, including current manager Art Howe, weren't so lucky. Howe lost so much money investing with the man that he had to sell his house.

Sambito said, "Every guy who wants to sell you something sounds so convincing: Arabian horses, wind turbines, time sharing. They make it sound good."

Sambito's nightmare was Peter Lemongello. Fortunately, he could handle the loss. Lemongello hasn't fared as well.

On March 2, 1990, Lemongello was brought to a Long Island hospital after taking an overdose of Valium. He survived. Police ruled it a possible suicide attempt.

With Kenny Landreaux AWOL for the two games against Winter Haven on January 18, the Pelicans were fortunate to come away with a split on the day. The Pelicans lost the first game in the ninth inning when reliever Dave Rajsich failed to retire Super Sox catcher Gary Allenson. With two outs and runners on first and third, Rajsich threw a sinker that Allenson lined into center for the game winner.

In the second game Hoot Gibson, who doesn't weigh more than 160 pounds, pitched a complete-game victory for the second time. He was hurling a five-hit shutout until the ninth, when he tired. Nevertheless, it was an impressive performance in a game in which Bobby Tolan had little healthy relief in the bullpen and desperately needed Gibson to go the distance. The question asked by his teammates was whether Hoot's arm would be able to take the strain.

The next day when Landreaux came back, Tolan kept him out of the game against Bradenton. With the score tied in the eighth inning, the Pelicans lost on a bunt. The batter was Stan Cliburn, the Bradenton catcher. Third baseman Roy Howell, playing on a sore leg, saw the ball drop in front of him, and in his haste he kicked it—toward the Bradenton dugout. As the ball rolled toward its ultimate destination, Howell raced after it. At the last moment he slid on his stomach, eating dirt, and watched in horror as the ball disappeared down the dugout steps.

But because second-place Orlando also lost and because Bradenton hadn't had as much success against the rest of the league as it did against St. Pete, the Pelicans maintained their lead at three and a half games. Even so, the players had become frustrated by their lack of success against the Bradenton Explorers.

After the game pitcher Milt Wilcox stood out by his van. He was upset.

"Tomorrow I'm going to beat them," he declared. "I beat them last time, and this time I'm mad. If we win tomorrow, we only lose one game in the loss column."

30

The Ace

Eleven games in the regular season remained. The next day, January 21, Milt Wilcox was good to his word, though the Pelicans didn't start off any better than they did the day before. The big right-hander allowed hits by Bradenton's Omar Moreno and Graig Nettles, and two throwing errors by first baseman Lamar Johnson brought Bradenton two first-inning runs. Despite the early runs and a thick fog that began to roll across Al Lang Stadium, the Pelicans weren't fazed.

In the bottom of the inning a single and a hit batter, followed by a double by Steve Henderson, brought across one run. Catcher Butch Benton then sent the Pelicans ahead for good with a hard single up the middle.

Benton, unknown to all but the most rabid Mets fans, was a force every time he played. He was a tenacious competitor, and when good things happened on the field, Benton often was somewhere in the vicinity. In addition, Benton finished the season hitting .374.

Because he was platooning with Dwight Lowry, Benton was denied the chance to hit often enough to qualify for the batting title and to be named the All-Star catcher. His teammates knew that politics often determine All-Star balloting. They were aware that the Pelicans were not a favorite team around the league, because Tolan was arrogant, and because they were too. Everyone on the Pelicans suspected that players like Howell,

Randle, Benton, Henderson, and Wilcox would probably be slighted when the votes came in.

In beating Bradenton when it counted, Milt Wilcox hiked his record to 11–3. There was only one other pitcher in the league, Juan Eichelberger, who won as consistently as he did, but Eichelberger was pitching on a deeper ball club. There had been days toward the end of the season when manager Bobby Tolan had to scramble to find nine healthy bodies. If *Sports Illustrated* had ever wanted to write about player injuries in the Senior League, now was the time to do it.

Through it all Milt Wilcox kept winning games.

"He's our ace," Tolan said. "He wins the big ones."

Milt Wilcox, who pitched in the major leagues from 1970 to 1986, had seen a lot, done a lot. Wilcox had confidence, character, and courage. He proved that in the minors when he refused to let the Cincinnati front office talk him out of rooming with a black teammate. He proved it again with Detroit when he stuck up for himself and refused to allow manager Sparky Anderson bury him in the bullpen. When Anderson finally relented, Wilcox spent the next seven years in Anderson's starting rotation.

As tough on the mound as they come, Wilcox nevertheless showed that any ballplayer has a breaking point. Faced with a divorce and with the loss of a considerable amount of money, he left the game in 1986 after suffering a nervous breakdown. Baseball had beaten one of the best of them.

The Senior League was giving Wilcox another chance to compete. Separated from his second wife, Wilcox would drive an hour to Al Lang Stadium from his home in Lakeland, often with his fourteen-year-old son Brian and their pet cocker spaniel, Ralph. Brian became a team batboy. Ralph became the team mascot.

The other players liked the kid, tolerated the dog—most of the time. But because Milt as the best pitcher stood at the apex of the pecking order, he was immune from their bitching. If Milt wanted to bring the pooch, he did so. And why not? Every fifth day Bobby Tolan would write his name on the lineup card, and twelve times in a three-month season Wilcox would come away with a "W" after his name in the box score. It was as impressive as winning twenty-five games in a season in the big leagues.

Milt Wilcox grew up in a suburb of Oklahoma City, and as a boy he could throw a baseball ninety miles an hour. When he was fourteen years old, he pitched a sixteen-inning game for his American Legion team. Throwing nothing but fastballs, he struck out thirty-four batters. He lost, 1–0. His catcher's hand was so battered that the boy had to hold raw meat on it for hours after the game was over.

By the time Wilcox was a sophomore in high school, scouts were watching him. Through it all Wilcox never got a swelled head. Wilcox was drafted out of high school in the second round by the Cincinnati Reds in June 1968. He received $24,000, plus a college scholarship, which he never used. He also got bonuses totaling another $12,000 if he made the majors.

Wilcox immediately found out that pro baseball wasn't always as glamorous as it seemed. He also discovered something about the promises that were made to him.

The Reds sent him to Sarasota, Florida, in the Rookie League. They told him he was going to get half of his bonus when he arrived. His parents, who didn't have a lot of money, gave him ten bucks for the trip. But when he arrived in Sarasota, he was told he wouldn't get his bonus money for three weeks.

His roommate, the Reds' number one draft choice, named Tim Grant, had been told the same thing. The two youngsters would have starved had not a nearby grocery store given them credit. For three weeks they ate baloney sandwiches. Neither of them had a car, and they couldn't afford a cab, so they had to walk over a mile to the park.

"We found out what it was like to be in the minor leagues real quick," Wilcox said.

He also learned something about the South, segregation, and baseball's reaction to Jim Crowism

The year was 1968. Milt Wilcox, who is white, and Tim Grant, a black from North Carolina, lived together in a small room in a hotel in Sarasota. Back then, baseball teams didn't like to disturb the local customs.

After about a week of spring training, Wilcox's manager, Bill Lajoie, told him that the Cincinnati general manager, Bob Howsam, had called.

"He said you have to get another roommate," Lajoie told Wilcox.

Wilcox, though a rookie, refused his request. "I don't have to get another roommate," he said. "I have a roommate."

"No, you can't room with Tim Grant."

Peter Golenbock

Milt and Brian Wilcox

Wilcox said, "Why can't I room with him?"

Lajoie replied, "Because you're white and he's black."

"*Whhaaaaattt*?" Wilcox exclaimed.

"Cincinnati doesn't like those kinds of things."

Wilcox told Lajoie, "I'm not leaving. Tim Grant is my roommate. We're good friends."

Lajoie then said, "I'll stand behind whatever decision you make."

Wilcox added, "I'm not going to get another roommate. I like Tim, and we get along real well together, and I don't care if he's green or purple or black or yellow. He's a nice guy, and I'm going to keep rooming with him."

Lajoie came back and said, "You know, Milt, they are really upset with you, and this could hurt your chances for getting to the major leagues."

"If that's what it is," Wilcox said, "that's what it is."

About a week later, Wilcox was sent to Tampa to play A ball. Right after the season, Bill Lajoie was fired from the Cincinnati Reds' organization.

"He always contended that the reason he got fired was because I wouldn't move out," Wilcox said.

Despite his stand, Wilcox continued in the organization as a top prospect. He threw in the mid-nineties and had good control. In his first game in Class A ball, he pitched against the Yankee farm club in the league, which was stocked with good young players like Johnny Ellis. Wilcox struck out fourteen.

With service in Vietnam on the horizon, Wilcox joined the National Guard in 1968 and spent six months on active duty, which set him back about a year. After finishing the 1969 season in A ball, in 1970 he jumped all the way to Triple A, Indianapolis, where he was 12–10, pitched a no-hitter, and was named Pitcher of the Year.

His year in Indianapolis was the first time Milt Wilcox had ever lived in a big city. It was also his first opportunity to experience all the possibilities that make up the lifestyle of the professional ballplayer.

"It was the first time when people really hung around you, wanted to be around you, what you call 'green flies,' groupies. It was my first introduction to those people," Wilcox said.

"I had never really gone out or drank much. There was a guy named George who owned a bar, and it was where all the ballplayers hung out. That's when I was turned on to what professional baseball was. Everything was so...so easy. Whatever you wanted was there. Everybody was throwing parties, and you were invited, and when you're a young guy in professional baseball suddenly you're on an upswing, everything is there, and you can see it, and you want to experience it.

"And being from Oklahoma and sheltered my whole life, I had never drank, never cussed, never smoked. It was an eye-opener. I began to see how the nightlife affected guys.

"At Indianapolis I played with pitcher Bo Belinsky. He had played with the California Angels in the early sixties, and he was on his way down. You always heard stories about Bo and how he partied and drank and took pills, and it was all true. He'd sit in the bullpen and drink brandy—he had a little flask with him—and I don't know if he was a hypochondriac, but he took a lot of pills. Here he was, so talented—he had thrown a no-hitter. He married Jo Collins, a Playboy Playmate of the Year. I thought he was real talented to do that. And she was there. But they were on the way out."

At the end of the 1970 season, Wilcox was called up to the Cincinnati Reds for the first year of the Big Red Machine. Wilcox pitched well.

At the age of twenty, Milt Wilcox had been sitting at the top of his profession. He helped the Cincinnati Reds defeat the Pirates to get into the World Series. Though he had lost a game in the Reds' defeat in the series to Baltimore, his future with Cincinnati looked bright.

Wilcox, however, had trouble with his catcher, Johnny Bench, and when a pitcher tangled with Bench, that meant he also had to battle the Reds' manager, Sparky Anderson.

"Sparky Anderson is great with young kids who are *not* in baseball," Wilcox said.

Wilcox liked to call his own game. He also didn't think catcher Johnny Bench was a very good signal caller.

"I figured I knew what I wanted to throw, so I shook him off a lot, and Sparky didn't like that. We had a couple of run-ins because of that."

His most public confrontation with Anderson occurred in San Diego as the Reds were getting ready for the playoffs. Bench called a pitch, Wilcox shook him off, and the batter hit a home run.

Anderson was miked for national television. When Wilcox returned to the dugout, Sparky walked him over by the camera and, on national TV, said, "How can a nothing pitcher like you shake off a superstar catcher like Johnny Bench?"

Wilcox replied, "I think I know what I can throw better than what Johnny Bench wants me to throw."

Anderson made it clear he didn't like the way Wilcox pitched.

"To be honest, it was probably just me," Wilcox said. "I didn't like Sparky too much at that time."

Sparky would have room checks, but Wilcox noticed that only the rooms of the young players like himself and Don Gullett got checked.

"Never the old players," Wilcox said. "He'd never catch Rose and Bench and those guys. Those guys were never in anyway, but he would never check them. So he had two sets of rules. He was really hard on young players."

The next year Wilcox's National Guard duty got in the way of his career. It was 1971, the year in which the Bobby Tolan-less Cincinnati offense had a "power shortage." The Big Red Machine didn't hit, didn't play well, and finished fourth.

Wilcox had been in the starting rotation, and he pitched his first game against the Cubs. But then the National Guard told Wilcox he had to go for two weeks of summer camp. So the Reds decided to send Wilcox down to Triple A and bring up pitcher Wayne Simpson, who had severely injured his arm in 1970. Wilcox will always remember Wayne Simpson and what happened to him. To Wilcox it is a prime example of how a club can ruin a young pitcher if it isn't careful.

Wilcox was Simpson's teammate when he got off to his great start in 1970. The young phenom was 13–1 at the All-Star break, but he experienced some shoulder problems and was sidelined. Toward the end of the year the Reds wanted Simpson to return to the starting rotation. But Simpson kept telling manager Sparky Anderson and the team doctor that there was something wrong with his shoulder. "A lot of pitchers go out and pitch in pain," he was told.

In those days players didn't have long-term contracts, and a player almost was forced to do what management ordered him to do. So Wayne Simpson gritted his teeth and pitched.

The Reds were playing in San Diego. Sparky came to Wilcox before the game and informed him that Simpson would pitch the first four or five innings, and he would pitch the rest.

"The first inning Wayne pitched very well," Wilcox said. "The second inning he was a little wild. The third inning he was throwing the ball all over the place. In the fourth inning he told them he couldn't pitch any more.

"I came in, finished the inning, and by the time I came back into the clubhouse, his whole shoulder had hemorrhaged. That was the end of Wayne Simpson."

When the Reds brought Wayne Simpson back up, they sent Wilcox down to Triple A, Indianapolis, where he went 8–5 with a 2.20 earned-run average.

"I felt then that my days in Cincinnati were numbered," he said.

Wilcox was right.

"I was twenty-one years old. I thought I had a great future, but after the 1971 season they traded me to Cleveland for Ted Uhlaender, who was on the downside of his career."

Wilcox is convinced that Sparky Anderson was behind the trade.

"He came out with some great quotes afterward, saying he didn't think I had much of a future, that I was not a complete-game pitcher, wasn't a starting pitcher of quality, stuff like that. And I had hard feelings about it."

With Cleveland, Wilcox became a regular. He lost more than he won, but so did the Indians, even though, during his three years there, they had the nucleus of a solid ball club with such players as Chris Chambliss, Graig Nettles, George Hendrick, Buddy Bell, Oscar Gamble, Dick Tidrow, and Gaylord Perry. The trouble with the Indians, according to Wilcox, was its management.

Wilcox said, "I put it this way. I was sentenced to three years in Cleveland. It wasn't a lot of fun."

In 1974 Wilcox finished 2–2 after having the heart of the summer cut out by military service. Just before the Indians were to start camp in February 1975, Wilcox was traded to the Chicago Cubs for Dave LaRoche and Brock Davis. In Chicago manager Jim Marshall didn't pitch him much. He never got to start.

The next year, 1976, Wilcox went to Wichita in Triple A. He played there about three months, and in June he was traded to Triple A, Evansville, a Detroit farm club.

Wilcox spent the entire 1976 season in Triple A.

When Wilcox was called up to Detroit in 1977, his career turned around. He won his first six starts for the Tigers and finished the year 6–2.

It had taken Wilcox seven seasons and four teams before he finally became a winning pitcher in the major leagues. That fourth team was the Detroit Tigers, and for seven years in a row there he won eleven or more games.

Sparky Anderson took over the reins in Detroit in 1979. Wilcox, remembering the way Anderson treated him in Cincinnati, was very unhappy about the move.

"I was still married to my first wife," Wilcox said. "We were driving down the expressway, and I heard the news on the radio. 'Sparky Anderson has just signed a six-year contract.'"

The Wilcoxes had just bought a house. Milt said to his wife, "Tell you what. We're not going to be here very long."

She said, "Why?"

He replied, "Sparky and I didn't get along too well in Cincinnati. He's going to come over here, and the first thing he's going to do is take me out of the rotation."

Sure enough, the first thing Sparky said to Wilcox was "You're only a five-inning pitcher. I can't have you in the starting rotation. You're going in the bullpen. I'm going to build my pitching staff around Steve Baker."

Wilcox said, "The Steve Baker *on our team?*"

"Yeah," Anderson replied.

"Sparky, you don't know what you're doing."

"You're telling me I don't know what I'm doing?"

Wilcox said, "Sparky, he can't even pitch in the major leagues. He doesn't have the head."

Wilcox told Anderson he didn't want to go to the bullpen. He was told to do as he was told. They talked more, and Anderson told him, "Tell you what. Give me six weeks with Steve Baker, and if he doesn't do the job, I'll put you back in." Wilcox agreed.

Wilcox said, "Six weeks went by, then seven, eight, nine, and I was still in the bullpen, and Baker wasn't getting anybody out. Million-dollar arm, nickel head. An old story.

"Sparky put me in in relief, the game was out of hand, and the White Sox hit three home runs off me in an inning and a third. The scoreboard was going off, the fireworks were exploding, and I said to myself, *That's it,* and I went to talk to Sparky. I had had enough. I had never gone up against management before. I don't like to do those things, but I felt I had to do something.

"I'm the kind of guy who has to psych himself up to pitch. As you get older, you really have to get yourself in the right frame of mind. And coming out of the bullpen, I was unhappy. I didn't want to be there, and I knew I could be starting for somebody."

Around the All-Star break Wilcox said to Sparky, "Time's up."

"For what?"

"You said six weeks, and it's been nine weeks."

"Go back to the bullpen and shut up. I'm running this team."

"I thought we had a deal."

"Look, when I'm ready to pitch you, I'll put you in there."

Wilcox balked. "It doesn't work that way."

"What do you mean?" Anderson asked.

"It doesn't work that way. I'm going to the press."

"You're not going to anybody. Don't you ever go to the press against me."

Wilcox went back to his room and called Tiger executives Bill Lajoie and Jim Campbell jointly. He told them, "The deal was six weeks. The team isn't going anywhere. I was your best pitcher last year. I want to pitch. And I don't want to go to the bullpen."

"You do what Sparky tells you," Lajoie replied.

Wilcox stood his ground. "I'm not going to."

"Don't you go to the press," Lajoie said.

"I can go to whoever I want," Wilcox replied. "You guys lied to me. Sparky lied to me. I want to pitch. Pitch me or trade me."

So Milt went to the press. The next day headlines in the papers blared Wilcox's trade demands. Sparky called him into his office.

"You did what I told you not to do," Anderson said, "but I'm going to give you a chance. You're starting the first game after the All-Star break."

"Really?"

"Yeah," he said. "Either put up or shut up."

"I looked at the schedule. We were to play the White Sox, the team that had just bombarded me. I thought, *Oh, gosh,* but I went out and shut out the White Sox, 1–0. I started for Sparky after that. All the way through 1984 I never made another bullpen appearance for him.

"If I had been a good soldier, I would have been like Jack Billingham and been forced out of the game a few years before I was supposed to. Sparky had come over and taken Jack out of the rotation. He didn't pitch him and sent him over to Boston. He was rusty and got knocked around, and Boston released him. The same thing probably would have happened to me."

After the initial row with his manager, Wilcox got along very well with Anderson. Wilcox was now an older player, and Sparky had mellowed. At Cincinnati Sparky was young and very intense, and years later when he came to Detroit he had learned that the sun would come up the next morning regardless of whether the team won or lost.

Wilcox also felt a little uncomfortable playing for the Tigers because management was always "playing games" with the players. Wilcox was particularly upset over general manager Jim Campbell's practice of clipping articles from newspapers around the country any time a Tiger player was quoted saying something negative about the team.

"He'd call you into his office and bring out the file and show you all the things you said," Wilcox said. "He talks to you about team loyalty, but when it comes down to it, what is team loyalty? It's like any other job. When they have no use for you any more, they broom you out, and they don't care a thing about you."

Another incident didn't sit well with Wilcox. This time the executive was Bill Lajoie, his old manager at Sarasota. Lajoie had become general manager of the Tigers. He accused Wilcox of trafficking in drugs.

Lajoie asked him, "What were you doing at the horse track before the game a couple days ago?"

Wilcox said, "They had early races, and I had a buddy who had a horse in the first race, and I wanted to stop by there."

Lajoie said, "We have reports from the Commissioner's office that you were seen talking to a drug dealer at the track, that you went back out into your car, and they feel you were doing something with drugs."

Wilcox said, "What are you talking about, Bill?"

He said, "We have it from undisclosed sources that they saw you go out to your car and put something in your car and come back in, and you were talking with this guy."

"I don't know who I was talking to," Wilcox said. "I went to the track, and a lot of people come up to you and talk to you."

"You are under investigation by the Commissioner of Baseball," Lajoie replied.

"For what?"

"For drugs."

"Bill, I've never taken drugs in my life. Any time you want to give me a drug test, any time you want me to go anywhere, I'll go. Put the people who have seen me take drugs in front of me, because I don't take them. I have no reason to take them. I was at the track, but that doesn't make me a criminal. I was at the ballpark on time. I've never been late for a game. Never been charged with anything."

"I just wanted to let you know, so just be careful who you hang out with," Lajoie said.

Wilcox is at a loss to understand whether Lajoie was being straight with him or whether it was just a ploy to keep him in Detroit by blackmailing him, an attempt to stop him from declaring free agency.

"Those are some of the tricks that have been played on players," Wilcox said. "I had nothing to hide, so it didn't scare me. There was nothing they could prove, because I knew I didn't do nothing."

In 1984, at the age of thirty-four, Wilcox won 17 games for Detroit, plus a game in the playoffs and a game in the World Series. That year he had seven cortisone shots in his shoulder, allowing him to continue on the mound all season long. He started 33 games and pitched exceptionally well, very consistently. A week after the World Series he went down to Columbus, Georgia, and had his shoulder operated on for the first time. He came back after the 1985 season started and pitched a few games, but he had returned too soon. His shoulder hadn't healed properly and needed another operation. In May Wilcox had it operated on a second time.

"That was it," Wilcox said. "My shoulder was gone."

After the 1985 season ended, Bill Lajoie told Wilcox the Tigers weren't going to re-sign him. Wilcox told Lajoie he intended to go down to the Dominican Republic and pitch winter ball. That winter he won six games. When Lajoie came down to watch him, Wilcox, who didn't want to leave Detroit, made it clear his shoulder was sound.

Nevertheless, in December the Tigers sent him his release.

Getting released by Detroit devastated Wilcox, who despite his protestations was indeed loyal to the Tigers. It was one factor in the buildup of pressure inside him that would lead to a breakdown.

"I was driving down the street after I came back from the Dominican Republic," he said. "I had been over to my ex-wife's, and we had a big argument. I just found out my accountant had been doing a lot of funny stuff the four months I was away and had cost me a lot of money.

"Everything was so mixed up. I had bought a house, and I gave him power of attorney for the house. He was buying stocks and putting me in insurance policies I didn't need, did stuff that cost me about $100,000. I only found out about it when I got back. I think I know what happened. I had a stress attack."

Wilcox had a queasy feeling in his stomach. Two hot pains went up the side of his head. He almost passed out behind the wheel. He went to the hospital, where doctors performed six hours of tests on him, including an EKG.

Wilcox said, "They released me and said there was nothing wrong with me. But I felt bad for about six months afterward."

The pathetic Seattle Mariners were the only team willing to take a chance on him. In spring training with Seattle, Wilcox would lie in bed and shake and shiver and sweat. "It felt like my heart was going to stop."

Wilcox pitched well for the Mariners, even though his record was 0–8. "Four of the games I was leading after six innings, but the team was just a bad team, and Seattle was not a good place to play."

Losing all those games finished him.

"What happened was, I'm not a loser," Wilcox said. "I feel like a winner, but I was losing all those games. All the pressure had built up, the arm and shoulder problems, problems with the accountant, feeling I wanted to play with the Tigers and couldn't, that everything, my family, was back in Detroit, so I went to the Seattle management and asked to be released."

They said, "Traded?"

"No," Milt said, "released. I don't want to play any more."

"We're not going to release you."

Wilcox would go home after games and say to his girlfriend, who later became his second wife, "I'm going to quit. I don't even like playing ball."

She'd say, "If you do that, you won't get your money." So he hung on. And about two weeks later, they finally released him.

Wilcox went straight home to Detroit. He didn't even try to catch on with another team, just got away from baseball, and about three months after that he started feeling good again.

A year later Milt made one final attempt to get back into the game. Roger Craig was managing San Francisco, and Milt called him to ask for a spring training tryout at the Triple A level. Craig gave him the go-ahead. Wilcox flew to Phoenix, and when he arrived, the manager of the team said he knew nothing about Wilcox getting a shot at making the team.

Wilcox, disgusted, got back on the plane and flew home. His career was officially over.

Now, as he travels Florida with his teenage son and his cocker spaniel, Ralph, Milt Wilcox enjoys himself. He owns some horses in Detroit, and at the end of the greyhound season in St. Pete he bought several dogs. He has been representing former Detroit ballplayers, lining them up for appearances and speaking engagements. Milt Wilcox is putting baseball back into his life.

"I am a winner again," he said. "That's what I am."

CHAPTER

31

Down to the Wire

As Winter Haven visited St. Pete for a pair of games, the season was winding down. With ten games left in the regular season, the Pelicans seemed especially confident. No one was going to catch them. One reason: The Pelicans knew they had Winter Haven's number.

The Pelicans once again routed Super Sox pitcher Bill Lee. Every Pelican batter hit safely. Most had two hits. In three at-bats, Lamar Johnson had two doubles, one to left and one to right.

In beating Winter Haven, Jon Matlack continued to impress. In the eight innings he pitched, he allowed only eight hits. He would have had a shutout, except that with two runners on base Kenny Landreaux lost a high fly ball in the cloudless Florida sun. Al Lang Stadium can be a tough place to see the ball in the early afternoon because of the glare off the silver seats ringing the top of the stadium. The ball fell behind Landreaux for a run. After two were out, second baseman Luis Gomez booted a ground ball to let in another run.

The win told the players that the pennant would be theirs. No one had to say it. Everyone just sensed it. It was in the air.

Before the game the next day, everyone was snickering, laughing, riding each other. If there was any pressure on the Pelicans, they didn't show it. Pat Zachry came into the clubhouse wearing a pink shirt and a multicolored hat with some pink in it.

Dave Chavez, the clubhouse manager, yelled across the room, "Hey, Zack, did you go out and match the shirt and the hat?"

"Hey, Chevy," Zachry shot back, "why don't you match my zipper to your lips."

Boistrous laughter erupted. Chavez laughed the loudest.

For the first time the players were trying to figure out the magic number for clinching the division title. Complicating the mathematics was the fact that the Pelicans had to eliminate both Orlando and Bradenton in order to win. The number had dropped to six. Any combination of Pelican wins with Orlando losses and with Bradenton losses totaling six would result in the division championship for St. Petersburg.

Hoot Gibson started for the Pelicans, but it was apparent that his two complete-game victories had taken their toll on his arm. Winter Haven scored four runs in the first. When the Super Sox returned to the attack in the third, Bobby Tolan removed him. Hoot Gibson would not be effective again for the rest of the season.

Despite the 5–1 Winter Haven lead, the same feeling of invincibility that swirled around the clubhouse before the game hovered about the dugout during it. The players felt there was no way the Pelicans were going to lose this game. The Pelicans knew if a key play had to be made, they would make it and the Super Sox wouldn't. It's hard to touch or feel group confidence, but in the Pelicans' dugout it seemed palpable.

Randy Lerch, inconsistent all year, made a rare relief appearance and ended the Super Sox's chances. He pitched through the seventh with control and confidence. When the Pelicans scored two runs in the fifth and five big ones in the sixth—Steve Henderson's three-run homer was the key hit—Randy Lerch had his fourth victory of the season.

In the eighth inning, Lee Sosa came in, but he needed help in the ninth. With runners on first and third and one out, Bobby Tolan brought in Dave Rajsich to finish off the Super Sox.

Razor quickly struck out Tommy Cruz, and then pinch hitter Glenn Brummer hit a lazy fly ball to center. The Pelicans were one game closer to clinching. Razor still had the broken pinkie finger on his pitching hand, but he had learned to pitch with it. He merely ignored the searing pain.

Wednesday, January 24, was an off-day. While the Pelicans played golf and fished, the Orlando Juice lost to Bradenton, reducing the Pelicans' magic number to three.

All season long, Orlando had gotten zero press from the local papers. Now, for the first time, the team began getting some ink. The team's owner, Philip Breen, had disappeared with $10 million he had allegedly swindled from his mortgage company. The FBI didn't know where Breen could be found. Neither did anyone in Orlando. Speculation was that he was either with Jimmy Hoffa or relaxing on a tiny Caribbean island somewhere.

This was a story the papers could understand. That the Orlando team's attendance rose dramatically during the last half dozen games of the season was no coincidence. Newspapers have that power.

The next day was the Pelicans' final home game, "St. Petersburg Times Day." Pushed by the promotions in the influential *St. Petersburg Times* and by ads on the radio, 4,425 enthusiastic fans packed Al Lang Stadium, a league attendance record, for a game against Earl Weaver's Gold Coast Suns.

Tex Williams, largely forgotten, pitched a masterful game. He allowed two cheap runs, making the tough pitches when it mattered and proving to everyone that he could compete in this league.

Soon after Tex came out of the Gold Coast game in the seventh, Lamar Johnson tied the game. With a runner on base he hit a towering home run way over the fence in left field at Al Lang field and into the palm trees beyond, the longest Pelican home run of the year.

In relief first Dick Bosman, then Dock Ellis, and finally Dave Rajsich held the Suns through the eleventh. With the speedy Hoot Gibson running for Lamar, who had walked, Kenny Landreaux bunted toward third.

Rafael Landestoy fielded the ball. But his throw to first bounced where the grass met the dirt in front of first baseman Rennie Stennett, who failed to get his glove down. The ball scooted by Stennett and rolled into right field as Hoot, fast as a jackrabbit, circled the bases with the winning run.

In the dugout right after the game one of the Pelican players voiced his opinion of the play. "It was a pussy throw and a pussy catch."

The magic number had fallen to two.

The pennant appeared to be in the bag, but after the game there was a piece of unsettling news. In the sixth inning, while diving for a ball hit by Orlando Gonzalez, second baseman Lenny Randle took a tumble and badly hurt his left shoulder and his right wrist. It was serious enough that Lenny might be through for the season. Could the Pelicans win in the playoffs without him? It was problematical. Alan Bannister would have to fill in for him.

The Pelicans drove to Orlando to play a 7:30 P.M. game against the Juice. In the afternoon Bradenton won its game against Winter Haven, so even if the Pelicans won, they still had to win one more game to clinch first place.

The players didn't care about only making the playoffs. From the first week they had assumed they'd be playing in Fort Myers in February. Their concern was winning the division title. Anything short of that would have been considered a failure. Thus, when the Pelicans beat up Vida Blue and the Juice, there was no celebration afterward. That would wait for the title clinching.

Orlando began the game with three runs against Milt Wilcox, but the Pelicans scored one in the fifth and one in the sixth, and Vida let the game get away in the seventh by giving up six runs. Steve Kemp, still playing every day since his sojourn at Disney World, was hitting .339 and making a strong case to be named to the Senior League All-Star team. As it turned out, his double in the sixth was the key hit in the big inning.

Kenny Landreaux, recovering from the trauma of his financial problems, again showed his ability to get big hits in key games. Landreaux had three hits against Gold Coast, following Kemp's double with a two-run single, finishing off the Suns. Kenny had boasted, "When it counts, I'll be there."

The final score was Pelicans 11, Juice 4. They had clinched a playoff spot. The winning pitcher, fittingly, was Milt Wilcox. It was his twelfth win against only three defeats, the most wins of any pitcher in the Senior League.

One more victory, and the division title would be theirs.

CHAPTER

32

The Pelicans Win the Pennant

On Saturday, January 27, 1990, the day the St. Petersburg Pelicans clinched the Northern Division pennant, starting pitcher Jon Matlack sat down for a breakfast of oatmeal. He was kidded for it, because during the first month of the season David Letterman had announced his Top Ten List of sayings from the Senior League. One of them had been, "That's not Morganna. That's Bea Arthur." Another was "Oatmeal, oatmeal, get your nice hot oatmeal," instead of "Peanuts, peanuts, get your red-hot peanuts."

Everyone had laughed hard when they heard that joke and even harder when they saw the oatmeal in Matlack's bowl. But Matlack was not the kind of guy to let a little kidding stop him from something he loved. After all, it was nearly twenty years since this old-timer broke into baseball.

As game time approached, it proved to be a warm, exquisite sunny afternoon in Orlando. It was "Frank Viola Day." The New York Mets ace threw out the first ball to great cheering. It was also "Clinic Day." On the field before the game hundreds of youngsters dressed in baseball regalia sat listening to the Juice players talk to them about the fundamentals of the game. The Juice, the weakest franchise in the Senior League, drew 1,529 fans, proving the interest was there if the promotion was strong.

Also contributing to the large crowd was the improved play of the Orlando team. Added to the team was Randy Bass, the large slugger who had been a megastar in Japan. With Bass hitting monstrous home runs, the Juice finished the season only half a game from making the playoffs.

Butch Benton ignited the Pelicans in the first with a two-run double, the twentieth straight game in which he had a base hit. Then in the fourth inning with a runner on first, Kenny Landreaux hit a home run over the FLEA WORLD sign in right-centerfield. Pitcher Jon Matlack did the rest, earning his tenth victory of the three-month season.

Matlack pitched masterfully—again. He threw with control, not walking a single batter over the six innings he worked. His pitches moved in the strike zone, and he was beginning to throw his fastball past the hitters. Tom Seaver, his teammate, once commented, "If you have location, movement, and velocity, you will win in the big leagues." On this day Jon Matlack had all three.

As always Matlack was stoical throughout. Like any great professional, Jon weathered the good and the bad in the field behind him with equanimity. He's handled life pretty much the same way.

Tall, lanky, composed, Jon Matlack still threw over the top with a classic, fluid motion. On the mound he was a fierce competitor, confident in his ability, a stable influence. Rarely when he made a pitching mistake would it occur a second time.

Off the mound, Matlack liked to laugh, enjoying the hijinks. In fact, Matlack was a serious, thinking, modest man, respected by everyone. His teammates actually address him by his nickname, Senator, recognizing his authoritative appearance. If asked, Jon always had an opinion, and in his stentorian voice always seemed to make sense, even if you didn't agree with him.

Once a star in the stellar pantheon of famous Mets pitchers along with Tom Seaver and Jerry Koosman, Matlack helped the Mets to a surprise pennant in 1973. Unfortunately, the Mets soon were run into the ground by an inept, unfeeling management that broke the hearts of their fans by trading away the nucleus of the team. The trades included the fabled Tom Seaver, who was sent to Cincinnati, and the dependable Jon Matlack, who spent the last six years of his thirteen-year career pitching for the Texas Rangers amid a flurry of managers and more bad management.

When Matlack was released after the 1983 season, he was so turned off by his treatment and by the heavy drug scene in baseball that he quit the game.

Once out, Matlack tried real estate and horse breeding, but the bottom dropped out of both markets, and he returned to the game as a pitching coach with the San Diego Padres. With the advent of the Senior League, he had to admit something he didn't think possible—he had missed the joy of pitching.

One of the better pitchers of his generation, Jon Matlack is self-effacing when he talks about himself. "I started out like a lot of Little Leaguers," he said. "My first year the coach told me to go out and play in right field with my back up against the fence. That way I could get in the least amount of trouble."

Matlack laughed. His favorite stories are ones in which the joke's on him. But at the same time Matlack has a lot of pride. Asked about their high school careers, some pro players are embarrassed because their performances were so dominating. Matlack recounted his accomplishments but always in the context of the team.

"In three years I was in high school we had very representative teams." he said.

"How representative?'

"We were undefeated for forty-one straight regular season games over a three-year period," he said.

Representative indeed.

"And you?"

"I was twenty-two and one. We lost the final playoff game in my senior year. I had six or seven no-hitters and a perfect game."

Despite his dominance, Matlack didn't feel like a superhero. He won, but as a high schooler he wasn't confident that his future success would be guaranteed.

"Even though I was winning, I felt like I was doing it by the skin of my teeth," he said. "Yeah, I got guys out, but it seemed to me like every time somebody swung the bat, the ball could leave the ballpark. Every pitch was a challenge. I didn't throw overpoweringly hard. I relied on control and a fairly good breaking ball. I felt I had to pitch every out."

Scouts had come by to talk to him, so he figured someone would draft him out of high school. When he was picked fourth in the entire nation in the June 1967 draft, Matlack was surprised but not excited.

"We were out on the athletic field, practicing for graduation, when Charles Peron, a quality coach, came racing out of the school, waving his arms and yelling that I had been the fourth player picked, by the New York Mets. I was nonplussed."

Matlack had been playing American Legion ball at the time, and there was an agreement that players wouldn't go to the minors until after the season ended. Matlack's team didn't lose. It won the pennant. It went to the playoffs and continued to win, and finally, around the end of August, the team lost in the state championships. When Matlack finally negotiated a deal with the Mets, there were only three weeks left in the minor league season. He was sent to Double A Williamsport, near his Westchester, Pennsylvania, home.

Matlack was seventeen years old. His roommate at Williamsport was thirty-one. He pitched twice and was hit hard.

"I was way over my head," he said. "I discovered professional baseball is a different game from the one I had been playing."

Matlack spent his first full season at Raleigh-Durham, playing half the games in each city. He and Mike Jorgensen lived in Raleigh. They loved to drag race. Matlack raced his GTO Pontiac against Jorgensen's Oldsmobile 442.

"When we played in Durham, we'd load up our cars with players," he recalled. "The twenty miles was pretty much an open road. We used to see who could get to the ballpark first. Thank goodness we never got into trouble, never blew a tire, never had a wreck, 'cause we were flying."

Another teammate had a Corvette. He was never allowed to join in those drag races, because Matlack and Jorgensen knew he had them outmatched. They also knew he was crazy.

One night the teammate was speeding in his 'Vette, and he decided to outrun the cop who caught him at it. He kept making turns and accelerating, and the last turn he made was up a driveway. He shot through a cyclone fence into a backyard.

"There was quite a hoopla, trying to get his Corvette back through the cyclone fence and trying to get him out of jail," Matlack said.

The next season he made a big jump to Triple A Portsmouth, Virginia. It was where the Mets played before moving into their Tidewater facility. Again Matlack won thirteen games, but his earned-run average jumped. It was a year of observing and learning.

His manager was Clyde McCullough, who fined him, the only time Matlack was fined in his career. One night in Portsmouth, McCullough was certain the opposing team was throwing at his hitters. He was equally certain that it was the catcher who was responsible.

The catcher was to lead off the next inning. McCullough called Matlack aside and in his deep voice said, "I want you to hit the son of a bitch."

Matlack had never thrown at a batter in his life. He wasn't particularly

The Pelicans

Jon   Matlack

upset or afraid to do it, he just didn't know how. The first pitch he hurled, the batter jumped out of the way. The ball went to the backstop. Ball one.

Matlack threw at him two more times. The batter twice more jumped out of the way, throwing his bat, diving to the ground, avoiding the ball.

Matlack had the catcher's attention, but McCullough had ordered him to hit the man, and he hadn't. And now he was in a mess, because he had run the count to 3–0 on the leadoff hitter. Matlack didn't know what to do. He didn't want to walk him, so he figured he'd better pitch to him.

On 3–2 the catcher broke his bat and blooped a single. When the inning eventually ended, Matlack returned to the dugout. Clyde had him up against the wall, reading him the riot act.

McCullough said, "It'll cost you $50, and I want it in the morning." Back then $50 was a lot of money to a minor leaguer.

When it was his turn to throw on the sideline, all Matlack did was practice throwing at hitters. Portsmouth had a player-coach named Wilber Huckle who got dressed up in catcher's gear. He stood up at the plate, and Clyde had Matlack do nothing for fifteen minutes but throw balls at Huckle.

"He showed me how you have to zero in on a spot just behind the batter," Matlack said. "It's the batter's natural reaction to back away from the pitch, and if you throw behind him, his first reaction will be backward, and he'll walk into it." After that experience Matlack never again had trouble throwing at batters or throwing inside.

Matlack said, "But when I think about it, it was *Jeez, how in the world did I get through that?*"

Matlack spent two more seasons in Triple A, playing under former Yankee star Hank Bauer. Bauer had a short burr haircut and was big and imposing. Matlack enjoyed playing for Bauer, which says something about Matlack, in that during his career he liked playing for other so-called "tough" managers, Gil Hodges and Pat Corrales, men other players complained loudly about for being too rigid and strict. The mild-mannered Senator was a lot tougher than he appeared.

"Hank was a tough Marine," Matlack said. "I always had to watch him in the clubhouse, 'cause he had a fetish for taking a fist that was the size of a cardboard box and planting it just under your ribs as a way of saying hello. And five minutes later when you got your breath back, maybe you could say hello back. Hank was good to play for. He never dropped off the deep end."

Each spring Matlack went to the major league camp and pitched a lot of batting practice, and each time he would be told, "We're pleased with your progress, but you're really not quite ready, and you need more seasoning."

Other players might have been impatient. Not Matlack. He saw who the Mets had in their rotation, Tom Seaver, Jerry Koosman, Gary Gentry, Jim Andrew, Don Cardwell, and Nolan Ryan. The Mets had won in 1969 with those arms, and Matlack knew they weren't going to make many changes. Moreover, he hadn't enough major league experience to feel confident he could get big league hitters out.

In his first spring training game in 1969, against the Red Sox, Seaver had pitched three innings, followed by three for Ryan. The two allowed one run. Matlack did fine his first inning, but the next inning allowed three home runs to four batters.

"The balls were flying into the orange groves that used to surround the ballpark in Winter Haven," Matlack said.

He came off the field. Mets manager Gil Hodges shook Matlack's hand, and he said, "Welcome to the big leagues, kid."

"I thought, *Sheeze.*"

At the very end of the 1971 season Matlack got called up by the Mets, pitched eight innings, and gave up one run against the Pirates. They asked him to go to winter ball. Jon played for Bill Virdon at San Juan, and the team won the league championship.

When Matlack came to spring training in 1972, his arm was ready to pitch nine innings Opening Day.

The other break for Matlack came when the Mets, in one of the worst deals in the history of the game of baseball, traded pitching prospect Nolan Ryan and three other players to the California Angels for a pretty good third baseman named Jim Fregosi. Ryan, of course, in 1990 pitched his sixth no-hitter, has struck out more batters than anyone in history, and undoubtedly will be inducted into the Hall of Fame as soon as he becomes eligible. Fregosi played the 1972 season, hit .232, and the next year after forty-five games was traded to the Texas Rangers. But for Matlack, something positive came of the trade. It enabled him to make the team, squeaking on as its tenth pitcher.

Matlack remembered the day. "The Mets were on the road the last day of spring training, and we came back to Miller Huggins Field to undress. I knew there had been some cuts made. I realized if there were twenty-five lockers still full of uniforms we were down to the limit. I tried to sit at my locker while I was taking off my uniform. I quietly counted the players around the room to see how many bodies I came up with.

"I didn't know it, but Gil Hodges was standing in the aisle watching me do this. And when I completed my count, I realized there were only twenty-five left, and I was one of the twenty-five. I was sitting there smiling, and he walked by and said, 'That's right, kid. You made it,' and he walked into his office."

He was embarrassed that Hodges had noticed him counting.

"I wanted to crawl under the carpet," Matlack said.

Some players feared Gil Hodges. Others didn't like playing for him, because Hodges had a chain of command and rarely spoke to a player directly, using his coaches as intermediaries. Matlack, even at the impressionable age of twenty-two, decided that rather than judge Hodges based on his personality, he would respond to him on the basis of his baseball acumen. Ever the observer, Matlack developed a respect for the man that bordered on devotion.

"I can remember sitting on the bench and watching Gil as things played out during a ball game. He would be telling people to get ready for a possible pinch-hitting role two innings before it happened. He seemed to be totally in tune with what was going on, anticipating everything that could possibly happen in a game.

"He kept you in the game. He would sit down at his end of the bench, and you'd be wherever you were. At some point during the game, he'd lean down and say, 'Matlack, what's the count?' I'd think, *Oh, my gosh,* and even if I did know, it was all I could do to get it out.

"He always kept you alert during batting practice and other drills by having a pocket full of baseballs and a fungo bat. He'd walk around behind the cage, and if a left-handed hitter was hitting most of the balls to right field and you were out in left, standing with some other guy talking, you might have a couple of rockets come your way. Gil would yell, 'You guys want a lounge chair out there?'

"He hit me in the chest more than once, not in the air but on one hop. I was scared to death of Gil to the point if I saw him in the lobby I'd go the other way rather than have to go by him and say, 'Good morning.' By the same token, if there was anything that came up that I needed to talk to him about, I knew the door was always open and he'd be fair about it."

At the end of spring training in Palm Beach, Gil Hodges went off to play golf. Before the round was over, he suffered a heart attack and died on April 2, 1972.

"To this day I don't think there was anybody I played for who kept better tabs on the game than Gil did. It was the passing of a great baseball man," Matlack said.

The man who replaced him was Yogi Berra, one of the game's great characters, who was very different from Hodges.

Matlack said, "Yogi was good people, but he was definitely different." After one flight the team got off the plane and was waiting around the terminal. Yogi had to go to the bathroom. He asked Matlack to make sure the bus didn't leave without him.

Matlack thought to himself, *That's strange. Why would they leave without the manager?*

He said, "Okay, Yogi, no problem." And Berra ducked into the men's room to go the bathroom.

When Yogi got to the bus, his pants were soaking wet. The players were snickering. They wanted to know what had happened.

Yogi said, "You won't believe what happened to me. I was in the bathroom taking a leak and another guy came and stood next to me. The guy looked over and saw it was me, and he turned and said, 'Hey, you're Yogi Berra,' and he peed all over my leg."

Yogi made Matlack his fifth starter. Jon won his first five games. The Met pitchers pushed each other to do well.

Matlack said, "Each good performance warranted a better one from the next guy. Seaver would pitch a ball game and win, and then Koosman would go out there behind him and pitch an equally good game, and if you had the next assignment, God forbid you do anything different. The inner competition to keep the thing going was really great."

Matlack, a rookie, didn't know the hitters or some of the subtleties of pitching the way Seaver and Koosman did. He learned a great deal from having his locker situated right between them.

"It was a very, very good location to be in," Matlack said.

If Matlack couldn't find the key to what it took to get through the lineup of a particular ball club, he would ask Seaver.

"I knew he would give me as much time as was needed to hash it around and come up with some different ideas," he said. "He and Jerry were both invaluable during the early years, helping me with unanswered questions both about opposing lineups and about conditioning, game-day preparation, diet, sleep habits, all the things you need to prepare for the day you gotta pitch."

Matlack calls Tom Seaver "the consummate professional." Matlack said, "For Tommy, pitching was a science and an art. At any point in time throughout those years he was a master. There were so many ways he was able to win. So many times he walked out on the mound and you watched him start a ball game, and you'd say, 'Man, he's never going to make it.' His stuff wasn't there, the ball was up a little, things just weren't clicking. But around the third, fourth, or fifth inning, it was like the previous innings had been 'get-ready,' and man, everything would come together. 'Put the bats away, because you're not gonna score now. It's all over for the rest of the game.'

"He would find a way with whatever stuff he walked out there with to be successful, until he could find the missing link that was keeping him from competing on that hard basis, and then it was, 'Close the doors, turn out the lights, the party's over.'"

Matlack remembered a one-hitter Seaver pitched against the San Diego Padres. It was an afternoon game. Seaver struck out the last ten batters.

"I don't think there was a foul ball," Matlack said, "and he didn't throw anything but fastballs. It was the most awesome display of sheer power location pitching I think I have ever seen. The guy was just phenomenal.

"He was a student of the game, studied what he did, talked about it, analyzed it, pushed himself regardless of the weather—if it was his day to throw, somehow, somewhere he was going to find a way to get his throwing in—he was just one of those people that, come hell or high water, he was going to be the best he could. And wasn't selfish about it. If he had knowledge and wisdom to impart to help somebody else, he was willing to share that."

In his six full seasons with the Mets, Jon Matlack won 15, 14, 13, 16, 17, and 7 games, a picture of consistency until his last year with them, and for him the highlight of those years was 1973, when the Mets surprised everyone by winning the Eastern Division title with an 82–79 record, and upsetting the Big Red Machine (99–63) in a five-game series to win the National League pennant.

"It was an overall effort where everybody pitched in and did whatever needed doing," Matlack said. "Somehow it got done."

For Matlack the playoffs were more fun and exciting than the Series. Most ballplayers feel that way. If you don't win the playoffs, you don't get to play in the Series.

Tom Seaver pitched the first game. Matlack kept the chart, because it was his turn to start the next day. The Reds beat Seaver, 2–1. Seaver had given up two home runs, one to Johnny Bench and one to Pete Rose. He struck out thirteen, which was a league playoff record. Other than those two pitches, he had an overpowering day.

Matlack said, "I sat there in the clubhouse after the game and reviewed that chart I don't know how many times and just thought to myself, *My God, how can you pitch that good and come away and get beat?"*

The next day Matlack faced Cincinnati's Don Gullett. Rusty Staub told Matlack before the game, "I've got his pitches," meaning, he knew when Gullett was throwing a fastball and when he was throwing a curve.

"Rusty was probably the best I've ever seen at knowing what pitches were going to be thrown from what a pitcher was doing," Matlack said.

Staub told Matlack, "Before the game is over, I'm gonna git him, so keep 'em close, 'cause I'm gonna get you at least one."

The Mets had an early lead, and then late in the game Rusty kept his word. He hit a three-run home run off Gullett and put the game away.

Matlack allowed two ground ball singles to Andy Kosko. That was all the mighty Reds were able to get.

Matlack said, "That was a real good experience against a very tough club. Oh man."

Tom Seaver pitched the last game of the playoffs. Jon Matlack became the leadoff Met pitcher in the 1973 World Series against the Oakland Athletics.

Matlack lost the opener when Felix Millan booted a grounder, Willie Mays made an error, and the opposing pitcher, Kenny Holtzman, doubled in a run. Jon lost, 2–1.

"We should have won the Series. We did not," Matlack said. "Really, the way I look at it, the real Oakland team did not surface until Game Seven. Whether it was our pitching that held them down, I'm really not sure. But in that seventh game it looked like the Oakland club we had heard about all year.

"I pitched, and I couldn't believe Campaneris could hit an outside curveball that far. He hit a fly ball to right field that proceeded to carry all the way over the fence for a two-run home run. I hung a curveball to Reggie Jackson, which he absolutely powdered. Deep. Another home run for two runs. And it wasn't that I made bad pitches. I did make that one bad pitch to Reggie, but the rest of the runs was just Oakland rising to the occasion. I don't know. Maybe they had seen enough of me that they could anticipate what I was going to throw and where I was going to put it or had a better idea of what to look for. But other than that one pitch to Reggie, and maybe one or two others, I wouldn't change what I did that day.

"They were just a very good ball club. And I thought the unsung hero of the whole Series was Joe Rudi."

After the seventh game, which the Mets lost, the locker room atmosphere was like a morgue. Rudi walked in and sat with Matlack, Seaver, Koosman, Cleon Jones, and Willie Mays and talked about the various plays, the pitch sequences, just talking baseball. He was there about twenty minutes before he returned to the Oakland clubhouse to celebrate.

"I thought that was a class act," Matlack said.

Jon Matlack was also a class act. The next season, 1974, he was 13–15 with a 2.41 earned-run average, and it probably was the best year he ever had. He led the league in shutouts, with seven.

At the end of the year Matlack was told by a baseball statistician that if he had played for Cincinnati or Oakland, his record would have been 33–3.

But 1974 proved to be a frustrating year for Matlack.

"There were a lot of games where I'd pitch my tail off and get beat 1–0, 2–1, 3–2. We were just coming up short. And Tommy that year was 11–11. He had leg problems, and he wasn't nearly as effective."

Yogi Berra, who had led the team to the World Series in 1973, was fired in 1975. Matlack respected Yogi, but his departure didn't seem cataclysmic.

"Yogi was a manager who would say, 'Here are the bats and balls. Go do your stuff.' When Yogi got fired, you sort of shrugged your shoulders. There was some sadness. Yogi was a likable guy. But for whatever reason, the team wasn't producing, wasn't winning, and it was felt that part of that was his responsibility. They made a change, though Roy McMillan didn't do any better."

Now it was time for the Mets to churn managers. The next was Joe Frazier. "He's sorta lost to memory," Matlack said. Frazier arrived in 1976, and in 1977 the team fell to last place.

After the 1977 season, the Mets dealt Matlack to the Texas Rangers. But before that, they traded Tom Seaver, the "Franchise," to the Cincinnati Reds, one of the greatest pitchers of his generation, the nearest to a perfect pitcher since the sainted Christy Mathewson (Nolan Ryan was the closest to Walter Johnson).

"Dick Young had Donald Grant's ear, and that was it," Matlack said. "I don't know why. I don't think anyone could give you any reasons that would explain the things that were done in 1977." Matlack's eyes blazed for an instant. He quickly regained his equanimity. "Ah, but nevertheless, they happened," he said. "The specifics are pretty vague right now. I just remember him going through a whole lot of hell, and to me, very much unwarranted. He couldn't get things worked out in his contract, and because of the negotiations all kinds of dirty stuff was being brought out in the press. And subsequently he was traded.

"We thought it was ridiculous," Matlack said. "To me that was the lowest point that I had experienced in my association with the Mets. They were rock-bottom."

Matlack was determined to do something about the sad state of the ball club. He and a couple of teammates went to see manager Joe Torre and general manager Joe McDonald. They told the two men how unhappy they were and expressed their desire for the club to do something to make the team better.

"If you're not prepared to do that," Matlack told them, "I and a couple others prefer to play somewhere else."

About a month before the winter meetings took place, Matlack received a conference call at his house with Joe Torre and Joe McDonald. After the pleasantries were out of the way, one of the first questions Matlack was asked was "Do you still want to be traded?"

The two men had missed the point of their earlier meeting. Matlack had said, "If you don't do something to improve the club, I want to be traded." He never said, "Trade me."

Matlack explained that to Torre and McDonald. Matlack never did answer their question. He hung up the phone and reflected on the conversation with his wife. She realized that Torre and McDonald had wanted him to say, "I want to be traded." That way they could tell Mets fans that they were only granting Matlack's wish.

Matlack told his wife, "Honey, we need to start reading the papers and listening to the radio, 'cause something's fixing to happen."

It was ironic because Matlack had bought a house in suburban Pound Ridge, north of New York, and had a three-year plan to change and renovate his home. The day they finished painting the screened-in porch, their final project, Jon was in the basement cleaning the paint brushes when the call came from Hawaii:

"This is Joe McDonald, and we have good news and bad news. The good news is we got Willie Montanez, Tom Grieve, and Ken Henderson, and in order to get them, the bad news is, you are now a Texas Ranger."

Matlack thought to himself, *Unbelievable*.

Going from the woeful New York Mets run by M. Donald Grant and Joe McDonald to the Texas Rangers under Eddie Chiles and Eddie Robinson was like going from the ridiculous to the depressing. That was the journey made by Jon Matlack after the 1977 season. Matlack finished his career in Texas and lives there today, after six straight years of frustration playing for Billy Hunter, Pat Corrales, Don Zimmer, Darrell Johnson, and Doug Rader, falling farther and farther out of favor. His final year was 1983, after which the Rangers released him.

Revolving-door owners like George Steinbrenner say that they are being decisive when they hire and fire managers so often. In reality they are impatient, foolish, arbitrary men whose enjoyment of the use of their power is more important than a successful team. And in baseball those who are hurt most by the revolving door are the players. The more managers, the more players are churned and discarded.

For Matlack in Texas, everything was fine under Hunter and then under Pat Corrales, who spent a lot of time with his star, during the offseason, working with him to strengthen his arm after surgery for bone chips. The surgeon removed twenty-one chips. Matlack saved them and brought them back to Texas.

The year 1981 saw another change of managers, this time to Don Zimmer. Zim had been the manager when the Red Sox blew the pennant to the Yankees in 1978, a disaster for which he is remembered. However, ballplayers say he is one of the better managers. In 1981 Zim led Texas to second place in the first half of the strike-torn season, third place the second half. In 1982 performance dropped, and he was fired.

"Zim was great," Matlack said. "He got a raw deal. They didn't give him half a shot. It was pathetic, a type of thing you'd rather forget."

Darrell Johnson came next, and Matlack and Johnson didn't see eye to eye. Johnson called Matlack by the nickname Square Root, because he felt Matlack was too much of a perfectionist.

Johnson lasted to the end of 1982, and in 1983 the Rangers hired Doug Rader. Matlack was too much a gentleman to say it, but he gave the impression he despised Doug Rader. If you churn managers long enough, eventually you hire one that really gums up the works.

Matlack said, "Rader really had it in for our catcher, Jim Sundberg. Doug literally crushed Sunny, publicly, privately, any way he could do it. Part of the spin was that he didn't feel Sunny was qualified to call the game, so Rader started calling the pitches from the bench. The other pitchers didn't have the intelligence to shake their heads and get the signs that they wanted. It became a job. Everything came unglued."

At the end of 1983 someone—Jon isn't sure who—wanted Matlack off the Rangers.

He received *five* independent notices of his release! "I got a phone call, a telegram, a certified letter, a letter...it was endless. On Halloween Day."

Matlack called his agent and told him, "The Rangers still have to pay me for two more years. All I want is a contract—anyplace. I can still pitch, and I'd like a chance to pitch for a couple more years." All a team had to do was offer him the minimum. He got no takers, and Matlack thinks he knows why.

"Somewhere along the line the word was put out that my elbow wasn't any good, that a bad elbow was the reason I had been let go," he said.

The interested teams said they would only give him a contract after he proved to them he could pitch. But Jon Matlack is a proud man. He had been in the majors for thirteen years, and he didn't feel he had anything to prove.

There was another factor in Matlack's decision not to go to spring training on a tryout basis. Drugs. He had seen the Mounted Police enter the Ranger clubhouse in Toronto and arrest pitcher Fergie Jenkins for drug possession. He became frightened.

Matlack is convinced that someone planted drugs in Jenkins's baggage and that Jenkins's arrest was a setup. To Matlack's thinking, the customs agents' version of the events surrounding Jenkins's arrest just didn't add up.

The customs agents had retained the luggage of four members of the Texas Rangers' entourage: Jenkins, Mickey Rivers, and two sportswriters. Matlack thinks that their search of the other three bags was a smokescreen for their intended target.

"Mickey Rivers wouldn't even take an aspirin tablet, let alone anything stronger," Matlack said, "and why check sportswriters? To my knowledge, they aren't into that scene at all."

Matlack remembers that when Jenkins's bags didn't show up in the clubhouse in Toronto the pitcher had an inkling that something was afoot.

"He was really frightened," Matlack said. The amount of cocaine and marijuana proved to be minuscule. Nevertheless, Jenkins was arrested. The charges were later dropped.

After that incident, Matlack became paranoid about someone planting drugs in *his* luggage.

"I packed my own gear everywhere I went," Matlack said. "I wouldn't let anyone touch it but me. I put it in the truck myself."

And so after no team would offer him a contract, Matlack didn't pursue one. He went to school, took real estate courses, and got his license. He continued raising horses and just went about his business.

Initially, it was a satisfactory life. He could stay home with his wife and kids, and the real estate and horse businesses proved to be fun.

Then life's realities set in. Matlack learned that in order to make certain real estate deals, he had to prostitute himself. It no longer was the quality of the deal, but whom he knew who could get the deal done. Politics, he soon learned, was the key ingredient to becoming rich in real estate.

"I couldn't bring myself to operate like that," Matlack said. "I don't know what I would have done if I had sold somebody something under false pretenses only to have it not work out and cause someone hardship."

The horse business, it turned out, was no better.

At the same time Matlack and his son went to a few Ranger ball games. He began watching baseball on television. Before he knew it, the bug had bitten him once again.

After a long argument with his wife, Matlack decided to coach. He prepared a résumé and sent it to every general manager. San Diego responded quickly. He's been coaching there the last couple of years, with the Padres' high A team in Riverside, California, and then with their Double A team in Wichita. His goal is to coach in the major leagues.

"I guess the competitive bug hadn't completely died either," Matlack said.

Jon Matlack made the kind of face that indicated he wasn't entirely comfortable with his baseball addiction. Addictions were what bedeviled others. But he smiled because he accepts his Baseball Jones. He was doing something he never thought he'd be doing again—pitching against other pros—and he loved it.

During the bottom of the sixth inning, the Orlando public address announcer intoned: "A final score: Winter Haven 3, Bradenton 2."

Their game was not yet over, but win or lose, the Pelicans had clinched first place in the four-team Northern Division. The Pelicans' six wins in a row left second-place Bradenton six and a half games back and Orlando seven and a half back. Either team could finish in second place, since five games were left in the season. Winter Haven, thirteen games back, was out of it.

On the bench the players smiled when they heard the news. A few shook hands. Winning at this point came as no surprise. They had felt for weeks that it was only a matter of time. Nevertheless, the satisfaction was palpable.

Bobby Tolan brought in Nardi Contreras to relieve Matlack, but after entering the game with two on and two outs in the sixth and getting the third out, Nardi threw one pitch to Ike Blessitt in the seventh. Ike fouled it off, and while everyone watched the ball, few noticed that Nardi had twisted his knee and was in great pain. He had to come out.

Elias Sosa took over. After taking his time warming up, Sosa dispatched the Juice, ending the game with a one, two, three ninth, getting Larvell Blanks to fly out to Steve Henderson in right field to end the game. All season long Sosa had pitched as Bobby Tolan had needed him, as a starter, a long man, or, in this case, a closer, and inevitably he came through. Though Sosa's record didn't indicate excellence, without him it is doubtful the Pelicans could have won.

As soon as the game was over, a mob of Pelican teammates surrounded Sosa on the mound. Everyone embraced. Animosities were forgotten—hurts and grudges no longer mattered.

In the clubhouse after the game, the celebration was joyous but not raucous. For a few players, it was their first pennant of any kind, and the moment felt special. Many of the players enjoyed surprising teammates by sneaking up and pouring entire bottles of champagne on their heads, down their shirts, and even into the front of their pants.

Randy Lerch, an old pro, was particularly adept at shaking the bottle and using his thumb to direct a spray of water at an intended target. Clubhouse manager David Chavez had anticipated the bubbly mess. Miraculously, he had arranged to cover the openings of all the lockers with a heavy plastic.

While everyone else celebrated, a lone figure sat on the trainer's table, a bandage wrapped tightly around his right calf. All season long Nardi Contreras had fought injuries for the privilege to pitch, to show people what he might have become, only to lose to his aging body. For someone who loved the game as much as Nardi, it was difficult to bear.

That night, ready to celebrate the championship in style, Randy Lerch, age thirty-seven, and his girlfriend went into a local Orlando bar. He was carded, asked to prove he was twenty-one. Randy was not carrying any identification.

"I have a thirteen-year-old daughter," he said.

"Prove it."

He couldn't and had to leave.

The next morning on the bus from the Holiday Inn to the Orlando ballpark, Pat Zachry said to Randy Lerch, "Hey, Blade, you're carrying Samsonite this morning."

"What do you mean?"

Zack pointed under his eyes. "The bags," he said.

Everyone else was just as sloe-eyed as they sat quietly looking out the bus window at the parade of ugly strip malls passing by. This was a day game following a night of revelry, and though their spirits were high the Pelican players weren't as young as they used to be.

CHAPTER

33

Bossie Wins One

Despite a constant barrage of injuries to important players, Bobby Tolan managed to win the division title. Lenny Randle had a fractured right hand, and Ivan DeJesus had a bad leg. Both were out. Roy Howell's leg was hurting, and so was Alan Bannister, though both of them continued to play.

While not all the players liked Tolan, most respected him. Many of the pitchers made it clear they were not fans of his pitching coach, Dock Ellis. Whether the pitchers were happy about the way they were handled or not, it was evident throughout the year that Bobby and Dock almost always had the right pitcher in the game at the right time. As a result, all of the pitchers ended up contributing.

It's hard to say whether some of the pitchers might have felt less hostile toward Bobby and Dock had they been white. A couple of them admitted race was part of the problem. But they had not done particularly well overall, and it might have been sour grapes.

Other white pitchers were upset with Bobby and Dock over the handling of Randy Lerch. Bosman, Matlack, and Wilcox had sought to help him. Ellis had not been happy about it. So there was tension over just that one issue. Other pitchers, inconsistent all year long, felt that Dock should have used them more. They expressed the feeling that Dock may have held it against them that they were white. But the fact was that all the pitchers were white. How could that have been a factor?

At the end of the season, one pitcher disgustedly confided, "I will never play for another black manager. I'll quit first." But before the start of the second season, that pitcher called to find out if Tolan had invited him back. He had.

Some of the bench players felt that Bobby tended to favor the blacks on the team, an interesting switch in light of how many Latin and black players have felt slighted throughout their careers by white managers and executives.

So, regardless of how anyone felt personally about Bobby and Dock, the proof was in the results. Under them, the Pelicans were division winners, and no one could ever take that accomplishment away from them.

All season long Dock Ellis said, "Kick ass and take names." And though the Pelicans were certainly the least popular team around the league in the eyes of the opposing players, that was exactly what the Pelicans had done.

At the end of the regular season, the standings read:

	W	L	PCT	GB
St. Petersburg	42	30	.583	—
Bradenton	38	34	.528	4
Orlando	37	35	.514	5
Winter Haven	29	43	.408	13

The St. Petersburg Pelicans had suffered setbacks all through the season. Injuries were cripplers, as they were for all teams. After the second week, the pitching staff never was intact. Leg pulls and other injuries took their toll on the fielders. But Jim Morely and Bobby Tolan had collected a nucleus of hard-nosed players: Butch Benton, Steve Henderson, Gary Rajsich, Lenny Randle, Roy Howell, and Steve Kemp. Their ability to play almost every day at the top of their game, combined with the excellent starting pitching of Milt Wilcox and Jon Matlack and the usually reliable relief of Elias Sosa, Dave Rajsich, Dock Ellis, and Joe Sambito, kept the team on a wire-to-wire victory course. Everyone else filled in and contributed. Late-season replacements like Lamar Johnson, Ozzie Virgil, Jr., and Ivan DeJesus proved invaluable.

Bobby Tolan, who had scrapped with authority every stop in his playing career, proved that past isn't always prelude. Still acerbic and sometimes arbitrary, there were days when certain players wished him dead. On other days they directed the same feeling toward Dock.

But in the end, how anyone felt—about Tolan's managerial skills, his color, his arrogance—proved irrelevant. To the victor go the spoils and the benefit of any doubts. The bottom line: Bobby Tolan showed he could assemble and manage a team of pros to victory.

There were still five meaningless games left in the season. The Pelicans lost the next four. Hoot Gibson started against Orlando and lasted exactly one inning. Before he got the third out, however, it looked like batting practice, as nine batters either walked or got hits. Hoot's arm was shot.

The next three losses were to Bradenton. It wasn't that the Pelicans didn't exactly try those last few games, but having clinched the pennant, the incentive was no longer there.

The other factor turned out to be injuries. Nardi Contreras and Hoot Gibson were finished, and Lenny Randle had a broken hand. Ivan DeJesus suffered a serious hamstring pull, and Bannister had bad wheels. Roy Howell had to have his knee drained to be able to play. Too, everyone was exhausted from the intense game-a-day season and cranky over having to play these pointless games.

On the final day of the season manager Bobby Tolan got into a car accident. He came late to the game when he couldn't get a tow truck that would rescue him.

Before the game Alan Bannister surprised everyone by announcing that a job opportunity in Arizona had forced him to leave the team. He had to drive there, so he would not be available for the playoffs. He felt bad, but Senior Baseball was not life. Selling stocks and bonds was.

If the Pelicans expected to have any chance at all in the playoffs, Lenny Randle would have to play second base, even with a broken hand. It didn't seem humanly possible. The bone was broken in the flat part of the hand, where the nerve endings would explode in pain every time he gripped the ball to throw it or squeezed a bat to hit.

But Randle confided that he would have played second base in the playoffs whether or not Bannister was there. He would merely will the pain away and carry on. A month before, Billy Martin had died a horrible death, inebriated in his pickup. Lenny Randle, a Billy Martin protégé, would have made Billy proud. He was a gamer. The only question was, gamer or not, with an injured hand would Lenny Randle be able to do the job?

On the final day of the season in the seventy-second game, with Milt Wilcox and Jon Matlack resting up for the playoffs and Tex Williams, Pat Zachry, Hoot Gibson, and Randy Lerch all hurting, the man in the doghouse, Dick Bosman, got to start his first ball game.

Bossie faced a hot Bradenton ballclub. Against the Explorers Bossie pitched five innings of five-hit, one-run ball, walking one and giving the few fans in attendance a reminder that Dick Bosman once had been a damn fine baseball pitcher.

Using the old Don Larsen no-windup delivery, Bosman kept his glove and ball at the waist, not bringing them over his head, hiding the ball from the batter. The follow-through was sidearm. After he completed his delivery, he always brought himself square to the plate, his head staring in at the batter, ready to field any ball that was hit his way. As a pitcher, his mechanics were perfect. As a fielder, Bosman was catlike.

A serious competitor, Bosman is a hardworking, blue-collar guy, a member of the clean-the-plate club. Nothing he ever achieved came easy. He proved himself on this day by throwing changeups, sliders, and occasionally his KY-jelly balls, dippers and divers. After each inning he would come in from the mound and give a little grin or a wink, as if to say, "I told you so."

The score was tied, 1–1, when Boz was told he would not be going out for the sixth. But in the top of the inning the Pelicans scored a run and the relievers made the run stand up. Bossie had his first and only victory of the year, his first win of any kind since 1976—a hiatus of fourteen years.

All along Bosman, who was almost forty-six years old, had felt he had the ability to complete in the Senior League. Now he had proved it to everyone else.

"That's good enough for me," he said after the game. "I don't have to do any more." He was smiling.

CHAPTER

34

The Championship

Bobby Tolan knew what it took to win a baseball championship. He had been there before. As a kid in St. Louis he had been part of two St. Louis Cardinals World Series teams, winners over Boston in 1967, losers to Detroit in 1968. Then with the Cincinnati Reds, Tolan and the Big Red Machine lost to Baltimore in 1970 and lost to the Oakland A's in 1972.

Other Pelicans had starred in a World Series or two. Dock Ellis had pitched for the 1971 Pirates against Baltimore and the 1976 New York Yankees against the Reds. Milt Wilcox had pitched for the 1970 Reds against Baltimore and the 1984 Detroit Tigers against San Diego. Jon Matlack pitched for the 1973 New York Mets against Oakland. Lee Sosa pitched for the 1977 Los Angeles Dodgers against the Yankees.

These experienced pitchers would lead the Pelicans into the Senior League championships.

Of the position players, Roy Howell had been the designated hitter in the 1982 World Series for the Milwaukee Brewers against St. Louis at the end of his career. Kenny Landreaux had played in the 1981 Series for the Dodgers against the Yankees. And Ivan DeJesus had played the infield for the 1983 Phillies against Baltimore and got one at-bat in the 1985 Series for the St. Louis Cardinals against Kansas City.

The other starters, Randle, Lamar Johnson, Benton, Lowry, Kemp, and Henderson, had never played in the Fall Classic. For these men, the

Senior League playoffs were to be their World Series. This was their chance to finally wear a championship ring.

After the Pelicans had clinched the division title and as the regular season was winding down, no one talked openly about the playoffs except manager Bobby Tolan.

"I want to win it all," he said. "I want to show them." "Them" meant every manager and general manager who had ever done him wrong.

The players didn't say much, I suspect, because in their hearts they knew it wasn't the World Series. This wasn't being played in New York or Los Angeles or Detroit in front of a huge crowd. It was Fort Myers in February in front of several thousand people in the stands and a small cable audience on TV. It wasn't best-of-seven. It was a single-elimination tourney. As a result, the players were feeling a little cheated.

The eight-team Senior League was faced with having to decide the format the playoffs would take. The owners wanted to involve as many teams as possible, but at the same time they didn't want their playoffs to include so many teams that it made the regular season meaningless, as in basketball and hockey.

In major league baseball, the regular season is meaningful, because only the four division winners get to vie in the playoffs. In football the division winners are invited, along with several wild card teams. In basketball and hockey *everyone* plays, except the few really dreadful teams.

Considering the alternatives, the Senior Professional Baseball Association playoff arrangement wasn't too bad. The first question was where to hold it. That was an easy decision.

The Senior League regular season ended January 31. On February 1, the major league teams were scheduled to arrive for spring training and would usurp the fields. The St. Louis Cardinals, for instance, were to begin training at Al Lang Stadium, and both Montreal and Atlanta trained where the West Palm Beach Tropics played. The Red Sox trained in Winter Haven, the Twins in Orlando. The Pirates invaded Bradenton, Texas trained in Pompano, and the Mets played in St. Lucie.

Only one Senior League team played in an unoccupied stadium: the Fort Myers Sun Sox. The Kansas City Royals had once trained at Terry Park in Fort Myers but left for a better deal.

Terry Park it would be.

The next questions were how many games should be played in the Senior League playoffs, and who should play them?

Three days of playoffs was all the league could afford. For every date scheduled, the teams involved had to pay for hotel rooms and food. With Orlando's owner having disappeared and the team unable to make its players' final payment, the other owners had to chip in and pay them. This, plus huge losses in cities like St. Lucie, Bradenton, Pompano Beach, and even West Palm Beach, had the league at the breaking point. The goal had been two thousand fans per game to break even. West Palm Beach, Fort Myers, and St. Petersburg averaged more than a thousand a game. Everyone else did worse. So three days it would be. The other question was who would participate.

Initially, the first-place team in the Northern Division was to play the second-place team in the Southern Division, and the first-place team in the Southern Division was to play the second-place team in the Northern Division. The winners of those two games were to meet in a final championship game. But after it was announced, no one seemed to like that arrangement, because it seemed too easy for the first-place teams to be eliminated from the finals, and so the league Solons decided to use a step-pyramid approach.

The two second-place teams would play. The next day the winner would meet the first-place team with the second-best record. The winner of that second game would play the team with the best record for the Senior Professional Baseball Association championship.

Bradenton and Fort Myers, the two second-place teams, were to meet first. The winner then played St. Petersburg, in that the Pelicans' 42–30 record was worse than that of the dominating West Palm Beach Tropics, whose record under Dick Williams was 52–20. The Tropics would be in the finals no matter what. St. Pete would have to win the semifinal game to get there.

The Pelicans arrived in Fort Myers on the Friday afternoon of February 2, hours before the opening-round game between Bradenton and the local Sun Sox. The Pelican players were angry when they arrived, because the Pelican officials, including Bobby Tolan, were staying at the Sheraton downtown near the ballpark, and the rest of the players were forced to stay at a cheaper motel that was several miles away. At the last minute, without explanation, the Sheraton had canceled the reservations for most of the Pelican team. David Chavez, who was in charge of the arrangements, was crestfallen, because he knew the players would blame him. And they did, even though it wasn't his fault.

The players had been expecting to stay at the best accommodations, and they weren't getting them. And when Bobby Tolan didn't switch lodging over to where they were, they directed their anger at him. Adding to the tension was the wait. That evening they had nothing to do while Bradenton played Fort Myers to see who their opponent would be.

There was another spirit-dampening issue in the wind. For months major league baseball had been threatened with a strike. The day before, February 1, the strike was on.

None of the players were optimistic that the major league camps would open soon. Salaries were skyrocketing. The owners proposed a salary cap, like pro basketball, a way to stop themselves from paying too much money to the players. The major league players were dismissive. They liked the system just the way it was. Market value would reign. The owners were pleading with the players to trust them in setting up a new system.

"The players have no reason to trust the owners," Milt Wilcox said. "The owners have never showed us good faith."

And so the likelihood was that after the Senior League playoffs were over, the ball fields around Florida would be silent, perhaps all spring long.

Terry Park was festive for the opening game. Bunting hung along the railing. Almost four thousand fans arrived for the game, in high spirits. Owner Michael Graham had built a strong following in Fort Myers. Under his deal with the city of Fort Myers he got to keep the concession money when the fans bought hot dogs, french fries, and beer. If his Sun Sox could reach the finals of the tournament, he stood to cut his losses considerably.

Graham, blond and dapper, was optimistic because he had the home-field advantage and 3,856 enthusiastic fans, most of whom came to root for his team. Even a forty-five-minute rain delay couldn't dampen the spirits of the local fans, who testified to the viability of the Senior League.

The Sun Sox blew the game.

Fort Myers looked like a winner as Steve Luebber relieved starter Rich Gale in the third inning and at one point retired fifteen straight Bradenton batters.

With two outs in the eighth, Luebber allowed a walk and a single. Fort Myers manager Pat Dobson went to the mound. Luebber told him he was running out of gas.

"Can you pitch to one more batter?" Dobson asked.

"Yeah, I can get one more hitter for you," Luebber said.

Jim Morrison flied out to right to end the inning. Luebber was done for the day.

So were the Sun Sox when Dave LaRoche and Doug Bird combined to lose the game in the ninth.

The Pelican players hadn't gone to the game. Most ballplayers love to participate, but they are not avid spectators. Watching a game is too much like sitting on the bench. Most stayed in their motel rooms and watched TV.

The next day, when they read about what had happened in the papers, the talk was mostly of Luebber's failure to go back out there and pitch the ninth.

Jon Matlack knew both Dobson and Luebber. The three were all pitching coaches for the San Diego Padres. Dobson was with the big club, Luebber at Class A, and Matlack at Double A.

Referring to why Luebber came out, Matlack said, "We'll never know the real story there."

"It came to nut-cutting time, and he didn't have it in him," another pitcher said.

Matlack knew how badly Pat Dobson had wanted to win. Matlack mused, "I wonder if this'll affect anything between Dobber and Luebber in the future."

Dock Ellis couldn't understand how Luebber could have begged out for the ninth. He said disgustedly, "The motherfucker said he was motherfucking tired."

And so, because the Sun Sox didn't have it when they needed it most, the Pelicans' nemesis team, the Bradenton Explorers, opposed St. Petersburg in Saturday's semifinal game.

With the game at hand, the blasé attitude of the Pelican players changed dramatically. True, it wasn't the World Series, but it was a game that meant something: an "us against them" shootout, with the winner reaching the championship and the loser going home. No one wanted early elimination, especially against the Explorers, of whom the Pelicans were particularly contemptuous.

It was the Pelicans' Milt Wilcox against Dan Boone, the little lefty. Boone, who was related to the Indian fighter, had been unhittable down the stretch and had been offered a chance to pitch in Triple A ball the coming year. He had pitched three straight complete games and had a scoreless streak of eight and two-thirds innings against the Pelicans.

The Pelicans weren't impressed. The players were wearing their arrogant faces, disparaging the Explorers, especially their starting pitcher. One would have thought the most veteran players would be unemotional about such a game. Rather, they were the most tense and vocal. Lenny Randle, Steve Kemp, and Milt Wilcox especially pumped themselves up by shouting remarks out onto the field. They were old pros, but the same remarks can be heard on Little League and high school diamonds. Baseball is baseball.

On the mound Boone was warming up. From the dugout on the first-base side Lenny Randle, cheerleading as usual, yelled out, "Let's have a laugher! This guy is easy to beat!" Lenny's name was written on the lineup card, despite his broken right hand.

"Take no prisoners," Milt Wilcox said to no one in particular. Milt also disparaged Dan Boone's chances.

"He throws that knuckleball," Wilcox said. "It's a hard pitch to get over. He doesn't challenge anybody."

Steve Kemp offered advice on how to neutralize Boone. "Expect to go on any pitch," Kemp told the other players. "If you get a good jump, you're gone. That'll take away his knuckleball."

"The guy has been a loser his whole career," Kenny Landreaux said snidely.

With the singing of the National Anthem, a mask of seriousness covered the faces of the Pelican players. Concentration and cool were the common denominators. The Pelicans were playing with an intensity you could feel. They were all business. They seemed to will all of the pressure onto the other team. The Pelicans were intent on forcing the Explorers to crack first. They did.

In the second inning, with Steve Kemp on second base, Boone fluttered two consecutive knucklers past catcher Stan Cliburn's glove. Kemp scored the first run.

Bradenton, who had played the Pelicans so tough all season long, cracked wide open in the fourth after tying the score.

Roy Howell bounced a shot off third baseman Jim Morrison's body. The official scorer ruled it an error. Steve Kemp then grounded to Boone on the mound, and throwing flat-footed, the Explorer pitcher threw far wide of second base and into center field. By the time the ball came back in, Howell was on third and Kemp on second with nobody out.

Kenny Landreaux, a lefty hitting a lefty, then blooped a single to center for the two go-ahead runs. Lenny Randle batted righty, and despite the intense pain he was feeling, he dumped a perfect sacrifice bunt.

When he returned to the dugout, Randle barked to the others, "Let's play some *hardball.*"

A double by Ivan DeJesus gave the Pelicans a 4–1 lead.

The Pelicans put it away with three more in the fifth. The players knew the result was ordained. They had had the best players and the right attitude and the strongest will. No one played the game like they did. No one wanted it like they did. This was a piece of cake.

And with the realization that Milt Wilcox was in command and that there was zero chance of the Explorers' winning, suddenly the mood on the team changed. From grim-faced seriousness, the players' mood lightened to where they joked on the bench with each other. Soon would come another mood: derision.

With a runner on first and Lamar Johnson up, Lenny Randle unexpectedly began discussing the huge amount of food that Lamar had eaten the night before.

"Ribs, key-lime pie . . ." Randle said.

As Lenny described Johnson's culinary binge, Boone threw Lamar a fastball. The large first baseman pulled the ball foul about 450 feet, way over the outfield fence in left. Half the team stood to watch. After he sat down again, Lenny continued to talk about Lamar's appetite.

Two pitches later the scrawny left-hander tried another fastball, and this time Lamar got it all and got it fair. The ball rose like a missile shot from a long-range gun. It was a high, arching drive that took what seemed like minutes to fly over a palm tree and land somewhere beyond the fence, a thing of beauty.

As Lamar was circling the bases—slowly, purposefully—the guys on the bench kept up their conversation about food.

Steve Henderson said, "Key-lime pie. Banana cream pie. Ice cream. Bar-be-cue."

Down the bench Jon Matlack, admiring Lamar's strength, said, "Hum, baby."

Butch Benton crossed the plate and waited for a smiling Johnson to score and gave him a high-five.

When Roy Howell walked, Hoot Gibson yelled at the Bradenton bench, "Stick a fork in him! He's done!"

Steve Kemp singled up the middle, and Howell circled to third. Clete Boyer went out to the mound to take out Boone.

Through the end of the game the Pelicans continued to deride the Explorers. Pride was involved. During the season, nine of their twelve games against Bradenton had resulted in losses. The Pelican players nevertheless considered themselves to be a superior team. Hence their hooting in the face of victory.

As Boone headed from the mound to the sanctuary of the dugout, Lenny Randle, reciting the Miller Lite beer slogan, shouted, "Tastes good, Boone, less filling!"

With the Pelicans ahead, 7–1, Jerry Royster led off the Bradenton sixth with a double. He was stranded there.

As the Pelicans returned to the dugout, Bobby Tolan exhorted his players to keep the pressure on.

"They're down!" he yelled. "Keep them down!"

"Pour it on," Wilcox said. "Let's go!"

"Let's get some more runs now," Hoot Gibson said.

As Bradenton's Rick Petersen warmed up before the start of the inning, Randle commented, "This guy is throwing shit. I'm glad they took Boone out."

In the Pelican seventh, Butch Benton batted against left-hander Earl Stephenson. Just a few days before the playoffs Benton had missed a game with a severely injured ankle. Against Stephenson, the Pelicans catcher pulled a ball into left field, and without hesitating, he raced into second, sliding hard to beat the throw.

"The bastard has a broken leg?" Jon Matlack said with admiration. "Boolshit."

Lamar Johnson grounded to short, and Benton, still charged up, made an unwise dash for third. He was thrown out easily.

As Benton sheepishly trotted back to the dugout, he was greeted by his teammates. He knew he had run the bases foolishly, but when you're ahead, 7–1, you can laugh about it.

"Attaboy, Kamo," Ozzie Virgil, Jr., said. "Butch Benton, the ka-mikazi runner."

After the Pelicans were retired and he was about to go onto the field for the eighth inning, Wilcox let his teammates know the game was as good as over. "You know," he said, "we have a hell of a chance to go to the dog track tonight." He was grinning.

In the Bradenton ninth, with the Pelicans still leading, 7–1, Wilcox retired leadoff hitter Omar Moreno on a lazy fly to right.

"No question," Bobby Tolan said, "Milt's the best pitcher in the league. He's done it all year long. He's won the big ones."

Graig Nettles grounded to Lenny at second. Two outs.

One out to go, but Wayne Nordhagen hit a solo home run to keep Bradenton alive.

"Too little, too late," Tolan said.

Jim Morrison was the batter. He struck out, swinging.

Everyone came out to the field to congratulate Wilcox and each other. It was handshakes, not frenzy. Today's game was important. Tomorrow's game would be everything.

Not a Pelican in the room doubted that they would win it. It's odd how a winning team almost always takes on the character of its manager. It's hard to say whether a manager picks players who have similar characteristics or whether the players adopt characteristics of their manager. Either way, feisty managers like Billy Martin, Dick Williams, and Tommy Lasorda often had feisty players. Laid-back managers often preferred laid-back players. Bobby Tolan's strongest characteristic always had been his arrogance. It became a common Pelican trait as well.

In the locker room after the game, outfielder Steve Henderson was asked about the Pelicans' chances against the favored West Palm Beach Tropics. The two teams were to meet the next day at four in the afternoon. The Pelicans had beaten the Tropics seven out of ten games, but West Palm Beach had been the dominant team in the league and still would be favored. Henderson appeared unimpressed. Jon Matlack was starting for the Pelicans. Hendu would take Jon over anyone the Tropics pitched.

When told that Juan Eichelberger would be pitching for West Palm Beach, Hendu spoke for the Pelicans when he said, "We know we can beat him. All we have to do is rattle him early and then take him out. We know we can do it, because we know we're the best team in the league."

Lenny Randle took it a step further. Cleverly, he made fun of Eichelberger's name.

"We've been eating burgers all year, so we'll handle that Whopper at four o'clock. Some of us will have cheese."

In the Pelican locker room two hours before the 4:00 P.M. finale the next day, the players were like soldiers just before a battle. Everyone sat around the lockers, thinking his own thoughts, lost in his own world. At the same time you could feel the boredom and the tension.

Outside it was raining—showers, but nothing serious. Though batting and fielding practice had been canceled, the game would still be played.

In the trainer's room the Pelicans' doctor conferred with Lenny Randle about his broken right hand. Randle insisted he could handle the pain. "I'm playing," he said. With Alan Bannister gone, Bobby Tolan could have kept Randle on the bench and played Luis Gomez. But Tolan was willing to chance letting Randle start, because he knew that just having him out there would be an inspiration. Randle could still bunt, still could steal if he had to. Could he handle the pain that came from catching a line drive or hitting the ball hard? Randle said he could. Randle was given permission to play.

A hearts game was in progress, but the usual loud kibitzing was missing. When the cards of the four players—Wilcox, Matlack, Dave Rajsich, Ozzie Virgil, Sr.—hit the table one after the other, someone would pick them all up and slap them in a pile, and another round would be played. Even when the queen of spades fell, the usual boisterousness was lacking. On this day playing cards became a way to kill time.

Behind them, stretched on the locker room indoor-outdoor carpeting, taking naps, were the large hulking figures of Dwight Lowry and Lamar Johnson, looking like Moby Dick and Shamu.

The Pelicans needed no added motivation, but the announcement of the Senior League All-Star team selections provided it anyway. No All-Star game was to be played. The team was honorary. The week before the playoffs all the players in the league had voted. A player could not vote for a player on his own team.

The players congratulated Steve Henderson, who made the first team. They felt Henderson was the league's Most Valuable Player. Milt Wilcox (12–3, 3.19 ERA) was picked on the second team after Juan Eichelberger (11–5, 2.90 ERA). There was some grumbling about that.

But what the players couldn't abide was the slap in the face by the opposing players when Lenny Randle at second, Roy Howell at third, Butch Benton at catcher, and Steve Kemp in the outfield all were left off both the first and second teams.

Tim Ireland and U. L. Washington beat out Lenny. Jim Morrison and Toby Harrah beat out Roy. Stan Cliburn and Sal Butera were chosen ahead of Butch, and when the players saw that, they laughed in derision. Since the players couldn't vote for their teammates, they had deliberately picked guys they believed to be the worst opponents in the league, so their teammates would win. A number of them had written in Butera's name.

As for Kemp, he had been as instrumental in the Pelicans' winning down the stretch as anyone. His teammates felt that he should have been at least on the second team, instead of Juan Beniquez, Tito Landrum, or George Foster.

When the sheet of paper with the All-Star team was handed out, the players flocked around it and from their angry response a surge of energy seemed to charge the room. The quiet was shattered and replaced with gutter expressions and sentiments of what the Senior League could do with its balloting.

Then, just before the players were ready to leave the clubhouse for the field, Milt Wilcox yelled out, "Remember, I want $20 from each of you for the batboys."

No one complained except Dock Ellis, who said, "I'm not paying. I want to know who's getting the money and how much."

Wilcox's son was one of the batboys. Wilcox screamed at him, "Don't pay! Be that way!"

They glared at each other. The tension increased as the rest of the players stood around, watching in detached amusement.

It was time to go out onto the field.

"Let's go get 'em!" Bobby Tolan said, as though releasing them from their cage.

As the players began to surge out the clubhouse door for the walk down the third-base line to the dugout along first base, the chatter began to intensify.

"Get, get, get, get, get, get, get up on it," Hendu was saying, almost in a chant.

"Let's kick their ass" was a sentiment expressed often.

"Let's kick somebody," Milt Wilcox said. "We're taking no prisoners."

The first ever Senior League championship game began with the gamest Pelican of them all, Lenny Randle, hitting a ground ball that went through the legs of All-Star shortstop Ron Washington, an irony that wasn't lost on the St. Pete players.

"All-Star, my ass" was the comment.

Randle, broken hand and all, stole second. When Hendu bounced a hard-hit ball past Eichelberger and into center field, the Pelicans took the lead.

In the Tropics first, Jon Matlack walked the first two batters. Ozzie Virgil, Sr., knew the Tropics manager Dick Williams so well that he knew Ron Washington wouldn't bunt.

"He'll go for the big inning," Virgil Sr. said.

Washington flied out. The runners held. Then Dave Kingman grounded to Howell for a force at third, and Tito Landrum popped out to the catcher.

The Tropics were done for the day.

Instead of winning humbly, the Pelicans did it the way the old New York Yankees used to. They won big and strutted.

Back in the 1920s, Yankee owner Jacob Ruppert once talked about his favorite afternoons at Yankee Stadium.

He said, "It's when the Yankees score eight runs in the first inning and slowly pull away."

Don't believe players when they tell you they'd rather win artistically, 1–0, than 10–0. Pitchers love big leads. Batters love to hit and hit and hit, like it was batting practice. True, during the regular season the Pelicans had taken big leads over the Tropics, only to have Williams's team battle back. On this day, with Jon Matlack at the top of his form, the Pelicans knew deep down from the start that they would win the championship.

After scoring one in the first, the Pelicans scored two in the second when Eichelberger's control left him and he had to come at the hitters with fastballs. The Pelicans are a fastball-hitting team. Four singles brought in the runs. Hendu had been right about getting to Eichelberger early.

"He's frustrated," Bobby Tolan observed. "He's trying to overthrow. He's outside his realm now." Tolan's eyes blazed. He wanted to beat his former mentor. He badly wanted the recognition he always felt he had deserved but never got. Perhaps if the Pelicans were to win, some of his bitterness would leave him. Of course, the possibility remained that his team would win, but the recognition still would not come his way. Then what?

In the third, Steve Kemp, the non-All-Star, led off against Eichelberger, the elected first-team All-Star pitcher.

Kemp's home run swing had been missing until there were only a couple of weeks left in the season. But like Kenny Landreaux, as the Pelicans entered the pennant stretch, his productivity increased to the point that he contributed something almost every day. Kemp had heard the trade rumors, and he too had something to prove.

Eichelberger threw, Kemp cocked his bat, swung, and jerked the ball— high, deep, and out of the park.

As one, all the players on the Pelicans bench leaped up, and they stood and clapped as he circled the bases. When he returned to the dugout, Kemp had a hint of a smile on his face. When each teammate approached him for a high-five, he smartly completed the ritual, slapping an upraised palm against theirs.

It was 4–zip, Pelicans. The next batter, Steve Henderson, stroked the ball up into the wind, and it was carried deep into center field, beyond the glove of the straining Mickey Rivers. Hendu, motoring, turned it on and steamed into third.

On the bench Kemp said mockingly about himself and his teammates, "We have no guys on the fucking All-Star team, and they have the fucking All-Star pitcher out there." He was looking at the scoreboard. When Lamar Johnson hit a long fly to left and Henderson tagged up and scored, the first three innings along the visitor's line read: 1–2–2.

After retiring the Tropics successfully in the fourth, Matlack came over to Henderson, who was resting on the bench. One can say a lot without saying much at all.

Matlack said to Hendu, "You all right, Stevie, you big dog?"

"Yes, sir," said Hendu smiling.

"Keep trucking," said the Senator.

Both were smiling. The Tropics, they knew, weren't going to come back this afternoon.

Steve Kemp led off the fifth inning with a single to right. Henderson struck out, but when he returned to the dugout, it was as though his at-bat had never taken place. With Butch Benton the next batter up, Hendu sought to agitate Eichelberger.

"Ike, you gotta give it up! Give it up, Ike!"

Benton kept fouling off pitches and then lined out to right. There were two outs. Lamar Johnson was the batter.

"Give it up, Ike!" Hendu hadn't stopped.

Ike gave it up. A fastball down-and-in went literally out of sight, over the left-field fence, over the palm trees.

Matlack, the major beneficiary, mused in awe. "I wonder if that came in as fast as it went out?"

"Naaaah" was the chorus.

Lamar Johnson, another player almost traded prematurely, would be named the Most Valuable Player of the tournament.

With the Pelicans leading, 7–0, Dick Williams went out to the mound to take out Eichelberger and bring in Paul Mirabella, a left-hander who would spend the next season pitching for the Milwaukee Brewers.

"Keep going!" yelled Hendu to his teammates. "We gotta keep going!"

The Pelicans kept going. Mirabella gave up two more runs in the fifth for a 9–0 Pelican lead.

From the start of the game the hitters had been promising Jon Matlack nine runs, something hitters often promise their starting pitcher. When Dwight Lowry crossed the plate with run number nine, Milt Wilcox told Matlack, "All you have to do is ask." They smiled at each other.

With each added run or two, the players' belligerence toward their opponents and arrogance about victory grew. These men had no intention of being gracious winners. They had been snubbed by their peers in the All-Star voting. The league had not shown them the respect they felt was owed them. Their intent was to shove their victory up everyone else's collective butt.

In the bottom of the fifth inning, the West Palm Beach fans along the third-base line began shouting, "Let's go, Tropics!"

Bobby Tolan said, "They can go, all right. They can go home."

Ozzie Virgil, Sr., had drawn a tic-tac-toe board in the third-base coach's box at the start of the game. When the Pelicans batted in the first, he had put a big "X" in the middle with his cleats. Williams had responded with an "O" when it was his turn to coach third. When the Pelicans kept scoring, Williams abandoned the game with Ozzie.

"How's the tic-tac-toe game?" Ozzie was asked.

"He won't play tic-tac-toe with the score the way it is." Ozzie laughed.

A six-four-three double play ended a Tropics threat in the fifth. When Matlack came into the dugout, he said to Hendu, "We're going to do it, Buddy. We're going to do it."

They embraced.

Sitting on the bench during the Pelicans' sixth, Lamar Johnson emanated a sound like Joshua at Jericho. His loud fart moved everyone, laughing, away from him. As Johnson sat there, fifteen feet from the closest teammate, Randy Lerch commented, "He's sitting with all his friends now."

If the Tropic players could have heard the raucous laughter, what would they have thought?

Ahead 9–0 in the bottom of the sixth, Bobby Tolan began reflecting on his expected victory. He seemed wistful.

"They won't give me Manager of the Year," he said. "They'll give it to Dick, even though we had injuries and I had to scramble. He didn't, but he had a better record. It's the story of my life."

In the Pelicans' dugout during the eighth inning Bill Denehy, a former Met pitcher and the color man for the Prime TV Network, interviewed Jon Matlack, who seemed not to mind that he might be jinxing the apparent victory.

"That's a buck for giving a postgame interview before the game is over," Milt Wilcox yelled.

"Five bucks," yelled Lenny Randle, the Chief Judge.

Dick Williams went to the mound to get still another pitcher. After Eichelberger, he had brought in Mirabella, and then came the march of Odell Jones, Will McEnaney, Tim Stoddard, and Tom Underwood. Yet another pitcher trudged to the mound.

Williams is the sort of man who never quits, regardless of the score. But the Pelican players thought he was overdoing it. They felt he should just lie down.

"Fucking asshole. Let's just get it over with."

"Oh man, come on."

The new reliever was Felix Pettaway, a fastball pitcher. Pettaway was throwing gas.

"Who is this guy, a truck driver?" asked a Pelican.

"That's exactly what he is." He was, too. Drove a cement truck.

The score was 12–4 when Lee Lacy singled to open the Tropic ninth against reliever Elias Sosa. The next batter, catcher Luis Pojols, flew out deep to center. Kenny Landreaux, hustling like he never had during the regular season, flew across the grass to corral it.

"The last two nights he's been playing his butt off," a teammate said.

With one out Rodney Scott was the batter. He fouled a high pop over by the Tropics' dugout along third base. Roy Howell charged toward the ball, oblivious to his surroundings. He reached out, not knowing he was nose-to-nose with an immobile, stolid television camera. They collided. Roy didn't get the ball. He did get contusions and abrasions.

When Scott ultimately walked, no one was concerned. Eight runs ahead, Sosa was in command.

As Wilcox yelled, "Sosa, you're throwing some nasty shit out there."

When Alfie Rondon, subbing for an injured Mickey Rivers, struck out, the Pelicans were one out from being champs.

Toby Harrah was the last hitter of this long first season. Sosa threw a hard breaking pitch. Harrah grounded to Ivan DeJesus at short. Smoothly Ivan devoured the ball, and effortlessly he flicked his wrist, the ball sailing toward first. When it settled in the ample mitt of Lamar Johnson, the game was over.

On the mound the normally undemonstrative Sosa leaped high in the air. His joy was unrestrained. The Pelican players raced toward him. This wasn't the World Series, but they acted as if it were. For an athlete to be energized, something has to be at stake, and on this day it was the championship of the Senior Professional Baseball Association. For this day, at least, these men were no longer salesmen or coaches or truck drivers or lost souls. They were professional baseball players at the top of their game. And as they hugged each other, dancing around, acting like little boys, the hurts and disappointments and tragedies of their pasts evaporated—if but for a moment. What mattered was the precious present, the celebration of continued youth that was taking place on this circle of dirt on a ball field in a sleepy town on Florida's Gulf Coast.

Afterward was anticlimax. The field was empty, except for the camera crews, who were closing up. The fans filed out slowly. The parking lot turned into a maze of blocked cars. There was one exit, too many people trying to get out. It would take an hour for everyone to leave the lot.

In the Pelican clubhouse, for a second time, the champagne flowed—122 bottles of New York's finest—mostly poured by the players over each other. Everyone drank from the large silver Championship Cup that had been presented to Jim Morley and Bobby Tolan.

While the bubbly was sprayed around the room, the reporters worked at getting their stories. One focus of the press questioning was the courage of Lenny Randle and Roy Howell, who symbolized the way the team had played hard all year long despite injuries and distractions.

The team physician said about Randle, "Nothing was going to get him out of the lineup, so we just let him play."

Lenny shouted, "Bring on the Oakland A's!" referring to the 1989 World Champs. "Give us a field and a hotel to stay in, and we'll take them on."

When Howell was asked about his collision with the television camera, he said, "The only way to play this game is full-out every play. You never give it a half-effort, no matter what the score. That's the only way I know."

Then he said, "We sent a message to a lot of major leaguers this season. If you want to play in this league, you better get ready. You better be in shape. The standards have been set."

Tom DiPace

Bobby Tolan and Jim Morley

During the celebration, Tropic manager Dick Williams came by the
Pelican clubhouse to offer his congratulations to Bobby Tolan. He had had
to walk a long way to get there. Williams hated to lose as much as anyone.
It couldn't have been easy for him.

"Enjoy it," Williams graciously said to Tolan.

"Thank you, Dick, I appreciate that," Tolan replied.

Bobby Tolan had his championship. He had worked hard, making the
right moves. Like his players, Bobby Tolan on this one day in early
February could say he was the best in all of baseball. On this one day he
stood alone.

Tolan said, "I guess this shuts everybody up."

But, of course, he was wrong.

It would be hard to say whether anyone would notice what Tolan had
done. Whether he will eventually make it to the major leagues as a

manager would be even harder to predict, because Bobby Tolan has never been a company man. In the corporate climb, Bobby topples off the ladder too easily. He is black, outspoken, arrogant, and proud, and he does not suffer fools gladly.

Bobby would need an executive who would overlook his abrasiveness and proud nature and focus on his ability, intelligence, and desire.

In baseball, which in so many ways is just like any other business, that's an awful lot to ask.

That championship celebration is remembered as though in a reverie. On reflection it didn't seem real. The senses remember the sweet taste of the champagne, the metallic taste of the large silver Championship Cup that everyone drank from, the sticky feel of the champagne as it clung to clothing, and the sickly smell of the clothing after being soaked only a short while.

The celebration, the culmination of a season of hard work, proved achingly short. It lasted about an hour. This one hour of shared joy was what the Pelicans had fought for since October, when a group of strangers came together on a practice field in St. Petersburg.

And then, after the handful of reporters finished asking their questions, and after the league officials walked around congratulating each other, and after the players took their final slugs of champagne, abruptly, the good times were over. It is the way baseball always ends.

No one ever wishes it to end. It just does. And so it was for the St. Petersburg Pelicans. After the final shower was turned off, the last uniform thrown into a pile, and the last locker emptied, each player went around the room and shook hands with teammates, aware it might be for the last time. The joy was mixed with a nostalgic sadness. It was the same feeling you got when you lay in your bunk at summer camp and listened to the bugle play "Taps" one final time. Where had the months gone?

One by one the players opened the clubhouse door leading to the parking lot. It was night. The palms in shadow rose majestically.

These men were going their separate ways again. Who knew what lay in store for them back in the real world? It wasn't something to think about as they got into their cars and rode off. For another couple of hours they would contemplate what they had just accomplished.

Tomorrow could wait for tomorrow.

Epilogue

The Senior Professional Baseball Association ended its first season in a sea of red ink. All teams lost money, which is the fate of new sports franchises.

Apparently, some of the owners feared losing more, as four of the eight original ownership groups dropped out. The St. Lucie Legends, Orlando Juice, West Palm Beach Tropics, and Gold Coast Suns ceased to exist.

Despite the financial problems, founder Jim Morley was able to interest two expansion franchises from the West Coast for the league's second season. The Sun City Rays from Arizona and the San Bernadino Pride from California joined four Florida teams: St. Petersburg, Daytona (which moved from Bradenton), Ft. Myers, and a traveling squad of renegades with no town to call its own. This sixth team, called the Florida Tropics, was funded by the rest of the league owners. This was necessary because the cable network carrying league games demanded that there be a minimum of six teams.

The league began play November 23, and was scheduled to continue through early February. When attendance through November and December was lackluster, players' salaries were cut. From the first week, everyone questioned whether the Senior Professional Baseball Association would survive a second season.

During the Christmas break there were rumors that the owners of the Ft. Myers Sun Sox were squabbling. One owner was rich, and the other was running the team but had contributed little money. The rich owner wanted the name owner to put up half the future losses. The name owner said no.

When Ft. Myers refused to fund a team for the rest of the season, Morley had run out of options.

On December 28, 1990, he reluctantly announced the cessation of competition for the year with a promise that he would do his best to resume the league the following year on a firmer financial footing.

Morley hopes to come back next season under a different concept. He wants to work together with the Japanese major leagues, and he also hopes American major league teams will send players seeking rehabilitation from injuries, regardless of age.

"The perfect roster will have ten senior players, five or six major leaguers and five or six Japanese players," Morley said.

Though the league folded, most players said they would return.

"The money was nice, and I could really use it," said Pelican infielder Todd Cruz. "But most of all, playing in this league, playing baseball, was the thrill of a lifetime for most of us. I'll come back next season if they do it, and I think most of the players will, too. We loved the idea of this league."

Index